THE AGE OF IDEOLOGIES

THE AGE OF IDEOLOGIES

A History of Political Thought in the Twentieth Century

KARL DIETRICH BRACHER

Translated from the German by Ewald Osers

St. Martin's Press
New York

© 1982 by Deutsche Verlags-Anstalt GmbH, Stuttgart
English translation © 1984 by Ewald Osers

Library of Congress Cataloging in Publication Data

Bracher, Karl Dietrich, 1922–
   The age of ideologies.

   Translation of: Zeit Der Ideologien.
   Includes bibliographical references and indexes.
   1. Political science—History—20th century.
I. Title.
[JA83 B68513 1984b] 320.5   84–15104

ISBN 0-312-01229-2
ISBN 0-312-01230-6 (pbk.)

For Dorothee

CONTENTS

Part III THE PRESENT
De-ideologization and Re-ideologization

PREFACE

Our century opened with the fateful transformation of political ideas into ideologies. This process has been repeated ever since: not least as the intellectual misinterpretation of developmental crises and as a susceptibility to totalitarian ways of thinking. In consequence, reliance cannot be placed on premature predictions of an end to ideologies; on the contrary, new challenges in the name of ideological claims to totality must be expected. There is, therefore, a greater need than ever for remembering and recalling those experiences which are capable of conveying political understanding and providing support against the confusion of concepts and values.

This book is dedicated to my wife. She has not only accompanied it, as she has all my work on politics and the history of ideas, for over three decades with indefatigable engagement but also promoted its realization by ideas which stood the test of time, during the most difficult period of our century, in the Bonhoeffer-Schleicher family from which she comes. My thanks go also to James Billington and to the Woodrow Wilson International Center for Scholars in Washington DC, where I was able to draft part of this book from December 1980 to February 1981. Some ideas and preliminary studies, of course, go back much further, indeed to my wartime and post-war experiences and to my doctoral thesis (1948) on ideas of decline and progress in classical antiquity. I hope to be able to supplement it with a further volume on the origins of modern political thought.

Karl Dietrich Bracher
Bonn, May 1982

PREFACE TO THE ENGLISH EDITION

The subject of this book has constantly engaged the author's interest over the past four decades while he was working on his studies of the Weimar Republic and national socialism, the history of European problems in the twentieth century, and the confrontation of democracy and dictatorship both in the past and at present. Invariably, these topics involved the question of the intellectual and ideological background of the great crises of the modern world – crises which are very largely those of thought as well as of political ideas.

The actual writing of the present book, however, was carried out in the face of the topical discussion about the profound change of social and political values in the seventies. It was carried out, moreover, amidst a German experience which, disturbingly and alarmingly, revealed the extent to which the special burdens of German history and German thought invariably affect questions of attitude and orientation, especially among the younger generation of Germans. The generation rift of the sixties was followed not by a generally predicted de-ideologization but by new waves of an ideological renaissance. When the realization of high-pitched political expectations was found to come up against certain limits, there was a revival of the confrontation of power and spirit, politics and ideal – a confrontation especially painful in Germany and one that was generally believed to have been overcome. There were new signs of that disruption of a normal relation with political reality which had caused the shipwreck of the first German democracy in 1933. A significant role was played in this connection by the challenge to and the questioning of institutional forms of education and upbringing, of family and school, under the impact of an unexpectedly rapid and radical upheaval of values. Belief in social progress and social emancipation had exerted a powerful reformist pressure on the era of the social-liberal coalition since 1969. Consequently, the crisis of growth after the mid-seventies was interpreted by an increasing number of contemporaries – either indignant or resigned – as a crisis of western civilization generally.

In this excited and exciting debate, which at times has the semblance of a throwback to the critical attitude towards democracy and civilization of the twenties, it is of particular importance to be clear about the great ideological arguments of our century. It is not enough to stare in momentary hypnosis at the mass 'movements' of our day, with their extravagant totalitarian claims. The author instead endeavours to present a critical survey of the ups and downs of the ideological enticements to which Europe, and the Germans in particular, have been exposed since the turn of the century, and thereby to reduce to their proper perspective the new confusions and threatening delusions with which the western democracies are confronted by old and new salvationist doctrines and their irrational effects. Intellectuals, young people and the churches in particular are emerging as exponents of revived crisis thought, with the threat of nuclear annihilation overshadowing everything.

These are ideas which carried a good deal of weight before and after the First World War, in the slogan of the 'Decline of the west'. We have witnessed the destructive negative force which an irrational charge and the political abuse, i.e. the ideologization, of such ideas can develop: wartime fatalism and communism, fascism and national socialism, authoritarian and totalitarian movements were the results which eventually culminated in the 'Third Reich's' regime of annihilation. Thus any re-emergence of the 'German problem', proclaiming a neutralist anti-western special road or a renewed quest for a German 'identity', deserves particular attention.

The division of Germany in a world which continues to be moulded by national states and characterized by the east-west conflict represents ideologically explosive forces. A historical and political understanding of the old and new ideas discussed in the present book should make it possible to examine these forces critically and to discover their rational and irrational modes of action.

Raymond Aron, having earlier made forecasts of de-ideologization, finally also spoke of the continuation, indeed the 'immortality', of ideologies and of the west's perpetual 'jeopardy from irrationality'. In Germany this manifests itself by the anti-concept of the 'movement', which, ever since the German Youth Movement of the turn of the century, has been charged as an ideally and morally justified counter-position to western civilization and politics, to parliamentary plural-party democracy. Its discrediting by the national socialist 'movement' does not prevent such attempts.

Here we find ourselves again confronted by the danger of an ideological way of thinking which, oriented towards an extreme ideal goal, devalues the fundamental importance of constitutional structures. Anyone reading the last ten years' writings on our (not merely ecological) crisis with a critical eye to ideology must at times feel reminded of the sense of hopelessness which rendered so many intellectuals between the wars vulnerable to the ideologization of their thought – so that finally they believed they were faced at the time with only the disastrous alternative of fascism or communism.

Ideological flight from reality can acquire pseudo-religious features; it can lead to the undermining of an open society and weaken its resistance to right-wing or left-wing dictatorships.

The new ideological movements – unless they put forward the totalitarian claims of sectarian or theocratic movements (as most recently in Khomeini's Iran) – still lack the closed structures of systems and theories of the kind that are typical of Marxism-Leninism and also of national socialism. But a typical feature is their use of persuasive 'empty formulas' such as we encounter at present in the peace concept of the eponymous movements: their function is dramatization and emotional mobilization. In the role of alternative movements, of ecological, anti-nuclear and anti-American colouring, they touch upon the foundations of the western concept of democracy whenever they see themselves as a fundamental opposition – *i.e.* an opposition to the system itself – and whenever (as with the 'Green' movement in Western Germany) they quite emphatically have one foot outside parliamentary democracy. Operating as they do in the boundary zone between democracy and dictatorship they might provide a nutrient for the incubation of totalitarian ideologies: preliminary stages and transitional forms of an ideologization process in which the struggle for position and the elimination contest have not yet been decided. *Vestigia terrent.*

Karl Dietrich Bracher
Bonn, November 1983

INTRODUCTION:
IDEOLOGY AND PROGRESS

The history of twentieth-century political thought is marked by the intersection of two major tendencies. It represents both the peak and the turning-point of those modern sets of ideas which had been maturing since the eighteenth century: liberal and democratic, conservative and national, socialist and revolutionary, imperial and racialist thought were invoked and also rebutted in a period of world wars and global transformations. At the same time, the seemingly irresistible advance of economy and society under the banner of science and technology, as part of a worldwide expansion of modern civilization, has been increasingly called into question since the turn of the century. It was the shocking breaks in progress during the great wars and crises of our century, long anticipated by cultural critics such as Nietzsche but nonetheless experienced as unexpected, which destroyed many rational certainties and made Europe receptive to irrational thinking. Ideologization and crisis of progress have become a fascinating motivation. They have also become a nightmare.

Both tendencies are jointly reflected in what is increasingly becoming also a directly politically effective clash of ideas and ideologies, capable of toppling long-established moral and value structures and ultimately leading to a threat fashioned by mankind against itself, a threat unprecedented in history in such close association with political thought and action. Hence also that new ferocity and that all-embracing claim to totality which characterize the process of ideologization in state and society, in the economy and in cultural life. Since the turn of the century there has been a rapid sequence of the blueprinting and realization of highly ideological dictatorial regimes of a new style. The groups and parties representing them make an uncompromising claim to the implementation of absolutely formulated ideas of extreme and radical character. Whether of conservative, democratic or socialist origin, they in fact constitute – and this increases their effective power – a highly explosive mixture of left-wing and right-wing radical, progressivist and romantically reactionary motivations. The age-old question about the significance of political ideas in their relation to political reality now moves into much sharper focus. The controversial concept of 'ideology', of the philosophical justification of political rule, is now given a

key part in the great debate of the century. And, at the same time, most
ideologies lay claim to shaping 'progress', and indeed present themselves as
its historical exponents. Both concepts are continually in need of clarification.

We are living in a century of ideologies. Optimistic talk of an imminent
'end of the ideological age' has proved a delusion of the fifties, as has the
prediction of the decline of the intelligentsia.[1] Not an 'exhaustion' or an
'ageing' of political ideas in the period following the Second World War, but
a recharging of ideological energies and intellectual allurements marks the
age of the post-European modernization of the world. This links the second
half of the century to the eruptions and errors of its early decades; these have
indeed been undergoing a revival since the sixties. The talk now is of neo-
Marxist, neo-liberal and neo-conservative movements: 'new' or not, the
ideological thirst has certainly not been quenched. Not even by the
realization that all that Europe seems to be capable of is a replay of
developments set into motion elsewhere, notably in America and in the
Third World: student revolts, youth revolts, anti-Vietnam movements and
the politics of *détente*, and finally human-rights initiatives and then once
more neo-conservative impulses from the New World.

Certainly there has always been reflection on politics and political
systems, on political ideas and blueprints for the future, including their
propaganda use and abuse to justify a striving for power and the exercise of
that power – indeed ever since human society, states and conscious history
came into being. Yet our ideological age is novel in three aspects.

First, in the question of legitimacy: never before did political systems and
forms of government, or politics itself – democratic and dictatorial alike –
display such an overwhelming need to justify themselves intellectually, to
establish the scope of their power in a comprehensive ideological manner
and to extend it as far as possible;[2] they require an 'ideological infrastructure'[3] of a kind that cannot be encompassed by the classical Marxist
superstructure theory.

Second, in the field of communications: never before has that justification
had such extensive technical equipment at its disposal; never before has the
world with its different political and social systems become so close-knit in

---

[1] Originally Daniel Bell, *The End of Ideology* (Glencoe, 1960); nowadays Peter Bender,
Das Ende des ideologischen Zeitalters (Berlin, 1981); also Thomas Molnar, *The
Decline of the Intellectuals* (New York, 1962).

[2] Dolf Sternberger, 'Arten der Rechtmässigkeit', *Politische Vierteljahresschrift* 3 (1962),
p. 2ff.; see Peter Graf Kielmansegg, Ulrich Matz (eds), *Die Rechtfertigung politischer
Herrschaft, Doktrinen und Verfahren in Ost und West* (Freiburg-Munich, 1978), p. 155ff. (also
Georg Brunner: 'in östlichen Systemen', ibid., p. 59ff.; Paul Kevenhörster: 'in westlichen
Demokratien').

[3] Karl Loewenstein, 'Über das Verhältnis von politischen Ideologien und politischen
Institutionen', *Zeitschrift für Politik* 2 (1955), p. 191ff.; Karl Loewenstein, 'Über die
Verbreitung der politischen Ideologien', op. cit. 3 (1956), p. 195ff.

terms of communications; never before, in consequence, have rivalry and conflict of political ideas assumed such global dimensions or acquired such direct and intensive effect on all groups of the population. Politics has become communication in the sense that the formation of 'public opinion' through the mass media has assumed decisive importance and indeed, in the hands of skilled politicians, is making history.

Third, however, the impotence of such public opinion is also very clearly revealed: power and rule go to strong and resolute regimes which make 'ideological' use of ideas without much regard to truth or otherwise and which are capable of manipulating public opinion in such a way that it tends to become 'publicized' or fabricated opinion. Time and again we see how difficult, or indeed impossible, it is to overcome ideological regimes from within so long as, and to the extent that, they are in sole control of the means of communication.

We thus find ourselves in the paradoxical situation of a simultaneous superiority and impotence of political ideas confronting the reality of power. The various political camps and regimes are conducting consistent and calculated power politics, while at the same time their efforts tend primarily towards an intellectual justification and propagation of their politics through a gigantic investment in the production and reproduction of ideas and their ever more effective mass-media dissemination as 'propaganda', from cultural propaganda to psychological warfare. It is this functionalization and instrumentalization of ideas in the service of the politics of power and influence which has resulted in an indissoluble fusion of the two elements and in the ideologization of political thought in all camps. That is why it has become particularly difficult and problematical to draw up a sober balance sheet of modern political ideas in the development of state society from the eighteenth and nineteenth century to the present day and to interpret their use and abuse.

No attempt will be made here to proceed from a preconceived notion of ideology. Instead we shall first observe the general process of the con-struction of an 'ideology', in the sense of the most comprehensive system of ideas possible, especially concerning the relationship Man–Society–Politics – a system capable not only of reducing reality to a formula but also of bending it or even concealing it in the interests of power politics.[1] Functionalization of ideas for political purposes is capable both of being a motivation for constructive action, in a positive sense, and, in a negative sense, of operating as a deception through falsifying exaggeration or simplification. Admittedly, the significance of ideologies can also be seen, in a value-neutral sense, in that they provide an action-oriented system of beliefs capable of explaining the world and of justifying decisions, of limiting

[1] *E.g.* the scientific-sociological approach of Karl Mannheim, *Ideology and Utopia* (London, 1954), p. 49. For a critique of his originally Marxist formulation see Edward Shils in *Daedalus* 103, No. 1 (Winter, 1974), p. 87f.

and identifying alternatives and of creating the most all-embracing and intensive social solidarity possible.[1] Fundamentally, however, ideologization is based on a conglomerate of deception and self-deception: pseudo-religious needs, idealism, and perfection mania ultimately support even the 'ideological self-authorization for power'.[2] Added to this religious-moral legitimation is a claim to 'scientific character' and simultaneously to the elimination of all conflicts through the magic formula of dialectics. From the idea of possessing the ultimate truth there follows eventually not only the justification but indeed the necessity of self-deceit and lie, of persecution and terror, in order to make that idea finally prevail.[3]

The profound ambivalence, indeed the great contradiction, of twentieth-century political thought lies in the fact that the critique of ideologies is similarly being developed more acutely and emphatically than ever before: a merciless questioning of all political ideas with the intention of revealing them as ideologies and thereby discrediting them. Simultaneously, however, such ideologies are being employed and utilized – often indeed by the critics of all other ideologies – more deliberately and consistently than ever before and raised to the position of the only truth. Thus our century has produced, at one and the same time, both the fiercest critique and the greatest glorification of ideologies, though admittedly it has also produced criteria and experiences enabling us to differentiate between various ideologies and their essential characteristics. In both instances the new significance of older sets of ideas and habits of thought emerges under the massive influence of changed living conditions and a changed world in an age of democratization and mass communications.

The present study attempts to do justice to this state of affairs by seeking to understand and interpret the process of ideologization and the weight of ideologies from four possible aspects. First, it accepts that a clear distinction of ideological and non-ideological statements remains open to question and that just this blurring of the idea content represents the core of the problem of modern political thought and the danger of it being abused.[4] Secondly, it must be stated that all political thought is subject to value orientations if it is to give rise to or affect policies, since it formulates in words the wishes and interests of the citizen.[5] Thirdly, this is why its intertwining with social and

[1] Paul E. Sigmund, *The Ideologies of the Developing Nations*, 3rd ed. (New York, 1969) p. 41f.

[2] Thus the eponymous article by Hermann Lübbe, in *Neue Zürcher Zeitung*, 28–9 Oct 1978, p. 65f.

[3] On the various elements of the construction of ideologies from the psychological point of view see Paul Watzlawick, 'Bausteine ideologischer Wirklichkeiten', in *Die erfundene Wirklichkeit* (Munich, 1981), p. 192ff.

[4] See Theodor Geiger, *Ideologie und Wahrheit* (Stuttgart-Vienna, 1953), p. 177ff.; further developed by Ernst Topitsch, *Sozialphilosophie zwischen Ideologie und Wissenschaft*, 2nd ed. (Neuwied, 1966), p. 15ff.; Kurt Salamun, *Ideologie, Wissenschaft, Politik* (Graz, 1975), p. 16ff.

[5] In this sense, for instance, Karl Mannheim's comprehensive, indeed 'total ideology concept'; see now especially Kurt Salamun, 'Ideologie, Erkenntnis und Wahrheit', in *Ideologien im Bezugsfeld von Geschichte und Gesellschaft* ed. Anton Pelinka (Innsbruck, 1981), p. 23ff.

economic conditions is important, even though the absolutization of this particular perspective in the Marxist concept of ideology can lead only to one-sided findings, as proved more particularly by its extreme Leninist development. Fourthly, and finally, a historical-political interpretation stands the best chance of leading to a comparative understanding and judgement: a historical derivation of the ideas together with the specific political and social patterns in which they appear or prove useful or necessary in legitimating and integrating a community, or negating and destroying it.

The character and effect of modern ideologies can best be seen in that most extreme and exclusive form that arises with the emergence of totalitarian political goals and styles of thinking. Totalitarian ideologies reveal with especial clarity the nature and function of the ideologization process in state and society, no matter whether they are seen as belonging to older layers of monocratic thought,[1] or derived from Rousseauism and the radical egalitarianism of the French Revolution;[2] or whether one prefers to see them as having arisen only from the right-wing and left-wing radicalization of socialism and nationalism in our century.[3]

At the centre of this process is a tendency towards an extreme simplification of complex realities: the claim that they can be reduced to *one* truth and, at the same time, divided into a dichotomy of good and evil, right and wrong, friend or foe, that the world can be grasped with a single explanatory model in bipolar terms, in the manner attempted more specifically by the Marxist class theory or the National Socialist racial theory. The creation of enemy stereotypes and of scapegoat strategies is just as important as a means of simplifying and integrating social and political plurality as are the rather vague promises and visions which in contrast represent the 'positive' content of ideologies. At the same time the need for orientation and security is met by the promise of true insights and principles underpinned both by faith and by (pseudo-)science. The assurance of absolute truth not just later in heaven but now on earth invests ideology with the character of a secularized redemption creed, one which excludes any ideological alternative by discrediting it in advance as 'bourgeois' or

[1] Thus principally Karl Popper, *The Open Society and its Enemies* (London, 1962), Vol. 1 ('The Spell of Plato') and Vol. 2 ('The High Tide of Prophecy: Hegel, Marx and the Consequences').

[2] Fundamentally Jacob L. Talmon, *Die Ursprünge der totalitären Demokratie* (Cologne-Opladen, 1961; English ed. 1952), p. 38ff. On earlier stages of ideologization now also Donald R. Kelly, *The Beginning of Ideology, Consciousness and Society in the French Reformation* (Cambridge, 1981). Talmon developed his statement through the nineteenth century (*Messianism, The Romantic Phase* (Cologne-Opladen, 1961)) and, before his death, down to the present in a posthumous volume, *The Myth of the Nation and the Vision of Revolution, The Origins of Ideological Polarization in the Twentieth Century* (London, 1981).

[3] Thus my contribution to the Talmon Colloquium at the Israel Academy of Arts and Sciences: 'The Turn of the Century and Totalitarian Ideology' (Jerusalem, June 1982).

'objectivist' without having to adduce any proof in support of such a truth.

The claim to and possession of this ideology makes its exponent, as an ideologist, a member of a self-appointed élite. His privileged insight and his monopoly of truth are simultaneously his legitimation to a claim to unlimited power, a claim he makes *vis-à-vis* all relative and limited forms of society and state, and which, if necessary, he asserts by revolutionary action: Plato's ruling philosophers, Lenin's *avant-garde* and Hitler's ss '*Ordensburgen*' (named after the castles of ancient orders of chivalry) belong to the same totalitarian understanding of ideology, one which absolves itself of any suspicion of being ideological. What distinguishes our century from others is that it exhibits a general susceptibility of the intelligentsia, and not just of the 'masses', to such forms of thinking in a particularly alarming and fateful degree. It has become the century of totalitarian seduction because it was, and has remained, an age of ideologies.

This was rendered possible and indeed promoted by the rifts and crises which the idea of progress, the force behind the mighty wave of modernization in our age, brought with it and eventually suffered itself. Today we are once more in the midst of such a crisis of progress.[1] The experiences gained in this century should warn us against mistaking this situation for an end to ideologies. On the contrary. The need for ideologies, as well as vulnerability to the use and abuse of political ideologies, becomes especially noticeable and mobilizable just at this moment of a new dramatic break in progress. Scientific and technological progress, far from equipping us to offer stronger resistance to ideological seduction, have in fact complicated the task facing the individual as a citizen: to think politics out for himself and participate in its shaping in order to oppose subjection to the exclusive claim of political creeds – and not the other way round, as ideologists have always wanted.

[1] K. D. Bracher, 'Fortschritt – Krise einer Ideologie', in *Geschichte und Gewalt* (Berlin, 1981), p. 211ff.; see Rudolf Wendorff, *Zeit und Kultur* (Opladen, 1980), p. 498ff.

PART I
THE TURN OF THE CENTURY

Signposts to the Modern Age

Prophesie being many times
the principal Cause of the Event foretold.

Thomas Hobbes, *Behemoth*

1. THE IDEOLOGICAL LEGACY

In the history of political ideas the last turn of the century represents more than a fortuitous caesura. There had been breathtaking scientific and technical progress. The year 1900 itself witnessed Count Zeppelin's first flight, the formulation of the physical quantum theory by Max Planck and the psychoanalytical interpretation of dreams by Sigmund Freud, while Haeckel's biological best-seller promised the solution of all 'cosmic riddles'. However, this prevailing progressive thought was matched just as decisively by an increasing scepticism. In the *fin-de-siècle* mood, more particularly in the culture of the Austro–Hungarian Empire, the slogan of the 'end of the world' began to come into fashion, crises emerged on the horizon or were brought on by being talked about – self-fulfilling prophecies.[1] Books such as Spengler's *Decline of the West*, written years before the disaster of the Great War, anticipated a final decline of western civilization. Such ideas even had been expressed before by a writer from the most prominent family of the land of progress, America: Brooks Adams's gloomy philosophy of history proclaimed 'The Law of Civilization and Decay' as early as 1896.[2]

[1] See Paul Watzlawick (ed.), 'Selbsterfüllende Prophezeiungen', in *Die erfundene Wirklichkeit* (Munich and Zurich, 1981), p. 91ff. The term 'Austrian experimental institute for the end of the world' was coined by Karl Kraus in 1914, in his obituary for the assassinated heir to the throne, with a later variation in his play 'The Last Days of Mankind' (1922). See also Hebbel's prophetic lines: 'This Austria is a little world in which the big one holds its rehearsal.'

[2] Brooks Adams, *The Law of Civilization and Decay, an Essay on History* (New York, 1896; republished in 1943 with an important introduction by Charles Beard). Ten years later there appeared, at first privately published, the more famous brother's critique of history and civilization, *The Education of Henry Adams* (1906), with its originally intended subtitle 'A Study of Twentieth-Century Multiplicity' as a companion piece to his medieval study *Mont-Saint-Michel et Chartres: a Study of Thirteenth-Century Unity* (1904). On *The Decline of the West* see now P. Ch. Ludz (ed.), *Spengler heute* (Munich, 1980), especially the essays by Hermann Lübbe, p. viiff., and Horst Möller, p. 49ff.; see further H. Stuart Hughes, *Oswald Spengler: A Critical Estimate* (1952, 3rd ed., London 1975), p. 2, when Spengler is seen as a 'manifestation of the enormous effort of intellectual re-evaluation that has characterized our century'. The historical figures of the idea of decline since antiquity are dealt with most recently in the symposium of R. Koselleck and P. Widmer (eds), *Niedergang. Studien zu einem geschichtlichen Thema* (Stuttgart, 1980). Also Egon Weber (ed.), 'Decadence', *Journal of Contemporary History* (Special Issue) 17/1 (Jan. 1982). For a balance sheet of 'materialism' at the turn of the century as a background to the critique both of Adams and of Spengler: Carlton J. H. Hayes, *A Generation of Materialism, 1871–1900* (New York, 1941).

However, the turn of the century was not marked by any event of a particularly dramatic political nature. Although the calendar of events might record new tensions between Britain and Germany, the anti-British turn in the century-old good relations was sealed only by the further progress of the arms race. A Franco–Italian agreement on Morocco prepared the ground for Italy's defection from the Triple Alliance with Austria and Germany, yet this was nevertheless renewed twice more, in 1902 and 1907. The Hague peace conferences of 1899 and 1907 admittedly produced no results; their epoch-making importance as an attempt to achieve a comprehensive regulation of international arbitration and disarmament remained theoretical, overshadowed by the impending World War.[1] The political and social disturbances in Russia, leading in 1905, in the wake of defeats by Japan, to general strikes and the establishment of the first 'soviets' (workers' councils), as well as to increasing radicalization, finally marked the beginnings of the split of the working-class movement into democratic-reforming socialism on the one hand and revolutionary-dictatorial communism on the other. The idea of revolution had undergone ever-new manifestations in the nineteenth century. It represented a European force of journalistic and intellectual striking-power, extending from the classical revolutionary ideology of France to the conspiratorial and subversive endeavours of Russia.[2]

Yet the road to the great historic dates of 1917–18 – Lenin's seizure of power, the communist slogan of world revolution, the outcome of the World War – was scarcely yet discernible. Only the war would change all this, even though the prerequisites were gathering from one year to the next.

In juxtaposing the beginning of the twentieth century to the end of the nineteenth century we should consider also the two decades before and after the turn of the century, decades which heralded truly profound transformations. Politically, the imperial race between the great powers since Bismarck's resignation in 1890 had moved to a climax. Mention should be made here of the extension of the USA's sphere of interest towards Central America and the Philippines through its war with Spain (1898) as well as of the international policy of intervention in China against the Boxer Rebellion of 1900; of the completion of the European colonial appropriation of Africa and the Boer War in southern Africa (1899–1902); but above all of the further reversal of European alliances through the Franco–British 'Entente cordiale' (1904) and its rapprochement with Russia (1907), and finally of the

---

[1] Now especially Jost Dülffer, *Regeln gegen den Krieg? Die Haager Friedenskonferenzen 1899 und 1907 in der internationalen Politik* (Berlin, Frankfurt/M. and Vienna 1981), pp. 8ff., 69ff., 300ff. and 329ff.

[2] In this sense see the fundamental and comprehensive work of James H. Billington, *Fire in the Minds of Men, Origins of the Revolutionary Faith* (New York, 1980), on the two great poles of the French and the Russian revolutionary prophecy, its nationalist and socialist ideological constructs in the nineteenth century.

exacerbation of the Balkan Wars (1912–13) in Europe's most sensitive crisis region following the disintegration of the Turkish Empire. The year 1902 marked the beginnings of that first major liberal-critical argument with modern imperialism in the work of the English economist John A. Hobson (1858–1940), which had an effect on the Marxist theories of imperialism of such as Rosa Luxemburg or Rudolf Hilferding and, in particular, of Lenin.[1]

The outbreak of the First World War in 1914 – regardless of the controversial question of responsibility and, more particularly, the disastrously mistaken decisions of the German and Austrian governments – must be seen as a result of foreign-political crisis developments which had their beginnings about the turn of the century. The intensification of imperialism and nationalism, needless to say, not only brought with it the collapse of traditional diplomacy and the European power system of the nineteenth century, but at the same time was a result of the transforming pressures of deep-set internal-political and economic developments. Above all, the road to the First World War, and indeed its progress and effects, cannot be understood without those intellectual and ideological transformations which emerged about the turn of the century and in fact set the principal signals and defined the battle-lines for the next few decades.

Any balance sheet of the history of political ideas forming the background to those transformations must take into account two fundamental starting-points. These are, firstly, those 'prophets of yesterday' who, both in Europe and in America, played such an outstanding part in the evolution and formulation of political thought on the great transformational waves of modernization from 1789 to 1914. Secondly, there is of the development of those major 'sets of ideas' which characterized and publicized political thought in close association with concrete social and political developments in the nineteenth century and which, at the same time, sought to integrate and utilize the numerous theories of philosophers, historians and politicians

---

[1] Hobson's book *Imperialism* (London, 1902), was largely the result of his experiences as the *Manchester Guardian* correspondent in South Africa prior to the Boer War. See also Rosa Luxemburg, *Die Akkumulation des Kapitals, Ein Beitrag zur ökonomischen Erklärung des Imperialismus* (Berlin, 1913); Rudolf Hilferding, *Das Finanzkapital* (Vienna, 1910); V. I. Lenin's *Imperialism as the Highest Stage of Capitalism* (1916), the continuation of the socialist debate, revised as a result of the war; on this see Hans Christoph Schröder, *Sozialismus und Imperialismus*, 2nd ed. (Bonn, 1975). Still instructive is the classic sketch by Joseph A. Schumpeter, 'Zur Soziologie der Imperialismen' (1918–19), now in *Aufsätze zur Soziologie* (Tübingen, 1953), p. 72ff. Generally, Wolfgang J. Mommsen, *Imperialismus – Theorien*, Göttingen 1977; as well as the studies, published by Hugh Seton-Watson under the title 'Imperial Hangovers', on the after-effects and hangovers of diverse imperialisms from Spain via Turkey, Austria, Britain, France, Italy, Japan, Belgium, Holland, America to Germany, in the *Journal of Contemporary History* 15/1–2 (1980): Russia alone – so far – has retained its empire, though now justified by a communist ideology (p. 205ff.).

by welding them into practicable models and prescriptions for political action.[1]

This was also a manifestation of a process of ideologization. The great simplifying systems for the guiding, influencing and propagating, and indeed also the justifying (legitimation) or refuting (revolution), of real politics sprang from that interaction of political and ideological change which during the first half of the nineteenth century led to the co-existence and confrontation of the more or less classical (but still effective) areas of ideas: liberalism and the idea of democracy, socialism and Marxism, conservatism and nationalist *étatisme*.

The next step, of course, marks the negative side of this development. Modernization of politics and thought has ever since the Enlightenment and the Revolution been marked by a genuine explosion of the idea of progress,[2] an idea to which even romanticism and conservatism have to pay (grudging) tribute, just as de Tocqueville's critical view of democracy did. Yet the process is attended by conflicts, resulting in continual confrontations between the old and the new, in expansion and destruction, civilizational progress and cultural self-questioning. The great achievements of industrialization and technicalization of life are confronted by painful losses. Very soon the dark sides of this headlong development appear: close on the heels of the positive 'isms' of the ideas, as direct implications of progress, there follow the negative 'isms' of crisis and decline thinking, like companion pieces to an increasingly ideologized belief in progress. The escalation of the clash of political ideas results in radicalization and self-destruction. The forms and effects of such radicalization are nationalism and racialism, anarchism and the idea of class struggle, technocratism and the belief in violence, the cult of violence.

By the end of the nineteenth century the two poles of the awareness of the age were at last confronting one another, with the various political and ideological currents pulsating between them: forward-thrusting progress-

---

[1] Hermann Heller, *Die politischen Ideenkreise der Gegenwart* (Breslau, 1926); Gerhard Masur, *Prophets of Yesterday, Studies in European Culture 1890–1914* (New York, 1965). On the intellectual climate at the 'watershed' of 1900, Jan Romein, *The Watershed of Two Eras, Europe in 1900* (New York, 1978). For the German historical and political background, G. Masur, *Imperial Germany* (New York, 1970); Michael Stürmer (ed.), *Das Kaiserliche Deutschland 1870–1918* (Düsseldorf, 1970). See also the studies of transition by H. Stuart Hughes, *Consciousness and Society, The Reorientation of European Social Thought 1890–1930* (New York, 1961). On central issues of the turn of the century, Hans Barth, *Masse und Mythos, Die ideologische Krise an der Wende zum 20. Jahrhundert und die Theorie der Gewalt: Georges Sorel* (Hamburg, 1959).

[2] From among the vast and varied literature the latest overall critical assessments deserve special mention: Robert Nisbet, *History of the Idea of Progress* (New York, 1980), pp. 171ff., 297ff., see K. D. Bracher, 'Fortschritt-Krise einer Ideologie' in *Geschichte und Gewalt* (Berlin, 1981), p. 211ff. On the old counter-concept see the symposium by R. Koselleck and P. Widmer (eds), *Niedergang*, op. cit., as well as my unpublished doctoral thesis, 'Verfall und Fortschritt im Denken der frühen römischen Kaiserzeit' (Tübingen, 1948).

ivism and *fin-de-siècle* cultural malaise, a challenge to scientific positivism from new concepts of the world, and theories of social progress and crisis.[1] They influenced not only the economic and social but also the scientific and philosophical models of the world which marked a transition from romanticism to technology, from a stratified to an egalitarian society in the state, from historicism to positivism. Simultaneously with the seemingly final triumph of science there occurred, paradoxically, a more acute ideologization of thought; indeed the total belief in science found itself a tool, or subject to the dictation, of the ideologists. It supplied political ideologization with quasi-absolute rearrangeable pieces of scenery; it became an instrument for the technological and industrial intensification of the use of political power.

The most extreme manifestations of this were the pseudo-scientific and technological creeds of socialism and communism on the one hand, and of fascism and national socialism on the other: class or racial thinking as driving forces and legitimation of totalitarian dictatorship owed their popular appeal and destructive levelling power largely to a vulgarized and ideologized belief in science, no matter whether sociologically or biologically founded.

Small wonder that these potential perspectives of scientific progress were confronted by profound scepsis. The moment of the supreme unfolding of human intellect, inventiveness and organizational skill became the eve of a war disaster for Europe. Many contemporaries of headlong progress had regarded such a disaster as impossible, others saw the war as a pacemaker of progress or the result of the deployment of forces, and scarcely anyone tried to prevent it.[2] The reason was that both sides, the optimists of national progress and the pessimists of an excessively powerful mass civilization, were rooted in the ideologically extremist and frayed battle-lines of the

[1] On this point see the accounts by Fritz Stern, *The Politics of Cultural Despair, A Study in the Rise of the Germanic Ideology* (Berkeley, 1961); Carl Schorske, *Fin-de-Siècle Vienna* (New York, 1979); Peter Paret, *Die Berliner Secession, Moderne Kunst und ihre Feinde im kaiserlichen Deutschland* (Berlin, 1981); George Mosse, *The Nationalization of the Masses* (New York, 1975); George Lichtheim, *Europe in the Twentieth Century* (London, 1972), p. 43ff. with the bibliography. On America in particular David A. Shannon (ed.), *Progressivism and Postwar Disillusionment 1898–1928* (New York, 1965); Yves-Henri Nouailhat, *Histoire des doctrines politiques aux États-Unis*, 2nd ed. (Paris, 1977), p. 75ff. ('Progressisme et imperialisme').

[2] See the studies by Roland N. Stromberg: 'The Intellectuals and the Coming of the War in 1914', *The Journal of European Studies* 3 (1973), p. 109ff.; 'Socialism and War in 1914', *Midwest Quarterly* 18 (1977), p. 268ff.; 'Redemption by War: The Intellectuals and 1914', *Midwest Quarterly* 20 (1979), p. 211ff. The way in which the impending war was anticipated in literature as a 'struggle between nations' of previously unheard-of technological total dimensions is shown by books such as *Das Menschenschlachthaus* (1912) by Wilhelm Ramszus. The ambivalent connection between war and progress was dealt with in particular by a colleague of the American war research pioneer, Quincy Wright (*A Study of War*, 1942); see John U. Nef, *War and Human Progress, An Essay on the Rise of Industrial Civilization* (New York, 1950, reprint 1968).

century that was drawing to a close. During that century autonomous national states and bourgeois parties, trade unions and working-class movements, industrial powers and special-interest pressure groups – in short, the structure of modern mass politics and its ideological direction – had been organized, enshrined in constitutions, and increasingly safeguarded by voting and civil rights. In consequence, however, the power of the states had been increased and ideologically hardened, both domestically and in the foreign-political confrontation of political forces and interests. To circumscribe and control them now became the principal problem of the modern mass and power state.

The First World War subsequently showed how strong was this ideologically excessive integration of the national states, how violently it seized mainly the 'new' nations (of Italy, Germany and eastern Europe) and how decisively the profoundly ambivalent claim to self-determination – to be practised either in a democratically peaceful or in a dictatorially expansionist manner – cut across and overlaid the supranational referential patterns of the great sets of ideas. The earlier federalistically democratic idea of the League of Nations, developed principally by President Wilson out of The Hague Conferences, remained controversial and largely ineffectual. The international dimension of an ideologically dogmatic policy later emerged far more powerfully in communism, fascism and national socialism, that is, under the banner of totalitarian, anti-democratic policies of hegemony and imposed uniformity.[1]

Naturally this dimension had existed from the outset, ever since the first great ideological revolution in France in 1789, the real starting-point of the crystallization of modern political currents and sets of ideas.[2] Bourgeois enlightenment and liberalism, the call for liberty and equality, government by the people and an awareness of an ideological mission, nationalism and

---

[1] See K. D. Bracher, 'Demokratische und totalitäre Europapolitik', in *Innen- und Aussenpolitik (Festschrift W. Hofer)* (Bern, 1980), p. 73ff. In spite of all fashionable fluctuations and taboos the author clings to the concept of totalitarianism. Its historical links not only with ancient despotic traditions but also with a radical idea of progress and democracy has been most impressively presented by J. L. Talmon, op. cit., p. 249: 'Totalitarian democracy, far from being a phenomenon of recent growth and outside the Western tradition, has its roots in the common stock of eighteenth-century ideas. It branched out as a separate and identifiable trend in the course of the French Revolution and has unbroken continuity ever since.' Talmon's chain of argument runs as follows: *volonté générale* means the social imperative of pure reason, which cannot therefore be legitimately opposed by anyone. It imposes a single system of values upon different people, and is therefore totalitarian and, simultaneously, radically democratic because implementation is linked with the active participation of all citizens. Similar ideas are also in Alfred Cobban, *The Crisis of Civilization* (London, 1941), p. 67: 'Dictatorship is both the logical and the historical consequence of the theory of the General Will. . . . The attempt to get the abstract idea of the General Will into practice produces dictatorship.'

[2] See Fritz Valjavec, *Die Entstehung der politischen Strömungen in Deutschland 1770–1815*, 2nd ed. (1977); Rudolf Wendorff, 'Die Entstehung des Fortschrittsdenkens', in *Zeit und Kultur*, op. cit., pp. 321ff., 391ff.

internationalism´ all then emerged virtually simultaneously, with all their contradictions. It was in the course of the French Revolution and of Napoleonic hegemony over Europe, practised in the name of those ideas, that the domestic and foreign-policy ideologization of politics first came fully into play.

Precursors of this phenomenon, such as the religious wars of the sixteenth century or the English Revolution in the seventeenth century, were predominantly associated with religious or traditionalist justifications of power politics, even though their effects may have transcended them. This is still true of the American Revolution of 1776, even though early liberalism and the vision of a 'new world' were powerful aspects of it; basically, however, it was concerned with ancient rights and with independence, and not with an ideological revolution for all of mankind, nor indeed with violent internal upheaval, in spite of the far-reaching consequences it was to have, not least for the French Revolution. It was the latter's national and, at the same time, humanistic, justification of political transformation, together with its supranational overspill, that irrevocably heralded in the new age of ideas and ideologies, both in action and reaction.[1] Existing political structures and social ties were called in question, and indeed made exclusively dependent on quasi-'politically-scientific' theories of reason, instead of, as before, on an authoritative religion or tradition.

This is true even of its effect on the declared opponents of secular upheaval and transformation. Even though modern conservatism essentially emerged as a reaction to the American and French Revolutions, it nevertheless, even with its first major champion (Edmund Burke), attempted to fit itself into the modern trend of ideas based on the autonomy of reason by proclaiming both the preservation of the existing *and* reform, both the enduring value of tradition *and* the continual improvement of the system. In fact, the claim of the new politics of ideas was and remained so powerful that, even in the age of reaction and the 'Holy Alliance', no state, however conservative, neither the Prussia of the authoritarian philosopher F. J. Stahl nor the Austria of Metternich, could afford to do entirely without the new ideological justifications or indeed remain aloof in future from the ideologization of its own political ends and means. If only because this ideologization went hand in hand with the two great demands of contemporary power politics (whose implementation alone was capable of providing security against the rising bourgeoisie and the growing working class) *viz.*, a tougher organization of the state and national–political integration.

The century of the modernization of political organization is thus at the same time (either as a necessary result or in spite of it) the century of the

---

[1] See now the latest survey in Fenske-Mertens-Reinhard-Rosen, *Geschichte der politischen Ideen* (Königstein, 1981), pp. 307ff., 319ff.

politics of ideas; in other words, of a politicization of ideas as much as of an ideologization of politics. It is from these premises that the subsequent examination of political ideas and of the ideologically determined political camps in Europe since the nineteenth century will proceed.

2. PROGRESS AND IRRATIONALISM

The idea of political progress is marked by two major opposing orientations. Its aim is change and improvement. Its means are dispute, conflict with existing traditions and systems. Progress ultimately justifies struggle and revolution. Yet the idea of progress has also invariably aimed at peace and its universal extension, promising a final solution of political problems. The idea of conflict and the idea of peace have emerged in acute confrontation since the end of the nineteenth century.

This political ambiguity of the idea of progress found its most extreme expression in the assertion that war was the mainspring of progress, that it promoted, above all else, material, scientific and also moral transformation. From Hegel to modern rearmament and military scientists the idea of power has been closely linked with a historical–political view of progress. On the other hand there is the belief of liberal enlighteners and democrats that political progress consists primarily in the steady and ever more universal extension of personal freedom in the world: increased knowledge and improved control of nature will become possible to the extent that obstacles to freedom are removed and that the political system ensures the full development of the individual.

This fundamental ambivalence was reduced to the formula: progress as freedom and progress as power.[1] And in fact the ideological development of progressivism can be traced in both directions. Active in the former sense are the ideas of thinkers such as Turgot, Gibbon, Adam Smith, the American founding fathers, Condorcet, Godwin, Malthus, Kant, Mill and Spencer, while Rousseau, Fichte, Hegel, Saint-Simon, Comte, Marx and Gobineau are seen as supporting the opposite trend. They counterposed the doctrines of nationalism and *étatisme*, of (socialist) utopianism and (populist) racialism to those of progressivist individualism. The imminence of the great clash has been perceptible since the turn of the century. It threatens to reduce the earlier belief in progress politically *ad absurdum* as its inherent contradictions are increasingly revealed.

The watershed between the nineteenth and the twentieth centuries was characterized by the political consequences brought about worldwide by the final triumph of the national state in Italy (1870) and in Germany (1871),

[1] Robert Nisbet, op. cit., pp. 179, 237.

simultaneously by the end of the Empire in France and the subsequent establishment of the Third Republic, by the comprehensive recovery of the USA after the Civil War (1865), by domestic pressure for reforms in every country, and by colonial imperialism. A multitude of innovations followed one another, resulting in profound changes first in Europe and America and soon throughout the world: electricity (1878), the motor car (1885 Daimler and Benz), film (the Lumière brothers 1895), wireless telegraphy (Marconi 1895), radio (1904) and finally the aeroplane (1895 Lilienthal, 1903 the Wright brothers) – rapid scientific progress in all fields. Voyages of discovery to both poles and the completion of the American 'frontier' movement to the West marked both the peak and the turning-point in the advance of civilization. In 1893 the American historian F. J. Turner (1861–1932) drew up a balance sheet of this movement: he saw progress as the advancement of the frontier and the penetration of democracy into barbarian countries. But this already posed the uneasy question about the future of progress under more restricted conditions, once 'the West' had been opened up.[1]

The history of ideas records the climax of the philosophy of Friedrich Nietzsche (1844–1900), followed by the first publications of Sigmund Freud (1856–1939) in 1893. Both, though in rather different ways, represented a challenge to the prevailing rationalism and faith in progress. This marked the emergence of crisis thought and of the irrational amidst a certainty that everything could be discovered and that the 'cosmic riddles' would soon be solved by science and technology, as proclaimed in a best-seller by the influential biologist Ernst Haeckel in 1900. The trite materialist monism of such books, which invested Darwinism with universal infallibility by assuming that man, originating from the ape, would pass through natural selection to an early final triumph over all the world's problems, produced not only a certainty of progress but also, alongside the reaction of the Churches, intensified philosophical and ideological conflicts concerning the social consequences of progress.

Nietzsche's critique of culture was concerned with the emergence of the man of the masses and with the significance of the élite and the strong individual. The social Darwinists and racialists transformed Darwin's doctrine of selection into a social theory of the struggle for existence and the right of the stronger nation or race to rule others. The new psychology was concerned with the internal exploration of man as against the belief that man's external conditions could be manipulated and brought to an assumed

[1] Frederick Jackson Turner, 'The Significance of the Frontier in American History' (Lecture to the American Historical Association 1893), published also in Turner's volume, *The Frontier in American History* (New York, 1920); on the set of problems, K. D. Bracher, 'Der Frontier-Gedanke: Motiv des amerikanischen Fortschrittsbewusstseins. Ein ideologienkritischer Versuch', *Zeitschrift für Politik* 2 (1955), p. 228ff. A second major theme emerging (as also in the discussion on antiquity) is the relationship between progress and slavery. See David Brion Davis, 'Slavery and the Idea of Progress', in Erich Angermann and Marie-Luise Frings (eds), *Oceans Apart? Comparing Germany and the United States* (Stuttgart, 1981), p. 13ff.

perfection through external progress. What all these views had in common were the beginnings of a profound doubt in society as it existed.

The consequences, of course, differed a great deal. The falsifications of Nietzsche's followers, with the philosopher's own sister in the vanguard, promptly refashioned his multi-level position of doubt and questioning which, in *Thus Spoke Zarathustra* (1883), in *Beyond Good and Evil* (1886) and in the *Genealogy of Morals* (1887) aimed at the supreme development of the individual, into a doctrine of the *Will to Power*; Nietzsche's last book (1888), arbitrarily compiled after his death, actually (quite wrongly) bears this title. Certainly it was possible to derive from Nietzsche's aphoristic insights and polemics something like a radical challenge to bourgeois-liberal society and its confident belief in progress, but there was equally an uncompromising critique of the imperial power states, especially the new German Empire, as well as the pseudo-scientific ideologies of the racialists and anti-Semites who experienced their first European flowering in the eighties and nineties.

As though in a burning glass Nietzsche gathered the scintillating surmises and theses of his day and intensified them in all their multiplicity and inconsistency. Just as with other emphatically original philosophical critics of their times, from Plato through Machiavelli, Hobbes and Rousseau to Hegel, his ideas were highly susceptible to subsequent ideologization. The deep personal resentments of this restless individual, his leapingly inventive, metaphorically poetical style, the subjective and ambivalent nature of his value-judgements, and finally his mistrust of the self-assurance of progress and of his age's trend towards mass democracy, countered by his justific-ation of the idea of an aristocratic power-wielding élite and of the trans-moral claim to power by the strong individual 'beyond good and evil' – all these offered splendid arguments for an anti-rationalist and anti-liberal critique especially from the Right, but also for the ideas of revolutionary violence from the Left. Just as had happened to Machiavellism, so Nietzsche's philosophy underwent an ideologization in this sense and became an ambiguous model, of truly massive consequences, in the 'pre-thinking' or 'idea prompting'[1] of authoritarianism and syndicalism, fascism

[1] 'Ideensouffleur': Thomas Mann, 'Nietzsches Philosophie im Lichte unserer Erfahrung', in *Schriften und Reden zur Literatur, Kunst und Philosophie*, Vol. 3 (Frankfurt/M., 1968), p. 41. On the falsification and manipulation of Nietzsche see especially Karl Schlechta, *Der Fall Nietzsche*, 2nd ed. (Munich, 1959); on categorization an early source is Hans Barth, 'Nietzsche und die politischen Idcologicn der Gcgcnwart', in *Fluten und Dämme* (Zurich, 1943); see also Friedrich Glum, *Philosophen im Spiegel und Zerrspiegel* (Munich, 1954), p. 134ff.; Paul-Laurent Assaun, *Freud et Nietzsche* (Paris, 1980). The most readable new overall portrayal is by Werner Ross, *Der ängstliche Adler, Friedrich Nietzsches Leben* (Stuttgart, 1980), p. 692ff. On the specialized question of fascism, Ernst Nolte, 'Marx und Nietzsche im Sozialismus des jungen Mussolini', *Historische Zeitschrift* 191 (1960), p. 249ff. His stylization into the pioneer of national socialism was performed chiefly by Alfred Bäumler, *Nietzsche der Philosoph und Politiker* (1931); see K. D. Bracher, *The German Dictatorship* (London, 1980), p. 45ff.; *Stufen der Machtergreifung*, 3rd ed. (1974), p. 420f.

and national socialism. Indeed nearly all the thought patterns and political concepts of the century following him reveal the lasting influence of the controversy about his ideas.

The significance of social Darwinism, of course, is far less ambiguous. Here we find a direct link not only with a quasi-scientific justification of the power-state principle but also with the populist theories of the racialists and the belief in the salvation of the 'superior' race through ruthless measures of 'racial hygiene', through racial struggle and the annihilation of the 'inferior'.[1] While Mussolini's thinking might have been derived, principally, from the idea of a socialist revolution, from Hegel's *étatisme* and from Nietzsche's élitist concept, Hitler and radical national socialism were influenced predominantly by racialist social Darwinism, subsequently amalgamated with imperialist and geopolitical theories of a struggle for 'living space' for the master race. So far, however, these are all-European ideas: the major contribution of French civilizational critique emerges also in Count Gobineau's racial theory and in the French Right wing's emphatic reaction to the ideas of the Revolution.

The third event in crisis thought, the foundation of psychoanalysis by Sigmund Freud, occurred considerably later than the other two – basically not until after the First World War. This does not rule out the possibility that the starting-point of psychoanalysis, the critique of a rationalist view of the individual and of the Victorian concept of morality, was, in a sense, in the air. Indeed it announced its arrival also in the upheavals in art and in music about the turn of the century, in the emphasis on the subconscious, in a transition from representational portrayal to an analysis of deeper feelings, towards Expressionism and an abstract approach.

In contrast to Nietzsche, the visionary philosopher of civilization, and to the pseudo-scientific vulgar philosophers of social Darwinism, Freud was an emphatically empiricist scientist. From this quarter, therefore, a questioning of the progressivist faith in science was bound to have especially painful consequences so long as it was founded on clinical investigation and formulated in terms of rational concepts.

The discovery of the unconscious and the subconscious, however, was overdue in an age when the influencing of the masses by means of modern

---

[1] Hedwig Conrad-Martius, *Utopien der Menschenzüchtung: Der Sozialdarwinismus und seine Folgen* (Munich, 1955); Richard Hofstadter, *Social Darwinism in American Thought* (New York, 1959); W. H. Koch, *Der Sozialdarwinismus, Seine Genese und sein Einfluss auf das imperialistische Denken* (Munich, 1973). See also Hans Günther Zmarzlik, 'Der Sozialdarwinismus in Deutschland als geschichtliches Problem', *Vierteljahrshefte für Zeitgeschichte* 11 (1963), p. 246ff.; K. D. Bracher, *German Dictatorship*, p. 27ff. Also the bibliography in Fenske, op. cit., pp. 406ff., 518f.; Rudolf Wendorff, 'Darwinismus und Marxismus', in *Zeit und Kultur*, op. cit., p. 400ff.

propaganda, 'mass psychology',[1] had already been technically developed, both for stimulating the economy through consumption and for legitimating government action through approval by plebiscite. This was true not only of majority rule in the democracies, with their free choice and competition for influencing the masses; it was more especially true of the seizure of power and exercise of government by minorities endeavouring to rule dictatorially in the name of and on the back of democracy, that is, endeavouring to create and manipulate public opinion through persuasion, pressure and compulsion.

The modern totalitarian movements, claiming as they did that they were implementing government by the people, based themselves on hitherto unsuspected possibilities of such manipulation. Admittedly, they tended to be the semi-scientific postulates of an emotionally controllable popular or mass soul, as subsequently exploited by Hitler in what is probably the most original part of *Mein Kampf* (1924) and applied by him at the mass rallies of his 'movement'. Nevertheless, modern propaganda succeeded in utilizing the growing insights into the importance of the unconscious and sub-conscious, of the non-rational. This meant, too, that the weaknesses of the liberal belief in progress, in the educability of man's rational nature, were revealed.

By contrast, Freud's psychoanalysis could not readily be allotted a political place. Its advance in understanding simultaneously militated against the basic axioms of the contemporary faith in progress. Marxism and the political Left in particular found its non-economic approach and its concentration on the individual unacceptable. The conservatives and the bourgeoisie regarded the moral implications of a thematization of sexual drives with suspicion and feared a threat to traditional family and social relationships. For a long time, therefore, Freudianism was of merely indirect significance to political thought; moreover, its effects were distorted by anti-Semitic hostility to the ideas.[2]

---

[1] *Psychologie des foules* by Gustave Le Bon (1841–1931) was published as early as 1895, and republished in numerous languages almost every year. Unscientifically generalized examples, chiefly from the French Revolution and the Paris Commune of 1871, were adduced to prove the antidemocratic postulates of a collective guidability of the 'masses'; the arguments of this mass psychology were repeated also in the relevant chapters of Hitler's *Mein Kampf* (pp. 197ff., 371ff., 530ff., 650ff.; see K. D. Bracher, *Die Auflösung der Weimarer Republik*, 6th ed. (1978), p. 112ff.). On social-science developments in France prior to the turn of the century, Robert A. Nye, *The Origins of Crowd Psychology, Gustave Le Bon and the Crisis of Mass Democracy in the Third Republic* (London, 1975).

[2] See especially Peter Gay, *Freud, Jews and other Germans* (Oxford, 1978), p. 29ff.; also L. L. Whyte, *The Unconscious before Freud* (New York, 1962); Paul Roazen, *Freud's Political and Social Thought* (1968), and *Freud and his Followers* (New York, 1976); Hannah S. Decker, *Freud in Germany, Revolution and Reaction in Science 1893–1907* (New York, 1977). Generally, George Mosse, *The Culture of Western Europe* (New York, 1961), p. 263ff.; William M. Johnston, *The Austrian Mind, An Intellectual and Social History 1848–1938* (Berkeley, 1972); R. J. Evans (ed.), *Society and Politics in Wilhelmine Germany* (New York, 1978); Rudolf Wendorff in *Zeit und Kultur*, p. 479ff.

Nevertheless it would be a mistake to underrate the new discoveries of psychology as a factor in the crisis of ideas merely because scientific and, even more so, academic acceptance of Freud's teachings was slow in coming. Freud published further pioneering works on psychoanalysis in 1910 and 1917, on *The Ego and the Id* (1923) and on *Civilization and its Discontents* (1930). Indirectly, through disciples and divergent theories (Alfred Adler, Carl G. Jung), its affinity with the needs for a psychopolitical understanding of the irrational has made it an important constituent in the upheavals in political thought and action since the turn of the century.

Another significant variation of crisis thought, one which attracted considerable attention to irrationalism even before the turn of the century, was represented, after 1889, by the books and lectures of the French philosopher Henri Bergson.[1] With a much more direct effect than Freud's analytical interpretations, and more respectable than Nietzsche's erratic ideas, Bergson's 'creative evolution' was hailed by contemporaries as an advance into unexplored territory, as the posing of new sets of questions, as a transrational creativity of thought and perception contrasting with trite rationalism. It was basically a neo-romantic attitude, culminating in a differentiation between the purely rational and conceptual intellectualism of an age believing in science and technology on the one hand, and an intuitively comprehending form of thinking oriented towards a deeper and more comprehensive truth than rational analysis on the other. Comprehension of the true, most inward, life by way of intuition, instinct, direct experience, 'vitalism' as an insight into an inner vital force instead of a merely mechanistically scientific intellectualism – this was the answer (not all that original, in fact, if one thinks of cognitive philosophy from Kant to Dilthey, but in line with the age) to the anti-rationalist questioning of the meaning and value of progress and to the question of the truth behind the external appearance of things.

To an emerging irrationalism in political and social theory this starting-point offered a respectable justification (one that was open to a variety of interpretations) of philosophies of action and volition to which radical ideologists and revolutionaries could refer and on which they could base themselves. On the emphasis on spontaneous action rather than reasoning intellect, on the entirety instead of the individual, on a transrational warm community instead of a cold, purely utilitarian society, on culture instead of civilization. The critique of intellectualism and of the intellectuals as the exponents of the idea of progress was to become one of the mainsprings of all anti-liberal movements, of authoritarian and totalitarian ideologies especially after the First World War.

By counterposing the demand for a 'creative evolution' of the world to the

---

[1] Especially Henri Bergson, *Matière et mémoire* (Paris, 1897). On this see Thomas Hanna (ed.), *The Bergsonian Heritage* (1962); and J. J. Gallagher, *Morality in Evolution: The Moral Philosophy of Henri Bergson* (1970).

prevailing Darwinism,[1] Bergson's mystically irrational, romantic philosophy seemed to indicate a new alternative of unsuspected strength. Its revolutionary effect was in no way diminished by its being dismissed as romantically reactionary or as an anti-modernist offence against technological and scientific progress or the achievements of democracy. On the contrary. It satisfied needs which were to arise directly amidst the political and social crises following the First World War but which had been powerfully signalling their arrival about the turn of the century.

As in the case of fascism and national socialism, the explosive power of anti-rationalism and irrationalism – underestimated by rationalist liberals and reformist socialists – lay in this very ambivalence, in the entangled combination of traditionalist and novel elements, in the interplay of reactionary and revolutionary needs which could not simply be measured by the yardstick of progress or retrogression.

Needless to say (and even more so than in the case of Nietzsche) there can be no question of a direct line leading from Bergson to the authoritarian-totalitarian ideologies. The religiosity and liberality of his thoughts ran counter not only to one-sided mechanistic materialism but most profoundly also to the authoritarian jackboot. His creative evolution was ultimately an affirmation of the individual against the technicalizing and collectivizing tendencies of the age of the masses; though admittedly it also harboured the danger of an ideologized and politicized irrationalism.

Closely connected with this trend, but different from the European crisis awareness because of a lesser historical burden and a greater measure of consensus with a democratic cultural development, there arose about the same time the American 'pragmatism' of William James (1842–1910) and John Dewey (1859–1952).[2] This theory of experience, oriented on the

[1] Thus Bergson's books, all with significant titles including *L'évolution créatrice* (1906), and *Durée et simultanéité* (1922). The German publisher Eugen Diederichs saw in Bergson a new irrationalist philosophy, comparable to the mysticism of Meister Eckhart: see Lulu von Strauss und Torney-Diederichs (eds), *Eugen Diederichs Leben und Werke* (Jena, 1936), p. 180.

[2] The most important works of William James are *Will to Believe* (1897); *Varieties of Religious Experience* (1902); *Pragmatism* (1907); of John Dewey: *How We Think* (1909); *Democracy and Education* (1916). See E. L. Moore, *American Pragmatism* (New York, 1961); also the principal comparative study by Paul K. Conkin, *Puritans and Pragmatists: Eight Eminent American Thinkers* (1968). Still of interest is Eduard Baumgarten, *Der Pragmatismus (Die geistigen Grundlagen des amerikanischen Gemeinwesens*, Vol. 2) (Frankfurt/M., 1938); also Thomas Löffelholz, *Die Rechtsphilosophie des Pragmatismus* (Meisenheim, 1961). On the intellectual history aspects, Roland N. Stromberg, *An Intellectual History of Europe*, 2nd ed. (Englewood, 1975), pp. 363ff, 438ff.; on the specifically American discussion of ideas, methods and research during the past few decades see also John Higham, Paul K. Conkin (eds), *New Directions in American Intellectual History* (Baltimore, 1980), pp. 64ff, 212ff.; Thomas L. Haskell, *The Emergence of Professional Social Science: The American Social Science Association and the 19th-Century Crisis of Authority* (Urbana, 1977); Alexandra Oleson, John Voss (eds), *The Organization of Knowledge in Modern America 1860–1920* (Baltimore, 1979); as well as the major article by Felix Gilbert, 'Intellectual History, Its Aims and Methods', *Daedalus* 100, No. 1 (Winter 1971), p. 8off.

practice of democracy, revealed the diverse, or indeed conflicting, possibilities which the political significance and effect of creative evolution could have. Pragmatism led to a theory of education for democracy which sought to do justice also to the non-rational factors, whereas in European thought the liberal-rational democratic principle and an anti-rational or trans-rational authoritarian community idea were being developed in increasingly uncompromising opposition to one another. Pragmatism represented a critique of purely 'intellectual knowledge', an emphasis on direct experience and a concept of reality which, just as the experience of music is based not only on notes but on hearing, comprised both and indeed attached the more profound importance to the latter.

Edmund Husserl's 'phenomenology', which succeeded Bergson and whose concepts go back to 1900, similarly reflected the strength and also the ambivalence of not-merely-rational interpretation patterns. Husserl was ostracized by the national socialists as a Jew, but his influential disciple Martin Heidegger, whose On Time and Being (1927) ushered in existentialism, in 1933 leapt the barrier to the ideology of national socialism, thereby proving both the affinities and the misunderstandings which marked the relationship between the new philosophy and authoritarian politics.[1]

Doubts of a definitive, abstract truth, the dependence of all 'truths' on the momentary 'act' of the acting individual, life as an open experiment whose reality we are ceaselessly testing: such theses certainly found an echo on both sides – among libertarian artists and writers and also among early fascists (such as the Italian pragmatist Giovanni Papini) and the later national socialists who were demanding a philosophy capable of endorsing the politics of action and ideological arbitrariness in the sense of a philosophy 'in tune with the people', in lieu of a rational 'objectivism' and supranational truth.[2] Irrationalism had a great many roots, fathers and disciples; it was equally capable of operating as a supplement to or as the destruction of modern civilizational and democratic evolution. It represented a relativization not only of science but also of faith, in the sense that the Catholic Church, for instance, could be both dismissed and admired as a 'splendid error' and a great myth – thus the pragmatist George Santayana, but thus also the Catholic Adolf Hitler in his negative appreciation of ecclesiastical organization and authority.[3]

[1] On the 'Heidegger case' mention should be made, among other things, of the address in which the philosopher, as the new Rector of the University of Freiburg, hailed the national socialist seizure of power – and resigned his claim to scholarship: 'Let not theses or ideas be the rules of your being! The Führer himself and alone is today and in future the German reality and its law' (in Martin Heidegger, Die Selbstbehauptung der deutschen Universität (Breslau, 1934), p. 22ff.).

[2] See K. D. Bracher, Die nationalsozialistische Machtergreifung, new ed. (1974), Vol. 1, pp. 364ff. and 556ff. with the bibliography.

[3] Alongside the much-quoted passages in Mein Kampf see also Hitler's illuminating conversation with E. A. Scharrer as early as the end of December 1922 in which he claimed that 'The Catholic Church deserves esteem because in championing its teachings it always remains consistently unshakable and does not compromise. It will retain its youthfulness forever because it invariably draws its best forces for the supreme ecclesiastical posts from below', in Eberhard Jäckel (ed.), Hitler, Sämtliche Aufzeichnungen 1905–1924 (Stuttgart, 1980), p. 775.

It is the plain consequence of any kind of ideologization that ideas are adopted as not (absolutely) true yet (absolutely) useful. This was bound to be especially true of the new subjectivism which relativized objective science just as much as social and political values. The most frightening example was *The Myth of the Twentieth Century* by which in the twenties the dilettante philosopher Alfred Rosenberg attempted to bestow an ideological consecration upon the racialism of national socialism – although Hitler expressly paid no attention to this 'unofficial piece of work'. But in replacing the idea of truth and of religion – and hence the denial of objectivity – by the myth, Rosenberg had no difficulty in utilizing that post-Nietzschean critique of rationalism and civilization which had also inspired his principal model, the widely-read *Foundations of the Nineteenth Century* (1899) by the English-born Houston Stewart Chamberlain, who had welded together racialism, 'Aryan' Christianity, idealism and creative evolution into a strange but exceedingly effective philosophy of history.[1]

The use of religion as a purely subjective experience, as a poetic adornment of life, as Jung's good 'psychotherapy', showed both its dissolution and its enlistment for service. Once again we have arrived at the transition point or the juncture of ideas and ideologies, as it emerged visibly about the watershed of the nineteenth and twentieth centuries. At the end of the First World War it gave rise to a universal ideologization of political positions, to the great new confrontation between democracy, fascism and communism, between the camp of rationalism and liberalism, and that of authoritarianism and totalitarianism.

The new irrationalism, originally a great inspiration mainly to literature and art, was abused and presently overtaken by the violent absolutisms of dictatorial movements from Right and Left, movements which, accelerated by the First World War, turned the question of truth into a basic question of power. Instead of the alternating rivalry of ideas there came the destructive struggle of ideologies: the decline of the one side into Hitlerism and of the other into Stalinism, the decline of Europe. The new philosophies were capable – just as much as the progress-intoxicated belief in technology, which they criticized – of lending support to all kinds of political movements provided these elevated action and dynamism into a principle. This was presently done by the war propagandists and before long by the future dictators.

---

[1] See Winfried Schuler, *Der Bayreuther Kreis von seiner Entstehung bis zum Ausgang der wilhelminischen Ära* (Münster, 1971); also the extravagant letter from Landsberg prison to Siegfried Wagner (5 May 1924), in which Hitler records his first visit to Haus Wahnfried in Bayreuth (early October 1923) and his meeting with the aged H. S. Chamberlain: Jäckel, op. cit., p. 1231ff. Hitler praised Bayreuth as the town 'where, first by the Master [Richard Wagner] and then by Chamberlain there was forged the spiritual sword with which we are fighting this day'.

3. POLITICAL RELIGIONS
AND THE BELIEF IN RACE

Simultaneously with a new wave of emphasis on man's subjective dimension and his unconscious, the progressive exploration of the external world had also led to profound crises within rational scientific thought. The philosophers of doubt were not by any means faced with a world of science that was solidly built and free from self-questioning. Indeed its latest discoveries tended to militate against the popular ideas of the mechanistic nature of the entire universe and of its subservience to laws which could be mastered. Nuclear physics, chemistry and biology were coming up against ever more complex patterns: while these did not prevent the most astonishing discoveries or inventions from being made, they certainly prevented the ultimate solution of the 'cosmic riddles' and instead called for new reflection on the limitations of natural science and its assured belief in causality. Albert Einstein's two epoch-making 'theories of relativity' (1905 and 1915), with their significant titles, also characterized the gulf between the structures of the universe and human capacity for cognition and conceptualization.

Thus the doubts which had brought a disenchantment with natural science to other spheres of thought were now being nourished also by scientific-technical and material progress. Traditional Christianity, challenged by the clergyman's son Nietzsche with his slogan 'God is dead', was described as a supernatural miracle religion incompatible with man's modern knowledge of nature and the world. Simultaneously it was being questioned by the historical criticism of its own Bible researchers, including the trend for the 'historical Christ', which produced even such curious blooms as Chamberlain's 'Aryan' Christ. Protestants, traditionally at loggerheads with each other, fluctuated between 'fundamentalists and modernists', Lutheran orthodoxy and a very considerable measure of rationalist 'liberalization'. Catholicism, still disturbed by the controversies on papal infallibility of 1870, adopted a critical stand towards the liberal and democratic doctrines because of the religious implications of scientific and socio-political modernization whenever these doctrines promoted progressivist scepsis and indifference.[1]

It was not political structure or ideology but the preservation of Christian principles and institutions that determined the policies of the Christian parties in France, Italy and Germany; these played an important part in the transition to democracy but equally displayed sympathy for authoritarian movements. They were eventually overrun by fascism and national socialism, while in the authoritarian dictatorships of Portugal, Spain and elsewhere their role tended to vacillate.[2]

The ambivalence of ecclesiastical policy, both of Catholicism and of Protestantism (the latter tending even more strongly towards the national authoritarian camp in Germany) led to a number of serious conflicts between liberal democracy and the Churches. In France especially, following the disturbing Dreyfus affair of 1894–1906, when anti-Semitic trends went hand in hand with ecclesiastic conservatism, an anti-clerical republicanism emerged, leading to a 'laicized' separation of Church and state in 1901, which further exacerbated the critical relationship between the Roman Catholic Church and modernism in society and the state. In Italy the unclarified situation between the temporal position of the papacy and the new state, which in 1870 had incorporated the Pontifical state, persisted with frequent tension until the advent of fascism.[3]

The difficulties of the Churches with the new fundamental currents of the times concerned not only their relations with science and liberalism (there

[1] Generally on this point George Mosse, *Culture*, op. cit., p. 245, still valid is Waldemar Gurian, *Die politischen und sozialen Ideen des französischen Katholizismus 1789–1914* (München-Gladbach, 1929); Hans Maier, *Revolution und Kirche, Studien zur Frühgeschichte der christlichen Demokratie 1789–1901*, 3rd ed. (Freiburg/Br., 1973); Helga Grebing (ed.), *Geschichte der sozialen Ideen in Deutschland* (Munich, 1969); Franz Prinz, *Kirche und Arbeiterschaft* (Munich, 1974); *Die soziale Frage und der Katholizismus. Festschrift zum 40 jährigen Jubiläum der Enzyklika Rerum novarum* (Paderborn, 1931); Michele Ranchetti, *The Catholic Modernists* (1970). On the philosophical and political problems also Hermann Lübbe, *Säkularisierung, Geschichte eines ideenpolitischen Begriffs* (Freiburg/Br., 1965).

[2] The comprehensive survey and latest state of research is by Wolfgang Mantl, 'Kirche und Staat', in *Katholisches Soziallexikon*, 2nd ed. (Innsbruck/Graz, 1980), col. 1346ff.; see in particular Hans-Peter Fagagnini, 'Christlichdemokratische Parteien', ibid., col. 369ff. Also Hans Maier, *Kirche und Gesellschaft* (Munich, 1972), pp. 82ff, 135ff.; Gert K. Kaltenbrunner (ed.), *Das Elend der Christdemokraten* (Freiburg/Br., 1977); Richard Konetzke, 'Die iberischen Staaten . . .', in Th. Schieder (ed.), *Handbuch der europäischen Geschichte*, Vol. 7/1 (Stuttgart, 1979), p. 65ff. On central problems, the volume *Christlicher Glaube in moderner Gesellschaft (Section 19)*, (Basle and Vienna, 1981), with major articles by Alexander Schwan, 'Humanismus und Christentum', p. 19ff., and 'Pluralismus und Wahrheit', p. 146ff., as well as Nikolaus Lobkowicz and Henning Ottmann, 'Materialismus, Idealismus und christliches Verständnis', p. 68ff.

[3] R. A. Webster, *The Cross and the Fasces* (London, 1960), and *Christian Democracy in Italy 1860–1960* (London, 1961); Francesco Margiotta Broglio, *Italia e Santa Sede, Dalla Grande Guerra alla Conciliazione* (Bari, 1966). On the German Concordat controversy of 1933 see also the fundamental articles by Konrad Repgen and Klaus Scholder, in *Vierteljahrshefte für Zeitgeschichte* 26 (1978), pp. 499ff. and 535ff.; as well as K. Scholder, *Die Kirchen und das Dritte Reich*, Vol. 1 (Frankfurt-Berlin-Vienna, 1977), p. 310ff.

were numerous instances of secession by 'liberal' wings) but even more so those with socialism, especially with its emphatically 'scientific', *i.e.* atheist, form. They led to the development of an alternative Christian social theory and of Christian workers' movements which moreover enjoyed papal support especially under Leo XIII (died 1903) and later under Pius XI (died 1939) through their social encyclicals *Rerum novarum* (1891) and *Quadragesimo anno* (1931), though they also gave rise to ever-recurrent conflicts within the Church on the scope and the interpretation of reforms. The assumption of numerous social duties had always been in line with Church tradition. However, attempts to make the Churches give greater priority to a radical engagement in favour of social reform than to a theological orientation, and thereby to bring them into step with the 'progressive' politico-social currents and demands of the age, or even to force them into a leadership role, have invariably resulted in major controversies between the Churches and their critics down to the present day. The idea of 'Christian socialism', or indeed a socialist Christianity, has found itself faced with justified doubts on the consequences of a total secularization or an ideologization of the Faith.[1]

Alongside progressive scientism and materialism there were also various spiritualist, moral and literary-aesthetic movements competing with the Churches and traditional religion, and rebelling against them. With an anti-orthodox Christian or even an anti-Christian orientation they were closely connected with crisis thought and the critique of drab rationalism and progressivism which they now extended to the established Churches which they saw as sharing responsibility for depriving the world of its soul. The new interest in the non-rational and suprarational dimensions of individuals swamped by science and progress and of a culture which had lost its assurance, of man's social and moral dilemmas in an age of rampant growth of the economy, the state, and civilization all favoured the rise of a non-ecclesiastical religiosity whose greatest exponent was the Russian poet Leo Tolstoy, the socially committed prophet of a return to primitive Christianity.

Private and oriental cults, theosophical and anthroposophical movements endeavoured to satisfy this need for extra-ecclesiastical and subjective religiosity in a world of upheaval and the collapse of traditional beliefs. Attempts to find new meaning amidst tempestuous change have often

---

[1] This is an issue of our century, manifesting itself especially in the (French) 'worker priests' and in a worldwide 'theology of liberation'; it still awaits scholarly treatment. See Adrian Dansette, *Tragödie und Experiment der Arbeiterpriester* (Graz-Vienna-Cologne, 1959); André Collonge, *Die Kirche und das Proletariat* (Darmstadt, 1958); Gregor Siefer, *Die Mission der Arbeiterpriester* (Essen, 1960). For a historical survey of the overall problem of a Christian – Marxist dialogue see the informative essay by Robert Banks, 'The Intellectual Encounter between Christianity and Marxism: A Contribution to the Pre-history of a Dialogue', *Journal of Contemporary History* 11/2–3 (1976), p. 309ff., with the international bibliography on the three phases prior to 1914, to the mid-thirties, to the Cold War in the fifties.

oscillated between de-ideologization and re-ideologization: before the First World War, with totalitarian tendencies in the twenties, with existentialism after the Second World War, with new 'alternative' movements from the sixties to the seventies. Time and again there has been, especially in connection with the religious element, this see-saw movement of rationalism and irrationalism, of progress and doubt, of scientific theory and political ideology, with successive generations and their horizons of specific contemporary experience playing an important part.[1]

The revolt against formal religion and rationalist institutionalization, which led Tolstoy to a kind of Christian communism, also had direct political and ideological consequences. Pacificism against war and all forms of violence, or political anarchism, now acquired a religious meaning, in total contrast to the atheist justifications of Marxist socialism which decidedly claimed the right to violence for itself. Tolstoy's world-wide literary influence for the first time disseminated the ideas of 'non-violent resistance' which were subsequently to achieve such effect through Gandhi in the Third World and then again, since the sixties, with the new Left.[2] Needless to say, they were unable to prevent or even to restrict, the outbreak of war or the transition to violent revolutions and dictatorships, any more than was international socialism. They often remained a theory abused by revolutionaries and militant movements, welcome for their partly religious impact but ultimately effective only in and against liberal democracies (as against Britain in Gandhi's India), but not against totalitarian occupations such as in Czechoslovakia in 1968 or in Poland in 1981.

It was also a kind of Rousseauism that enjoyed a rebirth in ideas and currents. The return to nature, as against the socio-political evils and moral doubts of an industrial society, remained on the programme. It had been moving towards a climax ever since the 1890s in the anti-bourgeois youth movements of the *Wandervogel*. The Great War, though sometimes hailed by them as a campaign against a materialist age, became the first nail in the coffin of this back-to-nature movement; the second nail was the blood-and-soil national socialism which either seduced or browbeat it. In line with the contradictions of the day it represented a paradoxical but effective blend of radical social criticism and romantic irrationalism, of anti-capitalism and anti-Marxism, of affinity with and opposition to socialism (that is, oppo-

[1] On religious movements and sects see Kurt Hutten, *Seher, Grübler, Enthusiasten, Sekten und religiöse Sondergemeinschaften der Gegenwart*, 8th ed. (Stuttgart, 1962); a classic balance sheet was first put forward in Ernst Troeltsch, *Die Soziallehren der christlichen Kirchen und Gruppen* (Tübingen, 1912); E. T. Clark, *The Small Sects in America* (Nashville, 1937); B. Wilson, *Religiöse Sekten* (Munich, 1970); F. W. Haack, *Von Gott und der Welt verlassen, Der religiöse Untergrund in unserer Welt* (Düsseldorf, 1974), and *Die neuen Jugendreligionen*, 2 vols (Munich, 1979).

[2] On the effect of Tolstoy see especially Erwin Oberländer, *Tolstoi und die revolutionäre Bewegung* (Munich-Salzburg, 1965); see W. Lednicki, *Tolstoi between War and Peace* (The Hague, 1965).

sition to 'scientific' socialism), of a demand for total reform and a vulnerability to authoritarian community and leadership cult. The opposition was equally to rationalist progressivism and cultural decadence, to liberal individualism and industrial collectivism, to the approach of mass democracy and to the survival of despotism. These currents, no matter whether promoted by Tolstoy's international fame or exploited by liberal and socialist revolutionaries, substantially contributed to the undermining of tsarism in Russia. In western constitutional states, on the other hand, especially in Italy and in Germany, they worked against the establishment and stabilization of a liberal democracy that was struggling hard against the consequences of war and depression: both fascism and national socialism subsequently saw themselves as successful youth movements against the political establishment and the evils of modernization. It was a very typical oppositional constellation. Parallels with anti-liberal and anti-civilizational movements today spring to mind.[1]

The revolt against materialism and capitalism, against the bourgeoisie and spiritual-religious flabbiness, sometimes intensified into a radical alternative, full realization or rejection of Christianity, had been developed into a political missionary idea even before the turn of the century by other influential writers, such as Dostoevsky, whom Nietzsche admired, as in the idea of the spiritual mission of pan-Slavism to save a decadent Europe. About the same time, also, the German propagandists of 'cultural pessimism', such as Lagarde, Langbehn and Moeller van den Bruck, hailed the revolt of the 'young nations' against western civilization as a new force in world history at the very moment of the *Decline of the West*, Oswald Spengler's famous book, which though not published until 1918, had essentially been mapped out as early as in 1911. 'The politics of cultural despair',[2] in conjunction with religious revival ideas and subsequently with racial and class-struggle movements, were able to grow into a nationalist ideology and ultimately to lend that ideology a totalitarian intensity (because it embraced all spheres of life), an intensity which, especially in Russia and in Germany, prepared the ground for unprecedented regimes of violence against civilization but with civilization's destructive tools. Thus, on the eve of the First World War, the important English historian and political philosopher J. N. Figgis (1866–1919) referred to a *Civilization at the Crossroads*, posing the question of whether European tradition was not

---

[1] On the connection between youth movement, civilizational critique and dictatorial tendencies in Germany see Harry Pross, *Jugend, Eros, Politik* (Bern-Munich-Vienna, 1964); there is present-day discussion in K. D. Bracher, 'Die doppelte Zeitgeschichte', in *Geschichte und Gewalt* (Berlin, 1981), p. 233ff.

[2] Fritz Stern's *The Politics of Cultural Despair* (Berkley, 1961) has emphasis on the precursors of national socialism such as Paul de Lagarde (1827–1891), Julius Langbehn (1851–1907) and Moeller van den Bruck (1876–1925). The quotation motto of Fritz Stern from *Jeremiah* 5, 31 is very appropriate: 'The prophets prophesy falsely, and the priests bear rule by their means; and my people love to have it so: and what will ye do in the end thereof?'

breaking up into a thousand fragments.[1]

Materialism and subjectivism, unreflected progressivism and prophecies of decline represented the extreme poles between which the great themes of the history of ideas were ground down. Anybody who could talk, write, paint or compose music could proclaim a new 'movement'. No doubt this promoted the variety of literature and art. These flourished, experimented, and pursued hitherto unexplored paths opened up by the collapse of traditional authorities. Art as a substitute for religion, as a subjective religion of its own, and the artist as a fully independent creator: these were views which brought in their train a rich flowering and exploration of the spiritual world. Such a religion of art, based on the creativity and aesthetics of the individual instead of on morality and responsibility for the whole, elevated up to lonely heights not only great works of art but also the artist's arrogance towards society and the state.[2]

Richard Wagner's unreserved claim for the 'total work of art' was an early instance (*Parsifal* in 1882 was the latest) with which, among others, the young Adolf Hitler intoxicated himself in the opera houses of Linz and Vienna. The politician as an intuitive total artist – that was a vision which, in conjunction with a totalitarian ideology, could, very differently from the mere sphere of art, lead to aberrations and presumptions of horrifying consequences. Typical of the results of a religion of art was the role of the Italian poet Gabriele D'Annunzio in the early years of fascism when, after the self-glorifying occupation of Fiume in 1919 he postured, as it were, as a Renaissance artist and politician beyond all morality. Inspired self-portrayal stylized into a signal for the militant realization of Italian nationalism.[3]

In political thought, unlike in art, fragmentation of ideas led to a state of confusion, opening up fatal possibilities the moment that, amidst all the experimentation and the cult of intuition, a sense of responsibility and a judgement of consequences were lost. Because just that fragmentation of political traditions implied also an opportunity for recombining the elements and slogans in a new way, for shaping new ideologies from the ruins, according to the attractiveness or propaganda value of one fragment or another, no matter whether this was done in accordance with an intuitive artistic claim, or with painstaking bureaucratic thoroughness, or with pseudo-religious zeal. National socialism and its 'philosophy', developed more by frustrated artists (Hitler, Goebbels, Rosenberg) than by bureaucrats (Himmler, Bormann) and sanctioned by 'German Christians' or even by a non-Christian 'German Faith community' (Wilhelm Hauer) was such a

[1] John Neville Figgis, *Civilization at the Crossroads* (1913).

[2] There is a good survey in Roland Stromberg, *Intellectual History*, op. cit., p. 397ff., and the bibliography.

[3] On D'Annunzio and his *coup* see Ernst Nolte, *Der Faschismus in seiner Epoche*, 5th ed. (Munich, 1979), p. 240ff., and especially also Michael A. Ledeen, *D'Annunzio a Fiume* (Rome-Bari, 1975).

conglomeration of ideas:[1] in some respects genuine invention but in many
others derived from the idea débris of the turn of the century, an eclectic
mixtum compositum of the most effective elements of national and social,
geopolitical and racialist, irrationalist and technical-progress theories,
opinions and catchwords. Not consistency but ideological value was the
yardstick, and indeed the strength, of such 'new' philosophies, in which the
much-deplored lost unity of political ideas and integral thought, following
fragmentation through modernization, seemed comprehensively re-
established.

This was the time of the creation of 'political religions':[2] pseudo-religious
ideologies with the dual claim to scientific validity and, simultaneously, to
religious absoluteness. They promised to reunite what modern science and
secularization had divided: harmony once more between culture and
technology, between politics and culture. They attempted to promise
everything to everybody, to be an all-embracing movement and an all-
embracing faith, while at the same time identifying and resolutely confronting the absolute ideological opponent in an ideology of simultaneous
integration and confrontation. The reverse of the medal was the emphatically one-sided militant and activist character of the totalitarian movements
employing these substitute religions. Fascism and national socialism, just as
Leninism-Stalinism and later Maoism, were both things at the same time:
promise of an eventual community – the 1000-year Reich or universal
communism – but meanwhile, and above all, mobilization ideologies for

---

[1] See Joachim Fest, *Das Gesicht des Dritten Reiches* (Munich, 1964), p. 391ff., and *Hitler*
(Frankfurt-Berlin, 1973), p. 59ff.; George L. Mosse, *The Crisis*, op. cit.; *Germans and Jews*,
op. cit.; Dietrich Orlow, *The History of the Nazi Party* (Pittsburgh, 1969), p. 299ff., and 'The
Conversion of Myths into Political Power, The Case of the Nazi Party 1925/6', *American
Historical Review* 72 (1967), p. 906ff.; Klaus Vondung, *Ideologischer Kult und politische
Religion des Nationalsozialismus* (Göttingen, 1971).

[2] The term is from Eric Voegelin, *Die politischen Religionen* (Vienna, 1938; 2nd ed.
Stockholm, 1939); see Waldemar Gurian, 'Totalitarian Religions', *The Review of Politics* 14
(1952), p. 3ff., and earlier *Der Kampf um die Kirche im Dritten Reich* (Luzern, 1936). This is
the starting-point of an attempt to identify the chiliastic and messianic eschatological features of
totalitarian ideologies. On this, alongside the great trilogy by J. L. Talmon (see p. 5 footnote
2), see also Eric Voegelin, *Wissenschaft, Politik und Gnosis* (Munich, 1959), and 'Religions-
ersatz, Die gnostischen Massenbewegungen unserer Zeit', *Wort und Wahrheit* 15 (1960), p. 5ff.
Fundamental also is Norman Cohn's *The Pursuit of the Millennium* (London, 1961). An
interesting new attempt at a contemporary application of this approach was made by James M.
Rhodes, *The Hitler Movement, A Modern Millenarian Revolution* (Stanford, 1980), with
reference also to the medieval apocalyptic movements from Joachim of Floris onwards. These
may be regarded not only (as Engels believed) as social-revolutionary precursors of
communism but also of a revolutionary right-wing radicalism, *i.e.* of any totalitarian ideology;
see, for instance, the neo-Islamic movements of our own day. For a Marxist interpretation see
Bernhard Toepfer, *Das kommende Reich des Friedens, Zur Entwicklung chiliastischer
Zukunftshoffnungen im Hochmittelalter* (East Berlin, 1964); for the significance of these ideas
in the developing countries see Wilhelm E. Mühlmann, *Chiliasmus und Nativismus* (Berlin,
1961); on the chiliastic idea of progress see K. D. Bracher, *Geschichte und Gewalt*, op. cit.,
p. 220ff.

battle with the total enemy. Incomparably harsher than all previous movements of ideas or conflict in their deployment for unremitting struggle against political unbelievers they were in every respect partial sociological movements with a stratum or class-specific character, while simultaneously proclaiming the final defeat of pluralism and the class society, the full implementation of the community, the total identity of rulers and ruled in the uncompromising sense of Rousseau's *volonté générale*, until then no more than an idea and a piece of wishful thinking.[1]

That was the novel and unprecedented element which achieved its first victorious advance in Lenin's revolution. Classical liberalism and its concept of society and the state, just as much as classical socialism, in so far as both of these had been oriented on the idea of libertarian democracy, were now opposed by absolutist variants from the Right and the Left which justified and totalized dictatorship in the struggle for power and integration but which, at the same time, declared their allegiance to all those concepts which in the past history of ideas had been developed for the improvement and fulfilment of society: political unity and social justice, government by the people and the historical mission of nation or class.[2]

Invariably irrational and rational elements came together. The former, initially, more markedly in fascism and national socialism, but soon also in the Bolshevik cult of personality and of the revolution, throughout two decades of Stalinism, subsequently also in Maoism and in the Ho Chi Minh or Kim Il-Sung cults of Vietnam and North Korea, and chiefly and all-embracingly in the quasi-religious cult of Lenin practised by international communism to this day. Irrational too were the forms in which the classical national and social ideas were employed as supreme values whenever the quasi-scientific concepts of race or class did not fit into standard slogans at national or international level. This happened in the Soviet Union during the periods of the New Economic Policy (until 1928) and of the Great Fatherland War (1941–5), and also at the time of the policy of coexistence and of support for national independence movements. Possible parallels in national socialism were the 'only' gradual application of racial policy (which

[1] Even leaving aside the long-contested interpretation of Rousseau, there can be no doubt about the significance of the absolute theory of democracy (put forward by this champion of the *volonté générale*) with its totalitarian tendency as the opposite pole to the concept of representative-parliamentary democracy. On these two fundamental exponents of tradition see mainly J. L. Talmon, *Ursprünge*, op. cit.; Ernst Fraenkel, *Die repräsentative und die plebiszitäre Komponente im demokratischen Verfassungsstaat* (Tübingen, 1958); Gerhard A. Ritter (ed.), *Vom Wohlfahrtsausschuss zum Wohlfahrtsstaat* (Cologne, 1973).

[2] The development of these right-wing absolute and left-wing absolute variants of a community ideology can be traced in German intellectual history of the nineteenth and the early twentieth centuries: on Right-wing German ideology see Hans Kohn, *Wege und Irrwege* (Düsseldorf, 1962); on left-wing analogues, with affinities and transitions to Marxism and communism, see Leszek Kolakowski, *Die Hauptströmungen*, op. cit., as well as the good resumé by David McLellan, 'Marx and his Gaps', *Government and Opposition* 14 (1979), p. 252ff.

led to illusions among many Jews up to 1938) and co-operation with the 'yellow' (Japanese) or the Mongolian 'race', as auxiliary troops during the War, and with the Arab, though anti-Jewish, 'Semites'. In spite of Göring's proud dictum: '*I* determine who is a Jew', a predominantly ideological irrationalism certainly operated in national socialism. Nevertheless, the rational component not only of communism with its ideological heritage of 'scientific socialism' but also of fascism and national socialism in their cult of technology and efficiency was also of considerable importance.[1]

Racialism, too, fluctuated between an ideology of decay and of progress. The turn of the century produced a book which instantly attracted widespread notice in Germany, from the Kaiser down to the village school headmaster: Houston Stewart Chamberlain's *The Foundations of the Nineteenth Century* (1899). It represented the most comprehensive and probably the most influential self-portrayal of racialism as a historical and cultural ideology. It is interesting that the two greatest prophets of this disastrous doctrine, which was to pervert a section of German political thought to such an extent in the future and lead German politics into the most terrible barbarity, were not native Germans. After the French Count Gobineau it was Chamberlain (1855–1927), son of an English admiral, who raised the racialist interpretation of history to its peak. True, he had received his education in France and Germany; he married a daughter of Richard Wagner and became a German subject. Towards the end of his life he still hailed Hitler as the 'great simplifier', concluding a birthday letter to the greatest racialist of all times with the sentence: 'May God, who gave him to us, preserve him for many years yet, as a blessing to the German fatherland.'[2]

Chamberlain combined the racial mysticism of Wagner, Gobineau and the anti-Semites into a philosophically coloured cultural history of the West by claiming all great ones as 'Aryans'; if they were not 'Aryan' racially then

[1] This was convincingly illustrated by the role of Speer as the confidant of Hitler in his architectural and technological ambitions; Speer's memoirs (1969), diaries (1975) and apologias (*Der Sklavenstaat* (Stuttgart, 1981)) also demonstrate the importance of technical endeavours in the Third Reich, such as the cult of the *Autobahnen* whose propagandist effect persists to this day. See my remarks in 'Die Speerlegende' (*Deutsche Diktatur*, op. cit., p. 545ff.), as well as 'Nur die Niederlage verhinderte den Sklavenstaat', in *Frankfurter Allgemeine Zeitung* 185 (13 August 1981), p. 6. Most recently, Matthias Schmidt, *Albert Speer, Das Ende eines Mythos* (Bern, 1982), p. 47ff.

[2] Walter Görlitz, Herbert A. Quint, *Adolf Hitler* (Stuttgart, 1952), p. 234; for anti-Semitism including the idea of a worldwide Jewish conspiracy and worldwide Jewish subversion see *Cosima Wagner und H. St. Chamberlain im Briefwechsel 1888–1908* (Leipzig, 1934), pp. 604ff and 641ff. On this also Winfried Schuler, *Der Bayreuther Kreis*, op. cit., as well as George L. Mosse, The Crisis, op. cit., p. 93ff. A recent very detailed study of Chamberlain is Geoffrey G. Field, *Evangelist of Race, The Germanic Vision of Houston Stewart Chamberlain* (New York, 1981); also Roderick Stackelberg, *Idealism Debased, From Völkisch Ideology to National Socialism* (Kent State, 1981); see the illuminating review by Peter Gay, 'A Homeland for Heroes', *The Times Literary Supplement* (4 September 1981) p. 997.

they were so spiritually and morally. To Chamberlain only the Aryans, and among them more particularly the Germanic nations, were capable of a 'creative' culture. Their intermingling with 'inferior' races would lead to decline, as the Roman Empire had drowned in 'racial chaos'; worldwide Jewish conspiracy and subversion were the explanation of the decline of modern civilization. No doubt these were purely intellectual constructs. As with Gobineau and Lagarde they were still canopied by a religiously coloured cultural philosophy, they bore a Christian anti-Jewish conservative stamp which even impressed broad circles among the educated. The radical biological racialism and anti-Semitism was developed simultaneously mainly in France and Germany, as well as in Austria, by journalists, pamphleteers and sectarian politicians like Daudet, Lapouge, Drumont, Marr, Langbehn, Schönerer, Lueger, Ahlwardt, Fritsch, and an alleged Jewish world-wide conspiracy of 1897 was finally pseudo-documented with the forged *Protocols of the Elders of Zion*.[1]

Such conspiracy legends, however, directed likewise against other 'worldwide threats' such as Freemasons, the Roman Catholic Church and the Papacy, were typical of the progressive confusion of thought. What they all had in common were, above all, two basic features: cultural pessimism and anti-democratism. And what made them so attractive, especially to disoriented readers like the young Hitler, was the comprehensive, profoundly ideological character of their explanation of the world, their viewing of culture and politics as deriving from one single cause. They appeared to hold the key to the interpretation of the problems of the present day; they succeeded in reducing the sense of crisis to a simple formula.

Certainly cultural pessimism and anti-modernism, the anti-liberal and anti-democratic formulation of the racial concept, were both the result and the obverse of the idea of progress. Racialism was based on the conviction that certain national and racial characteristics determined progress within a nation and hence also determined a nation's positive or negative contribution to the history of mankind. It was an old idea: a sense of 'national superiority' can be found in all civilizations throughout history. The classical confrontations between Greeks or Romans and barbarians, between the chosen and the damned, between the strong and the weak – all notions of national and imperial mission are thus inspired. So long as the religious concept of history was dominant the issue of ethnic or racial category was of

---

[1] First published in 1903 in Russia, later in exile 1920 and simultaneously in all western countries. See Norman Cohn, *Die Protokolle der Weisen von Zion, Der Mythos von der jüdischen Weltverschwörung* (Cologne-Berlin, 1969), pp. 12ff, 75ff, 216ff. This highlights in particular the pseudo-religious character of national socialist anti-Semitism with its roots reaching back to the Middle Ages. On Russian anti-Semitism see Heinz Dietrich Löwe, *Antisemitismus und reaktionäre Utopie, Russischer Konservatismus im Kampf gegen den Wandel von Staat und Gesellschaft* (Hamburg, 1978). See also the major work by Jacob Katz, *From Prejudice to Destruction, Anti-Semitism 1700–1933* (Cambridge/Mass., 1980), p. 245ff. (1879 is seen as the 'turning-point' and beginning of modern anti-Semitism.)

secondary importance. But ever since the voyages of discovery and the Reformation, in confrontation with new exotic people and in the religious wars between the persuasions, the religious framework had been broken and human progress, notwithstanding all ideas of universal humanity, had come to be understood as a revelation of the differences and as a contest between superior and inferior civilized nations, and indeed between more highly developed and backward races.

Colonial policy and modern nationalism were likewise largely based on at least a rudimentary racialist idea of progress, one which classified people and highlighted their cultural, political and also physical differences. What always mattered was the framework. The Christian universalist and subsequently the enlightened humanitarian concept of progress relativized a potential racialism; with the nationalist and cultural-critical dissolution of comprehensive universal systems of reference, however, the historical-political potential of racialism, especially during the nineteenth century, became more specific, and the scientific and biological discoveries associated with Darwinism further assisted a manipulative intensification of these tendencies.[1] This ideological intensification into militant racialism with its strategies for suppression and extermination was based in particular on the idea of a God-given, or nature-given, 'inequality'. It implied the radicalization of allegedly political-scientific discoveries concerning the 'inequality' of races – from neutral observation to a one-sided doctrine.

A basic pattern of all future conflicts emerged: progress either as a contested hierarchy of superior nations and races, or as a process of civilization in which all cultures and nations play a part. The former was in line with the concept of political struggle and of authoritarian nationalism, while the latter conformed to the liberally understood idea of equality in a democracy. Naturally this did not rule out the possibility of racialist and, more particularly, anti-Semitic concepts of history and politics emerging also in conjunction with liberal-democratic and socialist thought on progress. We find these even with that great enlightener Voltaire, who scoffed at Jews and regarded Negroes as incapable of becoming civilized; or with Marx, whose critique of capitalism did not lack anti-Semitic traits while his critique of tsarism also castigated a Russian incapability of revolution; or with David Hume, who saw civilization as the domain of the whites and thereby unwittingly provided a basis for the British imperialist concept of Rudyard Kipling. Scarcely any trend of thought was entirely free from that taint, as is shown by George Mosse in his latest account of the history of

[1] An example of importance to Germany is the far-reaching effect of the Darwinist zoologist Ernst Haeckel (1834–1919) with his best-seller *Welträtsel* (1899): on this Daniel Gasmann, *The Scientific Origins of National Socialism, Social Darwinism in Ernst Haeckel and the German Monist League* (London, 1971) – though the title is somewhat misleading: it deals with just one and not *the* root of the pseudo-scientific elements in national socialism.

European racialism.[1] The belief in science with its need for classification, the humanist cult of the beautiful mind *and* body, as encountered in antique sculpture – all these 'progressive' roots of a belief in a difference between the races and their contribution to civilization had led, ever since the end of the eighteenth century, to the simultaneous rise of the ideas both of race and of progress.

The greatest extension and dissemination, however, occurred between 1853 and 1900; by then the racial concept figured prominently in the confrontation between the optimistic and the pessimistic view of civilization. Extreme and systematic ideologization began with Gobineau's three-volume essay on *The Inequality of Races* (1853); it was taken up on both sides of the Atlantic and reached its climax in a series of works of entirely scientific pretension before the First World War. Outside Germany, too, attempts were made to explain all great minds and achievements, from an 'Aryan' Christ to the conquest of America and the world, by the superiority and inferiority of races. Apart from the authors mentioned already, and apart from Darwin himself who occasionally applied his doctrine of selection to British-American achievements, only two American books need be recorded here: the *Political Science* (1890) of the important scholar John W. Burgess, who referred to the special mission of the Teutons, and the Chamberlain-like book by Madison Grant (1916) on *The Passing of the Great Race or the Racial Basis of European History*, for which a leading natural scientist, H. F. Osborn, actually wrote the introduction.

The ambivalence of the idea of progress, together with its corruption, coincided, especially about the turn of the century, with the profound ambiguity and eventual ideologically-radical perversion of the national and racial concept. The same fundamental approach which had led Adam Smith, Jefferson, J. S. Mill and Herbert Spencer to the conclusion that mankind was moving towards a higher level of material flowering and moral harmony, and that this was due exclusively to greater personal freedom,[2] led Comte, Marx, Hegel and Gobineau towards doctrines in which, notwithstanding all

[1] George L. Mosse, *Rassismus, Ein Krankheitssymptom in der europäischen Geschichte des 19. und 20. Jahrhunderts* (Königstein, 1978), p. 10ff.; see also Eleonore Sterling, *Judenhass: Die Anfänge des politischen Antisemitismus in Deutschland (1815–1850)* (Frankfurt/M, 1969); fundamental also is Peter G. Pulzer, *Die Entstehung des politischen Antisemitismus in Deutschland und Österreich 1867–1914* (Gütersloh, 1966; English ed. 1964). On anti-Semitism on the Left see especially Edmund Silberner, *Sozialisten zur Judenfrage, Ein Beitrag zur Geschichte des Sozialismus von Anfang des 19. Jahrhunderts bis 1914* (Berlin, 1962); Zeev Sternhell, *La Droite Revolutionnaire 1885–1914* (Paris, 1978), p. 177 (anti-Semitism of the French Left); also Hans-Helmuth Knütter, *Die Juden und die deutsche Linke in der Weimarer Republik* (Düsseldorf, 1971), especially p. 123ff: unless Jews act 'progressively' they encounter the double disenchantment of the Left – since they offend against their anti-capitalist and their egalitarian doctrines.

[2] Robert Nisbet, *History*, op. cit., p. 259f. On the ideological substance see the comprehensive comparative study by Patrik von zur Mühlen, *Rassenideologien, Geschichte und Hintergründe* (Berlin-Bonn, 1977), p. 27ff.

avowals to freedom, it is ultimately power that triumphs, and, what is more, on philosophical–Utopian, political and racial grounds.

As an essential ingredient of totalitarian thought this concept of power, containing more or less racialist components, reached its most topical climax during and after the First World War. Hitler in particular was and remained fixated on it down to the final consequence of racial war and racial annihilation.[1] This is not to say that totalitarian policy is merely a consistent result of ideas: wars, crises and struggles for power have very real and specific material causes, and the organization of political systems depends on traditions and individuals which are not readily reduced to a formula – unless one were to succumb to a kind of inverted racialism or ideologism. Yet politicians, intellectuals and movements that, since the turn of the century, had been gaining increasing favour and impact among the growing 'masses' were after all more deeply pervaded and influenced by the power-political ideas of progress and race than belief in an ultimate rational solution of all world problems would have led one to expect. Confident belief in progress veered into very different directions about the turn of the century: democratic and totalitarian, progressive Left and progressive Right. As a result, fear of the consequences of progress, together with cultural pessimism and racial phobia, further intensifying the anti-democratic currents and undermining liberal self-assurance, remained closely tied up with the Utopian, supposedly idealistic, aspect of the great argument about progress or decay.

[1] See Eberhard Jäckel, *Hitlers Weltanschauung, Entwurf einer Herrschaft* (republ. Stuttgart, 1981); the most recent survey is in Peter Hüttenberger, *Bibliographie zum Nationalsozialismus* (Göttingen, 1980), p, 22ff.

4. HARBINGERS OF THE GREAT CRISIS

In order to understand the extreme potential and the realizations of the new political religions of pseudo-religious ideological politics, it is necessary to examine more closely the debris of those political ideas from which totalitarian ideologies sprang, and not just the ideologies themselves. In most studies so far this has not been done. The irrationalism of the turn of the century, which we have viewed mainly in its pre-political forms, contained not only the elements and driving forces of authoritarian and totalitarian ideas but also that modernization crisis of liberal, democratic and conservative thought which proved so decisive for the success of those authoritarian ideas. As the constituent force of the new national states in particular, liberalism showed itself lacking in self-assurance and possessing a low resistance. Here then was the principal difference as against the period after the Second World War, when experience of ideological dictatorships and awareness of a persisting threat prevented liberal democracy from displaying the same vulnerability or low resistance *vis-à-vis* anti-liberal ideologies, whether with or without a claim to democracy. Or at least this has been the case for three-and-a-half decades and an unsettling change of generations.

The political religions of authoritarianism and totalitarianism were above all, and without exception, anti-liberal; they were directed against the individual and his reason. Challenges to political liberalism and statements that it was dead had been numerous even at a time when it flourished in the economic and cultural spheres about the turn of the century.[1] At first, admittedly, this was an issue only among intellectual minorities from the Right and the Left, since even the Social Democrats appreciated the value of liberal rights for the working-class movement, and it was only the First World War that brought the radicalization of the 'masses'. But ideologically it was a disastrous in-between existence, with liberalism and the bourgeois concept of constitutional democracy being caught in the disputes between

[1] The polemical catchwords of 'late capitalism' and the 'end of the bourgeois era', which are again being bandied about, were not only greatly in fashion in the twenties and thirties but in fact date back to the turn of the century when they were used by right-wing as well as left-wing critics of the system. See K. D. Bracher, 'Ende des bürgerlichen Zeitalters?', in *Staat und Gesellschaft im politischen Wandel*, ed. W. Pöls (Stuttgart, 1979), p. 156 and *Europa in der Krise* (Frankfurt-Berlin-Vienna, 1979), p. 112ff.

progressivist and crisis thought, between materialist and religious interpretations of the world, between a bureaucratic-socialist strengthening of
the state's power and an apolitical individualism or indeed anarchism.

The fragmentation and distortion of the idea of liberal democracy into
nationalist and imperialist, anti-ecclesiastical and social-Darwinist fashion
trends resulted in a spiritual confusion which manifested itself especially in
their war tactics and battle cries. It led to the decline of the political Centre,
not only in Germany, with the lack of leadership and the excessive tolerance
shown by the liberal Weimar Republic to its enemies, but also in the
permanent crises of the French Third Republic; it showed itself most of all in
the early decay of democracy in Italy and in the inability of the newly created
states to function properly. Even the old democracies were not spared. The
USA, the main vanguard of progressivism and the technologically most
highly developed liberal democracy, withdrew from Europe and its crises
and eventually evolved the controversial ideas of the 'New Deal' –
strengthening of the governmental and social components of liberalism.
Only at the moment of catastrophe for European freedom did America
come to the rescue, and only the shielding of the re-emergence of democracy
in Europe after the Second World War against a persisting totalitarianism
finally rendered possible the ideological unity of the West in its plurality,
though of course at the cost of a divided Europe. The more seriously should
all tendencies towards anti-Americanism be viewed: at the turn of the
century this still played no part, between the wars it promoted the rise of the
dictators, and today, given the military-ideological presence of communism,
it represents a considerable threat aimed by European liberal democracy at
itself.[1]

Then, admittedly, the fundamental challenge came from the experience
of the non-rational and the irrational in politics. It based itself on the
observation that political ideas and convictions were not so much the
outcome of understanding or reason as of habit and unconscious influences,
as the British Fabian socialist Graham Wallas declared in his influential
book on *Human Nature in Politics* in 1908.[2] This observation, not exactly
sensational to us today, challenged a fundamental view, if not the very
dogma of liberal democratic thought. It was the classic anti-democratic
argument which the conservatives had used for so long against universal
suffrage: that the bulk of the citizens and voters were not even capable of
making the decisions which a majority vote would assign to them. Much as

[1] Anti-Americanism in the French context appeared especially as a phenomenon of
Gaullism. In the German situation it occurred in three contexts, separated in time and subject
matter: as the national socialist critique of 'plutocracy' in the thirties, as the Vietnam protest in
sharp contrast with the Kennedy enthusiasm of the sixties, and today as part of a
consciousness-changing succession of generations, as a crisis of *détente* policy and a left-wing
critique of the conservative anti-communism of President Reagan, entailing also a revival of the
discredited concept of totalitarianism. See below, pp. 47f., 81ff.

[2] See Roland Stromberg, *Intellectual History*, op. cit., p. 405f.

this scepticism may find itself justified by psephological research even today, in an age of continuous information and communication, it does not thereby refute the principle of the idea of representative democracy. This, after all, is founded on the experience that all other forms of government are even less capable of solving the problems inherent in human imperfection, on the possibility of error in human thought or action, that is, in any political decision – whether authoritarian monarchies or dictatorships, whether plebiscite systems or directed democracies.

In the argument about rationality or irrationality, however, in the argument about progress or decay of political culture in the face of the rise of mass democracy, Wallas's not necessarily incorrect but incomplete (because formulated without comparison to alternatives) remarks were bound to have an explosive effect – the more so as they came from the intellectual precursors of the English socialists, from the 'think tank' of the Fabians, and could not therefore be suspected of reactionary tendencies. But they were, of course, grist to the mill of both right-wing and left-wing radical anti-liberal élitists.

The arguments about the possibilities and alternatives of democracy implied both struggle *against* progress – as the crisis of rationalism – and ideological struggle *for* progress, which neither political camp could really do without, no matter what interpretation they put on it.[1] The question was merely how such progress was still compatible with the liberal premises which had accompanied and introduced it, and whether the anti-liberal answers might not prove more convincing or more cogent in urging a strong state, an integrated nation, and the creation of a socialist community. An important role was played also by the doubts which came from the vigorously developing social sciences, the offsprings of society's emancipation from existing structural patterns. Over a few decades they had 'swept over the western world like a natural phenomenon' (F. H. Tenbruck). In spite of their predominantly liberal or socialist origins these critical analyses, revelations and theories of a society in transformation contributed greatly to an increasing questioning of the democratic idea; some sociologists ended up in the sphere of élitist-authoritarian fascist or élitist-communist dictatorship theories – either from bitterness over disappointed socialist-democratic hopes, like the pioneer of party sociology Robert Michels, or as Realpolitik-oriented neo-Machiavellian critics of progressivist self-delusion like Georges Sorel, the inspirer of both Mussolini and Lenin, who elevated the theory of revolutionary violence into the real driving force of history.

Even before the turn of the century the Italian sociologist and professor of constitutional law Gaetano Mosca (1858–1941) had sharply and im-

---

[1] From this it became clear, even at the turn of the century, that the concept of progress was no longer suitable for scholarly use: its own ideologization had 'progressed' (see K. D. Bracher, *Fortschritt*, op. cit., p. 212ff.) The following quotation is from F. H. Tenbruck's topical introduction to the book by Michael Bock, op. cit., p. 13, see footnote 2, p. 42.

pressively formulated his critique of democracy; this took the form of an élitist theory. His principal work, first published in 1896 as *Elementi di Scienza Politica*, proceeded from the existence of two classes, a ruling and a ruled class, as the main factors of history. Politics were practised, even in a democracy, by a narrow stratum which controlled the press, the political parties, associations, and the selection of candidates, and did all this with an ideological trimming; the ruled were integrated by, among other things, the hope of rising into the ruling class. Thus a liberal starting-point was preserved by Mosca; later indeed he lent it greater emphasis and differentiated it from any kind of autocracy, though others who followed him (such as Michels and Pareto) focused on the authoritarian consequences of the élitist theory. At any rate it meant the definition of a clearly circumscribed ideologically based position; this was to prove of major importance to future sociological and politological critiques of democracy both from the Right and from the Left.[1]

Above all, however, the rigidity of the questions posed and the empirical penetration into the reality of society and politics, as well as the form of uncompromising 'analysis' (in the literal sense: dissolution) which tried to emulate the exact sciences, led to confrontations of idea and reality which frequently culminated in a fierce critique or indeed vicious negation of not only conventional bourgeois convictions but also of reform-socialist expectations of progress. This was true in particular of the second generation of the new sociologists who dissociated themselves from the progressivist-rationalist, enlightened-optimistic philosophy of history and society proclaimed by the great founders Auguste Comte, Herbert Spencer, and Karl Marx. Just as in religion and culture, the break-up of comprehensive binding doctrines and systems resulted in the acutely analytical, critically heightened separate systems of 'political sociology' whose most influential representatives were Émile Durkheim, Ferdinand Tönnies, Georg Simmel and Max Weber.[2]

Simultaneously, however, and closely linked with these empirical social theoreticians, there arose a front of deliberately one-sided, aphoristically and polemically arguing political sociologists, whose arguments and slogans were to provide the quasi-scientific background of anti-liberalism, anti-democratism and anti-social-democratism within the emerging authoritarian and totalitarian ideologies. Apart from the social Darwinists in all

[1] On these currents see especially Erwin Faul, *Der moderne Machiavellismus* (Cologne, 1961); I. H. Meisel, *Der Mythos der herrschenden Klasse, Gaetano Mosca und die Elite* (Düsseldorf, 1962).

[2] The manner in which the new sociology's claim to be an exact science, revealing the laws of reality, led to the advance of abstract, ideologized societal models and to the one-sided sociologization of thought, to a sociological substitute religion, is illustrated (especially with regard to the turn of the century) by the comprehensive study of Michael Bock, *Soziologie als Grundlage des Wirklichkeitsverständnisses. Zur Entstehung des modernen Weltbildes* (Stuttgart, 1980), p. 120ff.

countries, this group included more especially Georges Sorel, Maurice Barrès and Charles Maurras in France, Gaetano Mosca and Vilfredo Pareto in Italy, Robert Michels in Germany, Henry and Brooks Adams and the geopoliticians in the USA.[1] Each emerged, in his own way, with radical-revolutionary or with élitist-conservative conclusions from his analyses, as it were, as pre-ideologists, as proclaimers and utterers of ideas, as crisis prophets and subverters of the consciousness of their time in the diverse political cultures of Europe and the USA. Their actual effect as intellectuals and writers, and hence their intellectual responsibility for the destruction of political thought to come, its impoverishment into ideologies of battle and annihilation, is and remains rightly controversial. Certainly they did not reach the masses in the way the future demagogues and men of action did, and anyway that kind of intellectual 'responsibility' in the political and moral sphere of action is difficult to define so long as thought is declared to be free and so long as radical intellectual experiment in particular is regarded as an achievement of enlightenment and liberalism, or of scholarship generally. Here is the great distinction that applies also to the highly controversial concept of the *avant-garde*: in art it implies an engagement in favour of a claim to spiritual leadership in the radical rivalry of ideas and styles, but in politics (as Lenin would have it) it means support for the organization of the unified party by dictatorship over the masses and by the bloody annihilation of opponents.[2]

[1] Of major influence in America about the turn of the century was the book eagerly read by the young Theodore Roosevelt as well as by Wilhelm II (and later still by Franklin Roosevelt) by Admiral A. T. Mahan on *The Influence of Sea-Power upon History* (1890, see the introduction to the new edition, New York 1957). On the brothers Brooks and Henry Adams's ideas on decay see p. 9 footnote 2; still valid is Vernon L. Parrington, *Main Currents in American Thought*, Vol. 3 (New York, 1927), pp. 214ff. and 227ff.; see *Literary History of the United States*, Vol. 2 (New York, 1948), p. 1080ff.; Herbert W. Schneider, *A History of American Philosophy* (New York, 1946), p. 400ff.; and Charles Beard's introduction to Brooks Adams, *Law of Civilization*, op. cit., p. 3ff. On the further ideologization of geopolitical thought especially in Germany see Hans-Adolf Jacobsen, *Karl Haushofer, Leben und Werk*, 2 vols (Boppard, 1979), pp. I, 178ff.; see K. D. Bracher, *NS Machtergreifung* (1974), op. cit., p. 315ff., 544ff.; Peter Schöller, 'Geopolitik', *Erdkunde* 11–13 (1957–9).

[2] On the concept of the *avant-garde*, whose dichotomy between an outward claim to freedom and radical suppression within the framework of an idea continues in evidence in all 'progressive' movements to this day, see for the artistic-revolutionary significance Hans Egon Holthusen, *Avantgardismus und die Zukunft der modernen Kunst* (Munich, 1964); Bayerische Akademie der Schönen Künste (ed.), *Avantgarde, Geschichte und Krise einer Idee* (Munich, 1966); R. Poggioli, *Teoria dell'arte d'avanguardia* (Bologna, 1962); and for the alternative Leninist-Soviet claim of the communist leadership to represent the 'most progressive' part of the working class and, as a 'party of a new type' to assume the post-Revolution leadership in all spheres of life, see the article 'Kommunistische Parteien', in *Sowjetsystem und demokratische Gesellschaft*, Vol. 3 (Freiburg, 1969), p. 792ff.; Leonard Schapiro, *The Communist Party of the Soviet Union* (London, 1960), pp. 363ff., 488ff. Indeed (early) fascism also saw itself as an *avant-garde*: see George L. Mosse, 'Fascism and the Avant Garde', in *Masses and Man*, op. cit., p. 229ff.; also Paolo Nello, *L'Avanguardismo Giovanile alle origini del fascismo* (Rome, 1978). Others below, p. 96ff., 111.

In the history of political ideas, however, these neo-Machiavellians occupied a key position: on the social-science and intellectual plane they exerted an influence on the transition from the frayed and decaying sets of ideas of the nineteenth century to the political concretizations of the great ideologies, even though the violent upheavals of just these ideologies were soon to sweep over them. Yet even liberal scholars like Max Weber (1864–1920), probably the most important and – for today's controversies – still the most influential thinker among these then new sociologists, with his pointed theory of the 'value neutrality' of science *vis-à-vis* politics, lent support to those problems which arose from the collapse or from the denial of values. That sociology, with its claim to being an exact science, spotlighted the disintegration of the old society and its norms, that in the resulting disorientation it insisted on an alleged 'value neutrality' while at the same time providing the major ideologies with ammunition for their topical struggle, and moreover eventually entered the arena itself, this ambivalence and dichotomy of a presumed separation of social science and politics, emerges most clearly in the case of Weber himself, the 'value-neutral' analyst and committed national-liberal politician. It had, at an earlier date, been typical of the 'scientific socialism' of Karl Marx, who claimed for himself this dual role of analyst and prophet, of scholar and ideological politician in an admittedly highly one-sided manner. It has remained a basic problem of sociologists and economists, just as of political scientists.

A glance at a few details of the teachings of this 'political' science reveals the ambivalence between deliberately objective analysis (value neutrality) and its ideological prerequisites, implications and consequences. Max Weber examined the forms of political authority and economic development in history, with some emphasis also on the religious factors in social behaviour. This was the starting point for his epoch-making studies of the connections between 'Protestant ethics and the spirit of capitalism', between 'economy and society', and also of the special interest in the irrational aspects of politics and political leadership which at times brought him into compromising proximity to the champions of plebiscitarian democracy and charismatic leadership.[1] His championship of a powerful position for the

[1] On the discussion about Max Weber's position see Ernst Nolte, 'Max Weber vor dem Faschismus', *Der Staat* 2 (1963), p. 1ff.; also Wolfgang Mommsen, *Max Weber und die deutsche Politik, 1890–1920* (Tübingen 1959; 2nd ed. 1974); and Reinhard Bendix, *Max Weber, Darstellung, Analyse, Ergebnisse* (Munich, 1964). The difficult question about Weber's fundamental attitude towards liberal democracy has been most recently summed up by W. J. Mommsen as an antinomian conflict between two different value ideals, *viz.* that of the national power state and the liberal democratic, and also as a radical search for knowledge to the point of self-destruction, in a manner related to Nietzsche's: 'Die antinomische Struktur des politischen Denkens Max Webers', *Historische Zeitschrift* 233 (1981), p. 35ff., with a critique of the emphatically rational-liberal-democratic interpretations of Jürgen Kocka, *Neue Politische Literatur* 21 (1976), p. 282ff., also in *Historische Zeitschrift* 233 (1981), p. 65ff., Anthony Giddens, *Politics and Sociology in the Thought of Max Weber* (London, 1972), p. 55f. and David Beetham, *Max Weber and the Theory of Modern Politics* (London, 1974), p. 113ff. See

Reich President, the dualistic structure of the Weimar Republic, the presentiments of a caesarian age of strong individuals and ideological demagogues all pointed in that direction. Weber's famous distinction of the three types of authority – traditionally, legally-bureaucratically, and charismatically legitimated – reflected a transformation in his understanding of state and democracy which he shared with other contemporary critics such as Michels and Mosca. On the other hand, Weber emphasized the principle of 'rationalization' as an ever-present evolutionary trend: the importance of ever larger organizations in the social and political sphere, bureaucratization as an inevitable result of the application of modern scientific practices, and indeed of the historical process generally, a process moving from a magical to a rational control of the material world. The progressive expansion and rationalization of administration and government, their increasing institutionalization and systematic stabilization, however, would lead to an ossification and oligarchization of government not only in the state but also in social groups and organizations. The fact that this trend conflicted with the dynamics of political and social evolution and with the emergence of powerful personalities subsequently merely accelerated the dictatorial overpowering of democracy.

Max Weber's friend Robert Michels (1876–1936), half French, half German, and eventually elective Italian, in his classical analysis of socialist parties, even before the First World War (1911), had noted the 'iron law of oligarchization' and, after the war, had criticized it still more vigorously and decisively (in a new edition in 1925), until he eventually found a solution in the single-party system of fascism with its irrational mobilization of the masses.[1] Political parties as central organizations of political and social

also the posthumous observations of Karl Jaspers, *Die grossen Philosophen*, Vol. 1 (Munich, 1981), p. 649ff. Typical of the other sociologists of his day was the remark by M. R. Lepsius that what mattered most to Weber had been 'to dramatize these antinomies' (including that 'between formal and material rationality, of value and purpose rationality'): M. R. Lepsius, 'Max Weber in München', *Zeitschrift für Soziologie* 6 (1977), p. 114. See also the discussion at the 15th German Sociologists' Congress (1965) by Otto Stammer (ed.), *Max Weber und die Soziologie heute* (Tübingen, 1965).

[1] Robert Michels, *Zur Soziologie des Parteiwesens in der modernen Demokratie* (Leipzig, 1911; new editions 1925 and 1957), introduction by Werner Conze; its subtitle 'Untersuchungen über die oligarchischen Tendenzen des Gruppenlebens' indicated the direction in which the theory evolved, leading eventually to Michels's 'Psychologie der antikapitalistischen Massenbewegungen' in *Grundriss der Sozialökonomik* ix/1 (Tübingen, 1926) and in his critical notes 'zur Soziologie der Bohème und ihrer Zusammenhänge mit dem geistigen Proletariat' in *Jahrbücher für Sozialökonomie und Statistik 136* (1932), as well as on the 'Umschichtungen in den herrschenden Klassen nach dem Kriege' (Stuttgart-Berlin 1934). Michels's road to Italian fascism, like that of other élitists, came from a radical socialist, syndicalist critique of democracy, first displayed at a socialist conference in Paris in 1907, where he spoke on 'syndicalism and socialism in Germany' and where the socialist syndicalist leader Arturo Labriola reported on Italy; significant also were Michels's books *Sozialismus und Faszismus als politische Strömungen in Italien*, 2 vols (Karlsruhe, 1925), and *Storia critica del movimento socialista Italiano* (Florence, 1926). On these transitions see Zeev Sternhell, 'Fascist Ideology', in *Fascism, a Reader's Guide*, ed. W. Laqueur (London, 1979), p. 345ff.; Wilfried Röhrich, *Robert Michels, Vom soziologisch-syndikalistischen zum faschistischen Credo* (Berlin, 1972), p. 143f. stressing the influence of Max Weber, on whose doctrine of the charismatic politician Michels based his option for fascism.

evolution, and their adaptability and ability to take responsibility, were also very much at the focus of Max Weber's interest; especially in his writings between 1917 and 1920 this interest was time and again directed towards the ambivalence of rational-bureaucratic and non-rational-charismatic elements in party democracy. As rule became bureaucratized into government, he suggested, a 'demystification' simultaneously took place: a loss of political spontaneity and persuasiveness. Along with rationalization, with the dominance of the scientific and efficiency principle, would come an increased re-emergence of the pre-rational and irrational forces and needs of politics, for the creation of community and society – an indispensable component also of modern, democratically legitimated rule, an inevitable companion piece to inevitable bureaucratization. Institutionalized authority would control the system of rules, of normalized and standardized order. This would encounter its limitations especially at moments of crisis, when inspired and charismatically operating politicians, such as a Caesar and Napoleon, would break through that order by virtue of their own irrational authority, transform it, and bind it to their personal rule. Rationality and irrationality, bureaucratic and personal authority thus confront one another; and for a modern democracy, which hopes to survive and master its crises, everything depends on the combination of the two principles. The great external threat to it and its self-threat from within lie in the ossification and petrification of bureaucratic forms as against the dynamism of personal or party-linked movements.

The rise of authoritarian, irrationalist movements added a new dimension to this analysis, which found itself confirmed in the crises of the post-war period and in the emergence of strong individuals in opposition to the new democracies: a plebiscitarian-totalitarian dimension. Max Weber linked this mainly with charismatic leaders and their plebiscitarian self-endorsement. He died in 1920 and thus did not live to see the disastrous consequences of irrational politics: the pseudo-democratic, totalitarian integration parties,[1] which sought to extend their rise by the mobilization of the masses and the institutionalization of their leader's rule over the entire nation – rather like a counter-state with a total-democratic claim to an identity between rulers and ruled, leadership and the people. Max Weber's influence on the discussions about the constitution of the Weimar Republic was aimed at ensuring the charismatic leadership component in the shape of a strong Reich President elected by the people, to stand alongside and above parliamentary democracy. That was a dichotomous structure: a dual democracy – two bodies, both elected by the people, a parallelism of plebiscite and

[1] On this concept see Sigmund Neumann, *Die politischen Parteien in Deutschland* (Berlin, 1932; new ed. Stuttgart, 1965); also as editor of the volume *Modern Political Parties* (1956), with a juxtaposition of democratic and totalitarian 'integration parties' as the successors of liberal representational parties; see my introduction to the new edition of Neumann's *Parteien* (1965), p. 7ff.

parliamentary elections – can function only if the political trends coincide, as they did during the first half of the Weimar Republic under the presidency of Friedrich Ebert or as they have done so far in the French Fifth Republic. In the case of Weimar it failed mainly because of the extensive polarization of ideologies and because of the new phenomenon of totalitarian mono-parties which claimed to incorporate in themselves the state and the movement, society and leadership, as a single entity, and which either succeeded, because of the crisis-prone structure of democracy, in 'seizing' power in a quasi-democratic manner (as in Germany in 1933) or else exploited the revolutionary-plebiscitarian principle of creating an anti-parliamentarian dualism between government and councils, and subsequently captured power by a *coup d'état*, as did Lenin in 1917–18.[1] Mussolini, incidentally, used something more like the traditional method when he came to power under the king and with the preservation of the Italian monarchy: a model for most authoritarian movements operating within the framework of conservative or military dictatorships, though differing from these by the leading position of the fascist party and by its plebiscitarian methods. It is very largely this intermediate position which contradicts the equation of authoritarian, fascist and national socialist power organization under the concept of fascism, and it is the role played by a party and the total claim of its ideology which makes a comparison of the three great totalitarian movements possible and necessary, even though the right-wing and left-wing political substance of the different ideologies may differ a great deal.[2]

Max Weber's political theory, which has greatly influenced all theories of democracy down to our own day, was characterized by the intermediate position between traditional, representative liberalism, whose weaknesses he sought to offset by a strengthening of political parties and the authority of the state, and the plebiscitarian democratism of the advancing mass ideologies. The irrational force of the latter was still personified by him in

[1] On the concept of seizure of power and revolution see K. D. Bracher, *Europa in der Krise*, p. 52ff.; see also Paul Noack, *Die manipulierte Revolution, von der Bastille bis in unsere Zeit* (Munich, 1978), p. 13ff.; on a comparison between the Russian February Revolution and Lenin's October 1917 *coup* see Roger Pethybridge, *The Spread of the Russian Revolution* (London, 1972).

[2] This seems to me the decisive theoretical and empirical point of view in the rekindled fascism-totalitarianism argument of the seventies: see my *Zeitgeschichtliche Kontroversen*, 4th ed. (Munich, 1980); also (pro and con) the collection by Ernest A. Menze (ed.) *Totalitarianism Reconsidered* (London, 1981), as well as the discussion volume *Faschismus und Totalitarismus, Eine wissenschaftliche und politische Begriffskontroverse*, ed. Institut für Zeitgeschichte (Munich-Vienna, 1980). Z. Sternhell, *Fascist Ideology*, op. cit., p. 379ff., emphasizes the differentiation towards national socialism. Important as a specific comparative study is Aryeh L. Unger, *The Totalitarian Party, Party and People in Nazi Germany and Soviet Russia* (London, 1974). See the psychological balance sheet by Paul Watzlawick, 'Bausteine ideologischer "Wirklichkeiten" ', op. cit., p. 192f.: 'In contents' the two great ideologies show incompatible differences. 'Yet the practice of inquisition, concentration camps, the Gulag archipelago, or the terrorist scene reveal an undeniable, horrifying isomorphism.'

the figure of the charismatic leader; the power of totalitarian organization and the seductive power of the new faith were only beginning to be perceptible. Max Weber's epoch-making explanations of capitalism, of economic rationality and of political power led to the threshold of the great crisis which the idea of liberal democracy had to survive. Weber, however, unlike many of his sociological contemporaries and notably the Marxists, did not predict the end of capitalism; his sociological method, which regarded religion as a factor, saved him from the purely materialistic prophecies of progress or decline made by the ideologists, who were predicting (from the Left) the advent of the socialist-communist era or (from the Right) that of a 'national socialism', both of them dictatorial.[1] But he adopted a critical, and perhaps rather pessimistic, attitude to all aspects of a rational modernization of society and the state which was bound to lead to stagnation and to the eruption of non-rational forces.

The other great sociologist of the turn of the century was the Frenchman Émile Durkheim (1858–1917). His contribution to intellectual history was less directly related to politics. Critically developing the positivist historical sociology of Comte, he examined the 'final' phases of society in the light of the great changes wrought by population increase, urbanization of living conditions, growth of the cities, the crisis of traditional rural society and the profound effects of the industrial revolution in transforming the pattern of society and the individual. In his works on the elements of sociology (1889), the division of social labour (1893), suicide (1897) and the elementary forms of religious life (1912) Durkheim observed the disintegration of traditional social ties and 'solidarities' and attempted to find new solutions for abolishing 'anomia', the individual's loss of assurance following his loss or rejection of the old circumscribed, observable and well-defined social forms, models and authorities. What the American sociologist David Riesman, half a century later, under the catching title *The Lonely Crowd*, described as the characteristic of modern macro-societies,[2] remains to this day the conflict

[1] Among the most important theoreticians of capitalism mention must be made primarily of Werner Sombart, whose string of major studies was concluded with the book *Deutscher Sozialismus* (Berlin, 1934), which approached closely to the national anti-capitalist concept and slogans of national socialism and which was subsequently used as appropriate propaganda in the Third Reich's struggle against *international* capitalism and socialism. Sombart's earlier two-volume work *Der proletarische Sozialismus* (1924) had portrayed both Marxism and liberal capitalism in a very negative light; it became the 'standard textbook of the social conservatives': Bernhard vom Brocke, 'Werner Sombart', in H. U. Wehler (ed.), *Deutsche Historiker*, Vol. 5 (Göttingen, 1972), p. 143. On the overall picture see Wolfgang Hock, *Deutscher Antikapitalismus* (Frankfurt/M., 1969), as well as Avraham Barkai, *Das Wirtschaftssystem des Nationalsozialismus, Der historische und ideologische Hintergrund 1933–1936* (Cologne, 1977). See most recently Bernd Faulenbach, *Ideologie des deutschen Weges. Die deutsche Geschichte in der Historiographie zwischen Kaiserreich und Nationalsozialismus* (Munich, 1980), p. 279ff.

[2] For the external control of 'crowd' behaviour see David Riesman, *The Lonely Crowd* (1950). On Durkheim's place especially Jean Vialatoux, *De Durkheim à Bergson* (Paris, 1939); Anthony Giddens, *Capitalism and Modern Social Theory, An Analysis of the Writings of Marx, Durkheim and Max Weber* (Cambridge, 1971) (for comparison with Max Weber and Marx); Robert Nisbet, *Émile Durkheim* (Englewood, 1965), p. 11ff.; Steven Lukes, *Émile Durkheim* (London, 1973).

between an emancipation process promising liberation from earlier forms of order on the one hand, and a need for community and social harmony on the other, the conflict between rational individualism and the isolation of the individual in a mass society. Alongside the persistent survival of old strata we find a change in stratification through a new allocation of occupations and roles and the powerful influence of modernized social structures: on the one hand the party-political 'classes', used mainly by the Marxists, initially for agitation and then (after coming to power) inevitably elevated into absolutes, and on the other the de-politicized associations and mass organizations which could serve as substitutes for a community or as the exponents of ideologized integration in an atomized mass society. Durkheim's 'anomia' was curable – though at the cost of individual freedom.

Here again sociology and, in its train, the vulgarizing and ideologizing sociologism of the society it had analysed and thereby at times promoted to a one-sided point of reference, had performed a somewhat ambivalent service. Man as a social creature needed values, even in a sociological age, but this task was now assumed by the ideologists who replaced traditional Christian or humanist ideas of order with the myth of the proletariat or the *Volksgenosse*, the co-national, of the people or the nation, of the victorious class or race, of an absolute dependence on society or a bond with the community, and thus attempted to extinguish man as an individual. His 'loneliness' in a steadily expanding, impersonal macro-world, which refers him back to himself, flips over into a susceptibility to organizations and philosophies which offer him a new community and a substitute religion, which press them on him with new means of communication and propaganda, and finally force them upon him dictatorially.

5. THEORIES OF ALIENATION, THEORIES OF ÉLITES

What Durkheim diagnosed as the isolation or outsider's existence of modern man, and what he sought to solve by means of a system of social regulation, without however being able to foresee the political and ideological consequences of a threatening totalitarian collectivization, was summed up by the sociological and political precursors of authoritarian ideologies, and subsequently by the great simplifiers of political action, in the central and effective slogan of 'deracination', of 'uprooting'. From Maurice Barrès, the propagandist of the French radical Right, to Alfred Rosenberg and Joseph Goebbels, themselves uprooted intellectuals, from Mussolini, the socialist deserter, to Hitler, the frustrated artist, we are faced with a long row of nationalist demagogues who were now playing on that instrument of 'deracination' their battle songs in praise of a new root-taking, a new community, and a new faith.

On the other side, among the left-wing intellectuals and ideologists, as well as among the sociologists, the battle cries against man's 'alienation' through the modern division of labour and the industrial society were likewise becoming louder.[1] In both instances, therefore, the ideological formula was derived from sociological findings. Alienation, part of the arsenal of revolutionary terminology even before Karl Marx, was now taken up by the new psychology and individualistically refined. And in both cases it represented a challenge to the structure of modern society which contained both romantic-traditionalist and progressivist-revolutionary elements. The final objective was the 'liquidation' of deracination or alienation: on the one

[1] See Joachim Israel, *Der Begriff Entfremdung* (Reinbek, 1972), p. 32ff.; Franz von Magnus, *Normative Voraussetzungen im Denken des jungen Marx* (Freiburg-Munich, 1976); Arthur Mitzman, *Sociology and Estrangement, Three Sociologists of Imperial Germany* (New York, 1973); and, particularly critical of the ideological function of the concept of alienation, Leszek Kolakowski, *Leben trotz Geschichte* (Munich, 1977), p. 218ff. On socio-economic change between agrarian and industrial societies as a starting-point: Pierre Barral, *Les sociétés rurales du xxe siècle* (Paris, 1978); Jerome Blum, *The End of the Old Order in Rural Europe* (Princeton, 1978); David Landes, *Der entfesselte Prometheus* (Cologne, 1973; New York, 1969); Hans-Jürgen Puhle, *Politische Agrarbewegungen in kapitalistischen Industriegesellschaften* (Göttingen, 1975); Norbert Elias, *Über den Progress der Zivilisation*, 2 vols (Frankfurt/M., 1978).

hand by a 'return to nature', to blood and soil, or to a (proto-communist) pre-society existing *before* the corruptive progress of civilization, and on the other as a revolutionary, dictatorial break-through to a new people's community or the total society of the final era.

The parallels between right-wing and left-wing critiques are astonishing, but they are in line with the starting-point: socio-economic change, the diagnosis of psychological and sociological crisis accompanying it, and the universal search for comprehensive solutions looking both backwards and forwards, to a pre-civilizatory or a post-civilizatory world. The difference is in their point of reference: the global world-revolutionary vision of Marxism, even though already restricted by Lenin to a communist dictatorship, was confronted by the critics of deracination with an integral nationalism, with the nation (or race) and its living space as a rebuilt community. In the anti-communism of the one side and the anti-fascism of the other the ideological fronts appeared to become crystallized after 1917, though in fact they remained fluid until 1945.[1]

The meaning of the community concept first emerged clearly in the famous typifying juxtaposition which Ferdinand Tönnies (1855–1936) used as early as in the eighties in *Gemeinschaft und Gesellschaft* (1887) as a sociological description of the modernization process: community as the type of the integrated social group, small enough for it to be seen as a whole, yet comprehensive as a historical form of human existence; opposing it, and still advancing, society as a new macro-form, in its complexity (just as the new great states) no longer comprehended as a whole, consonant with both the freedom and with the lack of ties of modern man.[2] Similar ideas were expressed by Georg Simmel (1858–1918) in his analysis of the 'forms' of societal development: the autonomy, the spiritual and material opportunities offered to the individual by the new urban civilization, are purchased at the price of the loss of social ties and secure orientation, of the dichotomy and the pressure of powerful social forces to which the isolated individual finds himself exposed.

Simmel, along with Durkheim and Freud, Bergson and Husserl, reacted

[1] One should also remember the role of the 'Left people from the Right' (O.-E. Schüddekopf, 1960) in the Weimar Republic and the Right people from the Left under Mussolini's fascism, as well as of ex-communists such as Jacques Doriot and ex-socialists such as Marcel Déat in French right-wing radicalism prior to and during the Vichy period. On this see Bertram M. Gordon, 'The Condottieri of the Collaboration: Movement Social Revolutionnaire', *Journal of Contemporary History* 10 (1975), p. 261ff. On their ideological development since the turn of the century, Ernst Nolte, *Der Faschismus in seiner Epoche*, 5th ed. (Munich, 1979), p. 61ff.; Zeev Sternhell, *Fascist Ideology*, op. cit., p. 332ff. and *La Droite Révolutionnaire 1885–1914, Les origines françaises du Fascisme* (Paris, 1978), p. 27ff. Also Eugen Weber, *L'Action française* (Paris, 1962); *The National Revival in France 1905–1914* (Berkeley, 1968).

[2] See E. G. Jacoby, *Die moderne Gesellschaft im sozialwissenschaftlichen Denken von Ferdinand Tönnies* (Stuttgart, 1971); on the overall development of sociology still of special importance is Raymond Aron, *Hauptströmungen des soziologischen Denkens*, 2 vols (Cologne, 1971) (French edn Paris 1962); also his *Die deutsche Soziologie der Gegenwart* (Stuttgart, 1965).

as Jews with particular sensitivity to the problems of minorities and outsiders in this process of transition. It was they who, before long, found themselves discredited by anti-Semites and nationalists as philosophers of deracination. Thus the diagnosticians were declared to be the originators, and their observations were falsified and turned against them ideologically.

The next step, as it happened, was the invention and propagation of recipes for reintegration, with refined or with cruder means, and eventually with brutal ones. Progress now was no longer man's liberation or the extension of his potential; the new programme envisaged his recall or recapture. Civilization was declared to be retrogression and the decay of human culture; the objective now was the taming and instrumentalization of the modern age through the creation of a new community – though of course on the grand scale of the socialized and politicized nation, of the mass state or supra-state empire.

This was simultaneously a new form of re-barbarianization against the constitutional sophistication of political life. By far the most prophetic and impressive formulation, both for Right and Left cultural pessimists and neo-Machiavellianists, is that of the French journalist and political theorist Georges Sorel (1847–1922) in his *Réflexions sur la violence*. This first appeared as an essay in 1908, in the same year as his squaring of accounts with bourgeois *Illusions of Progress* and the *Decomposition of Marxism*: a burst of challenges simultaneously to the Right and Left. Sorel's life spanned the period between the revolutions of the mid-century and the new-style seizures of power by Lenin and Mussolini. Like many of his fellow radical thinkers he oscillated between revolutionary socialism and extreme nationalism, between romantic and progressivist political concepts. Sorel was one of a long procession of disenchanted Marxists, but his particular case was of one who had started at the extreme left. From Marx via Nietzsche and Bergson he arrived at an affirmative attitude to a revolutionary irrationalism which he held up against reformism and bureaucratization. Sorel's special importance lies in the fact that, emphatically as a socialist, he supported that irrationally-founded philosophy of action which, as a combination of nationalism and socialism, was to stand at the cradle of Italian fascism and German national socialism. Indeed two of their central ideas were already crystallized in his writings: the élitist idea as the structural principle of the power state, and of any rule which, to him, is based on violence; and the concept of the political myth, of that irrational emotional force, by means of which Sorel's élite would gain hold of the masses, in order to carry them along, by means of a general strike, by deeds instead of compromise, into action against bourgeois 'formal democracy'.

Once again it was primarily anti-liberalism, the critique of rationalism and materialism, the renunciation of the liberal and social idea of progress and its replacement by the true progressivism of revolution, no matter whether this was understood in (initially) a Marxist or (subsequently) a fascist sense.

That required an irrational myth, an apocalyptic faith like the one formerly represented by Christianity. The myth of a new religion following the decay of the old one – that was the promise of true revolutionary socialism. Sorel wrote his works in the face of the great wave of strikes in France, when programmes of sabotage and direct 'action' against capitalism and simultaneously the state were directly threatening the Third Republic which was still in turmoil after the Dreyfus affair. To Sorel the 'myth of the revolution' was the general strike, a kind of final battle by the faithful, whose revolutionary inspiration, as a sort of integrating value in itself, replaced society's belief in reason and progress, the bourgeois and social-democratic 'illusions of progress'. To him, socialism was not a rational 'science', as in orthodox Marxism, but simply a myth, a revolution. In practice this amounted to a form of syndicalist anarchism whose current forms, in Italy as in Spain and France, were a struggle of annihilation directed against society and the state itself. The only principle of order it was prepared to acknowledge was syndicalism, the action and self-government of revolutionary trade unions from below, on the basis of a working and production community: not peaceful anarchism of the Proudhon kind, but violence – self-liberation instead of state authority and oppression. And all this was predominantly aimed against 'democracy, the greatest mistake of the last century'; this had to be destroyed. On this point syndicalism and nationalism agreed.[1]

The Utopian traits of Sorel's influential writings were unmistakable, no matter whether based on Marxist collectivism or Neiztsche's individualism. Inevitable too were the abuse and the distortions which Sorel had to experience. The theoretical ideologist was engulfed by the ideological 'men of action' whom he himself had extolled and encouraged: above all Lenin and Mussolini. The essential point, clearly, was not the political label, which in Sorel's case had become blurred beyond decipherability: he remains the

---

[1] Thus the 'Déclaration', in *Cahiers du Cercle Proudhon* I (January 1912, p. 1) founded by Maurras with the participation of Sorel. Among the virtually boundless Sorel literature the following German interpretations deserve special mention: Michael Freund, *Georges Sorel, Der revolutionäre Konservatismus* (Frankfurt/M., 1972); Hans Barth, *Masse und Mythos, Die Theorie der Gewalt, Georges Sorel* (Hamburg, 1959); Helmut Berding, *Rationalismus und Mythos, Geschichtsauffassung und politische Theorie bei Georges Sorel* (Munich, 1969). On the French background especially Jean Maitron, *Histoire du mouvement anarchiste en France (1880–1914)* (Paris, 1951); also Robert Goetz-Girey, *La pensée syndicale française* (Paris, 1948). Also important are James H. Meisel, *The Genesis of Georges Sorel* (Ann Arbor, 1951); Hans Barth, *Die ideologische Krise*, op cit.; Irving Louis Horowitz, *Radicalism and the Revolt against Reason* (1961). Of Sorel's writings *Les illusions du progrès*, new ed. by Robert Nisbet (1979). Sorel's significantly simultaneous critique of Marxism was published under the destructive title *La décomposition du marxisme* (Paris, 1908); this was followed by his anti-intellectual challenge, *La Révolution dreyfusienne* (Paris, 1909). Sorel's 'Réflexions' had first been published as an article in the periodical *Mouvement socialiste* in 1906. In 1908–9, however, came his great outburst – an explosive mixture of critique of the Left and the Right, detonated simultaneously!

prototype and classical example of left–right radicalism with totalitarian features. The real point was the ideological method of the myth of struggle and violence, a myth which the great critics and subverters of liberal and rational social and political thought were able to exploit.

Glorification of direct action and of the great deed, which subsequently seemed to be represented by Lenin's revolutionary vanguard and later still by Mussolini's fascist civil-war troops, was followed by Sorel's great disillusionment – first with the reformist trade unions, which had functioned no better as exponents of revolution than had the socialists, and then with the 'revolutions' of Lenin and Mussolini, both of whom he had praised. Both revolutions, of the left and the right, were effected in the name of popular rule by small militant minorities, in an utterly élitist and anti-democratic manner. Until then perhaps Sorel's 'myth' might still have been valid. But the outbreak of power, the new dictatorship with its authoritarian or even totalitarian intensification of state power, ran counter to his idea of the abolition of government after the victory of the revolution. Instead, however, the myth acquired an independent life, became crystallized, and was turned into the state religion – the fate of all revolutionary ideologies. His critique of the *Duce* Mussolini's cult of the state and nationalism or of Lenin's oppressive dictatorship came too late: the 'myth' had served its purpose, its author was expendable. Fundamentally, however, there was no misunderstanding. Sorel quite clearly belonged to the direct ideologists of the rising totalitarianism.[1] What other interpretation can one put on the myth, now proclaimed as the new religion, of a revolutionary élite which liquidates bourgeois society and its values by violence – and, what is more, in the name of a good, uncorrupted, 'proletariat', of an ideal people arbitrarily definable, a people that was pure and unspoilt, yet also heroic and brutal? What other consequences could spring from this than the absolutization of a class, group or élite, and the legitimation of its new rule? Sorel's conviction that every society needed a faith, and that the lost liberal faith had to be replaced by the socialist creed, became, through the pseudo-religious glorification of revolutionary violence and its élitist champions, the tool of all future dictatorships.

[1] On this especially J. L. Talmon, 'The legacy of Georges Sorel. Marxism, Violence, Fascism', *Encounter*, February 1970; Jack J. Roth, 'Sorel und die totalitären Systeme', in *Vierteljahrshefte für Zeitgeschichte* 6 (1958), p. 45ff.; and *The Cult of Violence: Sorel and the Sorelians* (Berkeley, 1980); see Paul Mazgaj, 'The Young Sorelians and Decadence', *Journal of Contemporary History* 17/1 (1982), p. 179ff. Also E. Nolte, *Faschismus*, op. cit., pp. 203, 570, on Mussolini's relationship with Sorel, whom he once described as 'our master', though he later criticized him as a 'pensioned-off bookworm' and instead referred to Marx as the 'magnificent philosopher of workers' violence'. Recently also, highly important, is A. James Gregor, *Young Mussolini and the Intellectual Origins of Fascism* (Berkeley, 1979). As committed a disciple of Sorel as Eduard Berth in the twenties again switched from right-wing to left-wing radicalism: see Z. Sternhell, *Fascist Ideology*, op. cit., p. 348f.; the 7th ed. of *Réflexions sur la violence* contains a specific 'Plaidoyer pour Lénine' (Paris, 1930).

Sorel was not alone even then: the political sociology of Vilfredo Pareto (1848–1923), refined, academicized, not directly intended for daily use, pointed in a similar direction. Among the disciples of this Italian scholar, who taught in Switzerland, was for a while the still itinerant Mussolini. Pareto was the most important on the list of Italian élitist thinkers, a list which starts with the national liberal Gaetano Mosca's *Teorica dei governi* of 1884, and is eventually concluded with Robert Michels and the transition from socialist to fascist élitist theory. While Mosca operated with a fierce critique of the weaknesses of liberal democracy and its 'ruling class' in Italy, using a mixture of conservative and progressivist-critical and neo-Machiavellian arguments, Pareto attacked the problem in an entirely academic manner by means of brilliant analyses of leadership problems in modern society. As early as in 1902, in his book *Les systèmes socialistes*, he had, in spite of a fierce critique of socialism as a mystic Utopia, emphasized the élite-forming qualities of the class struggle. At the same time, however, his writings in the nationalist periodical *Regno* were directed against the weakly liberal bourgeoisie as much as against 'common socialism'.[1]

Pareto's grand-scale *Trattato di Sociologia Generale* of 1916 (English title: *The Mind and Society*) was a comprehensive treatment of economic and social structural problems on a mathematical basis. He distinguished between logical and non-logical action, the latter being based on fundamental, virtually immutable, motivations of human nature (the residuals) on the one hand, and their external manifestations and rationalizations as principles and theories (derivations) on the other. At stable periods government was in the hands of the tacticians; in crisis situations it was the men of action who brought about revolution for the periodic renewal of the state. The premise and method of Pareto's analyses were in the modern scientistic mould, but his findings were pessimistic. In contrast to Marxism, whose expectation of a final state he rejected as Utopian, and somewhat related to the social Darwinists, while lacking their biologism, Pareto viewed history and politics as a virtually inevitable perpetual power struggle between groups and classes. Victory of one side – including the Marxist – meant no more than the rule of a new élite against which others would rebel in turn.[2]

The drawback of this emphatically realistic diagnosis and prognosis, soon to be confirmed by communist élite rule, was of course – just as in classical

---

[1] Thus the preface of the editor, the former liberal Enrico Corradini, in the newly founded *Regno* (November 1903): 'Against the baseness of the Present'; see Nolte, *Faschismus*, op. cit., p. 237f. On Pareto, in addition to the voluminous Italian research by G. Busino, see Gottfried Eisermann, *Vilfredo Paretos System der allgemeinen Soziologie* (Stuttgart, 1962), and 'Vilfredo Pareto als politischer Denker', in *Bedeutende Soziologen* (Stuttgart, 1968); there is a clear exposition of élite theory in Günter Zauels, *Paretos Theorie der sozialen Heterogenität und Zirkulation der Eliten* (Stuttgart, 1968). See also the instructive correspondence between G. Mosca and G. Ferrero. For valuable suggestions I am indebted to Jens Petersen (Rome).

[2] See Zauels, op. cit., pp. 39ff., 47ff.

power-struggle theory since Machiavelli and Hobbes – that the social-anthropological portrait of political man was not only exceedingly pessimistic but amounted to a relativization of values, to a normative arbitrariness of politics. Naturally Pareto, the neo-Machiavellian, also esteemed freedom, but he was sceptical about its liberal release and tended to see a necessary circumscription in the continual rotation of élites. This famous circulation of élites would, through a continuous circulation of power, involve also the revolutionary potential of society. Pareto's cycle went through stabilization, rise of the tacticians, and internal decay of state life, to overthrow and new stabilization. The idea of a cycle, the oldest alternative to the idea of progress and decay, was applied here in a most ingenious way to the solution of the topical confrontation of progressivism, decadent attitudes and revolutionary thought. Added to this was Pareto's analysis of the nature of political ideologies – reminiscent of Thucydides or again Machiavelli – which he viewed as the justification of the power struggle and reduced to a definite number of basic human drives.[1]

Yet Pareto was by no means a value-neutral scientist, any more than the other sociologists of his day. He saw decay well advanced, the states weakened by liberal, democratic and socialist currents, an early revolution inescapable. Disillusionment and disenchantment with rational progressivist thought formed his starting-point and determined his 'realistic' dissociation from all ideals and values, his contempt for humanitarianism and parliamentarianism. The final stage of such a merciless critique of culture and society was a kind of heroic nihilism in the wake of Nietzsche, or a pseudo-scientific sociologism which at the same time questioned and justified everything.

Sociologism and psychologism served the power-political ideologies as stepping stones. Those things which, in their over-simplified way, they extracted from the complex system of this social philosopher, were sufficient to stamp him as a spiritual father of fascism: an eternal cycle instead of democratic progress, unshakable laws and, simultaneously, irrational determination of politics through blind power processes instead of through normative values. Pareto's corrosive relativism, his emphasis on élites and a random-value theory of power were readily turned, by just such ideologists, into welcome proof of the historical-philosophical necessity of revolution and in particular also into a justification of the new élite's power. Mussolini showed his gratitude for this unwitting support by promoting his famous 'teacher' from the days of his Swiss exile (1902–4) to the post of a fascist Senator in the year of his death. Pareto was subsequently glorified and criticized as a proto-fascist.[2] It is more correct to say 'that he looked forward

[1] See Zauels, op. cit., p. 79ff., 95ff.

[2] This kind of political narrowing-down of the rich and provoking work, a narrowing-down further intensified by Pareto's last remarks on the victory of fascism, for a long time determined judgement on him: the arguments for and against (together with a bibliography) are collected in Zauels, op. cit., p. 99ff. It would be going too far, after the exaggerations of mainly British-American criticism of Pareto, to attempt to deny any connection between him and the emergence of fascism, though even Nolte occasionally inclines that way (*Faschismus*, op. cit., p. 216ff.; see p. 199).

keenly to the advent of fascism because he saw in it the confirmation of what he had predicted for the parliamentary system and for democracy – to wit, their collapse'.[1] Pareto evidently shared an attitude familiar among many intellectuals and professors: confirmation of his own teaching, theory and prejudices meant more to him than the actual 'substance' or structure of fascism. Mussolini and Lenin had proved to him the remarkable thesis of his main work (§2 178): 'A mere handful of citizens, provided they are violent, can impose their will on the holders of power if these are unwilling to match violence by equal violence.'

Even before the First World War French right-wing radicalism had proceeded to formulate its authoritarian ideology very much more directly than Pareto, in a far more party-engaged manner than the 'Sorelismo' upon which Mussolini based his élitist-revolutionary activism (as *élan vital* of the creative-evolution philosophy) and subsequently the national-imperial authoritarianism of his fascist doctrine. Politicization of cultural and social critique, ideologization also of the new scientific sociology itself, received their organizational form from the monarchist Charles Maurras (1868–1952) with the foundation of the *Action Française* and its eponymous newspaper (1899). In the forefront was the idea of order as against the anarchical features of modernization and the democratization of the masses. French 'action' meant the glorification of the national community and authoritarian leadership by an intelligent and resolute minority whom the masses would follow. Amidst the decay of society and the state the radical monarchist '*Action*' was to enforce the new authoritarian order by its combat units (*Camelots du roi*) through agitation and street fighting. But this it never actually succeeded in doing in France itself. Right-wing radical inroads did not occur until the crises of the thirties (in the rebellion of the Croix de Feu in 1934) and following the defeat of 1940 under the Vichy regime – on both occasions with the employment of the legendary war hero of Verdun, Maréchal Philippe Pétain. Yet as an early model of fascist and national socialist actionism and its law-and-order ideology French authoritarianism occupies a pioneering place; this has been very impressively characterized in its political and philosophical context in Ernst Nolte's now classic study on *Faschismus in seiner Epoche* (1963).[2]

The basic concept of this anti-republican anti-democratism included the idea of 'corporativism', which played a part also in Catholic social teaching. This was a kind of modernized 'estator' state, which, instead of anarchical syndicalism and capitalism, was to be the exponent of a state-regulated new

[1] Zauels, op. cit., p. 104; see there also Pareto's last remarks, on the one hand dismissing fascism as a 'romantic episode' and Mussolini as an 'intriguer', while on the other being impressed by the massive rotational movement of the Italian élite that the new era seems to represent.

[2] See footnote 1 p. 51 above; recently also Paul Mazgaj, *The Action Française and Revolutionary Syndicalism* (Chapel Hill, 1979).

social order that would combine political and social authoritarianism. In Catholic countries such as Italy, Portugal and Spain corporativist theory and practice soon acquired an authoritarian-state significance in this sense – not so, however, in the totalitarian national socialist dictatorship which disappointed its conservative and authoritarian partners in this respect too.[1]

Traditionally anti-German and simultaneously anti-Semitic, anti-liberal and anti-parliamentarian, anti-democratic and critical of civilization all at the same time, Maurras's ideological agitation reached its climax in the nationalism of the First World War. However, it was extensively lacking in that other ingredient which subsequently lent such ideological striking-power to fascism and national socialism: 'socialism' alongside nationalism. This combination of the two great currents of the day was to lead beyond mere authoritarianism, beyond the predominantly traditionalist ideology of the usual authoritarian regimes of military or monarchist stamp, to the totalitarian dictatorship ideologies of Italy and, above all, Germany during the post-war period. Maurras's French right-wing radicalism can therefore be more correctly assigned to the ideologies of 'revolutionary conservatism', whose exponents in Germany were admittedly influential intellectuals but, as chiefs without Indians, could be likened to 'Trotskyites of national socialism'.[2]

Nevertheless French anti-democratism represented an important variant in the rise of the great ideologies. Its 'integral nationalism' was formulated amidst the exciting clash around the Dreyfus trial which was a watershed between the Right and the Left in French intellectualism; it also meant a notable defeat of French anti-Semitism which was never again to attain the strength or the power of German anti-Semitism. However, the persisting disaffection of the Right, the continual conflicts of the liberals and the Left, and finally the national upsurge of the Great War furnished sufficient arguments in favour of right-wing authoritarian integration ideologies. And following the defeat of the Third Republic, now of course under German influence, its national socialist version enjoyed a brief and deceptive flowering. Its principal exponent, alongside Maurras, the important writer Maurice Barrès (1862–1923) tended more strongly from the outset towards a harmonization and integration of nationalism and socialism: conservative monarchism was to be forced back and prominence given to the organic

[1] On the multi-layered historico-political problem of corporativism, which plays a part not only in authoritarian systems but also in modern welfare state democracy (*e.g.* with the concept of works councils), see Karl Loewenstein, *Verfassungslehre*, 3rd ed. (1975); Ulrich von Alemann, Rolf G. Heinze (eds), *Verbände und Staat, Vom Pluralismus zum Korporatismus* (Opladen, 1979), p. 38ff.

[2] As Armin Mohler formulated it for Germany in his fundamental study *Die konservative Revolution in Deutschland* (Stuttgart, 1950), p. 12f. He refers to an essay by Bertrand d'Astorg, *Introduction au monde de la terreur* (Paris, 1945), p. 186, which is admittedly aimed at the left wing of the NSDAP. For an appropriate characterization of French right-wing radicalism see R. Stromberg, *Intellectual History*, op. cit., p. 412.

decentralized unity of the entire nation, since it was in French centralism, above all, that Barrès saw the danger of that 'deracination' he never ceased to warn against. Admittedly, his was a somewhat agrarian-tinted national socialism, directed against the pull of the big cities and man's severance from his natural 'roots'. Following the defeat of the right wing in the Dreyfus affair he endeavoured to redeploy the anti-Semitic and anti-liberal forces by uniting them in a demand for strong authoritarian leadership of the state.[1]

Contemporary left-wing radicalism was likewise actively involved in the authoritarian ideologization of the pre-war and wartime period, often enough in a fluctuating exchange of ideas and arguments, slogans and individuals. This hostile common attitude of right-wing and left-wing radicalism emerged most clearly in the ideologization and concretization of élite and leadership theories. Very largely in parallel with Mussolini's ideological development, from Marx via Nietzsche to Sorel and Pareto, proceeded the transformation of Marxism by Lenin (1870–1924), who, in his Swiss exile, realized that the War provided the great opportunity, the real revolutionary situation.

Marxian determinism, however, a patient wait for an inevitable revolution, was no longer sufficient for a future revolutionary leader. He needed modern theories of action and élite, which could help create a revolution, even if it was totally undemocratic and by no means inevitable, but achievable only through a *coup d'état* by a minority. To justify this ideologically and to communicate it to the masses in the shape of a belief in revolution, to democratize (as it were) the *coup d'état* by the minority, required the theory of an élite which alone possessed the truth and the right to make it prevail. It was therefore not a case of the 'people's masses' of Bolshevik propaganda nor indeed of the overwhelming majority which Marxism had prophesied for socialism-communism.[2] The vanguard dictatorially replaced the proletariat, whose mandate it claimed to hold, and after its seizure of power also governed in an entirely dictatorial manner in the name of the people, of the workers, of the mono-party.

It was Lenin's totalitarian party theory (not Stalin's, as is generally believed) which first prepared the ground for the impending brutal reign of communism, requiring more than the vague concept of a 'dictatorship of the proletariat', a concept which anyway played scarcely any part at all in the laconic hints of the fathers of Marxism. In terms of intellectual history it based itself on the creative and leading action of the individual and his fellow

---

[1] See especially Zeev Sternhell, *La Droite*, op. cit., p. 348ff.; on relations between the two principal figures see their correspondence: M. Barrès et Ch. Maurras, *La République ou le Roi, Correspondance inédite, 1883–1923* (Paris, 1970). For a comprehensive treatment also M. Curtis, *Three against the Third Republic, Sorel, Barrès and Maurras* (Princeton, 1959).

[2] See Eleonore Sterling, *Der unvollkommene Staat, Studien über Demokratie und Diktatur* (Frankfurt/M., 1965), p. 216ff.; L. Schapiro, *The Communist Party of the Soviet Union*, op. cit., p. 159ff.; for the rest also, Thomas T. Hammond (ed.), *The Anatomy of Communist Takeovers* (New Haven and London, 1975).

conspirators, and simultaneously on the myth (Sorel's?) of the revolution, a myth preserved to the present day as an epithet in all self-portrayals of communist dictatorship, ritually observed and militantly protected against all apostates from the true faith, and indeed against anyone who might use the sacred term of revolution in a different context – be it right- or left-wing radical. In line with this arose the Leninist definition of 'counter-revolution': a collective term for all opponents of *its* revolution.

This was a long way from Marx, who saw universal suffrage and democratic reforms as the road to the victory of the proletariat; it was also a long way from Engels, who, shortly before the turn of the century, had expressed the opinion that the days of revolution by conscious minorities at the head of unaware masses had gone; it was even further away from the democratic socialists and trade unions who were improving the lot of the workers through legal progress within the framework of democracy. In total contrast to these, Leninism resorted to conspiracy and to action by a revolutionary élite; this held out a better prospect of success in a backward Russia – both against tsarist autocracy and later against the democratic transitional regime – than placing one's hope in the process of history.[1]

Lenin's proximity to Sorelism, therefore, may have been due to tactical methodological considerations: Lenin saw himself as Marxist, though under Russian conditions, and he repeatedly dissociated himself from revolution- ary adventurism and actionism. However, his 'modification' of Marxism also affected its substance: by breaking with the Russian socialists, first in 1903 and finally in 1912, and by placing his radical Bolsheviks in opposition to the (moderate) Mensheviks, he opted for a dictatorially-oriented and cadre- organized élite party, which would seize, and maintain, power by force.

Lenin laid the foundation for all this in his writings, during his long years of exile, and thus became, as the first great 'practical' ideologist of the century, a very real figure in the history of political ideas too. Above all, he saw himself as a revolutionary who, unlike other 'socialists' including Marx- Engels, combined his faith in historical determination with a will to power. This, of course, required a correct assessment and utilization of the historical process by the revolutionary leadership, an ability to strike at the right moment, to enforce the organization of the 'proletariat' in a disciplined and uncompromising manner for the execution of the revolution and subsequently for the implementation of socialism. That could be done only by an élite, by a vanguard, which was profoundly different from the democratic, reformist leadership groups of the European socialists. For this

[1] On Lenin's élitist party theory and on Leninism against the background of the evolution of Russian Marxism see S. V. Utechin, *Geschichte der politischen Ideen in Russland* (Stuttgart, 1966); David Lane, *The Roots of Russian Communism, A social and historical study of Russian social-democracy 1898–1907* (Assen, 1975); and recently Alain Besançon, *Les origines intellectuelles du Léninisme* (Paris, 1977). Generally important is Alexander Vucinich, *Social Thought in Tsarist Russia, The Quest for a General Science of Society, 1861–1914* (Chicago, 1976), as well as, in particular, James Billington (p. 10 above), p. 443ff.

reason it remains an open question whether Lenin really believed in an extension of *his* revolution into a world revolution.[1]

Most importantly, however, the theory of the vanguard party firmly established the character of political communism which, Marxist or not, has not changed over the sixty-five years of its realization: its monopolistic claim, its quasi-religious ideology, its definitive suppression of freedom after occasional brief intervening periods of loosening-up or deceptive liberalization (in the twenties, fifties or sixties) – in short, its fundamentally totalitarian character, both in its system and in its ideology. Whatever the former classical idea of communism may have signified in the heads of utopians and dreamers, its only real revolutionary triumph through Lenin's *coup d'état* and the subsequent permanence of dictatorship has proved it to be – alongside national socialism – one of the two totalitarian counterblows to the idea of liberal, constitutional democracy. Many had a share in this sudden turn from democracy to totalitarianism: not only Leninized Marxism but also the ideas of its opponents, of the right-wing anti-liberals, who brooded over an authoritarian and totalitarian refutation and overthrow of modern democracy, who hatched revolutionary actions and strategies, propagated radical ideologies and eventually, together with the constitutional state, suppressed and annihilated also the people who were standing in their way.

It is true that the ideas and ideologies which emerged in the great confrontations of the turn of the century did not inevitably point in this direction. Freedom of decision lay with politics. The First World War, however, substantially narrowed down that freedom and thereby, alongside the apparent triumph of democracy, also greatly enhanced the effectiveness of authoritarian and totalitarian ideologies. The main signals for the post-war period had been set, a massive front against democracy had been established, both from the Right and the Left. Its advance into the disaster of the War simultaneously provided unsuspected opportunities for inroads into the European political and social structures, economically weakened, socially undermined and shaken as they were from an awareness of the crisis. A great deal was to be decided in the five years from 1917 to 1922.

---

[1] On this controversial issue Piero Melograni recently developed and argued some very interesting points of view in 'Lenin e la revoluzione mondiale', *Mondoperaio* 7/8 (July–August 1981, Rome), p. 111ff. (This is his preliminary study for a book; a further article is due to appear shortly in the *Journal of Italian History*). According to Melograni, as on the issue of totalitarian dictatorship, it was not only Stalin who came into conflict with Trotsky; Lenin, as a realist in power politics, had opposed the ideology of world revolution ever since 1917–18 by concentrating on safeguarding his Russian dictatorship, as socialism in one country.

6. CHANGES IN LIBERALISM

The changes in political thought were connected with a profound structural transformation undergone even by the traditional views of fundamentally democratic parties. The modifications of liberalism and socialism call for particular attention here.

The inroads made by the state and its legislation into ever further areas of society and the economy represented a dual challenge to the evolution of liberal theories. On the one hand these inroads infringed the classical concept of a totally free and virtually automatic upward development: the rise of economic interest-groups and trade unions meant that group-political and state-political interventions were gaining in importance in the final quarter of the nineteenth century, and indeed it was the liberal parties which, contrary to their original principles, were largely involved in these. On the other hand, rivalry with the still powerful conservatives (and their agrarian policy) and with the emerging socialists (and their social policy) necessitated certain corrections to the pure doctrine, corrections which had been foreshadowed by John Stuart Mill[1] and which, about the end of the century, brought about a substantial change in ideas on the role of the state and the demands of democracy.

Liberalism had grown strong by its idea of progress. Now the belief in its inevitability and also in its sociological validity, had taken some painful knocks. This applied not only to economic *laisser-faire* liberalism itself but also to the belief in the political priority of liberty over equality, of the individual over the group. The pressing social problem, the expansion of imperialism, and finally a nationalism that was leading to war were all challenges to political ideas which far exceeded the basic individualist and rational axioms of liberalism. From one side, from England itself, came dire warnings of a menacing 'collectivization' that threatened to swamp the liberals even in the country of John Locke and Adam Smith. Liberals felt

---

[1] On conflict between the concepts of freedom and society in the face of progressive democratization see Heinz Rausch, 'John Stuart Mill', in *Klassiker des politischen Denkens*, Vol.2 (Munich, 1968), p. 240ff.; Walter Hübner, 'John Stuart Mills Freiheitsbegriff', in *Zur Geschichte und Problematik der Demokratie (Festschrift for Hans Herzfeld)* (Berlin, 1958), p. 97ff. See John M. Robson, *The Improvement of Mankind: The social and political thought of John Stuart Mill* (London, 1968); Pedro Schwartz, *The New Political Economy of John Stuart Mill* (London, 1972).

themselves forced on to the defensive.[1] The influential sociologist Herbert Spencer had, as early as in 1884, in a book with the alarming title *Man versus the State*, deplored parliament's increasingly frequent falls from grace in acting against the principle of a free market. On the other side both humanitarian and national sentiments were, in the face of headlong industrial and political developments, pushing even liberal theorists to a justification or even a championship of state measures which were dealing continual blows not only to their credo of the caretaker state but also to their belief in the free development of society.

It turned out that liberalism and humanism, personal rights and human rights, were indissolubly intertwined: the necessary reforms against the evils of industrialization and the abuse of power required a series of interventions in free development. The liberal dilemma was evident. Just as the conservatives were trapped between reaction and continuity, and the socialists between revolution and democracy, so the liberals were caught between their economic and their political postulates. And in each case the solution of the dilemma resulted in a strengthening of the state.

The deceptions and disappointments surrounding liberalism produced a variety of attempted adjustments and modernizations; yet each social or national modification robbed liberalism of some of its persuasive consistency and merely confirmed its critics on the Right and the Left in their impression that the liberal and bourgeois era was drawing to a close. In Britain, with its two-party system, it succeeded a little longer than elsewhere in halting its decline into a mere class party or interest party and in integrating its social component. On the Continent the rifts and struggles had long been patent; prior to and during the First World War they resulted either in a narrowing of liberal theory to one of specific political interests or else transforming it into a set of generalized postulates, thereby rendering a separate party dispensable to the extent that liberal views were taken over by other democratic parties.

In either case, however, the classical theory which had defined both economic and political liberalism by self-interest and happiness, usefulness and freedom for the individual was no longer correct. Relations between the individual and his social milieu – that was the age-old problem that was bound to concern especially the liberal social thinkers and critics of collectivist tendencies since Mill and Spencer, provided they wished to meet scholarly demands of factual accuracy as well as the moral demand for human validity. In Britain the problem was most clearly treated, about the turn of the century, by the 'neo-Hegelian' Oxford professor Thomas Hill Green (*Lectures on the Principles of Political Obligation*) and his disciples

---

[1] Thus A. V. Dicey, *Law and Public Opinion in England during the 19th Century* (1905). Also Carl Joachim Friedrich, 'Englische Verfassungsideologie im 19.Jahrhundert, Dicey's Law and Public Opinion', in K. D. Bracher, Ch. Dawson, W. Geiger, R. Smend (eds), *Die moderne Demokratie und ihr Recht (Festschrift Gerhard Leibholz)*, Vol.1 (Tübingen, 1966), p. 101ff.

Bernard Bosanquet (*The Philosophical Theory of State*, 1899) and Leonard Hobhouse (*Metaphysical Theory of State*, 1918),[1] and in Germany by the so-called academic socialists such as Lujo Brentano, and especially by the Protestant clergyman and 'national-social' politician and journalist Friedrich Naumann (1860–1919), whose friends included Max Weber and Hugo Preuss, among whose disciples, in turn, was his biographer Theodor Heuss.[2] Education in the broad sense of 'people's enlightenment' and also of the religious component of social affairs was considered by Naumann to be of particular importance. Social justice and participation of all citizens, both politically and in the fruits of progress, were part of the obligations of the liberal idea under present-day conditions.

Attempts at a conciliation of liberalism with contemporary social and national currents was, needless to say, at the cost of its unambiguity and stringency. As a result, long before its party-political shrinking, it found itself, together with rationalism and individualism, between the millstones of doubt, of a critique of capitalism and civilization, which supplied the irrationalism and collectivism of anarchical and authoritarian theories of state with the ammunition they needed to destroy the idea of progress and freedom.

This applied also to the belief in representative democracy, a belief deeply rooted in the liberal conviction of a constantly needed and valid self-determination of the citizen, while simultaneously fearing collective mass seduction by plebiscitarian movements. A liberal like Max Weber eventually saw the solution to the problem – entirely in agreement with Naumann – in supporting a mixed representative-plebiscitarian pattern, as provided for by the dualistic Weimar Constitution. Scepticism about winning the masses over and guiding them solely by parliamentary democracy had become too profound, and (national) conviction of the need for, or at least the inevitability of, leadership by a 'people's Kaiser' (Naumann), or a substitute Kaiser in the shape of a president directly elected by the people, actually standing above parliament and personifying national consensus, had become too overwhelming. Yet this could work only so long as president and parliament enjoyed the same political majority and endorsed democracy

[1] See George H. Sabine, *A History of Political Theory*, 3rd ed. (London, 1966), p. 727ff.

[2] Theodor Heuss, *Friedrich Naumann* (1937; new ed. 1968); F. Naumann, *Werke*, ed. Theodor Schieder *et al.*, 6 vols. (Cologne 1964–9); by Naumann, especially about the turn of the century, *Demokratie und Kaisertum* (Berlin, 1900). On the vacillation between liberal-social and national-imperial tendencies in this 'national-social' liberalism see Naumann's wartime study *Mitteleuropa* (Berlin, 1915). On Lujo Brentano (1844–1931), founder of the *Verein für Sozialpolitik* (1872) and leading representative of a combination of a pro-trade-union and liberal view of the economy, see his last book, *Mein Leben im Kampf um die soziale Entwicklung Deutschlands* (1931). James J. Sheehan, *The Career of Lujo Brentano, A Study of Liberalism and Social Reform in Imperial Germany* (Chicago, 1966), and *German Liberalism in the Nineteenth Century* (Chicago, 1978); and the still classic work by Leonard Krieger, *The German Idea of Freedom* (Boston, 1957).

itself; this was initially the case under Friedrich Ebert until 1925, but no longer under Hindenburg at the end of the Weimar Republic. Max Weber himself was disturbed by the pessimistic vision of a caesaristic overthrow or manipulation of modern mass democracy. However, he survived Friedrich Naumann by only one year, and then the misconstruction of Weimar was still totally masked by post-war crises.

What engaged the liberal 'revisionists' about the turn of the century was making full allowance for man's social nature, including his non-rational needs and susceptibilities. Naumann's social national concept, just as Green's neo-liberal philosophy, which was in turn influenced by German idealism, contained a critique of *laisser-faire* industrialism and its social consequences; by open-mindedness towards the powerful social current it was hoped that it might be won over or saved for liberal democracy, and that, in a renewed shape, responsive to the demands of the day and open to man's social and national dimensions, individualism and socialism might prove to be reconcilable. 'From Bebel to Bassermann', from the Social Democrats to the National Liberals – that was Naumann's coalition policy slogan; behind it were not just party politics but a liberal conviction of the compatibility of these philosophies on the basis of a democratic 'people's state'.[1]

The state not only as a negative limitation but as a positive tool for the safeguarding of freedom, both in its individualist and its civic-social dimensions, represented the decisive transformation towards the political modernization of liberalism. Admittedly, this might equally lead to a new threat to it from more tightly organized *étatiste* mass movements of the Right or the Left, once an increase in the state's range of competence and power began to encounter less and less resistance, or was even sanctioned by liberal-bourgeois justifications. In education and instruction, in cultural and social policy, in relations between the two sides of the economy right through to collective bargaining, in the combination of the principle of private ownership with the principle of the common good – everywhere there was a transition from the idea of economic freedom to that of the political constitutional state, an idea which increasingly also embraced social-state elements.

The essential point was that fundamental distinctions and division lines against both conservative and social democratic principles were in consequence being blurred and relativized. The combination of liberal principles with *étatiste* and social tendencies offered the prospect of a smoothly functioning democracy; at the same time the adoption of conservative and social-political concepts of the state deprived the liberal credo of some of its original force, it confused the great issues and postulates which had ensured its persuasiveness. Compared to more consistently self-sufficient socialist

[1] See Friedrich Naumann's study, *Die politischen Parteien* (Berlin, 1910), to this day of interest to party research.

and *étatiste* ideologies on the Left and Right, liberalism displayed less ideological rigidity and more tolerance *vis-à-vis* other currents. That, of course, was in line with its name and self-image but it also made it look inconsistent and ready to compromise, opportunistic and lacking in principles; its economic theory, moreover, lost much of its validity with the war economy and the crises of the post-war period.

The great moral substance of the liberal idea, the principles of civil and human rights, of checks on political power and arbitrariness, of national and international co-operation, which were reflected also in the politological ideas of the American President Woodrow Wilson, eventually fell victim – as he did himself – to disillusionment with wartime and post-war development. In the rivalry of ideologies, liberalism, which had introduced modern democracy, proved unable to keep pace. It was identified with its problems and crises, while the great left-wing and right-wing ideologies profited from them and, carried along on the waves of critique of democracy, satisfied the masses' craving for a political faith.

The great ideologies also benefited from the ambiguity which had surrounded the concept of liberalism itself during the nineteenth century and more particularly since the ideological debates of the turn of the century. It was no longer a case of just its economic and political meaning but also of differences existing between a narrower Continental-European and a broader Anglo-American understanding of liberalism. The resulting misunderstandings and misinterpretations were, and still are, innumerable – both in political discussion and in the scholarly literature. The narrower concept covered mainly the liberal's intermediate position between conservatism and socialism, it referred sociologically to the bourgeoisie and politically to a non-radical reformism. In this sense liberalism continued to be equated and opposed, especially by the Marxists, with capitalism. They even portrayed fascism as having logically developed from liberalism: the Marxist 'theory of fascism' was a deliberate falsification of the universally political, humanistic substance of the idea of liberalism; it represented its socio-economic narrowing down to a concept of selfish interest and struggle in the sense of *laisser-faire* and to a capitalist conspiracy for the (fascist) destruction of socialism.

By contrast, the broader concept of democratic liberalism, especially in the USA, where no socialism worth mentioning ever developed, described the basic attitude of a libertarian pluralist democracy generally: a politically and conceptually more comprehensive understanding, capable of including conservative and social-democratic currents and strata, the antithesis of autocracy and dictatorship, of authoritarian or absolutist-totalitarian movements and systems. In opposition to communism *and* fascism this democratic liberalism proved its 'ideological' force and, unlike Continental–European liberalism, maintained its position in the totalitarian era between the wars and, after 1945, actually made possible the rebuilding of democracy and acted as its ideological exponent.

Its core, along with the freest possible economy and society, is the preservation and further development of democratic institutions, of free elections and parliaments, and of the separation of powers, as well as of national self-determination and a social morality aiming at political liberty and equality for all, including particularly minorities and disadvantaged groups. Such a general democratic philosophy might view itself as progressivist in the sense of a more pronounced social or economic policy by the state, as in recent American development since Franklin Roosevelt's New Deal, where liberal tends to mean Left; but equally this general concept of liberalism comprised a 'neo-conservative' trend, as in the twenties and again in the seventies, even though it is increasingly dissociating itself from a left-wing, more welfare-state oriented and radical understanding of liberalism. Certainly it has not been narrowed down in class-political terms; it has, above all, been anti-dictatorial, anti-collectivist, anti-totalitarian. In resisting state interference and preserving democratic institutions it has seen itself, in this sense, as the high point and quintessence of western political tradition or indeed as the secular form of western civilization.[1]

This ambiguity of the modern concept of liberalism is reminiscent in many respects of the modern concept of progress, its economic and social, political and cultural dimensions and ambivalences, with which liberalism has been most intimately associated. Belief in man and his potential, the conviction of a not only material but also political and moral perfectibility of human systems, the idea of freedom and human rights had all been common to both. But this belief, at the moment of its highest development about the turn of the century, came under the fiercest attack. The undermining and narrowing-down of liberalism had been foreshadowed in the classic distinction between *citoyen* and *bourgeois* ever since the French Revolution, a distinction taken up by Marxism and intensified into total antagonism between bourgeoisie and proletariat. Nevertheless, there was reason to think that democratic evolution in the politically liberal sense might make a radical revolution unnecessary.

Only the Great War and its aftermath foiled and refuted this much-questioned and sharply criticized progressivist liberal optimism and lent fatal buoyancy to its worst enemies, communism and fascism. One might have been inclined to dismiss the ideas which heralded these as eccentric radicalism, but they were more deeply rooted in the general attitudes of the turn of the century than appearances before the war suggested. Not liberal democracy but a radical anti-liberalism and 'illiberalism'[2] occupied the

[1] Thus, in a specially comprehensive and impressive manner, Frederick M. Watkins, *The Political Tradition of the West: A Study in the Development of Modern Liberalism* (Cambridge, 1948). Western and liberal traditions, are here equated.

[2] Fritz Stern, *Das Scheitern illiberaler Politik* (Berlin, 1974), English edition, *The Failure of Illiberalism* (New York, 1972); as well as the important articles in the volume *Die Krise des Liberalismus zwischen den Weltkriegen*, ed. Rudolf von Thadden (Göttingen, 1978), including the historically exhaustive study by Martin Seliger, 'Authentischer Liberalismus, Grundideen, Entwicklungspotential und Krisen der Verwirklichung' (p. 31ff.).

extended field of political ideologies. In Friedrich Naumann's Germany and in Benedetto Croce's Italy, in particular, the more comprehensive ideas of liberalism had failed as early as in the twenties in the face of ideological polarization. Continental-European liberalism was overwhelmed by the authoritarian movements, or overlaid by a confrontation between fascism, national socialism and communism; in the British two-party system it was largely siphoned off between Conservative and Labour supporters. It was not the liberal and democratic compromise formula but the mass-and-élite concept of the critics of liberalism, both on the Left and the Right, which gained the upper hand ideologically between the two wars.

It took the experience of dictatorship and the Second World War for the fundamental anti-totalitarian attitude of liberalism, as well as of democratic socialism and of Christian-democratic ideas to find common ground for a more durable achievement of that interaction of individualistic and community-oriented views which, in the interests of both (liberal) freedom and (social) reform, would break the absolutist claim of the ideologies and safeguard the survival of a libertarian and social democracy. This generalization of liberalism, its integration in all democratic parties, has enabled it, though often declared dead, to become the basis of a revived western-libertarian parliamentary democracy.

7. SOCIAL DEMOCRATIC REFORMISM

The roots of a 'democratic socialism', dissociating itself, as a libertarian reformist movement, from revolutionary socialism and communism, and proclaiming a synthesis of socialism and pluralist parliamentary democracy, go back to the pre-Marxist ideas of the early socialists and, more particularly, to the co-operative and trade union movement of the 1830s and 1840s. Initially, it is true, the term social democracy was used rather vaguely to cover both revolutionary and reformist socialists so long as they were aiming at a transformation of existing economic, social and political conditions through social emancipation and political equality.[1] The objective was then, and still is, egalitarian democracy. The issue of civil liberties under socialism, however, led to major controversies after the foundation of socialist workers' parties in the latter part of the century, controversies which, under the catch-phrase of reformism, prepared for a division, as early as the turn of the century, and subsequently a split of socialism into a democratic and a communist stream. After the First World War an autonomous social democracy, in the sense of a non-dictatorial libertarian socialism, finally established itself; in view of the worldwide conflicts between totalitarian and libertarian versions of socialism it emphatically reconfirmed its programme after the Second World War. In its present-day meaning, therefore, it covers those socialist parties and doctrines which combine an avowal in favour of libertarian constitutional, pluralistic democracy with a readiness for political co-operation with the 'bourgeois parties' and with a belief in non-violent reform through legal methods and evolution.

This emphasis on the democratic and libertarian component of socialism,

---

[1] On this concept see Hans Müller, *Ursprung und Geschichte des Wortes 'Sozialismus' und seiner Verwandten* (Hanover, 1967). See also L. H. Adolf Geck on the penetration of the word *'sozial'* into the German language, *Über das Eindringen des Wortes 'sozial' in die deutsche Sprache* (Göttingen, 1963). On the history of the effects of Marxism see Iring Fetscher, *Der Marxismus*, 3 vols, 3rd ed. (Munich, 1976–7), and above all Leszek Kolakowski, *Hauptströmungen*, op. cit., 3 vols (Munich, 1977–9). The social democratic current of libertarian socialism, on the other hand, in its conflict situation between programme and practice, revolution and reform, is treated most lucidly by Susanne Miller, *Das Problem der Freiheit im Sozialismus* (Frankfurt/M., 1964); for a survey see also Helga Grebing, *Geschichte der deutschen Arbeiterbewegung* (Munich, 1966).

as against its authoritarian, dictatorial and compulsion-state aspects and motive forces, principally focused on the question of how and by what means society was to be transformed, and what its political form should be. Regardless of terminological fluctuations between socialism, communism and social democracy, this basic question has profoundly occupied modern socialism from its beginnings. Even during the Paris Revolution of 1848 a radical communist like Blanqui and a moderate social democratic trend, as seen in Louis Blanc, were present alongside each other. Until the First World War, however, in spite of all temporary separate groupings, these differences mostly existed in the form of wings within the overall socialist movement, without leading to a permanent split in the socialist parties.

The earliest socialist movement of social democratic stamp evolved in Britain. There the industrial revolution, the rise of capitalism and the growth of the proletariat had developed furthest; simultaneously the development of liberal democratic reformism in society and the state had deeper and stronger roots than on the Continent. Even though the reformist movement of the Chartists, which arose in the 1830s, soon declined again, the trade unions provided a new starting-point, first by the formation of a social reformist wing within the Liberal Party and subsequently, from the end of the century, as the Labour Party. Characteristically, this continued to lean closely on the Liberals, on whose electoral help it depended and whose government it supported. After a variety of disputes between different trends it acquired its own profile in 1918 under the impact of the socialist theoreticians of the Fabian Society. Its declared reformist aim was 'revolution by consent' (Harold Laski)[1]: a gradual progress towards socialism and the replacement of the Liberals as the major alternative party in the British two-party system, with the implication of full integration in the monarchist-democratic order. Labour first came into office in 1923; radical splinter groups, including the Communists, remained insignificant.

On the Continent, following protracted ideological preparation and conflicts between the Marxist doctrine and various reformist theories, permanently organized workers' parties with socialist objectives had come into existence in the second half of the nineteenth century. Ferdinand Lassalle first founded the *Allgemeiner Deutscher Arbeiterverein* in Germany in 1863; he hoped to realize the aim of social emancipation along an evolutionary and national road, by means of the existing state, as a 'revolution by ballot paper'.[2] This was followed in Eisenach in 1869 by the

[1] Especially influential is Harold J. Laski, *A Grammar of Politics* (London, 1925). On the further development of 'revolution by consent' see his wartime essay, *Reflections on the Revolution of Our Time* (London, 1943); see Herbert A. Deane, *The Political Ideas of Harold J. Laski* (New York, 1955); also A. M. McBriar, *Fabian Socialism and English Politics 1884–1918* (Cambridge, 1962).

[2] Discussion of the position of German socialism is invariably defined and pin-pointed with reference to Lassalle and Lassalleanism. See first Hermann Oncken, *Lassalle* (Stuttgart, 1904; 5th ed. 1966); Thilo Ramm, *Ferdinand Lassalle als Rechts- und Sozialpolitiker*, 2nd ed. (Meisenheim, 1966); also Shlomo Na'aman, *Lassalle* (Hanover, 1970) and H. U. Wehler (ed.), *Gustav Mayer, Arbeiterbewegung und Obrigkeitsstaat* (Bonn, 1972).

more Marxist-oriented counter-formation of a *Sozialdemokratische Arbeiterpartei* by Wilhelm Liebknecht and August Bebel; to the applause of Marx and in deliberate contrast to Lassalle's followers and also to Bismarck's newly created Lesser German Reich, this gave prominence to the concept of international socialism and revolutionary class struggle. A compromise between the two trends led to their amalgamation in Gotha in 1875 as the *Sozialistische Partei Deutschlands*; following its suppression by the Socialists Law (1878–90) this was re-established as the *Sozialdemokratische Partei Deutschlands* (SPD). Later its still largely Marxist programme acquired, through the growing influence of the trade unions and Eduard Bernstein's 'revisionism', a social-reformist stamp.[1]

Developments in other European countries were characterized by similar ideological controversies and issues of Marxist doctrine and reformist practice. A Social Democratic Party of Austria was formed in 1886–8 under the leadership of Victor Adler; initially this embraced all parts of Austria-Hungary, though later, with the exacerbation of nationality conflicts, it was increasingly restricted to Austria proper and in consequence developed the separate theoretical forms of 'Austro-Marxism'.[2] A decade earlier (1877) a Social Democratic Party of Switzerland had been established; other such parties were formed in Denmark in 1876, in Spain in 1879, in Belgium in 1885, in Norway in 1887, in Sweden in 1889, in Poland in 1890, in Holland in 1894 and in Finland in 1899. In France the first formation of the party in 1876 had been followed by a temporary split; in 1905, however, the socialist currents were successfully reunited in the *Section française de l'internationale ouvrière* (SFIO). In the *Partito Socialista Italiano* (PSI) of 1892 the conflicts had been more pronounced; the open split into a reformist and a revolutionary trend, continuing until Mussolini's seizure of power in 1922, had begun before the First War.

---

[1] Eduard Bernstein, *Die Voraussetzungen des Sozialismus und die Aufgaben der Sozialdemokratie* (Stuttgart, 1899; 7th ed. Bonn, 1977), *Texte zum Revisionismus* (Bonn, 1977); Peter Gay, *The Dilemma of Democratic Socialism: Eduard Bernstein's Challenge to Marx* (New York, 1954); Thomas Meyer, *Bernsteins konstruktiver Sozialismus* (Berlin, 1977); also Karl Kautsky, *Bernstein und das sozialdemokratische Programm, Eine Antikritik* (Stuttgart, 1899), as well as Walter Holzheuer, *Karl Kautskys Werk als Weltanschauung* (Munich, 1972). On the overall picture see Helga Grebing, *Der Revisionismus. Von Bernstein bis zum 'Prager Frühling'* (Munich, 1977), p. 16ff.

[2] See in particular the books of the sociologist and socialist theoretician Max Adler (1873–1937), *Marxistische Probleme* (1913); *Die Staatsauffassung des Marxismus* (1922); *Politische oder Soziale Demokratie* (1926); as well as the leading politicians Karl Renner (1870–1950), *Marxismus, Krieg und Internationale* (1917), and Otto Bauer (1882–1938) *Bolschewismus oder Sozialdemokratie* (1920). Also the fundamental studies by Peter Heintel, *System und Ideologie, Der Austromarxismus im Spiegel der Philosophie Max Adlers* (Vienna, 1967); Norbert Leser, *Zwischen Reformismus und Bolschewismus, Der Austromarxismus als Theorie und Praxis* (Vienna, 1968) and 'Austro-Marxism: A Reappraisal', in the *Journal of Contemporary History* 11/2–3 (1976), p. 133ff.; Peter Kulemann, *Am Beispiel des Austromarxismus, Sozialdemokratische Arbeiterbewegung in Österreich* (Hamburg, 1979).

The outbreak of the First World War intensified the implications of fluctuation between militant attitude and accommodation. Nearly everywhere the national, state-supporting trend of social democracy kept the upper hand; only in the course of the war and in the immediate post-war period did a final break take place between the democratic-revisionist majority and a radical revolutionary minority. This decisive turn was triggered by the Bolshevik revolution in Russia and by reaction to the victory of the revolutionary over the evolutionary line. In Russia, too, a Social Democratic Workers' Party (sDRPR) had been founded in 1898. Lenin, however, as early as in 1903, had broken away from it with a militant revolutionary fighting party; he elevated this to an independent party in Prague in 1912, and eventually, in the course of the 1917 revolution, succeeded in prevailing over the reformist majority by means of a violent coup d'état.[1]

Contrary to Soviet expectations, however, the result in most other countries was merely a secession of radical wings (which had until then stayed within their parties) and a purely temporary preponderance of communism. The main forces of social democracy, accustomed to reformist policy and encouraged by the partial implementation of political and social demands, were indissolubly wedded to the idea of a reformable democracy. Admittedly, the social democrats' readiness for co-operation continued to be obstructed by strong counter-currents within their own camp, and found itself under threat from both Left and Right. In Italy (1922), Germany (1933) and also Austria (1934) the social democrats were to share the fate of bourgeois-liberal democracy, in spite of large numbers of followers and voters; in Spain, during the Civil War (1936–9), and France, at the time of the Popular Front (1936–8), the attempt of a left-wing coalition with the Communists failed; eventually national-socialist expansion banished democratic socialism to illegality in most of Europe. Only in Britain and in the Scandinavian countries were the social democrats able to integrate themselves fully, as opposition or government parties, into the framework of democracy. In these countries, therefore, they progressed furthest in their development towards a state-supporting, though of course emphatically socialist, attitude to the libertarian democratic system.

The fundamental demands of modern socialism, which sought to realize the principle of equality on the issue of property, in labour and economic structure and in the political system, have undergone a multitude of variations and modifications in the course of history, and have been variously formulated, according to periods and countries, in the pro-

[1] In addition to L. Schapiro, The Communist Party, op. cit., see in particular Dietrich Geyer (ed.), Die russische Revolution, Historische Probleme und Perspektiven (Stuttgart, 1968); illuminating texts on Lenin's unconcernedly dictatorial tactics in his seizure of power in Alfred Schaefer, Lenin 1917 – Eine Aufklärung der Machtergreifung durch Lenin-Texte (Berlin, 1980), p. 18ff.

grammes of the individual parties. Whereas in western Europe, and more particularly in Britain, Marxism never quite succeeded in replacing the pre-Marxist and reformist ideas of the 'Utopians', or of the co-operative and trade-union movement, it has been, after prolonged quarrels and schismatic developments (especially Lassalleanism), the dominant doctrine in central and eastern Europe since the 1860s. The reasons for this lay both in the spiritual and in the political and social conditions of the countries concerned. In western Europe, simultaneously with industrialization and political emancipation, liberalism and the liberal version of democracy had been well advanced by the time socialism began its rise; its combination of the principle of equality with that other pillar of democracy, the principle of liberty, did not therefore face the same obstacles there as in the semi-absolute state forms of Germany, Austria-Hungary and Russia. Even though transfers between individual countries were always fluid, and even though the force of the idea of socialist internationalism militated against any nationalization of social democracy, it would nevertheless be difficult to overestimate the importance of these historical preconditions, which indeed emerged clearly even in distinctions between a north-German and a south-German mould of socialism. Certainly it must carry more weight than the always dubious derivation of differences from some 'national character' or a national typology.

Under the impact of the events of 1905, 1914 and 1917 the schismatic tendencies became almost irresistibly intensified. The various Socialist Internationals (First International 1864–76, Second International 1889–1914, re-established 1923 and 1951), being loose umbrella organizations, anyway possessed only limited significance for programmatic development in the different countries.[1] Although a declaration for Marxism was included in all party programmes, the urge for actual participation in policy making meant that the Marxist doctrine of revolutionary transformation instead of constructive participation had become, for the majority of parties and party

[1] On the idea and history of the 'Internationals' see in particular James Joll, *The Second International 1889–1914*, 2nd ed. (London, 1974); Julius Braunthal, *Geschichte der Internationale*, 2nd ed. (Berlin-Bonn, 1974); also Georges Haupt, *Socialism and the Great War: The Collapse of the Second International* (1972). The connection between 1905 and 1917 is emphasized in a study, devoted especially to Left trends and schismatic processes by Carl E. Schorske, *Die grosse Spaltung. Die Deutsche Sozialdemokratie von 1907 bis 1917* (Berlin, 1981), a very late German edition of the American publication of 1955 which also reflects a renewed ideologically nostalgic interest in the loss of socialist unity in our own day. Into the same category belongs the new edition of a contemporary account of German left-wing socialism by Eugen Prager, *Das Gebot der Stunde – Geschichte der USPD*, preface by O. K. Flechtheim (Berlin, 1980). See, on the other hand, the recent comprehensive documentation of schismatic problems, with an important introduction by Gerhard A. Ritter, *Die II. Internationale 1918–1919 – Protokolle, Memoranden, Berichte, Korrespondenzen* (ed. in collaboration with Konrad von Zwehl), 2 vols (Berlin-Bonn, 1980); also, on the wartime development of left-wing socialism and Lenin's participation, Horst Lademacher (ed.), *Die Zimmerwalder Bewegung*, 2 vols (The Hague, 1967).

adherents, just a romantic façade by the turn of the century. Reformist thought and revisionism found their way also into the discussion of programmes and in fact gained the upper hand. What mattered was participation in practical reformist politics and an avowal in favour of democracy, whose rule and power of decision was to be legitimated by the majority principle, based on universal, equal and free elections. Abolition of the monarchy was demanded only in those countries, where (as in Germany or Russia) it simultaneously meant an authoritarian regime. The dilemma of all party programmes of the period, the gulf between dogmatic Marxism and the doctrine of class struggle and revolution on the one hand, and inability or unwillingness to bring about a violent transformation of the existing order on the other, was resolved in this process of practical accommodation.[1]

The collapse of the Second International in the First World War and the splitting-off of communism accelerated this turn towards moderate reformist thought and lent greater weight to it. Whereas, however, the social democrats in the continually developing democracies of western and northern Europe were seeking to adjust to this trend, in the new democracies of Germany and Austria the fusion with the compromise construct of a parliamentary republic proved less than entirely successful in practice and almost totally unsuccessful in programme and ideology. The helplessness of social democracy itself and the weakness of democracy vis-à-vis its authoritarian and totalitarian opponents is largely a result of this indecisive vacillation between adaptation to a changed reality and clinging to an outdated tradition. The conflict, in spite of all the painful lessons and experiences, continues to this day; although, after 1945, even the programmatic statements of democratic socialism have emphasized the primacy of democratic over Marxist principles, powerful hostile forces continue to be at work, providing ever fresh nourishment to doubts and time and again calling the development of a universal reformist people's party into question. The persistence of anti-bourgeois feeling was most recently reflected in the British Labour Party's equivocal attitude to nationalization – down to the present day.

Between the arguments of a rather dogmatic and still strongly Marxist-coloured discussion around reformism and revisionism (Bernstein, Kautsky, Luxemburg) the pragmatic working-class and trade-union movements developed along their own lines; although Marxist socialism to them offered scientific prestige as well as elements of a faith, their policy was

---

[1] On the historical context before and after the First World War see mainly the recent studies by Susanne Miller, *Burgfrieden und Klassenkampf, Die deutsche Sozialdemokratie im Ersten Weltkrieg* (Düsseldorf, 1974). On the overall theoretical development to this day see the selection of texts by H. Flohr, K. Lompe, L. F. Neumann (eds), *Freiheitlicher Sozialismus, Beiträge zu seinem heutigen Selbstverständnis* (Bonn, 1973); Thomas Meyer (ed.), *Demokratischer Sozialismus, Geistige Grundlagen und Wege in der Zukunft* (Munich, 1980).

focused primarily upon their interests. Alongside doctrinaire disputes, however, which need not be discussed here in detail,[1] a psychological dimension had been emerging since the twenties, with new endeavours to define the moral and spiritually-philosophical foundations of socialism, such as the neo-Kantianism of Leonard Nelson and the ethical socialism of Willi Eichler.[2]

The efforts to provide a socio-psychological explanation and, at the same time, a progressive adaptation of socialism were formulated between the wars in the controversial views of the Belgian socialist leader Hendrik de Man.[3] In contrast to Marx he saw the concept of socialism in a free co-operative sense: not as a collectively proletarian anti-capitalist expropriating class movement but as an entirely individual reaction to the loss of man's right to 'independence, enjoyment of work and assured existence'. The workers, he argued, were rebelling not against the capitalist economic system as such but against the socially alienating circumstances which accompanied the origin of the system; indeed, they supported expropriation only to the extent that they wished to possess more property themselves, to compensate for their loss through the industrial revolution: the property-less society of communism ran counter to their own interests. Instead of the call for a violent overthrow of society and the state, with its consequences of dictatorship and bureaucracy, and indeed of a new class society, what was placed at the centre of the socialist idea here was a psychology of interests, a 'doctrine of social drives'. This viewed communism and the working-class movement as two totally diverse forces which were temporarily intertwined but were basically and ultimately antagonistic. To de Man it could not possibly be in the workers' interest for everyone to become proletarians; and, since not all could become capitalists, the practical co-operative methods and aims in societies were the ones which best represented socialism and working-class interests in a human-rights sense: 'awareness of

[1] See S. Miller, *Das Problem*, op. cit.; H. Grebing, *Revisionismus*, op. cit.; on the setting of signals in Europe before and after the First World War see also the special issue 'Conflict and Compromise, Socialists and Socialism in the 20th Century', *Journal of Contemporary History* 11, No. 2–3, (1976); Dan S. White, 'Reconsidering European Socialism in the 1920s', ibid. 16 (1981), p. 251ff.

[2] On the philosophical liberal-ethical justification of socialism by the Nelson circle (1882–1927) and its effect in the periods after the First and the Second World Wars see Minna Specht and Willi Eichler, *Leonard Nelson zum Gedächtnis* (1953); Ch. Westermann, *Recht und Pflicht bei Leonard Nelson* (Bonn, 1969).

[3] Especially in de Man's book *Untersuchung zur Psychologie des Sozialismus* (Jena, 1927 and 1931, new ed. 1976); see also his *Au-delà du marxisme* (Paris, 1926). The best treatment is by Peter Dodge, *Beyond Marxism, The Faith and Works of Hendrik de Man* (The Hague, 1966), and (ed.), *A Documentary Study of Hendrik de Man, Socialist Critic of Marxism* (Princeton, 1979). De Man's influence admittedly found itself in a dubious light as a result of the collaborationist willingness which, as the leader of the Belgian socialists and an old admirer of Sorel, he displayed in 1940 towards the victory of national socialism. See, for a critical account, Z. Sternhell, *La Droite*, op. cit., p. 404ff.

a human dignity without which all activity is but slavery'. In actual fact, the history of communism down to the most recent Solidarity trade-union movement in Poland (1980–1) shows that the human-rights concept of solidarity represents one of the principal mainsprings of the idea of socialism, provided this can develop freely instead of being manipulated in a single-party system.

In social-democratic programme discussion itself the experience of fascism, communism and emigration has resulted in priority being given to empirical-pragmatic over traditional-theoretical approaches to socialism. Eventually there was a deliberate turning-away from numerous postulates as well as from the terminology of Marxism, especially in its heartlands. Thus in 1960 the Austrian SPÖ, in the new programme by its chairman Pittermann, declared: 'The profession of Marxism is as much a private matter for the present-day socialist as the profession of religion.' In Germany the fundamental programme of the SPD (Bad Godesberg, 1959) endeavoured 'to counterpose to the brutal challenge of communism the superior programme of a new system of political and personal freedom and self-determination, economic security and social justice'. Reference was made, in particular, to the model of social democracy in Scandinavia, where Willy Brandt and Bruno Kreisky had found asylum in exile. The idea of freedom was now emphatically at the centre, and the economic demands on the welfare state were viewed chiefly as a means to attain that objective for all strata of the population. The road was to lead to an economic democracy with worker co-determination at factory level and with a mixed economy, a combination of public and private enterprise, of market economy and planned economy: 'As much freedom as possible, as much planning as necessary.'[1]

The relationship of democratic socialism to the intellectual currents of the age has been determined by this process of tranformation which started about the turn of the century. Absolute, pseudo-religious ideas about a future socialist order as the ultimate goal and fulfilment of mankind's progress have been replaced by specific, realizable and political-practice-related programmes. This 'secularization' of socialism represented a limitation of the chiliastically coloured claim to exclusiveness of the socialist picture of the world *vis-à-vis* other intellectual and political currents of the day. In conformity with this we now have programmatic statements such as 'socialism will always remain a task' or that its ideas are not a 'substitute

[1] On the circumstances surrounding the Godesberg Programme see in particular Susanne Miller, *Die SPD vor und nach Godesberg* (Bonn, 1974); Fritz Saenger, *Soziale Demokratie, Bemerkungen zum Grundsatzprogramm der SPD*, 3rd ed. (Hanover, 1964); Willi Eichler, *Grundwerte und Grundforderungen im Godesberger Grundsatzprogramm der SPD* (Bonn, 1971). On the theory principally Gesine Schwan, *Sozialismus in der Demokratie?* (Stuttgart, 1982). The most comprehensive modern account is by Kurt Klotzbach, *Der Weg zur Staatspartei, Programmatik, praktische Politik und Organisation der deutschen Sozialdemokratie 1945 bis 1965* (Berlin-Bonn, 1982).

religion' (Berlin Programme of Action, 1954). Anti-religious attitudes were being increasingly abandoned, though the justification for the existence of specifically Christian parties was questioned.

Emphasis thus switched from the determinist dogma of Marxism to a voluntarist attitudinal element. Socialism was comprehended, indeed with reference to the early (quasi pre-Marxist) Marx, as more of a spiritual and moral concern, one that should supply the correct impulses for a realistic analysis of economic, social and political conditions and for a blueprint of a 'better' order. Realization of the period-conditioned character, the errors and the gaps of the Marxist system meant that the spiritual justification of a libertarian-democratic socialism marked a redefinition of its relationship with culture and with the intellectual forces and trends of 'bourgeois' society; just as in practical coalition and co-operation policy this was intended not as co-existence for a limited period but as reciprocal discussion, penetration and fructification.

The problem which remained unsolved was, of course, how this was compatible with the claim of democratic socialism that it was in principle more than just a reformist party. This fundamental question, touching upon the conflict between tradition and revision, between ideology and practice, led time and again to new disputes with other social currents and with Christianity. Attempts to develop, 'beyond Marx',[1] more specific ideas and proposals for reform in the economic, educational, legal theory and constitutional policy fields, in social history and philosophy, were in line with the belief – lost somewhere in nineteenth-century socialism – that what mattered was not just a change in conditions and institutions but the full spiritual and moral development of the individual's personality in the realization of his freedom.

After the Second World War the Socialist International itself summed up these endeavours in a declaration on the objectives and tasks of democratic socialism (1951): these aimed at 'a world in which the development of the personality of the individual is the prerequisite of the fruitful development of mankind as a whole'. This represented a fundamental amendment to Marx's famous vision. The doctrine of the superstructure was replaced by the model of an essentially spiritually-determined 'socialist humanism',

---

[1] This was the slogan governing the Christian-social endeavours after 1945, endeavours which represented a main pillar of the CDU: thus Otto Heinrich von der Gablentz, *Über Marx hinaus* (1946), as well as the circle around Jakob Kaiser (see Werner Conze *et al.*, *Jakob Kaiser*, Vol. 3, *Der Politiker zwischen Ost und West 1945–1949*, Stuttgart, 1969). Recently, critically with interesting details, Peter Hermes, 'Sozialismus oder Volkspartei', in *Die politische Meinung* 25/193 (1980), p. 69ff. See earlier Gerhard Schulz, 'Die CDU', in *Parteien der Bundesrepublik* (Stuttgart-Düsseldorf, 1955), p. 82ff.; also A. R. L. Gurland, *Die CDU/CSU, Ursprünge und Entwicklung bis 1953* (Frankfurt/M., 1980); Rudolf Uertz, *Christentum und Sozialismus in der frühen CDU* (Stuttgart, 1981), p. 7ff.; recently also the Bonn dissertation by Herlind Gundelach, Die Sozialausschüsse zwischen CDU und DGB, Rolle und Selbstverständnis 1949–1966 (1981).

which acknowledges the primacy of the community-related individual over the collective, which historically relativizes the idea of the class struggle and the critique of 'capitalism' in accordance with the changed conditions of a levelled industrialized society, and which looks to a new relationship of socialism with culture and religion. Earlier searches for a 'Christian socialism' moved into a new light, the rooting of socialism in general western tradition was emphasized, spirit and religion were freed from the degradation of being a mere tool of a ruling class.

Nevertheless, decisive conflicts persisted on specific questions of cultural and especially educational policy: emphatic laicism (in particular on the part of French and Italian socialists) as well as questions of the integral school obstructed any rapproachement with the Churches, whereas relations with liberalism made better progress. More far-reaching criticism came from the Left: it declared the transformation process of democratic socialism to have been nothing else, from the very start, than a mere policy of adaptation, and repeatedly tried to re-tie it to its Marxist point of departure. As in the twenties and thirties, there were again numerous temptations of a relapse into 'pure' socialism during the sixties from south-European and British left-wing socialism to a 'Eurosocialism' which tries to obstruct social democratic and socialist tradition and tends towards new divisions. However, the democratic break with communism demonstrated the political and intellectual importance of reformist socialism in the worldwide conflict of the two post-war periods. The inroads of totalitarianism after the First as well as the Second World War had sounded decisive signals: any reform of the economic society must be linked with an internal consolidation of libertarian democracy against all authoritarian and totalitarian threats from the Left and the Right.

PART II
THE INTER-WAR YEARS
Intellectuals and Dictatorships

You can't build a Utopia without terror,
and before long, terror is all that's left.

E. V. Kohák, *Requiem for Utopia*

There is an ironic law
which causes revolutionary salvationist schemes
to evolve
into regimes of terror,
and the promise of a perfect direct democracy
to assume in practice
the form of totalitarian dictatorship.

J. L. Talmon,
The Myth of the Nation and the Vision of Revolution

1. AUTHORITARIAN AND TOTALITARIAN THOUGHT

To a liberal and a rationalist like the English philosopher Bertrand Russell 'the world between the wars was attracted to madness. Of this attraction Nazism was the most emphatic expression.'[1]

The beginning of our century, the stirring of its new ideas within the turbulent arena between progress and crisis, is eclipsed in retrospect by the emergence of new, unprecedented, forms of dictatorship and despotism. All that which had been considered as virtually overcome by the evolution of the modern constitutional state, soon to give way to a universal spread of democracy, of a peaceful and libertarian people's state, now suddenly reappeared in a new garb. The decline of the autocracies, their weakening through reforms or their disintegration through revolution was not followed by the expected advance towards universal liberalization and democratization of the states but by an incomparably more intensive form of dictatorship which now exploited the organizational achievements as well as the political ideas of the modern age, and which ideologized and manipulated them for purposes of power. Tradition and innovation, reactionary and revolutionary elements thus entered into a most effective combination; even the claim to 'government by the people', to democratic legitimation, was taken over and declared to mean the unity of people and leadership.

The manifestations of those modern dictatorships, most of which arose from the aftermath of the First World War, were certainly of great diversity. Nevertheless, they can be assigned to two 'ideal' types (in Max Weber's sense): to authoritarian and to totalitarian systems. Admittedly it is their transitional forms and variants which are of particular importance. That is why a simultaneous, if possible comparative, examination of their idea elements is both necessary and justified. The main point of interest here is not their philosophical substance but the political significance and ideological contents of those currents which regarded themselves as, or unwittingly served as, alternatives to modern democracy, as sources of ideas for dictatorial movements and systems of a new type.

In his (to this day) fundamental history of political ideas between the wars George H. Sabine wrote: 'Any account of the political theories of the recent

[1] Quoted by R. Stromberg, *Intellectual History*, op. cit., p. 445.

past must end with a comparison of national socialism and communism, and of both with liberal democracy.'[1] Two further complexes need now to be added: modern authoritarianism and neo-Marxism. However, Sabine's emphasis on the above three great manifestations of modern government continues to be correct, as are the comparisons, however unpopular these may be with all those who regard communism and national socialism as incompatible, or who consider liberal democracy to be an outmoded pattern and criterion of comparison. The fashionable left-wing tendency towards stretching the concept of fascism in an imprecise manner and apply it to all authoritarian systems, as well as to numerous non-Left democracies, will be avoided; national socialism will be called by its name and not disguised or underrated as 'German fascism' – a practice dating back to the Marxist theory of fascism prior to 1933.[2]

Above all, there must be no tabooing of the concept of totalitarianism. The point at issue will be a comprehensive comparison of dictatorial government technique and ideological justification, of political ideas and ideologies, of movements and systems which, no matter under what colour, have been fighting about modern democracy since the turn of the century. For this is what it is all about: a fight for or against modern democracy, concerning its concept and substance under the diverse conditions of national and cultural traditions, of socio-economic circumstances differing from country to country. They are all engaged in ceaseless argument about what is 'true' government by the people: this is what the struggle of ideas is now about, not traditional state-political doctrine – a struggle which is also a struggle about words and concepts, a 'battle of the books'.[3] Although mention will often be made of common features, of the authoritarian or totalitarian syndrome of modern dictatorial movements, the considerable differences, both national and political, in ideological pre-history will be kept under review. Even the conventional distinction between left-wing and right-wing radical ideas remains indispensable, no matter how important their transitional or mixed forms may appear. Differences in contents and similarities in the politics of government are both equally important.

The ideas of the extreme Right far exceed conservative criticism of modern democracy; their propagandists invoke a motley crowd of political thinkers. For the most part no attempt is being made to establish a consistent political theory; it is chiefly a critique of existing conditions and a declaration

[1] George G. Sabine, op. cit., p. 922.

[2] See K. D. Bracher, *Kontroversen*, op. cit., p. 14ff., with reference to the debate on fascism in the notes. Among recent attempts to develop a general theory of fascism mention should be made, alongside the studies by Ernst Nolte, of the fundamental books by George Mosse (*Masses and Man* (New York, 1980), pp. 159ff., 332ff.) and Stanley G. Payne (*Fascism, Comparison and Definition* (Madison, 1980), pp. 95ff., 195ff.). Both also point emphatically to its totalitarian features; these receive insufficient attention in the important book by Wolfgang Schieder (ed.), *Faschismus als soziale Bewegung* (Hamburg, 1976).

[3] K. D. and D. Bracher, *Schlüsselwörter in der Geschichte* (Düsseldorf, 1978), p. 17ff.

of war on liberalism. This is viewed as the principal enemy. Anti-liberalism is the clearest rallying-point, whereas attitudes toward socialism and conservatism, because of sympathy for the authoritarian elements in both trends, are highly ambivalent. A basic distinction from Marxism is, on the Right, the cult of the strong state and emphasis on the supremacy of the nation; a similarity between right-wing and left-wing extremist ideologies is the relativization of the individual, emphasis on the community or collect- ive, along with the acceptance of the historical force of power struggles, of revolution and violence; a further similarity is the claim to reduce the past and the future to a single historical principle of struggle, no matter whether by state, nation, people, race or class, community or society, by populist or collective 'socialism'.

Reference back to ideological ancestors and thought patterns similarly reveals many a point of kinship between right-wing and left-wing ideological ideas, different though their political conclusions may be. Time and again we find both the convergence and polarization of theories used by right-wing and left-wing authoritarian and totalitarian ideologists. Two great examples tower above the rest: Rousseauism and Hegelianism. The debate about understanding and application of the idea of *volonté générale* and of the identity of citizen and community is repeated in the struggle about Hegel's concept of the absolute spirit, translated and transformed into a secularized salvation story to which the individual has to submit. Whether primacy goes to the state or to society, an often Messianic challenge to liberal democracy is the outcome.[1]

Left-wing and right-wing Rousseauism, left-wing and right-wing Hegelianism are the starting-points for the progress and crisis theories which lead, on the one hand, from Marx and Engels to the radicalism of the Paris Commune and finally to Lenin, and, on the other, via the social Darwinists, racialists and revolutionary nationalists to Mussolini and a Hegelian- coloured fascist theory of the state (Giovanni Gentile). In between, as links between right-wing and left-wing radical ideologization, stand the anarchists and syndicalists, the neo-Machiavellians and élitists, the followers of Nietzsche, Sorel or Pareto, whose influence in both directions, regardless of the extent to which these great critics of their age have been distorted or even falsified, must always remain controversial. The formulation of ideological radicalism, the fact that it is ideologizable almost at will by the anti-liberal movements of the Right and Left, had by the turn of the century acquired a strength which contrasted markedly with the political radicalism

---

[1] Still as fundamental as ever, J. L. Talmon, *Totalitäre Demokratie*, op. cit., p. 6ff. ('rechter und linker Totalitarismus'), and *Politischer Messianismus, Die romantische Phase* (Cologne-Opladen, 1963). The third volume, completed by Talmon just before his death in 1980, leads into the twentieth century; it has recently been published under the title *The Myth of the Nation and the Vision of Revolution: The Origins of Ideological Polarization in the 20th Century* (London, 1981).

of the first half of the nineteenth century. Whereas this considered itself radical-liberal in the sense of bourgeois libertarian and human rights movements, the new radicalism, a way of thinking that rid itself of religious and natural-law ties and that was focused upon the roots and basic principles of politics as power, became an anti-bourgeois totalistic dismantling of the values of the liberal constitutional state.[1]

It was a twofold revolution, one of forms and goals, that was taking place, first at the level of ideas and later also in the political movements which claimed these ideas. No matter how ambivalent Nietzsche's critique of culture or Sorel's theory of violence may have been, the effect they produced was unambiguous: unwittingly heroized or deliberately falsified in operation by the political organizers and ideological standard-bearers of anti-liberalism. A telling example is the convergence of certain crisis concepts used in the challenge to liberal democracy and in the prediction of its inevitable early collapse. Such formulas are current again today: 'latter-day bourgeois' and 'end of the bourgeois era', 'latter-day capitalism' and 'end of capitalism', as the battle-cries of the anti-liberal front, from socialism to the Young Germany movement, and used by both left and right-wing critics of liberal society from the turn of the century onward, dominated the debate between the wars.

Much the same applies to the cult of violence. Even though orthodox Marxists may dissociate themselves from violence as a value in itself, evolving a sophisticated, if rather theoretical, distinction between individual and collective force – a distinction that can to this day be defined and manipulated almost at will – the ideologists of the Right and the Left both profit, on the eve of revolutionary upheaval, from the possibility of stylizing their revolution as a value in its own right, as the 'action' or 'deed' of a violent minority and a great leader, and of quasi-scientifically basing themselves in this on the ideological work of irrationalist social philosophers. Leninism and Stalinism, just like Mussolinism and Hitlerism, thus become a manifestation of an anti-liberal cult of personalities and action, a integral part in the realization of the political movement and goal in whose name they operate.[2] The worldwide continuous survival of Leninism, the most powerful individual cult of our century, testifies to this revolutionary transformation of the thousand-year-old idea of the great individual in history (in the ruler cult from Alexander and Caesar to Napoleon) into a

[1] Characterized most impressively by Sorel's example in the left-wing and right-wing totalitarian form of the cult of violence by J. L. Talmon: 'The Legacy of Georges Sorel', op. cit., p. 6ff.; see p. 52ff. above.

[2] On the historical and ideological parallels of Leninism and Mussolinism, Stalinism and Hitlerism see Leonard Schapiro, *Totalitarianism* (London, 1972), p. 72ff. What applied to Europe between the wars is now being repeated in the neo-Left revival of the sixties and seventies with regard to the Third World and in connection with the cult of terror in the name of 'liberation movements' which cannot be simply dismissed as anarchist let alone left-wing fascist. See p. 26off. below.

pseudo-religious legitimation of a collective all-embracing system of government and belief. Even the Marxist de-mythologization of a personality-
related interpretation of history subsequently fell victim to the communist
re-mythologization of party and leader by Leninism and Stalinism.

On the right-wing radicalist side the literary preparation and ideological
moulding took place in two stages. The essential elements had been
available before the First World War: much discussed but untested in
practice, underestimated, theoretical. The war itself and its revolution-
favouring conclusions subsequently supplied the political opportunities,
heightened the antagonisms, and weakened the forces of resistance. The
second stage was adaptation and concretization, the practical assembly and
application of those elements at the end of the war. The revolutionary,
authoritarian and totalitarian syndromes were further substantiated,
charged with real or imagined intolerable aspects of the end of the war, with
profound losses and disappointment among people and states, with phobias
and revisionist ideas, with political and socio-economic resentments.[1]

Psychological readiness to accept or support dictatorship systems and
susceptibility to ideological salvationist doctrines were indeed especially
marked in the defeated countries or those disappointed by victory. The
supposed triumph of democracy in the First World War proved a source of
new problems without solving the old ones. The new nationality states of
eastern Europe in particular were soon characterized by authoritarian
systems, while in Italy fascism was demonstrating the first non-communist
'model' of a practically applied anti-liberal doctrine of revolution and order
– alternatively claiming descent from authoritarianism and totalitarianism.[2]

But before then, left-wing radical revolution had achieved its break-
through – and, what is more, contrary to Marxist theory and its concept of
revolution in Russia. Hated, yet also admired by its right-wing rivals to
dictatorship, its success encouraged not only the cult of revolution on the
Left but also a militant anti-communism which henceforward became an

[1] There is a good comprehensive survey of the factors in Ernst Nolte, *Die faschistischen
Bewegungen* (Lausanne, 1969), p. 7ff., though too narrowly defined as premises of fascism *tout
court*, and by the particularly symptomatic example of Austria by Adam Wandruszka, 'Die
Erbschaft von Krieg und Nachkrieg', in *Österreich 1927 bis 1938* (Vienna, 1973), p. 20ff.; see
also, generally, Theodor Schieder, *Handbuch der europäischen Geschichte*, Vol. 7,1 (Stuttgart,
1979), pp. 70ff., 201ff. The socialist revolutionary component of Mussolini's fascism with its
affinities to Marxism and also to Leninism before and after 1917 is very informatively discussed
by Domenico Settembrini, 'Mussolini and the Legacy of Revolutionary Socialism', *Journal of
Contemporary History* 11/4 (1976), p. 239ff. Fundamental: Emilio Gentile, *Le Origini dell
Ideologia Fascista* (Bari, 1975); *Il Mito dello Stato Nuovo* (Bari 1982).

[2] Here undoubtedly lies the historic significance of the fascist seizure of power – as previously
that of Leninism. Both were of exemplary (or, to use Thomas Kuhn's fashionable term,
paradigmatic) character. But whereas the transition to Stalinism took place in one country and
one regime, fascism at best represents a prelude to national socialism and an intermediate form
between various types of authoritarianism and totalitarianism; for this reason it is not suitable
as an epoch concept or as a general concept, see K. D. Bracher, *Europa*, op. cit., p. 156ff.

essential element of all right-wing radical movements and improved their chances of capturing power in alliance with anti-communist conservatives, or even with sections of an alarmed bourgeoisie. Naturally this did not mean that these movements shed their anti-liberal character. The assertion, again widespread today, that there is an immediate affinity between liberalism and authoritarianism or even totalitarianism, not to mention that one-pot concept of fascism for all 'bourgeois' regimes, deliberately or carelessly mistakes that complex historical connection with a then very topical anti-communism. Faced with the terrorist events in communist Russia, which surpassed all past dictatorial systems of history also in terms of the oppression and annihilation of human beings, many people regarded any alternative as the lesser evil.[1] It soon turned out that this was a liberal bourgeois piece of self-deception because it underrated the violence of right-wing radicalism. After 1933 it became obvious that the national socialist regime outstripped even the Soviet example in an ideologized policy of oppression.

With the exception of Russia, it was right-wing radicalism which first achieved effective power in Europe as the exponent of authoritarian and totalitarian ideas; its extreme form was the Hitler regime. A balance-sheet of the main components of the right-wing radical idea syndrome – components readily available in the revolutionary situation of 1918 – must distinguish not only the two extreme cases of fascism and national socialism but also those national forms of authoritarianism with no developed ideology (military dictatorship) and those which emerged only in the train of others. Such an examination will have to consider affinities and reciprocities as much as delimitations. The fact remains that the general concept of fascism is not very useful in such a realistic consideration: it neither provides an answer to the question of the prototype (racialist-totalitarian national socialism or *étatiste*-monarchist fascism), nor does it solve the problem of delimitation (against military regimes or conservative dictatorship); indeed the concept of fascism today, as much as it was then, is open to the abuse of infinite extension.

---

[1] The predominant definition of fascism *tout court* as anti-communism or anti-Marxism, emphasized also by Nolte, runs a double risk: first, of underestimating both the anti-liberal and the 'positive' elements of right-wing radical ideologies, and secondly of misunderstanding the profound justification of bourgeois-liberal anti-communism and, at the same time, overlooking the numerous affinities and convergences of right-wing and left-wing radicalism. This makes it possible for pro-communist ideologies to label all anti-communists as, at least potential, fascists and to admit only a difference of degree between liberal and fascist (and, accordingly, also national socialist, 'German fascist') movements or systems. On this widespread attitude, and not only in communist publications, the books by Reinhard Kühnl (all too often used in Germany) are particularly trivial: for instance, *Formen bürgerlicher Herrschaft: Liberalismus-Faschismus* (Reinbek, 1976) (well over a hundred thousand copies sold by 1981!).

2. THE IDEOLOGICAL POST-WAR PERIOD, INTELLECTUAL SEDUCTIONS

Above the ending of the First World War, above the immediate impact of military victory and defeat, towered the far-ranging question of the long-term outcome of the war: how deep was the historic rift, how strong was the continuity of the pre-war world? Argument about the clarification of this issue, which transcends the surface military-political context, dominates to this day all serious historical discussion of that period. The war represented a climax and a reversal, the end of the principal trends of the nineteenth century; the war truly completed the turn of the century. Domestic and international developments which sprang from the great revolutions of the modern age had found their fiercest expression and release in this gigantic and convulsive clash, as well as their breakthrough to new, more intensive, realizations. The climax and outcome of the First World War represented a deep incision, a break with the past, and signalled a new beginning for an evolution of structures and systems which definitively went beyond any past history. New-type revolutions led to new-type dictatorships, established as totalitarian by new techniques of government. Simultaneously the monarchies by divine right tumbled. The victory of democracy seemed irresistible, a return to the pre-war world impossible.

The question of break or continuity, however, was only seemingly decided. In the power politics of the peace treaties, in the domestic and external share-out of power by the states, and even more so in the conflict between defenders and opponents of a post-war order seen by its radical critics as no more than a between-wars solution, the structures and currents of the pre-war world continued. The balance-sheet of 1914 to 1918 cannot merely be reduced to the simple formula of 'break or continuity'.[1] The war had rendered possible, or effected, decisions of enormous consequence to our entire century; but it was not simply the cause of them. Among its

[1] See the apt summary sheet in James Joll, *Europe since 1870* (New York, 1973), p. XIII: 'We can now see . . . that the First World War was not such a total break as it appeared to be, and that the movements and ideas which have conditioned the experiences of the later twentieth century had nearly all made their appearance before 1914.'

origins had been the accumulations of tensions and unsolved problems, all of which had been discernible even before the war and indeed far back in the preceding century.

This is equally true of the great slogan of the post-war period: the crisis of the European era. The nineteenth century witnessed not only the completion of the European occupation and penetration of the world, but world politics were equated with European politics. Even the American hemisphere and the eventual rise of Japan were seen as results of European policies and the extension of western civilization. It was the equation of European politics and world politics, not merely the huge scale of the conflict, which made people speak of a world war as soon as the European war began in 1914. However, Europe's domination of the world, which was expressed also in a transfer of institutions, ideas, and modern technology, had a number of gaps and penetration-points even in the nineteenth century, and these the First World War mercilessly revealed. To that extent it marked a turning-point from Europe's self-glorification to its self-destruction, which seemed to reach its final conclusion in the Second World War but which in fact began some decades earlier when the United States of America claimed its own hemisphere and imperially reached out across the Pacific, and when Japan, too, rapidly extended its imposed opening-out to the west into an imperial policy in the Far East. In historical retrospect the most significant penetrations were the USA's rise to the position of the deciding power in the European struggle; the over-extension of the European powers originating in their pre-war imperial and colonial policies; and a profound crisis of identity suffered by European civilization and society, shortly to be radically questioned by the two antipodal movements of Marxism and fascism.

By leading all this towards a preliminary decision the First World War simultaneously revealed the crisis of Europe's position in the world.[1] Admittedly, no conclusions were initially drawn from this fact; the fundamental problem of the period between the wars was just that misjudgement of real power relations, a deep discrepancy between imagined and real circumstances, apparently facilitated by the USA's withdrawal from world politics. Thus the great political ideologies and movements of the post-First-World-War period operated Eurocentrically. The Second World War again started as a European war but soon found itself in a global entanglement and eventually grew too big for Europe

[1] See the titles of Hajo Holborn, *Der Zusammenbruch des europäischen Staatensystems* (Stuttgart, 1954), and Felix Gilbert, *The End of the European Era*, (New York, 1970). On the German continuity question, mainly Andreas Hillgruber, *Kontinuität und Diskontinuität in der deutschen Aussenpolitik von Bismarck bis Hitler* (Düsseldorf, 1969), and *Die gescheiterte Grossmacht* (Düsseldorf, 1980); H. A. Jacobsen, 'Zur Kontinuität und Diskontinuität in der deutschen Außenpolitik des 20. Jahrhunderts', in *Von der Strategie der Gewalt zur Politik der Friedenssicherung* (Düsseldorf, 1977), p. 9ff. Controversial, as an American attempt at rehabilitation, is David Calleo, *The German Problem Reconsidered, Germany and the World Order 1870 to the Present* (Cambridge, 1978).

altogether. Europe's reconstitution in the illusory sense of the twenties and thirties has meanwhile been reduced *ad absurdum*: the old continent's international political dependence remains irrevocable, even though its rebuilding after the catastrophe of 1945 has astonishingly and unexpectedly given the lie to the pessimism of its contemporaries.

Most of the answers to the First World War, which were in consequence to determine European politics, led to the subversion and questioning of what the age of Europe had produced. Those answers were rooted in the spiritual and material world of the nineteenth century, even though their political implementation was manifestly the direct result of the Great War. Three predominant historic answers need listing here: Marxism–communism; liberal democracy; and fascism–nazism. They embodied the new and yet long-prepared: they were answers to the challenge not merely of the war but also of the industrial revolution, of modernization, nationalism and imperialism – in short, all those forces which were released in the war. It is these answers that provide criteria for the interpretation of the age, criteria more appropriate than the familiar idea of a global confrontation between revolution and counter-revolution, an idea then as now dominating chiefly left-wing polemics.[1] In all three instances the war directly triggered the transformation of nineteenth-century ideas into post-war forms of political rule. First, Marxism became the state doctrine in Lenin's revolution, more correctly described as a *coup d'état* – at any rate as the direct result of the old regime's military defeat and of the inability of the democratic revolution in Russia to put an end to the war and organize a parliamentary republic. Secondly, parliamentary democracy was regarded as the real victor in the war. Its diffusion throughout the old and the new states of Europe appears largely as the implementation of President Wilson's ideas, that is, the ideas of the USA, the decisive interventionist power. Thirdly, fascism and national socialism were the result of a national and authoritarian wave which in the countries frustrated by the war, notably Italy and Germany, turned against a seemingly victorious democracy. For these revisionists the struggle continued; their alliance under the banner of expansion would topple the peace system and eventually Europe itself.

These three answers to the First World War each in its own way presented a balance-sheet of the essential currents which had been carried to the surface by the war: socialism, democracy and nationalism. But they also represented the three misconceptions of the war by subjecting it to

---

[1] On the concept of revolution, Eugen Weber, 'Revolution? Counterrevolution? What Revolution?', *Journal of Contemporary History* 9/1974, p. 3ff. Operating with a wider concept and a theory of counter-revolution, on the other hand, Arno J. Mayer, *Dynamics of Counterrevolution in Europe 1870–1956* (New York, 1971); this also colours his most recent interesting attempt to explain Europe's road into the First World War from the persistence of the old regimes and structures, and not from new and forward-urging forces: Arno J. Mayer, *The Persistence of the Old Regime, Europe to the Great War* (New York, 1981), especially p. 189ff. ('Official High Cultures and the *Avant-Gardes*').

one-sided or unilinear interpretation. The collectivist misconception had seen the war as an irresistible pacemaker of future world socialism; the autonomist one as the final victory of self-determination and human rights; the nationalist one as the renewed rise or the perfection of the autarkic integral power state. The misconceptions were followed by disillusionment and false reactions: for the socialists the disillusionment that international revolution failed to materialize or failed to be accepted by the population; for the democrats the disillusionment that self-determination in the nation-states did not work and instead gave rise to new problems without necessarily solving any of the old ones; for the nationalists the huge miscalculation that a second round of world war would win them the power they had failed to gain in the first. Thus the misunderstanding of the realities and truths of the First World War was no less significant than the considerable measure of decisions and changes it actually produced. In this context four new main factors emerged in wartime and post-war development: the new importance of America; the conflicting structure of war and peace aims; the nationalities problem and the collapse of Austria-Hungary; and finally the success and the crisis of democracy.[1]

The new political constellation had a profound effect on the transformation of the major sets of ideas into pseudo-scientific theories and into political ideologies. After the intellectual changes of the pre-war period, the wartime and post-war period triggered off a new wave of doubt and of ideologization. The new and specific feature of this, however, was the fact that it was now no longer taking place at a philosophical-scientific remove from practical politics but in direct intimate contact with them: both influencing politics and being dependent on them, manipulating them and being manipulated. Admittedly, ethnocentric and étatiste nationalism continued to govern the disputes and interests of states. Simultaneously, however, ideological confrontations ran right across societies and communities. Whether these regarded themselves as democracies or as dictatorships, as parliamentary or as authoritarian systems – this question of political self-awareness, in its direct practical consequences, now far exceeded the theoretical and literary conflicts of the pre-war period.[2]

The war had changed everything especially in this respect. From the outset it had been conducted as a war of ideologies and not simply of states or nations. The passionate engagement of the intellectuals had been ideologically-oriented on all fronts. War proclamations and declarations of intellectual positions referred to the struggle of democracy (of the west) against autocracy (of the Central Powers) or despotism (of tsarist Russia). On the German side there was an even more marked concern with the spiritual confrontation between the concepts of 'culture' and 'civilization',

---

[1] On this more extensively K. D. Bracher, *Europa*, op. cit., p. 34ff.

[2] On the ideologization of wartime and post-war developments see the survey and bibliography in Th. Schieder, *Handbuch*, op. cit., p. 201ff.

which even Thomas Mann in his *Betrachtungen eines Unpolitischen* towards the end of the war still used in describing Germany's war against the West, as well as that 'genius of war and the German war' (Max Scheler) between 'tradesmen' and 'heroes' (Werner Sombart) – great intellects in the service of ideology.[1] Very often, of course, this was a very superficial propaganda dispute even by important thinkers, in which the chauvinism of earlier wars and the heightened self-assurance of Germany *vis-à-vis* western democracy re-emerged as a clash of ideologies. But it was really based on a meanwhile greatly enhanced ideologization of politics.

The 'ideas of August 1914' were a feverish eruption and release from the tensions of the turn of the century and their seeming solution through the colossal over-simplifications of an enthusiasm for the war which few were able to resist. Political Darwinism, democratic mass pressure, created a climate of 'ideological assumptions'[2] which made the war not only possible diplomatically and militarily but downright inevitable psychologically and philosophically: it was more popular with *everybody* than any other war before or since. Students, writers and artists who had been the exponents of the intellectual upheavals of the turn of the century went into the battles of 1914 as if these were setting the seal on something new, on some God-given and historically inevitable event for nation, progress and culture, something that would also solve the deeply experienced crisis of modernization.

Kaiser Wilhelm's proclamation, 'I no longer recognize parties: I only recognize Germans', was more than a welcome propaganda formula for domestic consumption. It was true of all nations and countries involved that, for one unforgettable moment which then became extended into four terrible years, the profound differences between the political battle-lines disappeared – admittedly, ultimately to reappear the more acutely and definitively, when many of that generation had been killed and others, embittered and ideologized, continued the struggle in peace-time, and above all now against internal enemies.

The long list of August 1914 enthusiasts reads like a great catalogue of culture – but its pages opened for a war of Europeans against each other: scientists and artists, poets and philosophers, conservatives, liberals, revolutionaries. On the German and Austrian side stood names like Thomas Mann, Sigmund Freud, Max Weber, Stefan George; on the French side

---

[1] Peter Graf Kielmansegg, *Deutschland und der Erste Weltkrieg*, 2nd ed. (Stuttgart, 1980), pp. 145ff., 205ff.; see Klaus Schwabe, *Wissenschaft und Kriegsmoral, Die deutschen Hochschullehrer und die politischen Grundfragen des Ersten Weltkrieges* (Göttingen, 1969); on the 'ideas of 1914', Hermann Lübbe, *Politische Philosophie in Deutschland* (Basel-Stuttgart, 1963), p. 173ff. The American turn-about is dealt with by Henry F. May, *The End of American Innocence, A Study of the First Years of Our Own Time, 1912–1917* (1959). On the general atmosphere among the 'war generation' see the symposium *War Generation* (New York, 1975), including D'Annunzio, 'The War as a Style of Life'.

[2] J. Joll, *Europe*, op. cit., p. 195, and his inaugural lecture of 1968, '1914 – The Unspoken Assumptions' (London, 1968), p. 6.

Henri Bergson, Emile Durkheim, Charles Péguy, and everywhere also the bulk of the socialists and even some of the Bolsheviks in Russia. Innumerable, in particular, were the writers, artists and professors who were hailing the war both as the defence of the 'most sacred possessions' and as an irresistible advance towards new shores. They eclipsed the few voices of reason, such as Romain Rolland and George Bernard Shaw, while Lenin, on grounds of revolutionary strategy, did not commit himself until the destruction and confusions of the war offered him his chance in 1917.

The war was the great self-deception to which all sides had hitched their hopes and fulfilments: critique of civilization from the Right and the Left, the call for spiritual renewal amidst bourgeois and materialist ossification, the revolts and visions of the Young Germany movement, a search for new forms of expression, for adventure, immediacy, irrational togetherness and personal action, and also a demand for technological and organizational application of the revolutionary achievements of science and industrialization. It was a welcome war, especially in the realm of ideas: the moods of 1914 very largely signalled irritation and a deep malaise at a peace which looked like a blind alley to the forward-thrusting forces and as a disaster to the pessimists; to both, the war seemed to be that new myth which, following the loss of all certainties, exposed new truths, bonds and solutions.[1]

The failure of such powerful international bonds as the (Second) Socialist International merely appeared to confirm the need to seek new paths now that the old certainty of progress had begun to crumble. Not only a heightened nationalism but also a novel 'socialism' of war caused the ideologization process of 1914 to rigidify into a continuing force in political thought even after the deep disillusionments of the great European War. In this sense the struggle over war aims was of decidedly ambivalent character: it called for a rationalization and legitimation of interests and at the same time for a transrational mythologization of the idea of a national-imperial mission which held out the promise of political orientation and fulfilment amidst the centrifugal trends of mass and class societies. Ideologization of the 'comradeship of the war' and the community of the trenches as the basis of a new socialism was one consequence. The other was a plunging from its blood and destruction into a fatalization of crisis thought. A profound questioning of accepted thinking was present also in the camp of the liberals and social democrats who eventually found themselves between these alternative battle lines of a militarist and a pacifist 'socialism'.

The war was of prime importance especially for the political revolutionaries: for Mussolini, now an up-and-coming figure as a newspaper

---

[1] See Wolfgang J. Mommsen, 'The Topos of the Inevitable War in Germany in the Decade before 1914', in V. R. Berghahn, M. Kitchen (eds), *Germany in the Age of Total War (Festschrift F. L. Carsten)* (London, 1981), p. 23ff.; also Klaus Vondung (ed.), *Kriegserlebnis, Der Erste Weltkrieg in der literarischen Gestaltung und symbolischen Deutung der Nationen* (Göttingen, 1979).

propagandist of Italian nationalism, and also for Hitler, who later in *Mein Kampf* elevated war propaganda itself, the forms of ideologization of politics as a battle, to the position of a key experience. The war had taught them the indispensability of a ceaselessly reiterated ideological explanation and justification of policies through pseudo-scientifically grounded theories, and what rational and irrational function they were to perform in a state of a modern mass communication society. Persuasion of the citizen and intellectual legitimation of policies had indeed become more necessary than ever before, and with their importance, in turn, also increased the political effect which those ideas and ideologies had on politics. Certainly these were predominantly nationally-oriented even in terms of language and effect. Even communism, following the failure of its world-revolutionary aspirations, evolved its theory of socialism in one country; its intellectual forms differed as much from country to country as did its political conditions and strategies: this emerges clearly from a comparison of German, Italian and French theories and arguments on political line during the twenties.

Alongside the activity of the Communist International (founded in 1919) Leninism itself provided, and continued to provide, an obligatory yardstick for all communist parties. Moreover, similar issues and problems, similar aspirations and illusions, existed in the fundamental currents of socialism and liberalism, as well as in Catholic and conservative groupings, in all European countries. To start with there was the great divide from (Soviet-type) communism; but there were also the (more or less ideologically based) domestic divisions into very different ideological directions and political cultures, as illustrated with exemplary acuteness in the rump state of Austria as a hostile co-existence of national, Christian and socialist camps.[1]

The cleavages into diverse political cultures, so much discussed at present, are nothing other than that profound conflict which runs across the powerful reality of the national-state tradition. This rift reflects not only specific socio-economic interest structures but, even more so, also operates as a direct irrational motivation of political attitudes and actions, a motivation seeking to engulf every citizen.

That, too, was an important result of the war which mobilized everything, organized everything and propagandistically intensified everything: an increased (and ultimately absolute) involvement of the citizen, his partici-

---

[1] On this point see the still classic analysis of Adam Wandruszka, 'Österreichs politische Struktur', in H. Benedikt (ed.), *Geschichte der Republik Österreich* (Munich, 1954; republished 1977), p. 382ff., and 'Österreich von der Begründung der ersten Republik bis zur sozialistischen Alleinregierung 1918–1970', in Th. Schieder, *Handbuch*, op. cit., p. 834; also W. B. Simon, 'Democracy in the Shadow of Imposed Sovereignty, the First Republic of Austria', in J. Linz, A. Stepan (eds.), *The Breakdown of Democratic Regimes*, Vol. 2 (Baltimore, 1978), p. 8off.; and the intellectual history survey in W. M. Johnston, *Austrian Mind*, op. cit. On the (later) cleavage theory see H. Boldt, 'Stein Rokkans Parteitheorie und die Vergleichende Verfassungsgeschichte', in L. Albertin, W. Link (eds.), *Politische Parteien auf dem Weg zur parlamentarischen Demokratie in Deutschland* (Düsseldorf, 1981), p. 91ff.

pation in general elections and exciting plebiscites, his party-political and group-political 'capture' and persuasion, or indeed indoctrination, now became the prerequisites of all politics. This was true of the parliamentary party-based democracies which had succeeded the limited constitutional forms of most pre-war states and were now based on universal suffrage, including women, on the complex mechanism of competition for support, and on majority creation in a pluralist society. However, it was true also of the conservative-authoritarian dictatorships which soon supplanted one democracy after another and were yet unable to turn the clock back entirely to before the age of ideologies, and therefore had to underpin their pressure on public opinion intellectually, albeit with the crudest pseudo-theories of corporatism and authoritarianism drawn from the arsenal both of history and of the most recent ideological clashes at the turn of the century.

This was overwhelmingly true of every direction of totalitarianism. This proclaimed the all-embracing politicization of all comrades (or *Volks-genossen*) and citizens, fixated it ideologically and perpetually nourished it with declarations on the society and the world, with political articles of faith and demands for endorsement because this total unity was, above all, a notional figment without which a modern dictatorship's claim to political unity – as distinct from earlier despotism through compulsion – was no longer conceivable. Ideological seduction and political compulsion had to interact with each other: that was the basic wisdom of Lenin and Mussolini, of Hitler and Stalin. Naturally, in these highly ideologized systems of voluntary compulsion there could be no question of intellectual movement or a discussion of ideas. This existed only below the surface in persecuted resistance, or at times of relaxation or power struggles, in the thorny path of dissidents and apostates, or through the effect of external pressure as in the early years of Mussolini and Hitler, under Stalin at the time of the 'Great Fatherland War', under Khrushchev and Brezhnev under the impact of international *détente* or human rights policies. Political idea or theory here meant the formulation of an obligatory ideology and its continually reiterated proclamation or abrupt transformation from above.

Not so in the democracies. Here there was argument, continually renewed verification, falsification and correction of political ideas before the eyes of the entire public as the criterion of their truth: that readiness of political ideas and systems to compete with each other which Karl Popper in 1945 defined by the concept of the 'open society' (and its enemies) which differentiates it fundamentally from 'closed' ideologies.[1] Even the division of intellectual history into open and closed forms of thought could acquire the features of an ideology if it were to block the view of different forms of closed ideological thought. It will therefore be necessary, to the extent that Popper's distinction is followed, to concentrate time and again on the

[1] Karl Popper, *The Open Society and its Enemies*, 3rd ed. (London, 1957); see K. D. Bracher, *Schlüsselwörter*, op. cit., p. 49ff.

possible variants of conceptual authoritarianism and totalitarianism: on the one hand, Leninism, Stalinism and the problem of the Marxist alternatives and totalitarian transitional forms, and on the other hand, fascism, national socialism, and other forms of authoritarian ideological structures. It will be necessary each time, for the purpose of comparison, to pose the ever topical question as to the different types and general concepts, above all the concepts of fascism and totalitarianism, as well as the question of the political contents these concepts define – or omit.

In spite of their ideological prehistory there can be no doubt that the new dictatorships of our century were principally a result of the 1914–18 war. It was the real disaster, from which political thought has not basically recovered to this day. The war cut short, re-shaped and fundamentally changed a lot of things. Ideological susceptibilities, delusions, enticements all now appeared with alarming clarity and effectiveness. But it is also correct to say that most of the ideas which were now turned into politics, or against politics, had already been thought through and mapped out by the time the great crises and revolutionary situations of the end of the war emerged. This was obviously equally true of Lenin's, Stalin's or Trotsky's communism as of fascism, national socialism and (in their wake) the authoritarianism of the newly founded states. On the one hand there was the ideological transformation of Marxian progressivism into Leninism: an enormous intensification and sharpening of dictatorial and totalitarian potential by revolutionary socialism. On the other hand there was the exacerbation of cultural pessimism into anti-liberal, national-social dictatorial thought with, at times, racialist colouring: the manifestation of political irrationalism in a pseudo-scientific garb.

And finally there were the controversial practical forms and theoretical problems of modern democracy.[1] A wide field of critiques of democracy was opening up: from the problems and weaknesses of the pluralist form of society and state, from the discrepancy between idea and reality in the empirical democracies, the conclusion was drawn that their principles were wrong and that alternatives needed to be sought. Intellectual discussion of the consequences of a mass society, of 'false' equality and a 'necessary' élite, of 'deracination' and 'alienation', and of new forms of society, was gaining immediate importance. The experience of the war and its aftermath had, as

[1] Classic in its day was James Bryce, *Moderne Demokratien*, 3 vols (Munich, 1923–6); see Peter Gilg, *Die Erneuerung des demokratischen Denkens im Wilhelminischen Deutschland, Eine ideengeschichtliche Studie zur Wende vom 19. zum 20. Jahrhundert* (Wiesbaden, 1965). Among contemporary politological literature see the books by Wilhelm Hasbach, *Die moderne Demokratie* (Jena, 1912); *Die parlamentarische Kabinettsregierung* (Stuttgart-Berlin, 1919); and, of special influence on the new German Constitution Robert Redslob, *Die parlamentarische Regierung in ihrer wahren und in ihrer unechten Form, Eine vergleichende Studie über die Verfassungen von England, Belgien, Ungarn, Schweden und Frankreich* (Tübingen, 1918); on this point, Detlev Stronk, *Gleichgewicht und Volkssouveränität, Eine Untersuchung anhand der Parlamentarismustheorie Robert Redslobs* (Bonn, 1976).

it were, changed the status of the argument about the correct order of state and society. Communism, authoritarianism, and democracy were no longer mere ideological constructs or fantasies but political realities for which one could opt in practice or to which one had to submit.

That was especially true of the new phenomenon of communism turned party and communism turned state. The future shape of post-revolutionary communist theory in Russia was determined primarily by consolidation of power: its idea content became meagre, emphasis was focused on justi-fication of the new regime and struggle against its opponents. This brought the issue of its further extension, of world-revolutionary strategy, into the controversial sphere of practical politics and personal power struggles. Trotsky's endeavours to preserve an independent line of his own, amidst the to and fro of ideologized decisions – one moment for world revolution, the next for socialism in one country – were doomed to failure even before his vain power struggle against Stalin, even though Trotskyism survived as a sectarian variant outside the Soviet Union.[1] The new Soviet Union itself at first gave free rein to a literary and artistic '*avant-garde*'s' high-pitched hopes of a new age. By 1925, however, the party had intensified a restrictive counter-course and by 1930 at the latest, with the suicide of the poet Mayakovsky, the once so extravagant expectations had been ruthlessly suppressed by Stalin himself. The 'Communist International', moreover, proved a tool of Soviet power politics: the break between socialist/social-democratic and communist parties became final.[2]

From that period of totalitarian unification under the cult of Stalinism, which, amidst the slogans of the 'building of socialism' and 'communism' produced little other than party and leader ideology, it was a mixture of Russian state policy and communist ideology that, at any given moment, determined the direction of the great oppression and extermination of those declared to be enemies of the state or 'class enemies'. To the intellectuals of Europe the last years of Leninism and the first years of Stalinism had little to offer in terms of new spiritual nourishment. But the rise of fascism and Hitler's seizure of power, and finally the Spanish Civil War, once more made them look towards communism. Throughout Europe the thirties were to become an age of sympathizers and 'fellow travellers', of new illusions and disillusionments.

In the twenties, by way of contrast, general pessimism was widespread. That was not surprising in view of the deplorable economic and social conditions during the post-war crises (until 1923) and later the worldwide

[1] Lev Trotsky, *The Permanent Revolution, Results and Prospects* (London, 1962); Isaac Deutscher, *Leon Trotsky*, 3 vols (Oxford, 1970).

[2] From Leninism to Stalinism: Max Gustav Lange, *Marxismus, Leninismus, Stalinismus* (Stuttgart, 1955); Bertram D. Wolfe, 'Leninism', in M. Drachkovitsch (ed.), *Marxism in the Modern World* (Stanford, 1965), p. 47ff.; Boris Souvarine, 'Stalinism', ibid., p. 90ff.; Robert C. Tucker, *Stalin as Revolutionary 1879–1929* (New York, 1973), and *The Soviet Mind* (New York, 1971).

depression (from 1929). The discovery that in Germany the outsiders had now become 'insiders'[1] also meant that criticism of culture and ideological polarization had become all-pervasive and did not allow the new democracies to come to rest. In defeated Germany, in particular, the 'decline of the West', Oswald Spengler's declaration of war on the idea of progress, first drafted before the war (1911) and doubly topical after its publication (1918), was very much an issue of the day. But even in the victorious west the critique of civilization was gaining ground as it was becoming increasingly obvious that victory had not solved the old problems and that the Paris peace settlements of 1919–20 had themselves laid the foundations of new crises, both economic and political. The search for political points of orientation and for spiritual values made matters even easier for the political simplifiers. An astonishing example was the intellectual support and the impressive adherents Italian fascism gained in its early days from the futurists via Pirandello, Puccini, Toscanini to the great Benedetto Croce. A major misunderstanding, of course, but a significant one. It was repeated each time a strong individual or a powerful ideology appeared on the horizon: national socialism was able to exploit the prestige of Gerhart Hauptmann and Richard Strauss, of Martin Heidegger and Gottfried Benn.[2] Between 1922 (Mussolini), 1933 (Hitler), 1936 (the Popular Front in France) and the pro-communist 'anti-fascism' of the thirties ran the lines of reference of a political thinking which largely exhausted itself in the pros and cons of critiques of fascism and socialism.[3]

[1] 'The outsider as insider' is the subtitle of the fundamental book by Peter Gay, *Weimar Culture* (New York, 1968). The political ambivalence of the development of culture during the 'golden twenties' is examined by Walter Z. Laqueur, *Weimar, Die Kultur der Republik* (Frankfurt-Berlin, 1976). On the overall problem, Mikel Dufrenne, *Art et Politique* (Paris, 1974); Donald D. Egbert, *Social Radicalism and the Arts* (New York, 1970); Theda Shapiro, *Painters and Politics, The European Avant-Garde and Society, 1900–1925* (New York, 1976); Renato Poggioli, *The Theory of the Avant-Garde* (New York, 1971).

[2] On fascism see Adrian Lyttelton, *The Seizure of Power, Fascism in Italy 1919–1929* (London, 1973), p. 46ff. ('The Fascists of the first hour'); p. 243 (Croce); p. 364ff. (Ideology and culture). On national socialism K. D. Bracher, *NS Machtergreifung*, Vol. 1, p. 392ff.; *German Dictatorship*. p. 311ff.; George L. Mosse, *Nazi Culture, Intellectual, Cultural and Social Life in the Third Reich* (New York, 1966), p. xix ff.; also Karl Corino (ed.), *Intellektuelle im Bann des Nationalsozialismus* (Hamburg, 1980), especially the introduction by Eberhard Jäckel (p. 7ff.) and Günter Maschke on the 'Irrgarten Carl Schmitts' (p. 204ff.): 'If one were to characterize Carl Schmitt with a catch-phrase, then as a man of "Sorel's Right wing" ' (p. 240).

[3] See W. Laqueur and G. L. Mosse (eds), *Left Wing Intellectuals between the Wars, Journal of Contemporary History* I/2 (London, 1966), especially p. 65ff. (Stuart Samuels, 'The Left Book Club'); *International Fascism 1920–1945*, ibid. 1/1 (London 1966), especially p. 183ff (Hugh Seton Watson, 'Fascism, Right and Left'). Many foreign politicians and intellectuals of liberal-conservative hue praised Mussolini's regime for Italy including, even still in 1933, G. B. Shaw and Winston Churchill, and Sigmund Freud, who sent the 'Duce' one of his books, with the dedication 'from an old man who greets in the Ruler the Hero of Culture', quoted from E. Jones, *Sigmund Freud, Life and Works*, Vol. 3 (London, 1957), p. 192ff. See Alistair Hamilton, *The Appeal of Fascism: A Study of Intellectuals and Fascism, 1919–1945* (London, 1971), p. 271ff.; A. James Gregor, *The Ideology of Fascism, The Rationale of Totalitarianism*, (New York, 1969) and *The Fascist Persuasion in Radical Politics* (Princeton, 1974); Raymond Aron, *Opium für Intellektuelle oder Die Sucht nach Weltanschauung* (Berlin, 1957).

But more than anything it was the crisis of faith in the liberalism and rationalism of the democratic era that provided the starting-point. European authoritarianism in the twenties and thirties lived not so much by a blueprint of the future as by its great anti-positions which promised a kind of salvation from the evils of modernization. Once rational evidence of the failings and injustices of democracy, parliamentarism and capitalism was submitted, the irrational conclusions were self-evident. The heroic nihilism of the 'conservative revolutionaries' like Spengler, Jünger and Moeller van den Bruck had the same attraction as emerging existentialism: literary pessimism was the order of the day, criticism of modern civilization determined the climate and the mood of the 'lost generation' in Europe as much as in America. Nearly all great writers were involved from D. H. Lawrence, André Gide, Ernest Hemingway and James Joyce to the Americans in Europe like T. S. Eliot, Gertrude Stein, and Ezra Pound. On the other side the intellectual seductive power of communism led to a transformation of cultural pessimism into new socialist progress: the scene was dominated by alternate immersion in enthusiasm and disenchantment.

In point of fact, the authoritarian ideologies can all be reduced to this common denominator: opposition to liberalism's rational theory of democracy. The demonstrative anti-communism, to which Ernst Nolte in particular relates 'fascism' generally, had a predominantly propagandist function. After all, its attitude to socialism, even to its authoritarian form, was marked by profound ambivalence.[1] Its followers were fond of describing themselves as 'socialists' but never as liberals let alone bourgeois; the quarrel about the internationalist or nationalist form did not touch upon that primal article of faith, the priority of society or community over the individual, which represents the real divide in the political argument between liberalism and authoritarianism. For communism, of course, this question was decided from the outset, but even Mussolini or Hitler, the one an ex-socialist and the other a racialist, have never left any doubt on this radical issue, on the primacy of the 'community'. Elitist ideas and the leader cult were not a contradiction but a confirmation: after all, party and leader were postulated as being identical with the whole, at one with the people's community.

The collectivist or holistic, anti-individualist credo of the great ideologies was one basic characteristic, the essence of a faith instead of individual thought and volition. The other basic characteristic was the impressive certainty of a firm hierarchy of values. What liberal democracy had failed to achieve – the establishment of a firm scale of values within pluralism – was guaranteed in the clear hierarchy of authoritarian thought, either in imitation of the military principle, internalizing military terminology as a fighting movement (like communism) or in imitation of the ancient model of an 'organic' order in which every 'member of society' contributes its own

---

[1] On the socialist component and (self-)assessment of fascism and national socialism see p. 103ff.

share, but related now to the modern age: corporativism as an up-to-date version of the estates state. In all instances it meant an abolition and restructuring of society in the sense of guidance from the top downwards; this was being increasingly set against the pluralist character of modern democracy.

The great differentiations in ideological critiques of democracy no longer resided in the substance or form of the alternatives offered but in their political reference to specific movements and ruling systems. The intellectuals, who were looking and calling for a revolution from the Right or the Left, who prided themselves on being a subversive force, who equated anti-liberal pessimism with revolutionary progress, regarded themselves as revolutionaries against the Establishment. They projected their own blueprints into the ideologies of which, as a rule, they did not know – or did not wish to know – anything beyond the fact that they were alternatives to liberal democracy.[1]

The psychological dimension of that simultaneous need for critique and political identification found expression in influential contemporary analyses such as Ortega y Gasset's *Revolt of the Masses* and Freud's *Civilization and its Discontents*.[2] The connection between outward progress and a general crisis of civilization, between man's technological potential and his deep self-questionings, emerged nowhere more clearly than in a mass 'fear and flight from freedom' (Erich Fromm) into new authoritarian ties. The consequences of emancipation called for new certainties, and these were offered mainly by those 'philosophies' which seemed to overcome not only (rationally) the permanent crisis of liberal democracy but also (irrationally) the vacuum of a value orientation by means of new certainties. Face to face with the frightening openness of secularized society it was the proclaimed 'closed nature' that contained the greatest seductive appeal. Not rational logic and harmony but an irrational assurance of salvation held together the large disparate elements of such philosophies: what mattered was not substance but the word.

The masters of such an eclectic piecing-together of scraps of ideas into

[1] Ideological concepts of society and community as fantasies of longing for the liquidation of the tension between individual and the whole! The demand returns in the famous slogan of the Paris students' revolt of 1968, with which the protest movement of the second post-war generation voiced its demand for total democracy, 'Power for fantasy!'. On the position of intellectual activity between tradition and fantasy see, in addition to the introduction (p. 1ff. above), the essays by S. N. Eisenstadt, Edward Shils *et al*., 'Intellectuals and Tradition', *Daedalus* 101, No. 2 (Spring, 1972), pp. 1ff., 21ff.; also Leszek Kolakowski, Seymour M. Lipset, Richard B. Dobson, Martin M. Malia *et al*., 'Intellectuals and Change', *Daedalus* 101, No. 3 (Summer, 1972), pp. 1ff., 137ff., 206ff. On American problems also Neil Harris, *The Artist in American Society* (1966).

[2] Both books appeared in 1930: the Spanish title 'La rebelion de las masas' does not seem to be too aptly translated by 'revolt'. Fromm's psychological interpretation of the problem in *The Fear of Freedom* (London, 1941) is able to include the disastrous events of the thirties and early forties.

all-embracing ideologies, however, were no longer the professors or men of the pen but the great orators and demagogues. The reason why so many intellectuals accepted it, or indeed temporarily sanctioned it, probably lay in admiration for the strong individual amidst a civilization that was uncertain of its orientation as well as in a need for close contact with the people, with the 'masses', from whom they were further removed than ever before and with whom they were the more anxious to identify. It was a combination of élitist thought and populism, a combination that seemed most directly embodied and realized in the harmony of strong ideologists with their mass following of believers. There is no doubt that, alongside curiosity about the great experiments in society and state, it was above all that dual claim of authoritarian ideologists to represent both élitist certainty of revolution and political religion for the masses that proved so fascinating. That fascination with the power of the great simplifiers caused many intellectuals to forget their role of guardians of spiritual truth and political humanity. The 'betrayal of the intellectuals'[1] weighed the more heavily at a time when moral values and political structures had been undermined and the political option of the theoreticians and idea producers was no longer, as before the war, a matter of playing with ideas but the legitimation of dictatorships, of regimes of violence and annihilation.

[1] On the now famous slogan of the 'betrayal of the intellectuals' see Julien Benda, *La trahison des clercs* (1st ed. Paris, 1928; as *The Betrayal of the Intellectuals*, New York, 1955). For the period after the Second World War, Czeslaw Milosz, *Verführtes Denken*, with a preface by Karl Jaspers (Cologne-Berlin, 1955); Raymond Aron, *Opium für die Intellektuellen*, op. cit.; Helmut Schelsky, *Die Arbeit tun die anderen, Klassenkampf und Priesterherrschaft der Intellektuellen* (Opladen, 1975). Even where the literature is strongly polemical, with anti-intellectual features as in Schelsky (very fierce, by contrast, is Dietz Bering, *Die Intellektuellen, Geschichte eines Schimpfwortes* (Stuttgart, 1978), p. 6ff., it nevertheless attacks a fundamental problem which emerged with particular clarity in the twenties and has emerged again since the sixties: the attitude of the intellectual interpreters in modern society fluctuates continually between alienation and Utopianism and renders many of them susceptible to dictatorial ideologies.

3. DICTATORSHIP AS A CONCEPT: FASCISM, NATIONAL SOCIALISM AND COMMUNISM COMPARED

The dictatorial movements of fascism and national socialism have their origin in three great sets of nineteenth-century ideas: conservative, national and social. Conservative critics of democracy initially viewed the early (still democratically-flavoured) nationalism with mistrust. But its subsequent combination with the idea of the power state – especially in the 'belated nations' of Germany and Italy – gave rise to a 'plebeian conservatism', and this paved the road for German populist anti-Semitic pan-Germanism and for Italian nationalist irredentism.[1] That, of course, was an involved and highly complex process, whose intellectual characteristics fluctuated between traditionalist and national-liberal modernistic variants. Whereas the old-style national concepts of Herder (1744–1814) extolled the positive variety of nations, they were beginning to be nationalistically remoulded and sharpened by Jahn (1778–1852), and during the nineteenth century increasingly moved away from their democratic old-style liberal origins; turning from the internal driving force of a constitutional movement into the foreign-political driving force of the modern power-state idea.

In Germany and Italy this change from a domestic-policy to a foreign-policy interpretation of the idea of national self-determination is most clearly reflected in the thought of Heinrich Treitschke (1834–96) and Giuseppe Mazzini (1805–72). Herder's idea of a universal historic mission of peoples and nations formed part of a universal principle, of progress towards a universal humanity. With the emergence of political romanticism, however, the idea of national independence was heightened into the thesis

[1] On the concept see Helmuth Plessner, *Die verspätete Nation* (Stuttgart, 1953; reissue of *Das Schicksal deutschen Geistes am Ausgang seiner bürgerlichen Epoche* (Zürich-Leipzig, 1935)). Still crucial is Hans Kohn, *Die Idee des Nationalismus* (Frankfurt/M., 1962), and *Von Machiavelli zu Nehru, Zur Problemgeschichte des Nationalismus* (Freiburg/Br., 1964). The best survey is Eugen Lemberg, *Nationalismus*, 2 vols (Reinbek, 1964); see Alfred Cobban, *The Nation State and National Self-Determination* (London, 1969); Heinrich August Winkler (ed.), *Nationalismus* (Kronberg, 1978); Otto Dann (ed.), *Nationalismus und sozialer Wandel* (Hamburg, 1978) (including Hartmut Ullrich, 'Bürgertum und nationale Bewegung im Italien des Risorgimento'); on Herder see also Rudolf Wendorff, *Zeit und Kultur* (Opladen, 1980), p. 307ff.

of the primacy of the nation: the national state was to embody the people's awakened political consciousness, simultaneously assuming the role of political integration domestically and of historic mission externally. Here we encounter the seeds of the two great deformations of the idea of the national state, and these, given the multiplicity of European nations, were bound to have a disastrous effect: domestic oppression of political or ethnic minorities in the name of 'the' nation and an expansionist imperial-mission policy externally – both pursued with the consistency of dictatorial power politics, though not at first thought through to its logical conclusion. Currents of a mission-inspired national imperialism surfaced in nearly all contemporary states from pan-Slavism via a French and British sense of mission all the way to the American expansionist ideology of a 'manifest destiny'.[1] Its potentially anti-democratic thrust was formulated in Germany with especial sharpness by the one-time liberal historian Treitschke in his significant abandonment of democratic thought: internally by a justification of élitist instead of parliamentary government, externally by an emphasis on the inequality of nations and races, and by a special national mission that the Germans should become aware of.

German and Italian propagandists took the view that belated national unification carried an obligation to catch up with one's national mission. The two nations were ancient and young at the same time; they could look back to famous forefathers – ancient Germans and Romans. But their political thought on this point became rigid. The most important protagonist of Italian unity, Giuseppe Mazzini, who was mainly active from exile, was a convinced anti-monarchist republican with a democratic and European outlook: to him the idea of self-determination for all nations aimed at a universal humanitarian goal, in whose service each nation would act in its own way, though, if at all possible, as a complete unit. However, even Mazzini's liberal republican national ideology, seeking ultimately the unity of all classes under the banner of the nation, eventually led him into the camp of power-state imperialist nationalism: following the unification of Italy, at the end of his life (1872) he called for an active Italian colonial policy

[1] See the classic presentation by Albert K. Weinberg, *Manifest Destiny, A Study of Nationalist Expansionism in American History* (1935, 3rd ed. 1963); highly critically Hans-Ulrich Wehler, *Der Aufstieg des amerikanischen Imperialismus, Studien zur Entwicklung des Imperium Americanum 1865–1900* (Göttingen, 1974) with an extensive bibliography; on these concepts see R. Koebner, H. D. Schmidt, *Imperialism, The Story and Significance of a Political Word 1840–1960* (Cambridge, 1964). Also Karl Epting, *Das französische Sendungsbewusstsein im 19. und 20. Jahrhundert* (Heidelberg, 1952); C. C. Eldridge, *England's Mission, The Imperial Idea in the Age of Gladstone and Disraeli* (London, 1973); John R. Seeley, *The Expansion of England* (1883) German, *Die Ausbreitung Englands* (Frankfurt/M., 1954). Hans Kohn, *Die Slawen und der Westen, Zur Problemgeschichte des Panslawismus* (Vienna, 1956); Frank Fadner, *Seventy Years of Panslavism in Russia* (1962); Leonard Schapiro, *Rationalism and Nationalism in Russian Nineteenth-Century Thought* (London, 1967); a recent major work, especially on the revolutionary component in the nineteenth century, is James Billington, *Fire in the Minds of Men* (New York, 1980).

in North Africa. He did so with a justification foreshadowing fascism, one which was at the same time traditionalist and in conflict with the liberal democratic idea of self-determination: 'After all, the Roman standard once flew over these countries when, after the fall of Carthage, the Mediterranean was called *mare nostrum*. We were the masters of this entire region until the fifth century. Now France is casting her eye on these countries, and she will have them unless we own them ourselves.'[1]

Here we have an early indication of fascism's subsequent identification of Italy with the *Imperium Romanum* of classical antiquity. It has been rightly remarked that philosophers of nationalism start out with supranational all-humanity goals as their final objectives while their own nation is weak, and that they make national-imperialist expansionist and autarky claims the moment a strong national state has been achieved;[2] from Italian irredentism to Bolshevik national imperialism and to the Third World – everywhere the supranational perspectives of nationalism were to prove the weaker. The original romantic idea of a peaceful co-existence of national states is forcefully brushed aside by the imperialist power state with its abuse of the national idea.

The main obstacle to proper elucidation has invariably been the imprecise nature of concepts, especially the highly ambiguous concept of 'socialism'. Like other political and ideological labels it has, since its pre-Marxist creation, been immensely stretched over the past 150 years and applied in mutually incompatible ways; it has become a readily manipulated formula of political faith. The dispute between its democratic and dictatorial trends began together with the rise of the working-class movement in the nineteenth century, simultaneously with the conflict between its international and national versions. Marxism, itself marked by numerous rifts, is only one of those trends, though the dogmatically most exacting of them; right from the start it raised its characteristic exclusive claim to proclaiming *the* authentic form of socialism, one which even Marx had practically

---

[1] Walter Theimer, *Geschichte der politischen Ideen* (Bern, 1955), p. 365: in Mazzini's later writings we also find the first demand for the Brenner frontier; Italy to him is the 'oldest and most capable colonial power on earth'. The significant contradictions between humanitarian and imperial national ideas are generally hushed up especially in the Italian Mazzini literature which is mostly inclined towards glorification. See Otto Vossler, *Mazzinis politisches Denken und Wollen in den geistigen Strömungen seiner Zeit* (Munich-Berlin, 1927); on the early phase see Franco Della Peruta, *Mazzini e i rivoluzionari italiani* (Milan, 1974); see Francesco Perfetti (ed.), *Il nazionalismo Italiano* (Milan, 1970). Fascism expressly saw itself in this tradition; Mussolini and his 'intellectuals' labelled him as a second, successful, risorgimento; indeed in 1943 Mazzini was claimed even for the then 'republican' and 'national-socialist' radicalization of the Salò residual regime. On this see Ernst Nolte, *Faschismus*, op. cit., p. 314ff.; also Francesco Leoni, *Origini del nazionalismo Italiano* (Naples, 1970) on the transition since the turn of the century, with a list of newspapers and movements, p. 119. Also L. Magagnato, *Nazione e rapporti internazionali nel pensiero di Mazzini* (Vicenza, 1943); Alessandro Levi, *La filosofia politica di Giuseppe Mazzini* (Bologna, 1917), new ed. 1955.

[2] W. Theimer, op. cit. p. 363.

equated with communism.

The package concept of socialism *as such*, a concept again much used today, blurs the fundamental distinction between a dictatorial and totalitarian concept and a reformist and democratic interpretation. Following Lenin's revolution and the split between social democracy and communism after the First World War that distinction acquired global significance.[1] At that time nationalist and dictatorial counter-movements also came into being, similarly, under the slogan of 'national socialism' and fascism, linking up with the collectivist and totalitarian, as well as with the anti-capitalist and anti-bourgeois, trends of revolutionary socialism. What unites the two totalitarian versions is their anti-liberal and anti-parliamentarian basic approach to politics; what divides them is their opposite attitude to the class struggle and the dictatorship of the proletariat. There is no denying that the deeper differences of ideological origin – from a social, supranational emancipatory movement on the one hand, and from a social-imperial, populist-racialist nationalism on the other – tend to be blurred as soon as dictatorial tendencies and totalitarian means of government become fully effective in the radical power struggle and in the all-round consolidation of power, classically illustrated in the side-by-side existence (and temporary togetherness) of Stalinism and Hitlerism.

Between those two totalitarian versions the only way social democracy can hold its own is by invariably applying the concept of socialism in an emphatically democratic sense and, time and again, clearly dissociating itself from communist and totalitarian versions. This, of course, is difficult as soon as the concept is used as a formula of a faith, a formula towards which young people in particular keep gravitating in their longing for universal solutions and one for which even many of the socialist parties in free Europe have a soft spot.

From its very beginnings, however, 'national socialism' claimed for itself the role of an emphatically social, though of course national, workers' movement. Indeed its earliest origins, in the then Austrian Bohemia of the turn of the century, were typical in this respect. Prior to the First World War a 'German Workers' Party' was confronting the Czech trade unions in the German-speaking regions of Bohemia; both its name and its declared 'national socialist' programme subsequently served the emergence of

---

[1] On the schisms and new foundations since 1917–18 see Walter Kendall, *The Revolutionary Movement in Britain 1900–1921* (London, 1969) and *The Labour Movement in Europe* (London, 1965); Leslie John Macfarlane, *The British Communist Party: Its Origin and Development until 1929* (London, 1966); John M. Cammett, *Antonio Gramsci and the Origins of Italian Communism* (1967); Annie Kriegel, *Aux origines du communisme français* (Paris, 1964), and Robert Wohl, *French Communism in the Making 1914–1924* (1966). Werner Angress, *Die Kampfzeit der KPD, 1921–1923* (Düsseldorf, 1973; American ed. 1963); Hermann Weber, *Der deutsche Kommunismus, Documente 1915–1945*, 3rd ed. (1973) and *Die Kommunistische Internationale* (Hanover, 1966). On the European context see K. D. Bracher, *Europa in der Krise* (Berlin, 1979) p. 64ff.

Hitler's Munich party after 1919. Indeed kindred, though at first rival, movements such as the 'German Social Party' (of Streicher, the publisher of *Der Stürmer*) made use of the socialist concept. National socialism largely owed its subsequent upsurge to an underestimation of its 'socialist' folklore alongside its nationalist pretensions.[1] Both the conservative Right and the Left, in particular the Marxist theory of fascism, failed to allow for the revolutionary, and potentially mass-mobilizing, component of that 'move-ment', because they tended to see it purely as an invention or as the product of anti-socialist, counter-revolutionary, monopoly-capitalist power politics. Of course it was all these things – but its attraction and unifying force arose primarily through its efforts to proclaim an alternative to communist socialism in the form of a nationalist people's comradeship, the egalitarian-ism of a people's community instead of class-struggle socialism, and through calling it 'national socialism'.

Gregor Strasser's notion of the 'anti-capitalist yearnings' of the masses[2] proved an effective tool at a time when, during the great depression, people had lost their sense of direction – no matter how trite the national socialist propaganda formula of 'work and bread' may have seemed. Use of the concept of socialism characterized both the earliest beginnings and the later rise of national socialism; in spite of Hitler's power-political twists and opinions it remained an important part of national socialist self-under-standing. Nor is it fortuitous that it has resurfaced in post-war neo-Nazi organizations and programmes: Socialist Reich Party, People's Socialists, Movimento Sociale Italiano are the titles they have given themselves.

Much as the currents, forms and contents of 'socialism' *throughout the world* differ from one another, and much as any national socialism may see itself as the counter-principle to Marxism, there is no mistaking the close kinship of its totalitarian, anti-liberal features or of its tendency to organize and regiment the people – a tendency that came to full fruition in the governing practice of the Third Reich. Certainly the 'Left' component of such a national socialism became totally submerged in Hitler's Führer absolutism; much the same happened to revolutionary socialism under Stalin. Anti-bourgeois radicalism emerged just as clearly in Hitler's regime of war and annihilation as it did in the extreme final phase of Italian fascism, when the one-time radical socialist Mussolini reverted to his revolutionary beginnings.

[1] See K. D. Bracher, *Die Auflösung der Weimarer Republik*, 6th ed. (1978), pp. 87ff., 100ff.; *Zeitgeschichtliche Kontroversen*, op. cit., p. 63ff. (Examples of an underrating of 'socialism' in the ideological attraction potential of national socialism are supplied, in particular, by left-wing theories of fascism, then as now.) See the verbal radicalism of Joseph Goebbels, *Der Nazi-Sozi* (Munich, 1931). In this context the Strasser brothers also emerged: on this see Udo Kissenkoetter, *Gregor Strasser und die NSDAP* (Series of studies of *Vierteljahrshefte für Zeitgeschichte* 37) (Stuttgart, 1978), pp. 22ff., 83ff.; see also Otto Strasser, *Hitler und ich*, (Buenos Aires, 1940) and *Mein Kampf* (Frankfurt/M., 1969).

[2] 'Antikapitalismus', *Nationalsozialistische Monatshefte* 3/28 (July 1932), p. 1ff.

The levelling, equalizing, quasi-socialist effects of such totalitarian movements and regimes are unmistakable. To follow the fashionable theories of fascism and refer to national socialism merely as 'German fascism' means a failure to take the concept of national socialism seriously or an attempt to taboo it just because it contains the hallowed word 'socialism'. This is the line invariably followed by the communists. Social democrats, on the other hand, remain dependent on a libertarian interpretation of the concept of socialism, more especially whenever some European or international nostalgia draws them towards a re-unification of all forces of left-wing socialism. But without a libertarian and democratic qualification socialism remains just a battle-cry to which far too many ideologists all the way from Left to Right have pinned their hopes, illusions and ambitions.

The idea of a 'national socialism' had been fairly current in Germany about the turn of the century, ranging from social-progressive liberals (like Friedrich Naumann) to radical racialists. What could be more tempting to ideologists than to combine these two most powerful currents of political ideologization aimed at the people generally, *i.e.* the nationalization and socialization of the masses, and thereby to create a clearly visible comprehensive alternative to the 'international socialism' of the Marxists and the social democrats? In Italy, following early agrarian-'fascist' protest movements prior to the turn of the century, the about-turn of the left-wing socialist Mussolini towards the nationalist propaganda struggle of the First World War represented just that combination. In Germany and Austria there were the social-nationalist trade-union movements, partly themselves the result of secession from social democracy, which emerged after 1904 in the border regions of Bohemia to oppose the Czech national movement. It was the struggle for national assertion with a simultaneous socialist colouring that underlay the early manifestos of 'national socialism' before the war.[1]

Here the profound difference between fascism and national socialism emerges very clearly: a national-imperial mission ideology with a touch of socialism and the powerful state as the highest value in fascism, and a populist anti-Semitic integrational ideology with the Germanic-Nordic 'race' as the highest value in national socialism – both emphatically anti-Marxist but equally emphatically anti-capitalist. This study is not greatly concerned with a systematic presentation of the two ideologies; for that recourse should be had to the books by Ernst Nolte, Eugen Weber, Renzo De Felice, Norberto Bobbio, James Gregor, Eberhard Jäckel and George Mosse, and to essays by the present author.[2] Their character of a strongly unifying battle ideology with a meta-scientific claim sharply distinguishes

[1] See Andrew Whiteside, *Austrian National Socialism before 1918* (The Hague, 1962); K. D. Bracher, *German Dictatorship* op. cit., p. 77ff.

[2] On similarities and dissimilarities in the ideologies of fascism and national socialism see the recent concise comparisons by Stanley G. Payne, *Fascism*, op. cit., p. 101ff.

both movements from Marxism – though admittedly less sharply from communist forms of faith. Its slight philosophical content need have no bearing on the weight and effectiveness of an ideology. What is essential is the relationship which fascism succeeded in establishing between ideology and reality, between actionism and authoritarian regime, at the moment when power seized by a minority had to be consolidated. Equally interesting is the question of how it was possible for the scant intellectual elements (such as race, living space, leader principle, people's community) which went to make up national socialism in Hitler's thought to be transformed into what would have seemed an inconceivable measure of support and eventually, just as unexpectedly, into consistent political realization.

A decisive aspect in this was, first of all, the hotch-potch character of the ideology. It operated through the interaction of traditional and revolutionary, of populist and social, of authoritarian and totalitarian elements. The parallelism and intertwining of these elements will be sketched out in a few key terms below·

Traditional: for fascism this meant the idea of the Roman empire and the national monarchical unified state as the fulfilment of the *risorgimento*; for national socialism it meant the 'Germanic Reich of the German nation' (Hitler 1937), the medieval concept of the Reich (of the Holy Roman Empire of the German Nation) and the greater-German idea (national rising, 1933).[1]

Revolutionary: this meant the outmanœuvring of all previous forces, moreover in a pseudo-legal and violent manner at the same time, followed by the overthrow of power structure and system of values.

Populist: this concerned the pseudo-democratic, plebiscitarian per-

---

[1] Adolf Hitler's speech at the *Ordensburg* Sonthofen on 23 November 1937, in Gerhard Ritter (ed.), *Henry Picker, Hitlers Tischgespräche im Führerhauptquartier 1941-42* (Bonn, 1951), Appendix p. 443ff. On the fascist concept of state and society see the different interpretations in Renzo De Felice, *Die Deutungen des Faschismus* (Göttingen, 1980), pp. 171ff., 247ff.; E. Nolte, *Faschismus*, op. cit., p. 268ff; Norberto Bobbio, *L'ideologia del fascismo* (Rome, 1976). Whereas national socialism very largely became Hitlerism even before the seizure of power, the difference between fascism and 'Mussolinism' emerges more clearly: see Piero Melograni, 'The Cult of the Duce', *Journal of Contemporary History* 11/4 (1976), p. 223ff.; now also in George Mosse (ed.), *International Fascism* (London, 1979), p. 73ff., with other important studies. More recent attempts at presenting the 'Hitler myth' as evidence of an allegedly polycratic structure of the Hitler regime such as Ian Kershaw's *Der Hitler-Mythus* (Stuttgart, 1980, with an angled introduction by Martin Broszat, p. 7ff.), disregard the ultimately totalitarian nature of the national socialist leadership system, which is inconceivable without Hitler. See, alongside the classic Hitler literature from Alan Bullock (1952) to Joachim Fest (1973), especially Eberhard Jäckel, op. cit.; also Klaus Hildebrand, *Das Dritte Reich* (Munich, 1979), p. 129ff., and 'Monokratie oder Polykratie', in *Der 'Führerstaat', Mythos und Realität* (Stuttgart, 1981), p. 73ff. (against most of the other contributions to the volume); K. D. Bracher, 'Probleme und Perspektiven der Hitler-Interpretation', in *Zeitgeschichtliche Kontroversen*, op. cit., p. 79ff.; on the distinction between fascism and national socialism ibid., p. 63ff. English version 'The role of Hitler: perspectives of interpretation', in W. Laqueur (ed.) *Fascism*, op. cit., p. 211ff.

suasion and manipulation of support in all strata of the population.

Social: this meant stressing the egalitarian patterns and collective pre-organizations of a 'people's community' of all 'workers', whether by 'brain or hand', instead of a class society and class struggle.

Authoritarian: this was the élitist structure of political struggle and decision-making, as well as the 'qualitative' idea of culture as against the merely 'quantitative' one of civilization.

Totalitarian, however, was the central idea of absolute identity of *Führer* and people, *Duce* and nation, party and state: the basic concept or basic fiction of modern dictatorship as an anti-liberal, totally-democratic people's government with one single head.

These effective axioms of fascist and national socialist governmental ideologies certainly were in glaring contradiction to the reality of the governmental systems. Yet the somewhat arbitrary character of actual decisions in fascist Italy or in Hitler's Third Reich does not invalidate the significance of the Führer cult or the brutality of the decisions to which the individual was subject. Any talk of polycracy let alone pluralism mistakes the profoundly anti-constitutional and anti-liberal form of just that 'authoritarian anarchy' over which the élite of party and ss, and finally the Führer himself as a semi-god, held sway. Here, too, a difference should be noted: in fascism the continued existence of the monarchy and the position of the Church prevented the rise of that pseudo-religious totality of Führer dictatorship which found its horrendous realization in the national socialist belief in race, and in the chiliastic oppressive and destructive fanaticism of the ss state. In both instances, however, the blending of rational and irrational, of bureaucratic and ideological forms was typical.[1]

Matters were different but comparable in communism. Its starting-point and framework was an elaborate 'scientific' theory with empirical pretensions, even though against a philosophically Utopian background. However, it was the adaptations to Lenin's revolutionary strategy and dictatorial rule itself which gave communist ideology its politically true shape both within and outside the Soviet Union: this was both authoritarian (the party élite) and, at the same time, totalitarian (the cult of Lenin and Stalin). This true shape, more particularly, meant enforced collectivism and a quasi-military structure, the individual's absolute submission and the persecution of all deviations, actual or alleged. Russian autocracy and imperialism likewise lived on, though under a new ideological label: dictatorship of the proletariat and socialist world revolution were now the

---

[1] See also the peculiar differentiation of fascism and national socialism in R. De Felice, *Der Faschismus, Ein Interview (with Michael Ledeen)* (Stuttgart, 1977), p. 34ff., with a most informative postscript by Jens Petersen, 'Zum Stand der Faschismusdiskussion in Italien' (p. 114ff.); on the sharp Italian controversies see also Michael A. Ledeen, 'Renzo De Felice and the Controversy over Italian Fascism', *Journal of Contemporary History* 11/4 (1976), p. 269ff.

justifications of a despotism which had previously been sanctified by the traditional pretensions of the 'Third Rome' and of pan-Slavism.[1]

If we compare this with the fascist and national socialist ideologies we find that the rational and progressivist core of communism – the liberation of the proletariat – which attracted so many intellectuals romantically or atavistically, is very largely propaganda. The emphasis on modernization and technology, which subsequently, under Stalin, characterized the communist claim to progress, similarly worked mainly in favour of an increase in power in the course of further development predominantly of military strength, while the economic and political infrastructure lagged far behind all promises. The further evolution of communist power was to base itself principally, in the post-Stalin era, on military strength both internally with the secret police, and externally.

Although the great army purges right into the thirties and the ceaselessly reiterated peace propaganda of the Soviet Union were designed to differentiate it demonstratively from the aggressive posturing and open warmongering of the 'fascist beasts', communist militant ideology nevertheless held a key position. So long as (world) revolution remained on the communist agenda, and so long as the internal class enemy (in spite of all annihilation campaigns) necessitated continuous struggle and a permanent militarization of social and political life, the militant terminology of its programmes and declarations was not all that different from the battle din of national socialist propaganda throughout all spheres of social life.[2]

A comparison of the main features of this form of government reveals the similarities between the regimes more clearly than their disparate historical and philosophical origins might lead one to expect.

Traditional: this was the long-term continuation of tsarist methods and objectives, of the traditional forms of oppression at home and great power policy abroad.

Revolutionary: this meant the pseudo-legal manipulation of the councils

---

[1] See Hildegard Schaeder, *Moskau, das dritte Rom*, 2nd ed. (1957); N. M. Zerno, *Moscow, the Third Rome* (London, 1937); Wilhelm Bettenbauer, *Moskau, Das dritte Rom* (1961).

[2] On militant terminology in communism and in national socialism see, for example, Lenin, *Agitation and Propaganda* (London, 1929); also *Kleines politisches Wörterbuch* (East Berlin, 1973); Ernst Richert, *Agitation und Propaganda* (Berlin-Frankfurt, 1978). On the other hand, Adolf Hitler's *Mein Kampf* and the extensive collection of quotations in Werner Siebarth, *Hitlers Wollen! Nach Kernsätzen aus seinen Schriften und Reden* (Munich, 1935), p. 91ff.; Wolfgang Bergsdorf, *Politik und Sprache* (Munich-Vienna, 1978), p.73ff., and *Die vierte Gewalt, Einführung in die politische Kommunikation* (Mainz, 1980), p. 114ff., and 'Die Sprache der Diktatur und ihre Wörter', *Deutschland-Archiv* 12 (1978), p. 1299ff.; especially on the GDR: Jean Paul Picaper, *Kommunikation und Propaganda in der DDR* (Stuttgart, 1976); see Cornelia Berning, Die Sprache des Nationalsozialismus, doct. thesis (Bonn, 1958); partially published, with a preface by Werner Betz, as *Vom Abstammungsnachweis zum Zuchtwart, Vokabular des Nationalsozialismus* (Berlin, 1964); J. P. Faye, *Totalitäre Sprachen* (Frankfurt/M., 1977); Aryeh L. Unger, 'The Totalitarian Party' (Cambridge, 1974); Dolf Sternberger *et al.*, *Aus dem Wörterbuch des Unmenschen*, 3rd ed. (Hamburg, 1968).

(soviets) alongside and above the state apparatus until that apparatus had been captured, followed by total imposition of party dictatorship.

Populist: communism's democratic pretensions differed from the Marxist expectation of a proletarian majority mainly by the enforcement of total support through party dictatorship and plebiscitarian endorsement.

Social: the egalitarian and collective reorganization of the whole of society had been intended to bring socialism to all 'working people'; some, however, were 'more equal than others' – the new class of revolutionaries, and subsequently the consolidators of power, had been pre-formed in Lenin's theory of the party.

Authoritarian: communism was and remained authoritarian in as much as the will of the party and its leadership – according to the euphemistically deceptive principle of 'democratic centralism' – was formed and enforced from above downwards; but even society itself, especially with regard to education, was marked by definitely authoritarian and hierarchical structures.

Totalitarian: from the beginning of the cult of Lenin, and certainly not later than Stalinism itself, the 'identification' ideology held sway, the equation of leadership and party, of proletariat and people; admittedly, this totalitarian unity principle was somewhat at odds with the continuation of the class struggle.

Communism in fact represented the first and most original variant of totalitarianism. This is true not only with regard to the time of its seizure of power. It also linked up, differently from fascism and national socialism, with the tradition of political rationalism and the French Revolution, though admittedly with its radical, Jacobine, phase. Just as Robespierre claimed the right to ensure the victory of truth by violence and terror against deviationists, so reference to 'pure' Marxism against reformist 'degeneration' and the 'betrayal' of other socialists provided the basis and the claim to exclusive validity of (Leninist) communism and its élitist-totalitarian party theory; this eventually resulted in a no less totalitarian bureaucratic dictatorship jointly by party and state. Not the 'withering away of the state' but an unprecedented intensification and permanence of that dictatorship became the future yardstick and substance of official, exclusively valid, Soviet-communist ideology; in spite of many a dispute this remained binding also upon all other communist parties. Totalitarian systems of belief, even if dogmatically and bureaucratically rigidified in the meantime, can recognize but one truth. Under Stalin, moreover, the theoretical and rational basis was distorted almost beyond recognition, even though it continued to be cultivated as an attractive façade for intellectuals by means of a scholasticism of quotations from Marx and Lenin.

What is and remains essential is the enormous extension of the idea of the dictatorship of the proletariat, together with the consolidation of the dictatorship of the party (which is always right) and the leadership élite (who know everything), without the possibility of any effective democratic controls since these can at all times be dodged or overridden by reference to the dictatorship. Totalitarian also is the treble ideological pretension by which subjection and oppression, hierarchy and government are justified in communism: government *for* the people, though not *by* the people but by the party, and within the party by its self-appointed élite, who regard themselves as the best representatives of the people but who govern without any effective constitutional checks because they possess the only scientific truth. Marxism-Leninism 'enables the party to find the correct orientation in any situation, to understand the inner connections of events, and to foresee their course not only in the present but also in the future' (*History of the CPSU*, 1939). The Stalinist final formulation of proletarian dictatorship is its equation with party dictatorship: 'No important political or organizational question is decided in our councils or mass organizations without guiding directives from the party. In this sense it can be said that dictatorship of the proletariat is in essence the dictatorship of its vanguard, the dictatorship of the party, as the most important directing force of the proletariat.'[1]

In whatever way the concept of totalitarianism may be seen in terms of constitutional and ideological theory, one aspect which the great anti-liberal ideologists had in common was a striving for monocracy or oligarchy in the name of government by the people, and the liquidation of all opposition. Arbitrariness and violence, if not altogether regarded as indispensable in the historical process, are sanctioned by the superior right of the revolution or of the new societal or governmental principle. Added to this is the claim to a systematic shaping of the inevitable social transformation by means of organization, mobilization and involvement of the entire population, and full utilization of the modern technical means which have equipped the dictatorships of the twentieth century with very much more effective tools of control and coercion: not only bureaucracy and police but also the widely ramified organizations of the party and indeed even the judiciary and educational systems. The extent to which they succeed in using these is another matter. But in terms of intention and potential, technological progress has enabled such dictatorships – and their ideologists of society and government – to make good their pretensions, beyond the political sphere, to the monocratic enlistment of the whole of society.

Invocation of 'the people', however, is no longer just a traditional tool of government, practised even by the tyrants of classical antiquity whenever they employed the 'shapeless multitude' (Plato) for purposes of power manipulation; 'government by the people' is now portrayed as a specifically 'democratic' dictatorship. Continual participation and ceaseless mobiliz-ation of the entire population is the pseudo-democratic axiom that is encountered very effectively in the totalitarian participation concepts of the

---

[1] Thus Stalin, in *Problems of Leninism* (1934). On the *avant-garde* theory see pp. 43; 96ff. above.

new Left.[1] In actual fact such a demand for total participation is not necessarily democratic but, on the contrary, highly susceptible to manipulation, more especially also against democracy. This emerges above all at times of crisis and transition to dictatorship, as proved by the end of the Weimar Republic with its high polling and high membership figures, especially of the dictatorship parties. We have here two different causes working together: the idea of emancipation as a demand for national or social participation, and communalization as a consequence of the mechanization and permeation of all aspects of life. In this process the rapidly developed new means of communication serve the control and manipulation of the public and not the free interchange of opinion. This, however, is justified by the ideologists of dictatorship with the argument that the open information process in a democracy is continually suspect, derogated as being inefficient and discredited by vested interests – a particularly well-tried method of all critics of liberal 'publicity' since Carl Schmitt, who thereby justify their critique of democracy (as well as by the anti-pluralist charge of polycracy).[2]

However, of central importance to both theory and ideology is the reversal of the role of the party in dictatorships. The liberal democratic idea of the pluralistic role of different parties in society, of parties necessarily incomplete and 'biased' in the sense of rivalry, is now confronted with *the* authoritarian-totalitarian party as the quintessence of all socio-political transmission processes: with a party bias (*Parteilichkeit*) now only in the sense of a complete embodiment and realization of the popular will, of the *volonté générale*.

This total reversal of the party concept, which indeed is a contradiction in terms and touches upon the roots of modern pluri-party democracy generally, is accompanied, on the one hand, by the greatest possible organizational enrolment of the people and, on the other, by a measure of ideologization of politics far surpassing anything experienced since the end of the First World War. The question to what extent the organizers and ideologists themselves believe in the pretensions of their policies has always been a controversial one. There can be no doubt that opportunism and

[1] On the almost arbitrary use and misuse of such central political concepts as democracy and participation by totalitarian regimes with their standard formulations and suggestions see Wolfgang Bergsdorf (ed.), *Wörter als Waffen* (Stuttgart, 1979), with contributions by H. Schelsky, H. Maier, K. Sontheimer, G. Schmölders, H. Lübbe and others, as well as the *Orwell Reader* (New York, 1956), the anti-Utopia of language control; also K. D. Bracher, *Schlüsselwörter*, op. cit., p. 85ff. National socialism's plebiscitarian-totalitarian pretension to democracy was repeatedly emphasized by Hitler himself during the phase of the seizure of power, 1933–4; see the evidence in K. D. Bracher *et al.*, *N.S. Machtergreifung*, Vol. 1, p. 472ff.; Vol. 3, p. 365ff.

[2] See Wolfgang Jäger, *Öffentlichkeit und Parlamentarismus* (Stuttgart, 1973), p. 6ff.; on pluralist critique also Hans Kremendahl, *Pluralismustheorie in Deutschland* (Leverkusen, 1977), p. 237ff.; also important is Wolfgang Mantl, *Repräsentation und Identität* (Vienna, 1975).

accommodation play a big part in dictatorial systems, especially in the ideological sphere. Time and again disenchantment with ideological formulas, and indeed cynical contempt for them, has been observed among broad circles of the population, and the real effectiveness of 'political religion' in the sense of the right-wing and left-wing political creeds has been called into question. This may be true of periods of ideological flagging in the post-Stalinist era or, earlier, at times of set-back for fascism. Nevertheless, the measure of acceptance of ideological creeds remains remarkable, even where these competed with strong ecclesiastical and religious traditions, as in Italy and Germany. The force of such creeds emerged with particular clarity in situations of extreme crisis, such as 1941 in the Soviet Union, or 1944–5 in Germany when the crushing of the Resistance and grim perseverance in a lost war was successfully suggested to the mass of the population by the miracle slogans of Nazi propaganda.

One thing is undeniable: ideologization of politics, while not unknown in antiquity under charismatic rulers such as Alexander, Caesar or Augustus, and steadily increasing since the emergence of the absolutist national state and the doctrine of people's sovereignty, reached its climax in modern dictatorship. What had emerged in outline in the English and later the American Revolution as the idea of justification and mission, first appeared openly in the ideologization phases of the French Revolution. Instead of the monarch's lordly reason of state it was now the downright mythical force of the popular will that was solely and wholly decisive. To invoke it meant to claim total control not only of power but also of moral values, as Robespierre and the Jacobins did. Ideologization of the popular will, which brooks no opposition, produces the totalitarian principle proper; it is the basis of any modern dictatorship beyond mere traditional dictatorial forms of military or authoritarian regime lacking any ideology.[1]

The less such a totalitarian ideologization of the 'indivisible unified popular will' reflects the reality of the situation, the harsher the means of coercion and the more fanatical the struggle to enforce it. The civil war situation demands (if necessary) the forcible establishment of unity; there can and shall therefore be only one authority above the clash of intérêts underlying such conflicts – the dictator, the monoparty. The ideologization which legitimates all this requires not only a unification that is at odds with the reality of the situation, but also a quasi-religious total obligation of political values and goals, and indeed the population's active and devout participation in the government's actions: total approval as coercion

---

[1] The concept of ideology was developed and critically examined in the twenties especially by Karl Mannheim; for his scientific-sociological studies after 1923 see, in particular, his book *Ideologie and Utopie* (Bonn, 1929 and 1930; 4th ed. Frankfurt/M., 1945). Ernst Topitsch and Kurt Salamun, *Ideologie* (Munich-Vienna, 1972); K. Salamun, *Ideologie, Wissenschaft, Politik* (Graz, 1975); also *Sozialphilosophie als Aufklärung (Festschrift for Ernst Topitsch)* (Tübingen, 1979). On the Marxist version Peter Chr. Ludz, *Ideologiebegriff und marxistische Theorie* (Opladen, 1976).

towards permanent participation. Such an ideologization of politics, first practised with complete consistency by the '*réligion civile*' of the Jacobins,[1] is based on the essentially totalitarian central principle of both Leninism and national socialism, a principle that links them both to political Rousseauism and makes them mutually comparable: it is the elevation of a *volonté générale* embodied by leader and party, and superordinated to all individual or group will, into an all-powerful authority.

The ancient search for a viable principle of all politics had reached its end in this ideologization process. It represented a powerful, infinitely attractive, overall alternative to mere individual endeavours by democratic theoreticians to find a viable compromise between individual and collective interest, between multiplicity and unity. Moreover, it seemed to eliminate the great doubt and the fundamental critique of the liberal-individualist belief in progress in favour of a true, social and national progressivism.

There was one other thing the great ideologies had in common: their claim to political and intellectual exclusiveness. Just as Leninism believed itself to have outstripped all other ideologies including religion, so both fascism and national socialism regarded all bourgeois philosophies as things of the past; only the Marxist philosophy remained to be 'exterminated', as Hitler used to put it. However, these declared ideologies or philosophies expressly excluded themselves from the suspicion of being just an ideology, a suspicion from which they otherwise profited a good deal (especially as intellectual criticism was predominantly directed at the liberal and later the social democratic interpretation of socialism) while casting fond glances at their anti-rational critics.[2]

Although this kind of claim to definitive validity was typical of all ideologies, in Marxism-Leninism it presented itself in a deliberately rational form – liberated, as it were, from any kind of superstition – and simultaneously in greater scientific elaboration than any other kind of political philosophy. Nevertheless it remained an ideology, both in terms of objectives and methods. Total liberty *and* equality in one, that was the Utopian faith it contained, and the *dialectical* method was the non-rational, or indeed irrational, element of that 'scientific socialism'. By applying this concept of flip-over or reversal of the historical process to any relationships whatever, which could always at will be proclaimed 'theses and antitheses', no limits at all were set on the constructive or interpretational potential of this method, and hence to the ideologizability of scientifically sanctioned

[1] See J. L. Talmon, *Ursprünge*, op. cit., p. 133ff.

[2] See the following chapters, p. 130ff. On the political tendencies of intellectual ideology critique see especially Jean-François Revel, *Die totalitäre Versuchung* (Frankfurt-Berlin, 1976), p. 20ff. ('Das Verlangen nach Totalitarismus'), as well as Raymond Aron, *Plädoyer für das dekadente Europa*, ibid. (1978), p. 23ff. (Europe's intellectuals 'mystified by Marxism-Leninism'). Hugh Seton-Watson in Mosse (ed.), *International Fascism* (London, 1979), p. 368f., aptly describes 'the whole half-century since 1927 – the decisive year in Stalin's rise to power – as the period of competition between totalitarian nationalism and totalitarian Marxism'.

developmental or intellectual processes. Such unlimited applicability largely determines the 'value' of an ideology. Thanks to its quasi-scientific character the dialectical method was even better suited to ideologization than the irrationalist voluntarisms of the fascist or national socialist philosophies; it found incomparably more, and ever new, intellectual adherents, whereas right-wing radical irrationalism was more specific in terms of period and nation. Neither, of course, has anything in common with science or with analysis of the real world.

Whether action philosophy or scientific socialism, what really mattered was that 'revaluation of values', so acutely formulated by Nietzsche, the struggle for old and new socio-political and moral norms which offered the ideologists the best points of departure. The struggle for values (of what kind?); the significance of individual theoreticians; the idea of war as a refraction of the concept of progress between the wars – these are three issues which our examination will have to attack now that our sight has been sharpened to political ideologies.

4. TOTALITARIAN PROGRESSIVISM
ON THE
RIGHT AND THE LEFT

The ideologies of fascism and national socialism are customarily mentioned only in a negative context within the idea of progress. They did in fact negate faith in a rational and universal improvement of the human condition, they were comprehended in terms of resistance and revolt against modernization, and they found their followers mainly in those strata of society which felt threatened by the concept of progress. Cultural pessimism and critique of civilization provided an effective background to the operation of the fascist and national socialist ideologies. Yet their relationship to progress was actually rather ambivalent. Like socialism and communism they proceeded from a comprehensive critique of contemporary liberal progressivist society. Many of the 'left-wing' arguments played a part also in 'right-wing' fascist and national socialist ideology: critiques of capitalism and democracy, anti-individualism, anti-parliamentarianism and anti-pluralism. Their methods, criteria and objectives were different, but the idea of change through power struggle and dictatorial rule produced entirely comparable forms of action and thought. The most striking difference was in the imagined, dogmatized, subject and exponent of the desired great transformation of the world: race or class.

A profound ambivalence emerges in their attitude to progress. Civilizational progress results in a threat to the nation as a race, or in the impoverishment of the proletariat as a class; at the same time, and by virtue of it, it becomes the driving force for the overthrow of existing conditions and their transformation into a new society or world order. This 'progressivism' was quite distinct from the liberal idea of progress. It presupposed a break and it aimed at dictatorship. Moreover, it put its trust in the irrational forces of history rather than in the rational forces of individuals. However, compared with bourgeois society, expectation of a 'final solution' to the problem of progress by means of a new order and a new human being, no matter whether based on the superior reason of the initiates or on the intuition of a leader, appeared entirely 'progressive' to the youthful followers of the totalitarian movements, who accounted for their great majority.[1]

The ambivalence of tradition and revolution, of criticism of culture and progressivism, was certainly more pronounced in fascism and national socialism than in communism. Communism was able to develop its revolutionary faith in progress quite impressively and consistently from a revolutionary *tabula rasa* situation, whereas Mussolini and Hitler were operating within the constraints of a coalition in a 'legal revolution'. Certainly this did not make the methods or goals of national socialism any less radical. There was complete agreement also on another point: their pronouncements on progress and completion dates were invariably vague and tactically flexible, avoiding any timetable. How long the period of the building of socialism would take, or when Mussolini's 'totalitarian state' of fascism would be achieved, or when the populist-racialist order of national socialism would be realized and superimposed on the traditional state – all these questions remained wide open. The only certainty was that they would endure a thousand years, definitely, eternally.[2]

All these instances, of course, were perversions of the classic idea of progress which envisaged progress as a gradual abolition of violence and an advance towards universal humanity, whereas the totalitarian ideologies sanctioned dictatorship as a means (of unlimited duration) or indeed as a final state; this distinguished their theories but not their practices. A chiliastically conceived progress which sanctified any means – that was the logical trap of totalitarian progressivism, the trap in which one got caught whenever criticism of the present was combined with anti-liberal and collectivist visions of community and unity, and their attainment defined as a law of history or of 'providence'.

National-socialist ideology, which was incomparably more far-reaching than that of fascism, provides a good illustration as a companion piece to communism. It represented, even more so than communism, an eclectic

[1] See both in fascism and in national socialism the invocation of the right of 'young nations', the slogan 'Move over, oldsters', the exploitation of the generation conflict and the importance of all-embracing youth organizations. The idealism and radicalism of sublime goals, and also the speculation (customary in all revolutionary movements) about personality changes, mainly benefited younger persons, and provided a stimulus, both in theory and in practice, for a well-above-average participation of young activists and members in totalitarian movements. On the generation problem see also p. 120ff. below.

[2] The notion of the Thousand Years Reich, as was shown in Germany in 1933, answered a readiness and a need that is generally typical of ideological breaks in history. Rome's eternity figure in the panegyrics of literary figures in the ancient Roman empire; the new age of the French Revolution was to be the final and supreme era of history. Fascism likewise enacted a new calendar, and the Germanists and philosophers of national socialism declared the 'Third Reich' to be the fulfilment of a thousand-year-old longing. Reichstag President Hermann Göring, of all people, gilded the lily by specifically (and brutally) declaring the elections of 5 March 1933 to be 'certainly the last for the next ten years, but presumably for the next one hundred years'. Documents in K. D. Bracher, *NS Machtergreifung*, op cit, pp. 114, 424ff.; *German Dictatorship* op. cit., p. 270ff. For communism's claim to finality see p. 125ff. below

'ragbag' ideology, drawn from a multitude of sources, and it lacked the kind
of classic bible that Marxism possessed. Yet in its concentration of
contradictory elements on one or a handful of points it combined both: a
quasi-existential starting-point for momentary perplexity and the expectation of a panacea-like community concept for the future. It is significant
that an anti-democrat so akin to it as Oswald Spengler was expressly
condemned for his 'pessimism' by Hitler himself.[1]

One of the more important causes of the rise of the national socialist
ideology following the unsuccessful putsch of 1923 was that literary trend
which has been paradoxically described as 'conservative revolution'. This
was part of a wider scene of anti-democratic ideology formation which
stemmed from reaction to the French Revolution and its aftermath. But it
differed from reactionary conservatism by the radical conclusions and
visions of the future which its very disparate representatives had drawn from
their experience of war and collapse. It has been suggested that this
conservative revolution was 'misunderstood', meaning that only the
thoughtless abuse of its ideas had turned it into a precursor and fellow
traveller of national socialist power politics. But there is no denying that the
writings which, in the twenties, came from this very motley camp contained
a great deal of that explosive with which the Free Corps, Young Germany
movement, radicalized students' unions and servicemen, political adventurers and intellectual power-worshippers operated. This was the post-
war anti-democratic wave in sublimated form. Exacting historical-
philosophical essays and anti-civilization aphorisms on the lines of Nietzsche
linked up in a new way with those pre-war currents which were discussed in
the first part of this book.

The genesis of such thought was the commonplace of the incomparability
and superiority of German nationalism, of its anti-western mission in the
struggle against the allegedly state-destroying and community-undermining
effects of liberalism and capitalism, of racial mixture and emancipation, of
international socialism and pacifism, of bourgeoisification.[2] Like the radical
pioneers of the Young Germany movement before them, the conservative
revolutionaries proclaimed the replacement of the 'bourgeois' age by a

[1] See Hitler's speech of 1 May 1935, in Max Domarus (ed.), *Reden und Proklamationen*
(Munich, 1965), I, p. 502; also earlier Arthur Zweininger, *Spengler im Dritten Reich*
(Oldenburg, 1933), and especially Johann von Leers, *Spenglers weltpolitisches System und der
Nationalsozialismus* (Berlin, 1934), p. 5, with a sharp condemnation 'from the national socialist
point of view'. On the following section in greater detail see my analysis in *Auflösung der
Weimarer Republik*, p. 96ff.; *German Dictatorship*, p. 183ff.; *Zeitgeschichtliche Kontroversen*,
p. 71ff.

[2] On the ideology of the separate German road see now Rudolf Vierhaus, 'Die Ideologie
eines deutschen Weges der politischen und sozialen Entwicklung', in Rudolf von Thadden
(ed.), *Liberalismus*, op. cit., p. 96ff.; in greater detail Bernd Faulenbach, op. cit.; also more
recently the essays by Thomas Nipperdey, Ernst Nolte, Kurt Sontheimer, Michael Stürmer,
and K. D. Bracher, in Horst Möller (ed.), *Deutscher Sonderweg – Mythos oder Realität?*
(Munich, 1982).

specifically German, Prussian nationalist, truly conservative 'socialism', based on organic instead of numerical thought, that is, on quality instead of quantity, on the people's community instead of on class and mass. The generation hardened in the 'storms of steel' of the war, whose 'ideas of 1914' had overcome the destructive 'ideas of 1789', would replace the Republic, that unworthy heir to the Second Reich by the ultimate Third Reich of the future.

Admittedly such romantic and irrationalist fantasies, lacking as they were in any specific practical or political aims, were exceedingly heterogeneous and vague. But as an anti-democratic ferment such thought produced considerable effects among the semi-educated bourgeoisie and in the universities. German post-war society proved more susceptible than any before it. Most importantly, there was no real boundary against national socialism, which succeeded in diverting these literary dreams into its own channels by filling its specific organizational and agitational techniques with its substance. Conservative revolution, which tended to see itself as an élitist movement and which generally looked down with contempt on the 'plebeian' petit-bourgeois movement of national socialism, was in fact extremely vulnerable to such manipulation. After 1933 it divided into deserters to national socialism, resigned individuals, and opponents who, from disillusionment, sooner or later, but ultimately too late, might find their way into the Resistance.

Anti-western resentment went furthest in the group of 'national Bolsheviks'. Nationalists like Ernst Niekisch were fascinated by certain aspects of the Russian revolution and regarded the system of soviets as a model of a corporate order for 'creative' people in place of parliamentarianism. Germany's position between east and west was to give rise, through a decisive orientation towards the east, to a new great power liberated from the fetters of Versailles. The basic Utopian character emerged in ever new and different interpretations and patterns; its real effect was the undermining of the Republic and thus – directly or indirectly – the upgrading even of the crude national socialist 'philosophy', which gained respectability as it moved into closer kinship with respected writers and poets. Among these was the widely read Oswald Spengler with his *Preussentum und Sozialismus* (1920), proclaiming 'barbarian Caesarism' as the governmental form of the future. Arthur Moeller van den Bruck had programmatically claimed for Germany 'the right of the young nations' (against the west) as early as 1919 and in his book *Das Dritte Reich* (1923), while not actually foreseeing the subsequent reality of Hitler's Reich, at least supplied him with the formula. Ernst Jünger wrote about the bath of steel of the war and provided the heroic accent of what was to come in *Die totale Mobilmachung* (1931) and in *Der Arbeiter* (1932), in which he stylized the worker into the soldier of technology. Edgar Jung in his anti-republican mammoth work *Die Herrschaft der Minderwertigen* (1927) called for a permanent élitist state; Hans

Grimm in his bestseller *Volk ohne Raum* popularized the break-out from confined space into living-space politics. The Austrian Othmar Spann in his book *Der wahre Staat* (1921) had propagated a corporate state of fascist stamp, with considerable effect on fascist and national socialist theoreticians, as well as on the experiments of Dollfuss and Schuschnigg. Carl Schmitt, Hans Freyer (*Revolution von rechts*, 1931) and the circle around the periodical *Die Tat* (Hans Zehrer, Ferdinand Fried, Giselher Wirsing) with their fantastic ideas on state and social policy also belonged to the extensive group of forerunners, contributors and deliberate or unwitting assistants of national socialism.

On the poetic and literary level Stefan George's political lyrics had a considerable sectarian, pseudo-religious effect; in his volume of poetry *Das neue Reich* he exquisitely extolled an ideology of anti-democratic struggle and élitist leadership – though in 1933 he died in his Swiss exile, an embittered man, and his disciples either emigrated or (like Stauffenberg) joined the Resistance.[1] It was a splendid scene of exalted prophecies, all grounded in a blurred irrationalist mysticism. They were specific only in their anti-western critique, in their haughty condemnation of the democratic present. But their stylized or expansive emotions and thoughts fell upon fertile ground, no matter how different, or how much more 'lowly', the intellectual world of the populist movements and, within it, the ideology of the revived Hitlerite party might be.[2]

The national socialist movement itself had three principal roots. Ideologically it lived by the dual protest of nationalism (outwards) and anti-parliamentarianism (at home). Economically it was rooted in a 'panic of the middle class', which transferred its fight against economic, social and prestige decline to the plane of chauvinism and imperialism. Psychologically the movement largely profited from the generation problem and the romantic protest of youth. All this was topped by an ideology of unity, in which the heterogeneity of social ties and interests of followers, the antagonism of petit-bourgeois small peasants, discontented intellectuals and nationalist adventurers were to be turned into a mystical community, with pent-up aggression forcefully directed outwards.

Particular importance attached to the youthful following, attracted by the movement's romantic radicalism and emotional appeal; these proved the magnet also for the Young Germany movement which had little success in gaining a foothold in the democratic parties and which in the National Socialist German Workers Party (NSDAP) found the most consistent

[1] See Christian Müller, *Oberst i.G. Stauffenberg, Eine Biographie*, 2nd ed. (Düsseldorf, 1970), p. 44ff.

[2] On 'conservative revolution' in addition to the books by Armin Mohler see especially Jean Neurohr, *Der Mythos vom Dritten Reich* (Stuttgart, 1957); Klemens von Klemperer, *Konservative Bewegungen zwischen Kaiserreich und Nationalsozialismus* (Munich-Vienna, 1962); Kurt Sontheimer, *Antidemokratisches Denken in der Weimarer Republik* (Munich, 1962); Otto-Ernst Schüddekopf, *Linke Leute von rechts* (Stuttgart, 1960).

declaration of the leadership idea: 'National socialism is the organized will of youth' ran the official slogan.[1]

These young people witnessed and experienced with outrage the difficult and often unjust conditions of their existence and the numerous constraints of the present. To them the movement was an outlet for their need for action, perverted as it was by unemployment and uncertainty about the future. Those under thirty lacked comprehension of the historical circumstances and political possibilities of the Weimar Republic. They protested against the seeming inactivity of the older-generation politicians, who had in actual fact fallen down on the task of political education. Only in this extreme protest movement – and in the Communist Party – was there an apparent chance of rapid upsurge. 'Move over, oldsters!' demanded Gregor Strasser.[2] Here was an organization which demanded a 'real man', which held 'the old ones' guilty, which satisfied the need for a community, a 'movement' which promised to overcome this 'lukewarm present' and a bourgeois order disintegrated by crises with a more resolute leadership. Community now meant 'socialism'; action and leadership now meant 'nationalism'. The false confrontation of socialism and nationalism was to be smashed, socialism was to be separated from Marxist internationalism, nationalism was to be severed from capitalism. The ringing synthesis of national socialism shaped a collective out of naïve Utopias of social libertarian enthusiasm, a collective which resolved all questioning in obedience to unquestioned Führer dictatorship. The community and leadership idea of the Young Germany movement, which had predominantly cultivated small units, was thus perverted into a centralized bureaucratic collective organization. No matter how deliberately the Hitler Youth adopted the terminology and the style of the Young Germany movement, its uniform organization was totally out of keeping with the individualist basic principle of the Young Germany groups.

The well-nigh incomprehensible success of this ideological conglomerate cannot be explained without the peculiar position of national socialist propaganda. Its astonishing effect was intensified by a masterly use of new techniques of public opinion manipulation. But it was, at the same time, a genuine phenomenon of religious psychology. Just as the concept of 'faith' held a central position in the postulates and self-confirmations of national socialist politics, so the 'philosophical' foundations of the movement and its objectives represented the backbone of all discussion. They eluded the grasp of rational criticism by continuous invocation of a biological mystique: it was from the 'singing of their blood'[3] that the faithful should draw their fanatic strength for action. Whether the effect of such political religions is attributed

[1] Otto Dietrich, *Mit Hitler in die Macht* (Munich, 1934), p. 135.
[2] Thus his eponymous article of May 1927 in Gregor Strasser, *Kampf um Deutschland* (Munich, 1932), p. 171ff.
[3] Gregor Strasser, ibid., p. 222.

generally to a need for faith on the part of the uprooted masses in a secularized world, or whether it is attributed mainly to the specific political, economic and social hardships and wishful thinking of post-war Germany, a Germany of crises, disappointments and resentments – either way patterns of a hymnic adoration of the Führer developed early in the NSDAP foreshadowing the boundless Byzantinism of the Third Reich. Certainly such forms were quite deliberately employed for the manipulation, regimentation and metaphysical buttressing of the movement's totalitarian leadership structure. But they undoubtedly met with a growing echo in a democratically free society, and they proved to be the most effective tools of a propaganda which proclaimed not only gain and greatness but, with increasing success, also salvation and security. Long before 1933 grotesque evidence of religious devotion began to accumulate, such as notices of deaths in which God was replaced by Hitler, testifying to the faith-creating effect of Führer propaganda.

But it was chiefly in an 'inner' sense that Hitler was presented as the revealer of a new meaning to life, one which absorbed his followers' need to surrender themselves, to serve him and to submit to him, to shed their weariness of responsibility, and as one who alone was capable of translating this need into the release of political action. He was the incarnation of the 'people's community'; thanks to his intuition and leadership talent he was always right, he was the unchallengeable interpreter of their interests. For this reason he was not subject, even *vis-à-vis* his own followers, to any rules of law. Such a sense of mission even overrode a monarchical sense of legitimacy: even in the eyes of a Hohenzollern prince (August Wilhelm) Hitler became the 'God-sent leader'.[1] It was on him, therefore, that the entire argument about national socialism was centred.

The revolutionary 'quality' of national socialism was based on its close intertwining of domestic and foreign policy, of ideology and practice. The effect produced by national socialism was typical, both in traditional and in radicalized circles, when it laid claim to 'legal revolution' or to 'national revolution': a manœuvre to deceive all groups from Right to Left. Typical also was the ambivalent and, at the same time, indissoluble interrelation and interaction of both attitudes and convictions: they were nearly always found simultaneously also in most other leader figures of national socialism. The almost dialectical connection of domestic and foreign policy, of theory and practice, of pretensions to tradition and to revolution, represented the new, highly attractive and effective element in national socialist (and, to a lesser

---

[1] Thus as early as 1931 at a meeting in Braunschweig: *Berliner Tageblatt* of 17 June 1931. On the significance of the Führer cult see Albrecht Tyrell, *Vom 'Trommler' zum 'Führer'* (Munich, 1975); also Ian Kershaw, *Der Hitler-Mythos, Volksmeinung und Propaganda im Dritten Reich* (Stuttgart, 1980) although Kershaw has a tendency to underestimate the totalitarian component. See, on the other hand, Klaus Hildebrand, *Das dritte Reich*, op. cit., p 132ff., and 'Monokratie oder Polykratie?', Lothar Kettenacker, 'Sozialpsychologische Aspekte der Führer-Herrschaft', ibid., p. 98ff.

degree, fascist) politics in the transitional period from liberal notability to democratic mass societies.

A few examples of the dovetailing of traditional and revolutionary elements:

(1) The principal notion of national socialism, the reconciliation of labour and the national state, struck at the very heart of the problems of the day and has retained its epoch-making significance if one considers the 'socialism' of the developing countries and the ceaselessly propagated 'third road' between capitalism and communism.

(2) The basic idea of a racially structured and graduated humanity represents a radical alternative not only to the liberal-humanitarian concept of world civilization but also to the current idea of the national state. It is the conviction of the role of racialism as a world-revolutionary principle which will replace traditional nationalism and determine historical movement in accordance with the racially superior nation's right to living space: herein lies the universal world-political mission concept for national socialist domestic and foreign policy.

(3) The social-Darwinist starting-point of these basic national socialist principles again operates in both directions. As an assertion of the superior right of the stronger it is in line with a more or less conservative theory of politics, with the thesis of men making history. But the underlying pessimistic note of the social Darwinists, which after all also determines anti-Semitism with its invocation of an alleged danger of extinction through 'over-alienation', is virtually turned upside down in the transformation of the 'doctrine' into politically active ideology and thereby revolutionized: as a motive force for totalitarian power politics and racialist extension of rule.

(4) The national-socialist concepts of the structure of society contain a strange combination of conservative cultural romanticism and economic-technological progressivism; their contradictory nature is typical also in the justification and implementation of practical cultural, social and economic policies at various periods and in various fields. Here too national-socialist ideology benefited from certain seductive trends of the day: industrialization and technicalization in the sense of a new romanticism as the fulfilment of long-cherished human yearnings for praise or for the glorification of the worker as the embodiment of a new people's community. Of course this implied a grotesque distortion of the social structure in the modern industrial state, but as an alternative to an equally unrealistic class struggle theory it proved most effective both in taming and in mobilizing the population.

(5) This combination of opposites appears in the most striking manner when the most up-to-date manipulation of the mass media and the technique of mass rallies are employed for such traditionalist, rurally romantic events as the Reich Peasants' Rally on the Bückeberg. Under this heading comes also the inventive elaboration of a political mass liturgy and generally the

character and effect of a political religion with fanatical believers and a pseudo-Germanic or a pseudo-Christian Führer cult. National socialism's roots in nineteenth-century anti-modernist and anti-industrial currents are, in a sense, offset, or indeed, overtaken by a cult of technology and efficiency, as reflected in such emphatically *avant-garde* enterprises as the autobahnen, the Volkswagen, the people's radio set, or in the thoroughly planned nationalization and mobilization of the masses under a superb stage management of public life.

In the military sphere – a central area of foreign-political thought and action – this modernism emerges with particular clarity. Hitler's much admired knowledge and oft-praised understanding of downright revolutionary new forms of warfare clash, on the other hand, with the most traditional ideas on war and foreign policy. The contradictory character, the rapid switch from one perspective to the other may seem to be the real problem, but is also the secret of national socialism's success in that it has time and again upset the assessments and expectations of both friend and foe and indeed to this day impairs a clear judgement.

(6) Thus a mystical political religion and the adoration of technical success, ancient German rural romanticism and modern mass show, the socialist May Day and national socialist worker romanticism are all slotted together, each performing its function in the amalgamation of opposites, in radiation in both directions. Hitler's speech at the *Ordensburg* Sonthofen on 23 November 1937, shortly after the *Führer* Conference of 5 November in preparation for the war, similarly implied that characteristic ambivalence in its concept of the 'Germanic empire of the German nation'. In that secret speech on German history and the German destiny, made to the young leadership cadres, ancient and modern goals of racialism and living space ideology were bracketed together; amalgamating diametrically opposed elements they resulted in a historically draped design for worldwide dominion, a design that cannot be denied a revolutionary quality any more than could, 150 years earlier, the nation-state seed of political revolution and transformation of international relations. The most profoundly traditionalist element may be seen in the mystical elevation of the concept of the Reich. Yet this vague concept, ambivalent though it had been even during the history of the Second Reich, fluctuating between an old-German conservative and an imperialist interpretation of the Reich concept, was now eminently suitable for the plans and dreams of world rule, aiming at the break-up of the existing system of states and at new forms of political life and political organization, as eventually presented by Hitler in his table talk of 1941–2. Wherever one searches in the documents of thought, planning and action, which national socialism has left in such bewildering profusion, one encounters everywhere that basic trait which makes it impossible to employ a simple formula to dismiss national-socialist ideology as traditional or revolutionary, counter-revolutionary or modernist, improvised or planned.

In contrast to fascism and national socialism, and to the authoritarian dictatorship theories, but equally in marked contrast to a despised and 'revisionist' 'social democratism', communism always laid claim to a scientifically infallible and, simultaneously, politically closed doctrine. In this lay not only its great strength *vis-à-vis* supporters and sympathizers but also its extremely intolerant and coercive character. Not only the party and the system of government, but the ideology of communism itself is designed in an utterly dictatorially authoritarian manner. One collective magnitude governs all politics and has greater value than the individual: the class, the proletariat. All individuals are subordinated to that collective and merely act as its executive organ.

Basically, therefore, in spite of all its pretensions to a scientific character, communist policies are something mystical, something surpassing the rational capability of the individual, something fully accessible only to the collective and its leadership, to an exclusively informed élite. Their determination, in contrast to fascism, does not primarily depend on irrational categories such as instinct, intuition or genius, although these were not unknown to the Stalin or Mao cults and are part of the Lenin cult to this day. It is the science of history's true progress to socialism and communism, a science mastered by the initiates of the communist élite and to be imparted to the new generation of leaders by indoctrination. Yet Lenin's slogan, 'Take the fortress of science by storm!' does not mean just any, or a pluralist, search for the truth by the individual but the discovery of the *one* genuine truth of Marxism-Leninism. This is occasionally re-interpreted, amended by excisions, in line with changing power relations: from Lenin to Stalin and under his successors, from the Mao era to the post-Mao era, in the programme changes of communist parties especially during the factional struggles of the twenties and subsequently under the banner of 'Eurocommunism' which, in the seventies, even questioned the doctrine of the dictatorship of the proletariat while yet adhering to the 'hegemonism' of the party.[1]

But the real core of its ideological self-understanding presents communism as a political religion with a closed Church and an unassailable dogma, designed to hold the faithful in the grip of an appropriate sense of community. It was the scientific pretension by the political élite to make final decisions on moral and intellectual issues just as much as on man's interests by referring to its historical-philosophical expertise. Since it was familiar with the course of history and its inevitability, in God's place, as it were, no limits were set to that élite's suprapolitical competence: thanks to science it personified *the volonté générale*; alternatives were ruled out by definition, since there was only one true science of Marxism-Leninism.

It is this intellectual and moral totalitarianism, pseudo-scientifically

[1] See Klaus Hornung, *Der faszinierende Irrtum, Karl Marx und die Folgen* (Freiburg/Br., 1978), p. 141ff.

justified and politically enforced, that represents both the strength and the weakness of communist ideology. It was able to bring salvation from doubts in a modern complex world, but it was bound, time and again, to come into conflict with the facts of that complexity. Crises of faith were and still are inevitable, conversion and apostasy sharply confront each other, and the refutation of the ideology itself, its wear and tear and its increasing loss of credibility have repeatedly been diagnosed or forecast.[1]

This ideology, of course, was not only rooted in the Leninist doctrine of revolution, as suggested by those reformers who believe that a return to proper Marxism is possible in a 'socialism with a human face'. Marx himself, in his critique of the Gotha programme of the German Social Democrats (1875), first made the famous observation that during the transitional period from capitalism to communism the state could not be anything other than the dictatorship of the proletariat, without anything being ever said about the duration of that totalitarian rule. Marx's doctrine, alongside his expectation of an irresistible proletarian majority revolution, certainly also contained the idea of an élite-controlled minority revolution in as yet underdeveloped countries – and that was what Leninism could invoke. Admittedly it claimed to be the further development of Marxism 'in the period of imperialism and the proletarian revolution', as Stalin stated canonically in his *Foundations of Leninism*. Whether it is not instead an adaptation of Marxism to Russian conditions has been the great intra-Marxist argument ever since.

Nevertheless it remains a fact that the enormous importance and attraction of Leninism lies in just that dual claim, and that its topical and specific strength as a creed and its worldwide influence are due to that claim – and not only in eastern Europe, as Bender rashly concludes when he equates an ideological crisis there with the disintegration of communism. It is that dual claim of administering Marxism as a canonic doctrine and of presenting its revolutionary realization in the Soviet Union which sustains Leninism to this day. What matters is not outward conflict but the inward relationship of the two claims: that of historical theory and that of revolutionary practice – and their fusion into a single system of political beliefs and action beyond good and evil, answerable only to the recognized progress of history. Marx, the genius philosopher, and Lenin, the genius strategist: that was an ideal combination, the totalitarian version of a religious-ecclesiastical constellation between God and his first prophet.

The dual aspect of the communist ideology, as classic Marxism for the capitalist countries and as a revolutionary doctrine for developing countries, has always ensured a remarkable flexibility of interpretation of history, one which compensated for the rigour of historical determinism. True, no

[1] Thus most recently and optimistically, Peter Bender, who once more proclaimed '*Das Ende des ideologischen Zeitalters* (Berlin, 1981), meaning primarily the decline of the communist ideology.

Marxist revolution ever succeeded in any 'capitalist' country. But the Leninist revolution offered a second model to take its place. Leninism might well be described as an adaptation of Marxism to non-industrialized societies with a predominantly peasant population – and the world was and is full of such societies.

This dual strategy of communism was matched by a dual significance of Marxist teaching. To Lenin and his successors it had the significance of a dogmatic faith and of a religious symbol, the integrating force of a supreme value: ceaseless quotations from Marx, and later from Lenin, and at times from Stalin and Mao, served the scholastically irrefutable confirmation of one's own policies; they were intended to crush the opponents and to confirm the faithful. The extent to which the leaders actually believed in it has always been a controversial question. Belief in an *inevitable* socialist revolution was certainly as deeply rooted as was Hitler's conviction of racial revolutions. Additional to this quasi-religious function of communist faith, which also lends a moral justification to all political decisions, was the role of Marxism as the ultimate philosophy, which had all the ideas for the correct intellectual analysis and lent scientific exactitude and unassailability to all political decisions. Every communist leader followed Lenin's example – and that of the distant Marx in the British Museum Reading Room – in being an eternal student of Marxist literature. Here lies an essential difference from the fascist and national socialist action religions which allowed the books of nationalism and racialism no more than a supportive role and saw the intuitive will of the Führer as the ultimate source of political truth. Hitler's *Mein Kampf* was considered the most widespread book but it was not much read even by adherents; as for Alfred Rosenberg's *Myth*, Hitler himself dismissed it with a shrug.[1]

Not so Lenin's Marxism as the bible of communism. No matter how flexible practice was, it always – if need be by scholastic tricks – had to be intellectually aligned with the pure doctrine, and that was why this had to be mastered 'scientifically'. The didactic character of communism, just as much as its intellectual pretensions, was apt and bound to bring faith, science and politics into unfailing harmony. If the leaders were continuous students of Marxism-Leninism, then surely students of Marxism might regard themselves as the most apt leaders of communism: Plato's dream of the philosopher-kings finally come true. It was a powerful and enduring source of attraction for intellectuals that knowledge of the books and the ceaseless study of them had an overriding importance in communism as in no other ideology. The same was true of the central claim to the 'unity of theory and practice', whereby theory was taken entirely seriously and continually displayed.

Naturally enough, the inner conflict between western Marxism and Soviet

[1] See my chapter on 'Nationalsozialistische Weltanschauung' in *Stufen der Machtergreifung*, op. cit., p. 362ff.

communism has never come to rest in the theory and practice of Leninism itself. This became obvious during the first major course-settings following the seizure of power in Russia. There was, above all, the question of world revolution or socialism in a single country; this has remained controversial to this day. Could Stalin and his successors, or maybe even Lenin, have given up the concept of world revolution and with it the revolutionization of the west and instead assigned priority to dictatorship in an underdeveloped Russia and its spread to underdeveloped colonial countries, thereby abandoning the Marxist doctrine of the priority of socialist revolution in the industrialized countries?[1] Be that as it may: the practice of communism did not match up to the rigidly held primacy of theory either in the early days or since. But the great falls from grace of communist policy, the most striking being the 1939–41 pact with Hitler, could always be explained and belittled as temporizing tactics along a historically correct road, so long as one clung to the basic substance, belief in the inevitability of the socialist revolution and the superior knowledge of the élite. And that faith was ultimately strengthened afresh and confirmed by victory over Hitler and the worldwide expansion of communism since 1945.

Some thorns of doubt nevertheless remained in the flesh of theory. First, the stagnation of revolutionary development on the western parade ground of Marxist theory: the non-occurrence of the great turn from capitalism to socialism; second, the difficulties of explaining fascism and national socialism as mass movements; third, the unexpected survival and astonishing rebirth of liberal democracy after 1945; and finally, the attraction of bourgeois values (declared dead) and the strength of social-democratic alternatives to communism; only in France and Italy have these left communism any revolutionary roots, and their influence has even radiated into a coercively-managed eastern Europe. However, the great challenges to present-day communism and its great weaknesses should not lead one to the erroneous conclusion that it has abandoned its historical-theological consistency or lost the strength of its ideological faith for good. Whatever improvisations and adaptations the theory of communism may have undergone, they were always on the basis of Marxist philosophy and thereby met the first demand of a political religion: to supply scientific revelation, truth and a political explanation of the world at the same time. The writings of Marx, Engels and Lenin provided an inexhaustible reservoir which might be drawn upon whenever practice fell short of expectations. They reinforced the believers and provided a theoretical explanation and justification for any new start, simply because they never provided precise dates or substance for the believers' expectations of the future (and these alone matter in a political religion, not the questionable means to an end) but instead kept ultimate communism as a secret for the initiates alone.

Lenin's theories on the party and the state, his voluminous arguments

[1] See now the thesis of P. Melograni, p. 61, footnote 1 above.

with other exponents and currents of Marxism, his grasp of dialectical materialism, of history as a sequence of social revolutions and of the final revolution of the proletariat all have to be seen in this light. World revolution came to mean not merely or primarily the overthrow of economic capitalism but, far more comprehensively, the overthrow of its politically generalized and abhorred consequences throughout the world – the overthrow not only of imperialism but also, in the broadest sense, of any non-communist form of government. This made it possible – vaguely perhaps but convincingly – to deny any conflict between revolution in one country and world revolution; Lenin's theory of imperialism was to prove particularly effective during the de-colonization phase, even though his rival Trotsky's theory of permanent revolution remained relevant and useful whenever perpetuation of dictatorship was required.

As for the actual political system itself, what mattered now was no longer the classic 'bourgeois' issues of majority government and checks and balances, of the separation of powers, or individual freedom, but the primacy of revolution and the aptitude of the political rulers to execute it.[1] Democracy and dictatorship of the proletariat were identified with each other in the revolution and subsequently under the system of government itself. Concentration of power and 'democratic centralism' as the authoritarian organizational principle of party and state ranked above any liberal objection: the end hallows the means, and it does so absolutely. To be sure, it took the power of the Soviet Union and the totalitarian dimension of dictatorship to turn communism from an attractive doctrine into a worldwide political power. Its strength lies in the interaction of political power and political creed, and its inhumanity is equally contained in their equation and fusion. The totalitarian chiliastic ideologies represent both the highest peak and the deepest humiliation of the western idea of progress.

---

[1] On the primarily anti-liberal, anti-bourgeois thrust of communism and national socialism and on their intellectual attraction amidst the 'anti-bourgeois wave' of the years between the wars, see K. D. Bracher, *Geschichte und Gewalt*, p. 151ff.

5. FORMS OF CRISIS THOUGHT

The great disillusionments of the post-war years sent up two different shoots: defiant revolt against the new reality and an increased return of pessimism. All reflection on culture and politics was now aware of the immediate proximity of disaster; it was no longer foreboding but experience. At the same time, however, it was profoundly marked by an ideologization which the thoughts and ideas of the turn of the century had meanwhile undergone in such a specific and distorting manner, differing from country to country, but everywhere as a further jolt to rational progressivist thought. This did not rule out some form of ideological progressivism, such as that put forward mainly by communist propaganda from the new Soviet Union, the 'fatherland of all working people', a last hope to many basically pessimistic intellectuals, who had rebelled against the bourgeois restoration of Europe in the cultural upheavals of the 'roaring twenties', to the dictatorial reality of which they shut their eyes for a long time or indeed (as subsequently Bertolt Brecht) permanently.[1]

Added to this was the disappointment of the expectations that had been placed in a new peace system, in Wilson's 'open diplomacy' and in a supranational League of Nations instead of old-style power politics. Profound scepsis concerning all liberal-democratic progressivist thought once again seemed to be justified. Many intellectuals now viewed the period since 1914, which they had once extolled, as a failure of politics. Yet the 'No more war' of the post-war era soon proved an equally illusory phase: it finally weakened society's defences against the great revisionists who, with old and new philosophies of violence, were using their struggle against the outcome of the war for reactionary and revolutionary challenges to 'bourgeois-capitalist' or 'plutocratic' democracy, the alleged culprit of post-war misery, and for a new ideological mobilization of the discontented 'masses'. There is no doubt that this pessimism and pacifism unwittingly benefited Hitler's advance in Europe, when he presented himself as the last alternative to the

---

[1] On the phenomenon of the pro-Bolshevik enchantment of the 'fellow travellers' see David Caute, *The Fellow Travellers* (1972), *Communism and the French Intellectuals, 1914–1960* (London, 1964), and *The Left in Europe since 1789* (London, 1966); Neal Wood, *Communism and the British Intellectuals* (London, 1959); and the accounts of the disillusioned in Richard H. S. Crossman (ed.), *The God that Failed* (1949).

'decline of the west', both against Bolshevism with its dictatorship and against the 'decadent' west with its democracy.

Renewed doubts on the fundamental tenets about the practical viability of liberal democracy were not dispelled even by social democratic theoreticians. The state of democratic socialism after its wartime and post-war divisions was marked by deep-going insecurity. In Germany it fluctuated typically between a Marxism whose theory still governed its programmes and a somewhat reluctant co-operation with the bourgeois parties,[1] between the decisively anti-Marxist anti-fascism of the younger generation (Hermann Heller, Julius Leber, Kurt Schumacher, Carlo Mierendorff, Adolf Reichwein) and a leaning towards an authoritarian concept of the state (Hendrik de Man, August Winnig).[2] This in-between position became more than obvious in the fatal development of the Weimar Republic which, in the end, found no one ready to defend it – largely because political value concepts had more or less dissociated themselves from the Republic, not only among the radical but also among the democratic parties. The 'spirit of Weimar' found itself, thanks also to the vacillating behaviour of its adherents, in the vacuum of a value-neutral attitude, of toleration instead of defence of the Republic.[3]

An early illustration had been the failure of the Italian socialists between 1919 and 1922, when, being unable to make up their minds whether to support the existing 'bourgeois' state or fight it as revolutionaries, they thereby left a clear field for Mussolini.[4] Faced with unfulfilled expectations

[1] Of significance is the enduring influence of Rudolf Hilferding's Marxist analysis (*Das Finanzkapital*, 1910) in spite of Hilferding's own reformist policies as Reich Finance Minister in 1923 and 1928–9. On the dilemma of the S P D see the contemporary analyses by R. Michels, *Zur Soziologie*, op. cit., pp. 43ff., 215ff.; and Sigmund Neumann, *Parteien,* op. cit., p. 28ff.; now also the special studies by Susanne Miller, *Die Bürde der Macht, Die deutsche Sozialdemokratie 1918–1920* (Düsseldorf, 1978); and Heinrich Potthoff, *Gewerkschaften und Politik zwischen Revolution und Inflation* (Düsseldorf, 1978); on the further development see especially Hagen Schulze, *Otto Braun oder Preussens demokratische Sendung* (Frankfurt-Berlin-Vienna, 1977).

[2] A typical instance is the critique of the S P D, following its end, written in Nazi detention by Julius Leber, 'Gedanken zum Verbot der deutschen Sozialdemokratie Juni 1933'. See also Hermann Heller, *Europa und der Fascismus* (Berlin-Leipzig, 1929); *Rechtsstaat oder Diktatur* (Tübingen, 1930); *Sozialismus und Nation* (Berlin, 1931). On Adolf Reichwein, Theo Haubach, Carlo Mierendorff *et al.*, see Annedore Leber, W. Brandt, K. D. Bracher (eds), *Das Gewissen steht auf* (Berlin, 1954), pp. 60ff., 211ff. Winnig's road from social democracy to national socialism is reflected in his writings: *Vom Proletariat zum Arbeitertum* (Hamburg, 1930); *Der Arbeiter im Dritten Reich* (Berlin, 1934); *Aus zwanzig Jahren, 1925 bis 1945* (Hamburg, 1951).

[3] The argument about the first German Republic's excessive tolerance and weak resistance has now acquired renewed topicality with the challenge to the principle of a democracy ready to defend itself, a principle proclaimed shortly after 1933 by clear-sighted contemporaries such as Karl Loewenstein and Karl Mannheim (see below, p. 231ff.), and on the need for which, as a guarantee of freedom, there was extensive consensus at least after 1945; see Eckhard Jesse, *Streitbare Demokratie* (Berlin, 1980) and *Die Demokratie der Bundesrepublik Deutschland* (Berlin, 1978), p. 20ff.

[4] See A. Lyttelton, op. cit., p. 37ff.; most instructive also in (moderate communist) retrospect is Giorgio Amendola, *Der Antifaschismus in Italien, Ein Interview (von Piero Melograni)* (Stuttgart, 1977), p. 36ff.

of revolution, the guilty conscience and shattered confidence of the European socialists reflected their position between bourgeoisie and communism. In spite of their key position, especially in Britain and Scandinavia, their 'reformist' thought earned itself contempt or disregard in the political theories and intellectual controversies of the post-war period. Instead the confrontation of fascism against communism, as supposedly the only pair of alternatives, eventually gained the intellectual following which liberalism, democracy and even socialism were losing. And faced with this 'alternative' a great many conservatives gave their sympathies and support to the anti-Bolshevism of the radical Right wing, thereby lending it respectability.[1]

Equally important, however, was the fact that, for the first time since the war, a growing number of intellectuals were finding themselves face to face with the real possibilities and limitations of politics; their often Utopian designs and aspirations had been hardly compatible with political reality, which in their eyes spoke against politics.[2] After all, it was not a new age of well-planned peace that had sprung from the war as the main driving-force of practical politics but heightened nationalist fears and passions. The more bitter were the disappointment, the protests and the self-accusations in the face of the failures of what few starts had been made to an international peace policy, now playing only a pitiful role in negotiations in Paris and Geneva in the League of Nations; the USA, having decided the war and heard its President Wilson promise the great peace, had once more withdrawn from Europe and handed it over to the *Realpolitik* of states and parties, no matter how distasteful that was to idealists. Even the short-lived spring of a Franco-German policy of understanding under Briand and Stresemann failed, in the late twenties, to spark off many intellectual

[1] The way this polarization to the extremist formula 'communism or fascism' about 1930 effected the conversion of a liberal intellectual and journalist to communism is impressively described by Arthur Koestler, *Arrow in the Blue* (London, 1952), p. 221ff., with significant headings for the process: 'Liberal Götterdämmerung', 'The Psychology of Conversion', 'Rebellion and Faith'.

[2] One illustration was the massive participation of intellectuals in the council movement, especially the experiment of the Munich Republic of Councils of 1919; see Ernst Toller, *Eine Jugend in Deutschland*, 2nd ed. (Amsterdam, 1936), p. 144f., also dramatized in Toller's *Masse Mensch, Ein Stück aus der sozialen Revolution des 20.Jahrhunderts* (Potsdam, 1921); Ernst Niekisch, *Gewagtes Leben, Erinnerungen eines deutschen Revolutionärs*, Vol. 1 (Cologne, 1974), p. 65f.; Erich Mühsam, *Von Eisner bis Leviné* (Berlin, 1929), p. 42f.; Rosa Leviné, *Aus der Münchner Rätezeit* (Berlin, 1925), p. 12ff.; Martin Buber (ed.), *Gustav Landauer, sein Leben in Briefen* (Frankfurt/M., 1929), Vol. 2, p. 413f.: 'I am now Commissar for Public Enlightenment, Education, Science, the Arts and some more. If I am allowed a few weeks I hope to achieve something; but quite possibly it will only be a few days, and then the dream will be over.' (Picture postcard with his own portrait to his friend Fritz Mauthner, 17 April 1919.) A 'happy, irresponsible government of coffee-house anarchists' – Robert G. L. Waite, *Vanguard of Nazism* (Cambridge/Mass., 1952), p. 82ff. On this also Allan Mitchell, *Revolution in Bavaria 1918–1919* (Princeton, 1965), p. 304ff.; Walter H. Sokel, *The Writer in extremis, Expressionism in Twentieth Century German Literature* (Stanford, 1959), p. 196ff.

impulses; what few there were were presently trampled on by the jackboots of the dictators and by Hitler's 'New European Order'.[1]

The disappointed hopes of the political progressivists on the one hand seemed merely to confirm the gloomy pessimism of the decadence and crisis thinkers on the other. It was a tense interplay of spiritual emotions and expectations which were fixed upon new political decisions but had, since the shattering experience of the war, lost their academic innocence and were now headed for frightful realizations. The storm of political ideas which had broken over Europe in 1914 and over Russia in 1917, which in 1918 had swept away the monarchies of Austria-Hungary and Germany, continued to rage in central and eastern Europe. In Italy fascism was the answer, in most of the new democracies it was an authoritarian regime, while in Germany and in Austria radical criticism of democracy paralysed all political life. It counterposed the wrestling for 'the decision', a decisionism which saw the essence of politics in just this friend-foe relationship and which called for 'crisis-inspired thought', contrary to the idea of parliamentary democracy.[2]

Yet this was more than just an Italian and later a German special case. Certainly the consistency with which Hitler eventually steered crisis thought into an ideologically based policy of rule and annihilation under the German banner was unique: the way he – a century after Heinrich Heine's gloomy forebodings – made totalitarian action succeed the ideological thunder of ideas. Yet this process would have been inconceivable without the loss of faith in reason or without the vacuum of moral values, or without Europe's alternate immersion in intellectual Utopias and pessimism. Although the post-war intelligentsia, labelled the 'lost generation', was capable of quite extraordinary efforts and achievements, the philosophical-theological and literary renaissance of the twenties was like dancing on a volcano. Belief in progress and civilization was shattered, and the search for a substitute all too often resulted in the *sacrificium intellectus* of violent ideological solutions or in an apolitical contempt for real problems, in aloofness, despair or cynicism.

Most of the writers of the period, from James Joyce, André Gide, Ernest Hemingway and T. S. Eliot to D. H. Lawrence and Knut Hamsun, and indeed to the 'critical theory' of the Frankfurt School, found themselves in this oppositional attitude to western civilization – not to mention the intensified anti-western tradition of cultural pessimism and 'illiberalism',

[1] See Walter Lipgens, 'Europäische Einigungsidee 1923–1930 und Briands Europaplan im Urteil der deutschen Akten', *Historische Zeitschrift* 203 (1966), pp. 46ff., 316ff.; recently also Klaus Schumann, 'Von der europäischen Idee zur europäischen Wirklichkeit: Aristide Briand', in Thomas Jansen, Dieter Mahnke (eds), *Persönlichkeiten der europäischen Integration* (Bonn, 1981), pp. 71ff., 88ff. Also, critically on the overrating of the European component of Stresemann, Werner Weidenfeld, 'Nationales Interesse und internationale Verständigung: Gustav Stresemann', ibid., p. 289ff.

[2] See especially Christian Graf von Krockow, *Die Entscheidung, Eine Untersuchung über Ernst Jünger, Carl Schmitt, Martin Heidegger*, (Stuttgart 1958).

and of 'conservative revolution' in German wartime and post-war literature against the Republic.[1] True, there were, by way of contrast, such positive demonstrative instances as Thomas Mann's turning towards democracy. However, the strictly stylized and heroic war literature of the anti-democratic Right wing was opposed by an equally sharp left-wing critique of the Republic from Erich Maria Remarque's *All Quiet on the Western Front* to the literary journalism of Kurt Tucholsky and Carl von Ossietzky. Like any other self-fulfilling prophecy the assertion (made with the benefit of hindsight) that intellectuals had foreseen the course of events prior to and after 1933 a lot more clearly than professional politicians need not be taken too seriously.[2] Their merciless exposure of the shortcomings of the Republic, though democratically intended, was not apt to bolster confidence or to narrow the gap between the idea of a special German situation and western civilization, any more than did the general pessimism in European literature and philosophy.[3]

Thus, even before, and alongside with, political expulsion by the dictators, there were the literary exiles who, like D. H. Lawrence, James

[1] See the concepts in Fritz Stern, op. cit., and Armin Mohler, op. cit.; also the presentations by Peter Gay (Weimar Culture) and Walter Laqueur (Weimar) as well as my examination of the anti-bourgeois thrust of intellectual critique in *Geschichte und Gewalt*, op. cit., p. 166ff. In Laqueur (p. 263) we read on the final phase of the Republic: 'Given the paralysis of social democracy and the suicidal policy of the communists the Weimar intelligentsia found themselves by and large outside any party framework. Yet, their comments on current political problems do not reveal a greater astuteness than those made by the spokesmen of the parties, and this although the intellectuals kept silent not from a mistaken feeling of responsibility and loyalty (like the Social Democrats) nor because they were gagged by Comintern instructions (like the KPD). (English ed., 1974.)

[2] Thus also the great critic of Weimar culture Alfred Kerr in his exile diaries, and with him a good part of literature on the 'golden' twenties. On the political significance of left-wing literature in and towards the Republic see, in addition to W. Laqueur and K. D. Bracher (previous note), especially George L. Mosse, 'Left Wing Intellectuals in the Weimar Republic', in *Germans and Jews*, op. cit., p. 177ff.; Istvan Deak, *Weimar Germany's Left Wing Intellectuals* (Berkeley-Los Angeles, 1968), particularly on the periodical *'Weltbühne'*; the formulation of this latter title by O. E. Schüddekopf, op. cit., first in Kurt Hiller, 'Linke Leute von rechts', *Weltbühne* 28–31 (2 August 1932). On the concept of the intellectual especially also Joseph A. Schumpeter, 'The Sociology of Intellectuals', in G. B. de Huszar (ed.), *The Intellectuals* (Glencoe/Ill., 1960); on misuse comprehensively and copiously Dietz Bering, *Die Intellektuellen, Geschichte eines Schimpfwortes* (Stuttgart, 1978), especially under totalitarian dictators like Hitler: 'I don't want any intellectuals' (see J. Fest, *Gesicht des Dritten Reiches*, op. cit., p. 338ff.) or Lenin: 'The intellectuals must always be gripped with an iron fist' (in D. Bering, op. cit. p. 1).

[3] On the strength of a separate German consciousness especially in historiography see Bernd Faulenbach, *Ideologie*, op. cit., p. 293ff.; Rudolf Vierhaus, 'Die Ideologie eines deutschen Weges der politischen und sozialen Entwicklung', in Rudolf von Thadden (ed.), *Die Krise des Liberalismus zwischen den Weltkriegen* (Göttingen, 1978), p. 96ff., also the instructive contributions by S. N. Eisenstadt ('Europäische Tradition und die Krise des europäischen Liberalismus'), Yehoshua Arieli ('Deutsche Geschichtsschreibung und die liberale Tradition'), and Werner Jochmann ('Der deutsche Liberalismus und seine Herausforderung durch den Nationalsozialismus').

Joyce and Ezra Pound, escaped from their own civilizations to distant countries or more ancient cultures. And even a liberal progressivist optimist such as H. G. Wells, who had once declared the world 'safe for democracy' and had seen the 1914 war as having put an end to all wars, now believed that European civilization was rapidly declining.[1] The consciousness of decadence could result in grand literary visions such as T. S. Eliot's, or in a flight into ideologies: for Pound to fascism, for Gide to communism. No doubt these were essentially unpolitical identifications in the expectation of alternative movements promising a charismatic, pseudo-religious, creative rejuvenation of the old Europe but which in fact brought anything but a free flowering, and indeed new disillusionment. It was the ideological 'God that failed' – mostly of course the communist one, towards whom, from the thirties to the fifties, continual crowds of intellectuals turned and again turned away from.

Another road attempting a trans-political mastery of the crisis led by way of new theological and philosophical gods. Here too, especially in the Germany of the Weimar Republic, major and far-reaching spiritual advances were made, but these again produced, if anything, negative political effects by further complicating an already disturbed awareness of reality and by leading to further extremes in thought. A comparative survey of the German scene must highlight in particular the representatives of dialectical theology (Karl Barth), of personalism (Martin Buber) and religious socialism (Paul Tillich), of neo-Marxism (Georg Lukács, Karl Korsch) and of decisionism (Ernst Jünger, Carl Schmitt).[2] Most significant of all was the development of existential philosophy (first adumbrated by Kierkegaard) through Martin Heidegger and Karl Jaspers, and its subsequent political reshaping by Jean-Paul Sartre. Radical reduction of human questionings to the individual and his lonely existence, to a pre-rational being, to *angst*, to 'being dropped' into time and the abysmal depths of history could lead to very divergent political answers: to philosophical-rational renewal and endorsement of liberal democracy as the exponent and expression of human freedom, as in Jaspers; to irrational delusion regarding the 'explosion' of a national socialist spirit of power and of the age, when the 'lonely towering individual' would emerge as the leader – albeit temporarily, as in Heidegger; or to a variety of individualist variants of Marxist cultural

[1] See W. W. Wagar, *H. G. Wells and the World State* (1961). On the following see p. 130, footnote 1. The most important crystallization point of intellectual left-turns in the thirties were the illusions of a 'Popular Front' policy not only in France and in the face of the Spanish Civil War but also with European consequences, especially on emigrés. Ten different countries are treated in the symposium 'Popular Fronts', *Journal of Contemporary History* 5/3 (London, 1970).

[2] Fundamental now is Alexander Schwan, 'Zeitgenössische Philosophie und Theologie in ihrem Verhältnis zur Weimarer Republik', in *Weimar, Selbstpreisgabe einer Demokratie* (Düsseldorf, 1980), p. 259ff.

and social criticism, as in Sartre before and after 1945.[1]

In theological argument about the consequences of the secularization of Christianity and about the recapture of solid faith the critique of liberal rationalization of religious thought led to the Catholic renewal movement of neo-Thomism (Jacques Maritain) and to a return to a Protestantism concentrated upon the fundamentals of being a Christian (Karl Barth). In the place of a lost belief in progress and its humanist ethic, which had allegedly been shallowly optimistic and unable to stand up to the great wartime and post-war tests, crisis theology, notably that of Karl Barth, endeavoured to find an answer to the eschatological questions and needs of the day.[2] Instead of an historicizing and relativizing theology with its liberal accommodation and its idealistic or even national features it demanded the direct step into an existential confrontation with the Christ of a world crisis (in antiquity and the present) and with the apocalyptic aspect of Christianity. Instead of a betrayed trust in human nature it called for a pessimistic confrontation with the tragedy of a world which had turned away from God: held out into nothingness (as Heidegger formulated it), but now prevented from falling into nihilism by an existentialism understood in a *Christian* sense. Barth also in consequence (unlike Heidegger and also many of his formerly liberal theologian colleagues) resisted the enticements of national socialism and revised his extreme anti-political position, while younger crisis theologians went as far as deliberately choosing political resistance, for which, like Dietrich Bonhoeffer, they were to suffer the deadly vengeance of pseudo-religious national socialist totalitarianism.[3]

Barth's theology first emerged in 1919, in the year of immediate post-war disenchantments. His challenge was to the equation – widespread among the

[1] See Alexander Schwan, *Politische Philosophie im Denken Heideggers* (Cologne-Opladen, 1965), p. 95ff.: 'The approval which Heidegger, principally in his Rectoral Address of May 1933, accorded to the national socialist seizure of power, and by which he committed the university, arises logically from the basic elements of his thought at that time. Heidegger saw in the seizure of power the sudden historic eruption of the "splendour" and "greatness" of a historic "new beginning", of a new movement of epoch-making state-shaping that would leave the past behind it and transform it.' See also Philip Thody, *Jean-Paul Sartre, A Literary and Political Study* (London, 1960); Thomas Molnar, *Sartre, Ideologe unserer Zeit* (Munich-Vienna, 1970); and on the further development, D. G. Copper, R. D. Laing (eds), *Reason and Violence, A Decade of Sartre's Philosophy 1950–1960* (Paris and London 1971); also Wilfried Desan, *The Marxism of Jean-Paul Sartre* (New York, 1965); Rudolf Wendorff, *Zeit und Kultur* (Opladen, 1980), p. 470ff.

[2] In his commentary on the Epistle to the Romans (1919, revised 1921), p. 410ff., Karl Barth, with considerable self-assessment, announced the new dialectical theology as the 'great upheaval' to liberal ethic and democratic politics. See A. Schwan, *Zeitgenössische Philosophie*, op. cit., p. 262ff.

[3] Comprehensively, Eberhard Bethge, *Dietrich Bonhoeffer* (Munich, 1967) on the attitude to K. Barth see p. 101ff.; on Barth's position to Resistance and democracy see especially *Rechtfertigung und Recht* (Zollikon-Zurich, 1938), p. 42ff. The criticized background for the new start is outlined in Barth's work *Die protestantische Theologie im 19.Jahrhundert* (Zurich, 1947).

educated bourgeoisie – of civilizational and Christian progress. However, in his attack on the Christian tradition in its fundamental significance to the modern concept of progress as a secularized, moralized version of the doctrine that history is continuous divine action with humans, he simultaneously struck at political liberalism, at modern democracy, at western civilization, all of which were based on belief in man's rational capacity for understanding and decision-making. Barth's critique, put in an extreme form, meant 'a levelling of all political yardsticks and criteria on the grounds of a fundamental condemnation of their self-assessment'.[1]

Crisis theology, therefore, merely deepened the crisis which it tried to solve. Herein lay its confounded ambivalence, one which it shared with crisis philosophy and with critical social theory, with neo-Marxism and also with the sharp critique of democracy by disenchanted 'progressive' intellectuals. The clear-cut separation of world and God, which it counterposed to both the Christian and the Hegelian belief in progress, the 'clear distance of theology from politics',[2] tended to widen the vacuum of political ties and values unless there was a readiness to perform the great leap across that divide. Otherwise the philosophical-theological crisis theories merely increased the danger that the dilemma of an imperfect human being in an increasingly perfected society would be a temptation to take the great leap into pseudo-religious ideologies.

The political label of such doctrines, which might lead even to 'sheer irrationality' in the *Political Ethic* (1932) of Friedrich Gogarten, the Lutheran co-founder of dialectical theology (1887–1967)[3] and to the authoritarian-totalitarian Nazi state, continues to be uncertain: they contain both liberating and hardening, emancipating and enslaving, modernizing and orthodox reactionary elements. In conjunction with the period's laments of decline they represented a powerful challenge, both renewing and dividing theology and the Church before the great seductions of national socialist political religion swept over them.

Even before the First World War a number of authors had claimed for themselves the scientific refutation of belief in progress. Now, under the direct impact of war and self-destruction, the title and theses of Oswald Spengler's book produced a particularly persuasive effect. His ideas of a cyclical rise and fall of all cultures admittedly acquired an anti-scientific aspect by his emphatically 'intuitive' method and the inadequate empirical coverage of his vast subject, as well as by his symbolist style and the equating of civilization with nature; this led to opposition among historians and other

---

[1] Thus A. Schwan, op. cit., p. 264. On the political context see also R. J. Zwi Werblowsky, 'Die Krise der liberalen Theologie', in *Die Krise des Liberalismus*, op. cit., p. 147ff.; Hans-Georg Geyer, 'Die dialektische Theologie und die Krise des Liberalismus', ibid., p. 155ff.

[2] Ibid., p. 263ff. Barth did not take much part in the exciting debates with Marxism and communism: see Richard Banks, 'Christianity and Marxism', op. cit., p. 319f.

[3] Schwan, op. cit., p. 266.

specialists. *The Decline* was seen as a primarily political book: herein lay both the opportunities and the limitations of its controversial effect.[1]

Not so the other great work whose first volume appeared one and a half decades later (1934): Arnold Toynbee's encyclopaedic *Study of History*. This gigantic work also arose from the experience of the First World War, though its twelve volumes were only completed after the Second World War which had once more, in the most frightful manner, confirmed the questioning of progress. Toynbee claimed to provide a comprehensive comparative analysis of all known civilizations, though he too met with only divided scholarly approval. Yet his work was impressive for its exceptionally rich substance and effective by its striking (if not entirely new) fundamental thesis whereby origin, rise, flowering, decay and death of cultures is determined mainly by the ratio of 'challenge' and 'response'. As for the present and future of western civilization, Toynbee unlike Spengler, while convinced of its deep crisis, did not believe in its final decline. This English-western nuance, connected with Toynbee's esteem for western-Christian values (whereas Spengler emphasized the anti-western and caesaristic elements of development) was stressed even further by Toynbee at the end of his work in view of western Europe's unexpected recovery after 1945 and the worldwide extension of western forms of civilization.

For the period between the wars, however, this comprehensive philosophy of history represented a further challenge to historical progressivist thought. Coming as it did from a victorious country of the west, applying the classic scientific methods of universal history in contrast to Spengler's visionary and intuitive style, and imbued with deep spiritual and religious convictions, it provided a highly learned confirmation of crisis moods among a non-scientific public. Although no certain decline was being predicted, the sickness of present civilization was identified. Yet the warning reference to the decline of other cultures was bracketed with a glimpse of a possible termination of the cyclical up-and-down of past history in a world civilization. It was the ambivalence of progress and crisis, with the possibility of breaking the cycle, with the prospect of a worldwide order with new spiritual and moral dimensions, which was the goal of Toynbee's philosophy of history. For the thirties, on the other hand, it belonged to the realm of crisis thought, no matter how inexact or novel Toynbee's 'laws' in their rather vague generalizations might appear to historians and social scientists. As in Spengler's case before him, the methodological and comparative-culture discussions produced exciting effects for decades to come and, as a political counterpart to the German writer's conservative-revolutionary

---

[1] See especially Horst Möller, op. cit., p. 49ff.; H. Stuart Hughes, *Oswald Spengler, A Critical Estimate*, 2nd ed. (London, 1962). Reference to contemporary civilization-critical theories: Karin E. Eckermann, Oswald Spengler und die moderne Kulturkritik, doct. thesis (Bonn, 1980), p. 182ff. On topicality and relation to contemporary 'decline' literature see also Northrop Frye, 'The Decline of the West', *Daedalus* 103, No. 1 (Winter, 1974), p. 1ff.

cultural pessimism, the liberal-Christian universalism of the Englishman embodied the potential and the limits of a historical crisis theory amidst the political-ideological clashes of the era of the world wars.[1]

Toynbee's background, of course, was a situation in the west which Spengler could not know and which he only partially surmised: the great confrontation of communism, national socialism and democracy in the face of a specific threat to civilization, and not just the intellectual debates and social constructs of the turn of the century which had been Spengler's principal inspiration. True, Spengler's *Years of Decision* (1933) came right up to the threshold of the thirties, and the prophet of decline, wooed though he was as an anti-democrat, resolutely refused to be identified with national socialism. Yet Spengler remained rooted in the problems of the immediate pre-war and post-war periods, while Toynbee was able to turn his gaze to the more distant consequences of the great conflicts of powers and ideologies, to the real global decisions of the Second World War and its aftermath (with which his subsequent writings were then concerned). Questionable though their claim to scholarship may be, their very subjective character made these two great philosophies of history touch upon the same fears and confusions about progress and decay which were heralded in the coming of the First and then the Second World War.

These historical diagnoses, including Toynbee's, have been aptly described as a 'vast prose poem lamenting the sickness of a civilization'.[2] By being just that and by a seeming conformity with a natural law, which lent them the appearance of science, they confirmed a mood that was then in the air, which engaged all literature and which erupted at the point of rapid further modernization and technicalization of material culture and society. Technological 'progress', of course, had not stopped either before or after the war, no matter how emphatically one might wish to assess the war (rationally) as a barbarian relapse or (irrationally) as a heroic experience. Discrepancies between an accelerated advance of science and technology during and after the war, together with their social and political applications on the one hand and the cultural, economic and moral-political consequences of crisis on the other, deepened further. The great worldwide recession after 1929 further highlighted the glaring conflict between progressivist and catastrophic thought; the interpeters of decadence, along

---

[1] Toynbee's development from the twenties to the forties is readily reflected in his articles, at different times and on different subjects, in *Civilization on Trial* (New York and Oxford, 1948); also *The Future of the West* (Munich, 1964; lectures of 1961). See Joseph Vogt, *Wege zum historischen Universum* (Stuttgart, 1961), p. 98ff., especially p. 111ff. (on Spengler, p. 51ff.). In his unpublished BA thesis 'The Meaning of History: Reflections on Spengler, Toynbee, and Kant' (Harvard University, 1950) Henry Kissinger emphasizes in Spengler the inevitability of disintegration and decline, and in Toynbee the pressure of external circumstances as the decisive interpretative pattern. For a comparison now also Northrop Frye (previous footnote), p. 11ff.

[2] Roland N. Stromberg, op. cit., p. 497.

with the Spanish philosopher Ortega y Gasset, were awaiting the *Revolt of the Masses* against European culture, and deploring the impossibility of democracy – as Plato before them had seen it as a disaster – and its levelling of values, the values which science and the intellectuals themselves had so enduringly relativized.[1]

Once more the battle lines intersected: on both the Right and the Left (capitalist or socialist) progressivism emerged in confusing confrontations, as did (conservative or anti-capitalist) crisis slogans. Much the same impression was conveyed by the new humanities, principally sociology and psychology, which, optimistically and pessimistically, with revolutionary and with unsettling discoveries, further deepened the rift which had opened between the helpless individual and an over-powerful society, between material progress and the crisis of culture, between democratization and the élites, between the liberal concept of freedom and toleration and the call for state efficiency and security, for strong men and regimes.

But above all there were the recurrent economic crises. 'Economy is destiny' (Rathenau), said the philosophizing men of industry, and not only the Marxists. But this rapid economic progress itself led, through unpredictable consequences of expansion, to economic mass depressions such as had never before been experienced, and self-assured modern economists now began talking fatalistically about cycles, about ups and downs instead of about onwards and upwards, about inevitable unemployment and indispensable national indebtedness. After much helplessness in the face of the crises of the twenties and the failure of the reparations policy the new theory of 'deficit spending' put forward by John Maynard Keynes (1883–1946) eventually confirmed what strong individuals like Roosevelt (with his New Deal) or ruthless dictators like Hitler (with his boosting of the war economy) had been bold enough to do in the face of classic liberalism.[2]

Yet the most significant new ideas and doctrines were based not on progress but on crisis. Even an expert on the human psyche like Sigmund Freud, unlike some of his progressivist disciples who saw themselves as successful engineers of the soul or as revolutionaries, now proclaimed the rather pessimistic realization that civilization was possible only at the cost of a psychological restriction or inhibition, indeed the neurosis of the individual through the sublimation of his aggression. Freud's *Civilization and its Discontents*, which he diagnosed as the downright inescapable manifestation of a permanent tension between the individual and society, was matched, on the eve of Hitler's seizure of power, by the critique of the

[1] See the shrewd observation illustrated by the Spanish bestseller: Geoffrey Clive, 'Revolt of the Masses, by José Ortega y Gasset', in *Twentieth-Century Classics Revisited* (*Daedalus* 103/1, Winter, 1974), p. 75ff.: it was not any novelty about Ortega's thesis but its specific relevance at a critical moment in European history that produced its great impact.

[2] See the comprehensive collective volume by Seymour E. Harris (ed.), *The New Economics, Keynes' Influence on Theory and Public Policy* (New York, 1950); Lawrence B. Klein, *The Keynesian Revolution*, 2nd ed. (New York, 1963).

philosopher Karl Jaspers whose approach was likewise from the side of psychiatry. In a significant misunderstanding of political structures and power relations, like most intellectuals from the Right or the Left, he presented in *Man in the Modern Age* (1931) a mainly pessimistic critique of culture and deplored the 'rule of the masses'.[1] However, the 'decision' they were all talking about, whether 'socialist' (Tillich 1932–3) or 'total' (Jünger 1931), but either way directed against liberal 'bourgeois' democracy, was not made in the field of sceptical or existentialist cultural critique. The 'socialist decision against the bourgeois principle' and 'for the primeval forces', for an alliance between proletarian and conservative revolution (Tillich), added religious arguments to that declaration of war on pluralist democracy (both bourgeois and social democratic) which had already led to its destruction in Italy, and which in Germany rendered possible the legitimation of the 'total state' with its 'friend-foe' ideology (in Carl Schmitt's 'decisionism') and which eventually drove nearly all of the cultural critics into emigration.[2] The uncertainties and uncanny ideas which technological and scientific progress under the banner of Einstein's theories of relativity and of Heisenberg's indeterminacy principle had introduced also into the belief that the universe was subject to regular laws can hardly have been reflected in a more striking manner than by the English writer Aldous Huxley, himself the grandson of an eminent progressivist scientist. His haunting literary work of the twenties illustrated the relativization and the 'nihilism' of values in the post-war decade, while his anti-Utopian fiction

---

[1] Jaspers's work was published in English in 1933 as *Man in the Modern Age*. See on this, Klaus Piper, Hans Saner (eds), *Erinnerungen an Karl Jaspers* (Munich-Zurich, 1974), *e.g.* pp. 77 and 186; Hans Saner (ed.), *Karl Jaspers in der Diskussion* (Munich-Zurich, 1973); P. A. Schilpp (ed.), *The Philosophy of Karl Jaspers* (London, 1957). See, on the other hand, the very apt critical assessment of Jaspers's work in Alexander Schwan, *Zeitgenössische Philosophie*, op. cit., p. 273ff. Jaspers's work is extensively marked by culturally-pessimistic and politically-critical terms such as technology, apparatus, mass existence, mass rule, mass order, fragmentation, compromise, random decisions, outsmarting, corruption through private interests, accidental leader, a blindly evolving reality. His conclusion is that 'The question of what is left today has to be answered: the *awareness of danger and loss* as an awareness of the radical crisis.'

[2] Paul Tillich, *Die sozialistische Entscheidung* (1933, written in 1932); Ernst Jünger, *Die totale Mobilmachung* (1931); Carl Schmitt, 'Die Wendung zum totalen Staat' (1931), also in *Positionen und Begriffe im Kampf mit Weimar-Genf-Versailles 1923–1939* (Hamburg, 1940). The strange fascination exercised by Carl Schmitt is evident from a vast and still growing secondary literature from all directions: most recently Günter Maschke, 'Im Irrgarten Carl Schmitts', in *Intellektuelle im Bann des Nationalsozialismus* (Hamburg, 1980), p. 204ff. On Jünger especially Hans-Peter Schwarz, *Der konservative Anarchist, Politik und Zeitkritik Ernst Jüngers* (Freiburg, 1962). See also Eduard Heimann, 'Tillich's Doctrine of Religious Socialism', in C. W. Kegley, R. W. Bretall (eds), *The Theology of Paul Tillich* (1961), p. 312ff.; more critically on the shipwrecked illusion of a combination of Marxism and Christianity, Richard Banks, op. cit., *Journal of Contemporary History* 11/2–3 (1976), p. 316f., who sees the significance of the Tillich trend more in a future relaxation of the understanding of Marxism by emphasis on the pre-materialistically prophetic Marx.

Brave New World (1932) portrayed the future of a world that was technologically perfect but drained empty of humanity.[1]

Doubt on ultimate certainties in all spheres of past progress not only undermined belief in progress itself and in its human consequences, long before the great self-threat of nuclear physics and its bomb, but also exacerbated the confrontation between a profound civilizational scepsis and the totalitarian temptations of the political promises of salvation held out by the substitute religions, those totalitarian enticements of the thirties and forties. The notion of a return to nature and instinct was shared by a number of authors critical of civilization; but they also shared a weakness for the combination of romantic and technological faith, as proclaimed by fascism and national socialism, or for the socialist myth of a perfect society to be found in communism.

It was a heightened sensitivity face to face with the social and political conflicts of the age of progress that brought a wealth of outstanding achievements and experiments – the modern age of western culture proper – first to light and then to full flower. The 'golden twenties', however insecure their foundations and however irresponsible their disintegrating effects may have been, seem to this day an inexhaustible source of questions and answers. Renewed contact with its abruptly cut-short flowering and rediscovery of contemporary achievements – even though these may have been too uncritically opposed to a changed present – was yet to contribute to a 'cultural revolution' in the sixties and to a subsequent new loss of bearings of our (western) civilization.[2]

However, the political break of the thirties was no accident. Political thought was in no way adequate to the artistic and literary renaissance; instead it suffered considerable strain as a result of it. The reason was that what was essential about the new spirit and intellect was directed against reason and moderation. It was immoderate in criticism and expectations of society and state. It made excessive demands on the political capabilities of voters on the difficult road towards democracy, which lives by reason and moderation; moreover, it underrated the forces of discontent and the hunger for a faith – both the traditionalist and the revolutionary potential these forces were able to arouse but not to satisfy. The intellectual and his relations with politics were and remained the problem. This too was a replay of the pre-history of the First World War from the turn of the century. The 'golden' age of crisis thought in the twenties was followed by the new 'iron' age which was to demonstrate the great dilemma of ideas and their ideologization, the game of ideas on the brink of civilization, the close proximity of progress and barbarism as a political danger, the great vacuum

---

[1] Especially his books, *Antic Hay* (1923), *Those Barren Leaves* (1925), *Point Counter Point* (1928). A later retrospect is in *Brave New World Revisited* (1958).

[2] On the renaissance of the twenties see p. 206ff. below.

left behind by intellectual neglect of a political value ethic because rational critique and experiment had not gone hand-in-hand with forward-looking or responsible thought.[1]

Hatred of self and misanthropy on the one hand, and cynicism and obsession with Utopias on the other, were a heavy price to pay for the glitter of the new. The intended shock to the bourgeoisie and élitist contempt for the masses were matched by their indifference, mistrust and reciprocal hatred of the new – only to be mobilized, at the moment of great political crisis, by resolute ideologists and dictators. They, too, were acting on behalf of civilizational critique, but over the heads of the intellectuals whom they were hounding into persecution or emigration. That was true mainly of Germany. Yet remoteness from a sense of political responsibility and from public life was a serious drawback of fundamental cultural pessimism generally, in that it forced modernism into an art-for-art's sake attitude or one of distortion of reality, misjudging its political effectiveness.

What swept over Europe now was not just an intellectual 'revolution of nihilism',[2] which drove many into emigration and silenced others, but actually a skilfully fanned revolt of the masses, mobilized by anti-modernist resentments and national-revolutionary ideology, and styled as an alternative to cultural pessimism, even though in fact it sprang from it. Its radical spearpoint, however, was racialism, and more especially anti-Semitism, with which the massive anti-movement now nourished its charges against modern civilization and its disaster. Hitler's struggle against the 'racially inferior' and the Jews, his quasi-scientific-technical annihilation policy against them, whose 'fault it all was', and the frightening, oversimplifying scapegoat ideology of the Third Reich were directed against western civilization as such, with all its contradictions.[3]

Hitler's cultural pessimism, intoxicated with Wagner's and Nietzsche's tragic heroism, translated into reality the ideas with which Gobineau and H. S. Chamberlain, Lagarde and Langbehn had falsified the entire history of racial struggle about the turn of the century. He was the only ideologist who did not just talk about action but who actually implemented his racial policy as a solution to the crisis of civilization, all the way to the 'final solution', as the cold national socialist terminology described the bureaucratic extermination of Jews, Slavs and other enemies. His ultimate failure once

[1] See also James Joll, *Intellectuals in Politics* (London, 1960) and *Europe*, op. cit., p. 300ff.

[2] Thus the former national socialist and acquaintance of Hitler (*Gespräche mit Hitler*, Zurich 1940) Hermann Rauschning: *Revolution des Nihilismus* (Zurich-New York, 1938). The nihilistic interpretation is frequently encountered, though it does not explain much. See also Heidegger's contribution to nihilism, *Der europäische Nihilismus* (Pfullingen, 1967), as an interpretation of Nietzsche.

[3] On the anti-western thrust of national socialism see, clear-sighted at an early date, Aurel Kolnai, *The War against the West* (London, 1938), pp. 106ff., 230ff., 558ff., 672ff. See K. D. Bracher, *German Dictatorship*, op. cit., p. 38ff.

more revealed the abysmal pessimism which the mythical invocation of political 'faith' and 'triumph of the will' by his satellites Goebbels, Hess and Rosenberg had merely glossed over but which nevertheless sprang from the same source as the cultural critique of his contemporaries: from the vacuum of values and from fear of uncertainties, of the complexities, demands and conflicts of modern civilization. The ambivalence of progress and crisis thought revealed, above all, the failure of a self-glorifying progressivism to lend political and moral forms to material progress, forms which would match up to its social consequences. It was here that both the high-flying *avant-garde* and the political system concepts of state jurists and parties failed.[1]

Two major questions of political theory, however, remained. They concerned the attitude of the citizen and the 'masses' between liberal democracy and authoritarian systems, and they were exploited both by the critics of democracy and by the authoritarian ideologists of the Right and Left. First: how could the desired liberal freedoms and the unstable openness of democracy, upon which the intellectual freedom of the intellectuals was based, be combined with the stability and efficiency of the political system that was demanded by 'the people'? And second: to what extent is unlimited intellectual mobility, the questioning of this system, of its society and civilization, actually possible if this stimulates a demand for new values and norms, for a new inner security of the individual amidst the upheavals of ideas and of the existing order, without being able to satisfy it – except by political religions and dictatorial creeds which abolish that freedom? This was the fundamental question about unlimited 'emancipation', a question to which there was no answer that did not lead into deepest scepsis or to new violence. The failure of numerous intellectuals was paralleled by that of the Churches, which reacted with progressively unstable institutions or with a retreat from politics; it was paralleled also by the parties and interest groups which, at most, made half-hearted declarations in favour of pluralist democracy but were unable to contribute greatly

---

[1] The lack of constructive realistic theories opposing the ideologisms of the Left and the Right had its reflection in the helplessness of not only conservative but also liberal and social democratic policies in the face of the enticements of anti-democratism: a kind of 'public poverty' of ideas and a demonization of heroic nihilism. See, for instance, Benedetto Croce's attempt to gain a foothold in historical thought against and between the dominant currents of mathematical-scientific and speculative-determinist thought: *La Storia come Pensiero e come Azione* (1938); also the symposium 'Conflict and Compromise, Socialists and Socialism in the 20th Century', *Journal of Contemporary History* 11/2–3 (London, 1976); and on the German issues Arnold Metzger, 'Das Dämonische im deutschen Denken', in *Dämonie und Transzendenz* (Pfullingen, 1964), p. 156ff. How largely incapable of a constructive-realistic political theory even 'democratically' oriented thinkers like Jaspers, Buber or Tillich were at the time is shown by A. Schwan, *Zeitgenössische Philosophie*, op. cit. p. 273ff. (see p. 163, footnote 1 below).

to the key question of value fixation or the defence of the democratic state.[1]

Thus the great conflict faced by twentieth-century political theory between the two great wars remained unresolved. On the one hand everything had become relative. Even in the much admired natural sciences the old laws seemed to have been undermined; 'the theory of relativity' and 'indeterminacy' had become concepts of symptomatic significance even for humanist scholars and laymen who had come to take their cues in the 'scientific age' from the supposed exactitude and dependability of science, and to identify general progress with ever new discoveries. Certainly this applied to the multiplicity and growing complexity in society and politics, which, following the collapse of the absolute monarchies, now called for pluralist systems. But did this not also imply that political values and their truth were pluralist? Could such pluralism itself be viewed as a supreme value, or was it just a makeshift solution – and hence the appropriate form of democracy? Was it not too much to expect the citizen to accept a value-relative or a value-neutral concept of democracy – as all too many political theoreticians did, only to be surprised at the speed with which such a democracy was dropped the moment a promise of a new absolutism with a binding philosophy appeared on the horizon?[2]

And on the other hand: was it enough to make the relativist assurance that democracy, at any rate, was the least bad political system even if it was not a good one? Memories were still fresh of rigid systems and state doctrines which had certainly regarded themselves as the best, and there was therefore a good deal of attraction in new obligatory value and state systems which promised once more to fill the vacuum of relativist uncertainty. Now that the old orders had failed the need for security and a 'reduction of complexity'[3] demanded new, non-relative, orientations and orders. These would, at the same time, represent alternatives to the much-quoted failure of liberalism and its ability to guarantee rational solutions in the sense of progressivist

[1] Typical is the relativist concept of party and democracy represented even by emphatic democrats like the social democrat and Minister of Justice Gustav Radbruch (1878–1949) in his fundamental study 'Die politischen Parteien im System des deutschen Verfassungsrechts', in *Handbuch des deutschen Staatsrechts*, Vol. 1 (Tübingen, 1930), p. 285ff. Not until after 1945 did Radbruch perform his turn towards a concept of democracy grounded in natural law: Erik Wolf (ed.), *Rechtsphilosophie*, 5th ed. (Stuttgart, 1956). See 'Die Kritik am Parteienstaat', in K. D. Bracher, *Auflösung*, op. cit., p. 34ff. (giving the different theoretical positions). On the overall complex see Wolfram Bauer, *Wertrelativismus und Wertbestimmtheit im Kampf um die Weimarer Republik* (Berlin, 1968), p. 54ff.

[2] On the continuing issue of pluralism see especially Ernst Fraenkel, Kurt Sontheimer, Bernard Crick, *Beiträge zur Theorie und Kritik der pluralistischen Demokratie*, 3rd ed. (Bonn, 1970).

[3] Thus especially Niklas Luhmann, 'Komplexität und Demokratie', *Politische Vierteljahrsschrift* 10 (1969), p. 314ff.; more extensively as 'Soziologie des politischen Systems', *Kölner Zeitschrift für Soziologie und Sozialpsychologie* 20 (1968), p. 705ff. On the problems (then as now) of the growing welfare state and the poverty of political theory alongside it see also his *Politische Theorie im Wohlfahrtsstaat* (Munich-Vienna, 1981), p. 12ff.

thought also to politics and society. Thus the attraction of authoritarian and totalitarian philosophies lay not only in their older nationalist, socialist or even racialist 'substance' but in their coincidence with political crisis thought generally and with the normative vacuum in which they operated. It sprang from the (also political) relativization of liberal rationalism and, simultaneously, was seeking new certainties of being *as such*, of existence *as such*, certainties which were incompatible with the pluralist reality of a modern society 'freed' from past ties, unless their general validity was – dictatorially – enforced.

Crisis thought, in consequence, resulted, at best, in an ambivalent, critically aloof or half-hearted, and certainly rather negative, endorsement of pluralist democracy,[1] though it might equally well result in authoritarian thought and in the acceptance of dictatorial solutions[2] – or else in being misused for these. Anti-intellectual though these trends and solutions might be – and anti-intellectualism grew into a massive force not only in Germany – they were very largely the arguments of intellectuals themselves, whose comprehensive critique of civilization and whose discontent with pluralist democracy and its exacting difficulty[3] had, together with the promise of old or new key explanations, made possible the rise of political religions and their work of destruction.

[1] Examples are Barth, Jaspers, and Buber (A. Schwan, op. cit., p. 262ff.).

[2] Examples are Heidegger, Gogarten (Schwan, op. cit., p. 265ff.).

[3] An understanding of the relativity of human existence and order, its openness and contradictoriness, to which that form of democracy alone does any kind of justice, demands a political maturity which is time and again in jeopardy, even though theory today, unlike then, is aware of the illusory nature of perfect Utopias of truth and order. See, for instance, the limitative theories of the modern mathematician Gödel in Douglas Hofstadter, *Gödel, Escher and Bach* (New York, 1980): 'No formal system capable of rigorous distinctions between truth and falsehood can ever be both, consistent and complete.' Democracy is not – but it is capable of distinction and of tolerating opposition. This makes it, simultaneously, irreplaceable and forever threatened.

6. THE STRUGGLE FOR VALUES AND ORIENTATIONS

Just as the nineteenth century had been dominated by the emergence of nations and the demand for national states, so the twentieth century was dominated by the clash between nationalisms and ideologies, between independence for each separate state and new universalisms. Wars and revolutions blurred the battle-lines. These were shifted by the growth crises of scientific and technological progress and by the social consequences of economic expansion; by the extension of the state, by tense waves of democratization and anti-liberal movements; by imperialism and colonial policy, and also by decolonization and neo-colonization. These have been perceptible in North and Latin America since the eighteenth century and have, since the two world wars, given rise to the problems of a 'Third World'. They were all challenges to political thought, touching on the very substance of traditional norms and values.

The struggle for old and new orientations was reflected more in the numerous artistic and literary, philosophical and social-science controversies, than in the great ideologies and their fellow travellers. Their positions had been pre-formed even before the First World War; they exhibited only a limited and passing receptivity to new impulses, such as did Soviet communism to the artistic *avant-garde* until 1925, Italian fascism to futurism in the early twenties, and national socialism to architectural monumentalism. For the rest they resolutely opposed 'bourgeois' or 'degenerate' art, and withdrew into national or 'socialist realism', designed to be 'accessible to the millions', as the Central Committee of the Communist Party of the Soviet Union demanded in 1925.[1]

Inasmuch as the period after the First World War produced a literary renaissance and a new upsurge of philosophical thought, these proved, in the long term, to run against the grain of the ideologically collectivist movements. Of course there was also a lot of vanity and artistic mania,

---

[1] Simultaneously a number of far-reaching decisions set the seal on Stalin's dictatorship: in 1924 Stalin proclaimed the construction of socialism in a single country; all 'factionalism', *i.e.* intra-party democracy, was banned, and Lenin died. (See George Sabine, op. cit., p. 862ff.). For a comparison of 'socialist realisms' see Martin Damus, *Sozialistischer Realismus und Kunst im Nationalsozialismus* (Frankfurt/M., 1981), p. 7ff. (p. 156, footnote 2).

gesturing in a totalitarian manner itself, such as the (significantly self-labelled) Russian 'suprematists' (1914–25). Large-scale experiments with abstract forms in art and (atonal) music, in poetry (Dadaism) and in philosophy (mathematical logic, existentialism) had in fact – in spite of extravagant ideological self-assessment – very little to do with the ideological confrontations of fascism and communism, democratic and nationalist socialism, or messianic revolutionary movements.[1] They were primarily concerned with a new emphasis of individual human 'existence', and with the renewal of a religious fundamentalism after the relativizations of liberal secularization. Simultaneously there was a call for a reality-related 'material value ethic'. With this demand Max Scheler (1875–1928), an aesthetically sensitive, undogmatically flexible philosopher of life, endeavoured, unlike Bergson, to place the problem of objective values at the centre of social thought. Like many others he had been concerned, since the war, with the problem of how unity and community were feasible in a pluralist society, but unlike the pessimist cultural critics of the Right and Left, he was convinced of the existence of lasting value structures in human society; they only needed rediscovering and reasserting. At times close to Catholic social teaching, Scheler thereby raised a fundamental issue of contemporary political thought: the argument was between relativization and dogmatization of values.[2]

Democratic theory suffered most from the 'value neutralism' practised in the interpretation of the constitution. Eminent constitutional lawyers like Hans Kelsen and Gustav Radbruch supported a relativist view, according to which political institutions could be interpreted almost at will. This value neutralism, especially that of its convinced democratic interpreters such as Anschütz and Thoma, surrendered the almost defenceless Weimar Republic to the value-emphatic attack by its right-wing and left-wing opponents. Too late was it realized that a democracy can be overthrown by its own instruments, pseudo-democratically and pseudo-legally, if it leaves the monopoly of value definition to its adversaries. From this realization some critics of the system concluded that value-pluralist democracy now only possessed a formal legality, while losing its essential legitimacy to those

---

[1] Conflicts between the demand for extreme artistic and philosophical freedom and totalitarian-collectivist imposed order was bridged by a pseudo-religious absolutization of the myth of the Revolution. On the delusions of a totalized concept of the revolution see Hannah Arendt, *On Revolution* (London, 1973), p. 215ff. (idea of councils); G. Siebers, *Psychologie der Revolution* (Stuttgart, 1976); Paul Noack, *Die manipulierte Revolution* (Munich, 1978), p. 9ff. Above all, Norman Cohn, *The Pursuit of the Millennium, Revolutionary Messianism in Medieval and Reformation Europe and its Bearing on Modern Totalitarian Movements* (New York, 1961); and recently, James M. Rhodes, *The Hitler Movement, A Modern Millenarian Revolution* (Stanford, 1980).

[2] On Max Scheler see Maurice Dupuy, *La philosophie de Max Scheler*, 2 vols (Paris, 1959); Manfred S. Frings, *Max Scheler* (Pittsburgh, 1965); Ernst Wolfgang Orth et al., *Husserl, Scheler, Heidegger in der Sicht neuer Quellen* (Freiburg/Br., 1978).

who overcame that value neutrality by the proclamation of a political creed. What was not sufficiently realized or appreciated was the fact that the interplay of different political forces in itself represents a high value, a great achievement and a challenge.

The lesson, then learned, that value relativism and value neutrality implied political helplessness, led, after the fall of the Weimar Republic and that of the national socialists to a deliberate value-emphatic constitutional understanding, at least in Germany, even though this is once more being challenged today.[1] A similar vulnerability to that of democracy was shown by the political theories both of liberalism and of social democracy, the latter especially weakened by its theoretically uncommitted intermediate position between Marxism and reformist legalism. Attempts to fill the gap by a neo-Kantian idealism (Leonard Nelson) or by a left-wing Christian socialism (Paul Tillich) never succeeded except in small groups. It was Catholicism, above all, that proved able to counterpose a value-oriented doctrine of society and state[2] to the political value vacuum – which the aggressive salvationist ideologies threatened to fill. In papal encyclicals, in professional and workers' organizations, in its own educational institutions and parties, political Catholicism attempted to resolve the problems of modernization with its own social doctrine, and in so doing achieved a remarkable stability of the Catholic electorate even during the crisis of the Weimar Republic. Admittedly, at the moment of state crisis, when ecclesiastical interests were at stake and compromises were entered into, it was incapable of an unequivocal decision between democratic and authoritarian options. In Italy, Germany and Austria it cleared the road for the latter – regardless of the subsequent importance of its role in the Resistance. Its position above or between the ideologies and political systems did not sufficiently underpin a democratic concept of the state: the gulf of mistrust of liberalism, in spite of

[1] See Friedrich Karl Fromme, *Von der Weimarer Verfassung zum Bonner Grundgesetz* (Tübingen, 1960); the concept of 'militant democracy' in fact goes back to specific contemporary experiences and conclusions of constitutional and social science scholars of Weimar democracy; see, in particular, the exiled constitutional lawyer Karl Loewenstein, 'Militant Democracy and Fundamental Rights', *American Political Science Review* 31 (1937), pp. 417ff., 638ff., and *Verfassungslehre* (1959), 3rd ed. (Tübingen, 1975), p. 348ff.; also the influential sociologist Karl Mannheim in an early book, *Diagnose unserer Zeit, Gedanken eines Soziologen* (Zurich, 1941), p. 9ff. See now also Hans Vorländer, *Verfassung und Konsens, Der Streit um die Verfassung in der Grundlagen-und Grundgesetzdiskussion der Bundesrepublik Deutschland* (Berlin, 1981), p. 63ff. K. D. Bracher, 'Zum Verfassungsverständnis der Bundesrepublik in historisch-politischer Sicht', in *Verfassung und Geschichte der Bundesrepublik Deutschland im Unterricht (Schriftenreihe der Bundeszentrale für politische Bildung)* (Bonn, 1980), p. 31ff.

[2] On efforts to develop a politically value-emphatic Catholic social doctrine and state theory see especially the great collective works such as *Staatslexikon* (1st ed. 1889–97; 6th ed. 1959); A. Klose, W. Mantl, V. Zsifkovits (eds), *Katholisches Soziallexikon* (2nd ed. Innsbruck-Graz, 1980; 1st ed. 1964), pp. 1290ff., 1306ff., 2894ff.; Alfred Klose, *Katholische Soziallehren* (Graz, 1979); Nikolaus Monzel, *Die Katholische Kirche in der Sozialgeschichte* (Munich, 1981); Anton Rauscher (ed.), *Der soziale und politische Katholizismus, Entwicklungslinien in Deutschland 1803–1963* (Munich, 1981).

the Catholic parties' practical coalition policy, was still too wide. Never-theless the Catholic camp, whether orientated more towards Christian socialism or bourgeois culture, exhibited stronger resistance to the on-slaught of the great ideologies than either Protestantism, with its mainly right-wing stance, or liberalism, which had relativized its own value; social democratic reformism, finally, still sitting on the fence with a guilty conscience, remained in a virtually paralysed oppositional position to the ideological dictatorial movements of the Right and the Left.

Political and ideological confusion and helplessness in the camp of democrats and liberals, and indeed also of moderate conservatives and Christians of both denominations, increased to the extent that the con-frontation between the two totalitarian ideologies was adopting also increasingly political forms with the rise of national socialism and the intensification of the communist movements since the end of the twenties. Typical of the collapse of a libertarian democracy was the fate of the Weimar Republic between 1932 and 1933: the crushing of the political centre by the extremes of Right and Left, and the transformation of a great power vacuum, which was above all an *idea vacuum*, into a totalitarian dictatorship with the monopoly of a radical intolerant ideology.[1] The worldwide depression as an apparently definitive confirmation of the decadence and hopelessness of existing organizations, the loss of faith in the effectiveness of liberal democracies and the advance of authoritarian theories promising a solution all led political thought in the thirties either into deep resignation or rather into desperate attempts at salvation, which presently proved as confusing as they were illusory.

There was an increasing over-simplification of political reasoning and emotions, a narrowing-down to a few ideological alternatives, and finally their reduction to *the* alternative of fascism or communism, displacing all more complex or differentiated thought in terms of democratic categories and alternatives.[2] This applied in particular to the ideas of liberalism and

[1] On this now see the volume *Weimar, Selbstpreisgabe einer Demokratie*, op. cit., with a bibliography of research by Hagen Schulze, p. 25ff., and a final summary by K. D. Erdmann, p. 345ff.; there is also a retrospective reference to my thesis of the power vacuum: K. D. Bracher, 'Demokratie und Machtvakuum', p. 109ff. See my earlier 'Auflösung einer Demokratie', in *Faktoren der Machtbildung* (Berlin, 1952), p. 41ff.; also *Die Auflösung der Weimarer Republik*, 6th ed. (1978), pp. 24ff., 463ff. On the international contexts and constraints of the great depression as a break in world politics, leading to major political escapist movements, see Josef Becker and Klaus Hildebrand (eds), *Internationale Bezie-hungen in der Weltwirtschaftskrise 1929–1933* (Munich, 1980). (Final observation by K. Hildebrand.)

[2] The scale of accommodation or desertion certainly varied from country to country. The attraction and the circumstances of ideologization are belittled as (youthful) idealism and 'spirit of the times', and the scale of intimidation and oppression, of persecution and voluntary falling into line varies widely – most clearly and most radically eventually in the totalitarian movements and systems themselves. On cultural-political uniformization in Italy, A. Lyttelton, op. cit., pp. 346ff., 394ff.; in Germany, K. D. Bracher, *Stufen der Machtergreifung*, op. cit.,

socialism. In a growing number of European countries these two trends of democratic thought were displaced and persecuted the more the authoritarian wave advanced. Towards the end of the thirties only the two ancient democracies, Britain and France, as well as – still in the lee of the 'new' politics – Scandinavia and Switzerland, remained 'open' states in the sense that they tolerated all political currents and left the formation of political attitudes to the rivalry of ideas.

The old and new political ideas and concepts, which had battled so furiously against each other in the twenties and which had undergone such extensive, rich, and also extreme development, now gave way to a great impoverishment and narrowing of the arena of ideas. Even the drumbeats of the fascist and national socialist policy of violence and expansion, which from 1935, in Abyssinia, Spain, Austria, Czechoslovakia and Albania, had heralded in the new era of the dictators, finally setting seal to it with the outbreak of the Second World War, almost exclusively produced defensive reactions, their clearest expression being the western 'policy of appeasement' and the Munich agreement of 1938: capitulation by the west, justified as preserving the peace. Ultimately, however, this was the result of years of disorientation of political thought in the western democracies, of both the Right's and the Left's tactical vacillation between challenges and political abstinence or seduction – a moral decadence of Europe.[1]

In Britain, however, it was not only the conservatives' illusions about national socialist anti-Bolshevism that played a part, but also the pacifist

p. 36ff.; as well as the series of lectures, *Nationalsozialismus und die deutsche Universität* (Berlin, 1966); *Deutsches Geistesleben und Nationalsozialismus* (Tübingen, 1965); in Russia and worldwide, Jürgen Rühle, *Literatur und Revolution, Die Schriftsteller und der Kommunismus* (Munich-Zurich, 1963). On the Left see also the essays and texts in B. Dinkerneil *et al.* (eds), *Literatur und Gesellschaft, Dokumentation zur Sozialgeschichte der deutschen Literatur seit der Jahrhundertwende* (Frankfurt/M., 1973); on the problems of the Right: G. K. Kaltenbrunner (ed.), *Konservatismus in Europa* (Freiburg/Br., 1972); on German leadership and élitist thought alongside K. Sontheimer, *Antidemokratisches Denken*, op. cit., Walter Struve, *Élites against Democracy, Leadership Ideals in Bourgeois Political Thought in Germany, 1890–1933* (Princeton, 1973): from the 'Challenge of the 1890s' to the 'Sources of National Socialist Élitism', with highly critical sketches of F. Naumann, M. Weber, Rathenau, Nelson, Spengler, Keyserling, Edgar Jung, Zehrer and Jünger.

[1] Thus Jean-Baptiste Duroselle, *La Décadence, 1932–1939* (Paris, 1979), especially, on French foreign policy. The idea and phenomenon of appeasement contains two mental processes of central importance to specific foreign policy and security relations then as today: on the one hand the conservative idea of a taming (and utilization) of radical forces, on the other an ideological pacifism to the point of unilateral rejection of all military defence. Thereby domestic seizures of power and foreign-political extortion have been rendered possible and indeed legitimated. There is a copious and controversial literature on the appeasement issue. See its balanced discussion in Reinhard Meyers, *Britische Sicherheitspolitik 1934–1938* (Düsseldorf, 1976), p. 19ff.; the latest fundamental overall presentation is by Gerhard L. Weinberg, *The Foreign Policy of Hitler's Germany, Starting World War II, 1937–1939* (Chicago, 1980), p. 52ff.; K. D. Bracher, *Europa*, op. cit., p. 222ff.; *NS Machtergreifung*, op. cit., p. 324f.

leanings of the Left, especially among the intelligentsia. Regardless of opposition to fascism 'as such' in general terms, regardless of the close if passing engagement with which the Spanish Civil War had been followed, reservations about any kind of power politics or rearmament were still great. The result was a total misjudgement of the actual political situation. Thus John Strachey, the English aristocrat converted to communism, in a widely read book predicted in the fateful year 1932 not only the victory of communism over Nazism in Germany but indeed a final struggle of dying capitalism between Britain and the USA[1]; considerable influence also attached to the pro-Russian attitude of the 'Red Dean of Canterbury', Hewlett Johnson. Whereas their critiques of democracy and their anti-capitalism remained implacable, numerous intellectuals in Britain and France compensated their sense of political weakness by an idealist inclination towards the communist alternative. But this, too, time and again ended in deep disillusionment over Soviet behaviour: in the Spanish Civil War (1936–9), when Moscow put ruthless action against all deviationists above the fight against 'fascism'; in Moscow's own great show trials and bloody purges (1936–8), a mockery of all noble communist ideals; and finally in the pact between the two totalitarian despots Hitler and Stalin (1939), which exceeded the worst expectations, refuted all illusions, and forced Europe's last democracies, isolated and unprepared, into a new world war.

This was the collapse of that ideological alternative of fascism or communism, which had all too persuasively served as a signpost to political thought and emotions in the thirties. The struggle for old and new political values was revealed as a process of illusions and disillusionments, which was not even concluded in 1939: it revived after Hitler's attack on the Soviet Union (1941) with new hopes among the anti-Hitler coalition of east–west co-operation and democratic-communist reconciliation in a new world order, with the liberal concept of 'one world', and even survived the rifts of the Cold War.[2] Distaste of fascism and, subsequently, horror at national socialist totalitarianism were more than understandable. Any alliance

[1] John Strachey, *The Coming Struggle for Power* (London, 1932); Hewlett Johnson, *The Socialist Sixth of the World* (London, 1939). See, in particular, the excellent description of left-wing illusions and indoctrination in George Watson, *Politics and Literature in Modern Britain* (London, 1977), p. 36ff, with numerous examples testifying to the extent of pro-communist leanings in the thirties – and their resumption by the 'New Left' (p. 15ff.). On the overall problem in historical perspective see Raymond Williams, *Marxism and Literature* (New York, 1977), *Culture and Society 1780–1950* (New York, 1958) and *The Long Revolution* (New York, 1961).

[2] Important starting-points after 1945 were provided by the popular post-war existentialism around Sartre and the anti-nuclear movement with its links with a pro-Soviet peace movement, and finally the arguments about the start of the Cold War and McCarthyism which are invoked especially by anti-American 'revisionists' among western historians and sociologists: see K. D. Bracher, *Europa*, op. cit., pp. 281ff., 476ff.; also especially Ernst Nolte, *Deutschland und der Kalte Krieg* (Munich, 1974), p. 173ff.; and Hans-Peter Schwarz, *Vom Reich zur Bundesrepublik*, new ed. (Stuttgart, 1980), p. xxxvff.

seemed justified. Writers like André Gide opted for the communists who, moreover, seemed to be fighting against fascism and national socialism with the greatest sacrifices. The communist Popular Front strategy since 1934 reinforced these illusions, and too few then remembered the communist struggle against the Weimar Republic and against the social democrats who were still being slandered as 'social fascists' in 1932–3.

However, that 'anti-fascism' was not just a political decision against the dictatorial and totalitarian principle. This turn came much too late, especially in practical politics, and not consistently enough. This was predominantly an ideological decision, and Stalinist Russia, itself engaged in a steady intensification of totalitarian one-man rule, was in fact anything but an alternative to 'fascism'. True, intellectuals with Marxist and pro-communist inclinations, critical of democracy, were able to point to the persecution of all Marxists in Hitler's Germany. But they were overlooking not only the fact that non-Marxists were equally being persecuted in Germany but that an alternative, ideologically opposite, regime of persecution in the name of Marxism-Leninism was dealing hardly any less rigorously with its own dissident intellectuals and minorities.

The real miracle was, and still is, that the idea of communism scarcely suffered as a result of communist practice – either then or now.[1] Evidently it differed not only from the fascist and national socialist ideologies but also from liberal and social democratic concepts of politics in that it possessed a number of particularly attractive features, which made that great misjudgement of the thirties possible: the belief that fascism could be fought by pacifism, communism and excessive critique of democracy, and that the struggle for orientations and values in favour of man and his culture, in the sense of true progress, could be won at the same time. This was in fact the Utopia – more a feeling or a delusion than logically thought out – of the achievability of a just society in the face of the undeniable injustices of one's own system which caused sensitive people in particular to develop a guilty conscience. Yet it remains a paradoxical phenomenon that writers and artists, philosophers and intellectuals, who more than anyone else are dependent on freedom and uncontrolled thought, seem to develop a strange weakness for revolutionary but intellectually closed systems of ideas, and one such system was offered by communism amidst the relativization and

---

[1] The continuing attraction of communism on successive generations and élites, intellectuals as well as propagandists, can only, in view of the paucity of actual results of communist policy, be explained in pseudo-religious psychological terms: as a surrogate God, a secularized God, and later also as 'apostasy from the Red God'. See the eponymous chapter in Jürgen Rühle, *Literatur und Revolution*, op. cit., p. 400ff. (on Gide, Capek, Malraux, Hemingway, Spender, Sperber, Sartre, Koestler, Orwell and Auden). Now also the memoirs of Malcolm Muggeridge (*Like it was*, London 1981) who, as the *Manchester Guardian* correspondent in Moscow 1932–3 recorded the more than fifty-year-old contradictions to the communist ideal with which visiting western sympathizers found themselves face to face but which, for far too long, they did not see or want to see.

degradation of all past value systems.

It was this prospect of a supposedly new future, contrasting with the crisis of the liberal and social democratic idea of progress, that made such influential pioneers of English Fabian socialism as the Webbs, who hailed 'Soviet civilization' as a liberation from landowners and from capitalism (1935)[1], whereas in fact Stalin's Russia was marked by the destitution of the peasantry and the persecution of intellectuals. True, Lenin had once opposed war, had terminated it prematurely and, following an admittedly violent consolidation of his power, had raised the idea of peace to the centre of Soviet policy. People wanted to see only that 'peace-loving Soviet Union' and its worldwide peace propaganda, and not its pretensions to world revolution, the dictatorial pressure of the Comintern, the quasi-military development of the communist system. People continued to believe in the 'defensive' interpretation of Soviet imperialism, though in fact it persisted along the road of tsarist expansion and eventually legitimated the Soviet Union as the last and only colonial empire in the world to have retained all its nineteenth-century imperial conquests.

Anti-capitalism and peace propaganda, social revolution and equality of all men – these were inspiring value concepts which could now be projected upon a notoriously unknown Russia; any destruction or oppression could be excused with Marxist arguments as prerequisites of a better future. This, too, was a totalitarian logical trap. Such is the nature of politics, and 'wo gehobelt wird, fliegen Späne' ('you can't make an omelette without breaking eggs'): thus conservative politicians had been justifying Hitler's 'national revolution' to themselves and their own standards.[2] National socialism could be belittled by the international Left as the final, expiring, stage of capitalism and excused or praised by the international Right as a bulwark against communism. The October Revolution, as the only comprehensive 'social revolution' of the century, on the other hand, provided a great historical model, and the 'struggle against fascism and war' proved an equally effective political platform for identification with communism. It

[1] Sidney and Beatrice Webb, *Soviet Communism: a New Civilization?* (London, 1935; the 2nd ed. 1937 omitted the question mark), aptly called by A. J. P. Taylor, 'The most preposterous book ever written about Soviet Russia' (with other examples in G. Watson, op. cit., p. 51ff.). Beatrice Webb's cynically doctrinaire comment on a transport of starving political prisoners *en route* to Siberia was that 'You can't make an omelette without breaking eggs'. Typical also was the view of W. H. Auden in the 1935 symposium 'Christianity and Social Revolution' (p. 156 footnote 1 below), that the Christian must admit 'the necessity of violence and judge the means by its end'. Other shocking examples in G. Watson, op. cit., p. 67ff.

[2] Thus the classic self-appeasement of Hitler's 1933 German national partners under Hugenberg's leadership, who frequently used the slogan: K. D. Bracher, *German Dictatorship*, op. cit., p. 249; *Stufen der Machtergreifung*, op. cit., p. 97ff. On passing sympathies, especially among British conservatives, for the Third Reich, matching left-wing sympathies for Soviet communism, see ibid., pp. 325 and 547 (Lord Rothermere and the *Daily Mail*); on the effect of anti-communism see Sigmund Neumann, *Permanent Revolution, The Total State in a World at War* (New York and London, 1942), pp. 257ff. and 282ff.

also had all the answers: war and fascism as the consequence of the dynamics of capitalism and the armaments industry. And communism, now equated with Marxism, also seemed to be alone in possessing all those values which had been lost in cultural-critical argument with the western democratic idea of progress or which had lost their credibility in the debacles of the war and its aftermath – and more especially so for the younger generation which saw this, simultaneously, as a struggle against the Establishment, against the outworn 'rule of old men'.[1]

On this point the totalitarian ideologies resembled each other in their attraction to the young, except that communism claimed the more humane, universally-human values and further heightened its anti-positions (which it shared with militant anti-communists) by monopolizing the idea of universal peace and justice for its own 'socialism'. Fascism and national socialism, on the other hand, did in fact demonstratively support the idea of struggle and élite, the idea of the (national and racial) inequality of mankind and the oppression of nations and minorities. But then communism had done the same – and not only during its supposedly excusable practice of transition to 'socialism'. Although the theory of struggle and dictatorship was eclipsed by the dazzle of the idea of peace and justice, it was nevertheless deeply rooted in the concepts of class struggle and the dictatorships of the proletariat, and in that of a party élite – some of it already in Marx, decisively so in Lenin, and further extended by Stalin through the dictatorship of the victorious and infallible leader and teacher.

To many intellectuals the great difference was not, therefore, in the ideas themselves but in the consistency of radical change and of the new life that went with it, and also in the remoteness and strangeness of the place of its realization; this invested it with Utopian features. The Soviet Union had, at best, been briefly visited and then left, by some in a sobered-up condition. Fascism and national socialism, on the other hand, had arisen and were rampant in the middle of Europe, in one's own civilization and experience: they were the outcome and extreme result of one's own mistakes and errors. Until as recently as 1914 all those ideas, including anti-Semitism, had been an entirely all-European phenomenon; now the struggle against them and simultaneous mistrust of 'bourgeois' anti-communism was therefore a struggle against one's own evils, part of one's conflict with one's own civilization and of the struggle for new orientations and values: these, it was believed, were more likely to be found in the radiant distance of communism

[1] On the generation conflict as a vehicle of radical ideologization see generally Karl Mannheim, 'Das Problem der Generationen', in *Vierteljahrshefte für Soziologie* 1928. Specifically, Sigmund Neumann, *Parteien*, op. cit., pp. 8off. and 133; also the effective propaganda of the national socialists: Gregor Strasser, 'Macht Platz, ihr Alten!' (1927), in *Kampf um Deutschland* (Munich, 1932); see K. D. Bracher, *Auflösung*, op. cit., p. 101. Similarities and differences in the two post-war periods are discussed in the symposium 'Generations in Conflict', *Journal of Contemporary History* 5/1 (London, 1970), especially p. 175.

than in the crisis-ridden proximity of democracy.[1]

There were also other motivations. The important impulses of the Russian *avant-garde* and its excitingly 'progressive' exponents continued to be effective for a long time. Most of these had emerged before the Revolution even though they had largely identified themselves with the Soviet regime; admittedly many came to a tragic end or fell silent. The 'young' Soviet Union represented an idealistic counter-pole to the decadent moods of the west, moods which one tried to escape. New 'positive' values were beginning to take shape after a long period of negative culture critique. This need for a new cultural-revolutionary start was likewise a rather ambivalent phenomenon: one need only think of the role of futurism in the early years of fascism or of the 'clean break' of national socialism which culture-critical experimenters such as the expressionist poet Gottfried Benn so decisively hailed in 1933. However, the Soviet experiment proved an incomparably stronger and more permanent answer to the intellectuals' needs of future-oriented change, of social deeds as a release from mere critique, of a truly 'social realism' – a term which subsequently, under the knout of Stalinist levelling (much as painting in the 'Third Reich'), served the aesthetically trite glorification of the 'achievements' of dictatorship and its ideological, allegedly conflict-free, mastery of reality.[2]

The number of intellectual fellow travellers or even believing converts, whose romantic yearnings and illusions the writer Arthur Koestler later classically described by the example of his own conversion to communism about 1930, grew amazingly: authors like George Orwell and W. H. Auden in England, John Steinbeck, Upton Sinclair and John Dos Passos in the USA, Henri Barbusse, Jules Romain and Malraux in France, Bertholt Brecht and Anna Seghers in Germany were the best known names of those

---

[1] On this affinity of 'anti-fascist' and pro-communist, or at any rate anti-capitalist, 'progressive' thought on the European intellectual scene, which prevented any closer, especially any critical or moral, examination of Soviet totalitarianism see Roland Stromberg, op. cit., p. 466ff.; George Watson, op. cit., p. 85ff. ('Left and Right'). There was an important initiative in the various endeavours to achieve a synthesis of Christianity and socialism/ Marxism/communism which occurred in the thirties, and exhibited their attraction especially on 'progressive' non-communists. This happened in America too: see the writings of the American philosopher John MacMurray, *The Philosophy of Communism* (1933); *Creative Society, A Study of the Relation of Christianity to Communism*, (1935); or the symposium 'Christianity and the Social Revolution' (1935), in which the subsequent leading American theologian Reinhold Niebuhr participated; see his books *Moral Man and Immoral Society* (1933); *Reflections on the End of an Era* (1934); he later reversed his views in *Christian Faith and Social Action* (1953). Among Catholic attempts mention should be made in particular of the essay of the Jesuit Gaston Feassard, *Le dialogue catholique-communiste est-il possible?* (1937). On these and other (counter) currents see Richard Banks, 'Christianity and Marxism', op. cit., p. 317ff.

[2] See Martin Damus, *Sozialistischer Realismus und Kunst im Nationalsozialismus* (Frankfurt/M., 1981), p. 7ff.; the instructively comparative analysis unfortunately uses the concept of fascism in too general a manner without adequately inquiring into the totalitarian substance of left-wing and right-wing culture.

who switched from the scepsis and social criticism of the twenties to the positive engagement of the thirties. What lent wings to their leap and to their 'arrow in the blue' (Koestler) was not direct communist 'organization' but a powerful sympathy for the New and, most of all, a horror of fascism. This need has been aptly called 'mock-proletarianism'[1]: the pessimistically individualistic aesthetes of the twenties now tried to become optimistic radical democrats with a collectivist-communist vision and to discover a positive social content for their civilization-criticizing emotions and art forms. Herein, without any doubt, lay the forward-pointing significance of such processes and the explanation for the lasting attraction this literature has to this day.

However, the *political* effect of pro-dictatorial sympathies and options in the confusing struggle for new motivations and values which shook the thirties is quite another matter. Party communists and their Moscow centre made use of this literary support for buttressing their Popular Front tactics which were designed to bring the bourgeois-liberal, social democratic and revolutionary currents of anti-fascism under communist influence. Yet the interests of Stalinist rule had priority: the stifling of free cultural activity and the bloody purges which dominated Moscow politics from 1936 onwards showed no concern whatever for western sympathizers. Their option, when all was said and done, was not so much political as personal. Frequently it resembled an escape from intellectual despair into the solace of a faith, from the 'tragic' mood of decline into the safety of a 'closed system' which left no room for hesitation or doubt.

It was not a case of communism as a 'science' but as a surrogate religion, capable of demanding the *sacrificium intellectus*. True, this clashed sharply, for instance, with the expectations of the great Pablo Picasso who had hoped to find in communism the fresh clear spring of art, the greater liberation and creativity. Yet even after the great disillusionment at the end of the thirties the memory of the intellectual thrill and, simultaneously, mental discipline of their Marxist-communist period remained entirely dear to some of them (like Koestler) as *ex-post* confirmation of the aesthetics of totalitarian enticement. Others stayed with it, like Brecht, who willingly admitted the *sacrificium* of submission. The countless confessions of ex-communists are of psychological rather than political interest. But their effect at the time remains alarming.[2]

[1] Thus Roland Stromberg, op. cit., p. 449. Significantly there is a return of this idealized proletarianism in the New Left of the sixties and seventies: see p. 203ff. below.

[2] On the problems of ideological conversion, substitute religion and 'hanging on' see p. 98ff. above. Koestler's books are *Arrow in the Blue* (1952); *The Invisible Writing* (1954); and especially *Darkness at Noon* (1941). Finally typical of Brecht's deliberate 'hanging on' out of weakness was his ambivalent attitude to the East Berlin Rising of 17 June 1953: see G. Lichtheim, *Europe*, op. cit., p. 192ff.; also Jürgen Rühle, *Literatur und Revolution*, op. cit., p. 201ff. (also on the large number of those writers and émigres who after 1945 associated themselves, more or less permanently, with the GDR: Arnold Zweig, Anna Seghers, Ludwig

It should be pointed out that even the 'reform communist' variants of Marxist theory, some developed as early as in the twenties, mainly by the Hungarian Georg Lukács (1885–1971) in his widely discussed book *History and Class Consciousness* (1923) and Carl Korsch (1886–1961) in *Marxismus und Philosophie* (also 1923), were anything but politically constructive in the sense of a conciliation of communism with liberal democracy. On the contrary, they were aimed in particular against the Social Democratic Party and its 'reformism' as a state-supporting element of the Weimar Republic, and they remained within the realm of Leninism just as much as all other (west European) versions of communism to this day: from Italian resistance communism of the twenties (Gramsci) to the Eurocommunism of the seventies. Fundamental, even for Lukács, was the totalitarian interpretation of the *volonté générale* of communism: 'Renunciation of individual freedom . . . conscious subordination to that collective will is destined genuinely to produce genuine freedom. . . . That conscious collective will is the communist party.'[1]

It was obvious that almost anything could be interpreted into Marxism, Leninist or otherwise. But there were other weighty factors of disorientation. The worldwide depression magnified the great waves of 'anti-capitalist longing' about which Gregor Strasser, the exponent of the socialist wing of the NSDAP, had been enthusing in March 1932 and from which Hitler later benefited. Socialist ideas like state planning, abolition of profit and unemployment, co-operative and socialized production were more popular than ever with both Right and Left, whereas the liberal democrats alongside the social democrats were in the dock together with capitalism. Nearly all of them tried to profit from the socialist wave, but only the authoritarian movements and systems succeeded. Success demanded a strong state, and not one in the process of withering away, and that was why Mussolini and Hitler, just as Stalin, were able to promote the development of dictatorship in spite of the patent clash with Marxist dogma. Again it was the radical social experiments and the interventions of collectivist labour and community policy which attracted attention, especially from intellectuals, while the much more efficient economic and social *dirigisme* of 'national socialism'

Renn, Johannes R. Becher, Stefan Heym, Alfred Kantorowicz, also Ernst Niekisch, Ernst Bloch; Heinrich Mann died in California in 1946 before his planned move to East Berlin). It is said that on 17 June 1953 Brecht commented on the situation in the GDR Writers' Union by saying, 'The writers are putting up their barricades: their readers are coming.' A comparable situation arose on the other side in 1968 for the exponents of the 'critical theory', when students put it to a violently revolutionary test: Adorno did not survive it, Habermas withdrew to Lake Starnberg.

[1] Georg Lukács, *Geschichte und Klassenbewusstsein* (republished Amsterdam, 1967), p. 317ff. See George Lichtheim, *Georg Lukács* (London, 1970), as well as his discussions of Marxist literature of different trends in the twenties and thirties, in G. Lichtheim, *Europe in the Twentieth Century* (London, 1972), p. 211ff.; also Raymond Williams, *Marxism and Literature* (New York, 1977).

in Hitler's Third Reich was underrated, in line with Marxist theory on fascism, as a mere continuation of bourgeois capitalism – followed by great astonishment that, right to the end of the regime, 'the masses' in particular, including the workers, by no means rebelled against it.[1]

The western-Marxist explanation that this acceptance and the functioning of national socialism was due solely to the war[2] is inadequate. Anti-capitalism and socialism simply were not – as communist ideology insisted they were – inevitable future steps and phases of mankind as a whole. They were vehicles of change and also of modernization, functioning (or not functioning) irrespective of ideological categorization, according to whether they were backed by an efficient organization and an effective myth. In national-socialist Germany it was the idea of the hierarchical state system and the national-populist community myth, in Russia a blend of despotic tradition and Marxist-Leninist myth, that determined the face of socialism. But the great five-year or four-year plans with which the dictators operated contrasted effectively with the apparent helplessness of the democracies and their capitalism. Even the 'new' economic intervention theory of Keynes (1936), though intended merely as a corrective to the market economy, might look like a liberal confirmation of the dictatorships: like *étatisme* and, if not actually socialism, at least a road to the welfare state which was bound to appear to an old-style liberal theoretician like Hayek as already a 'road to serfdom'.[3] At best the New Deal of Franklin D. Roosevelt, who as the new President of the USA in 1933 ordered a far-reaching economic and social anti-recession programme, might arouse some intellectual sympathies with liberal-democratic solutions. But America was felt to be far away and different; after years of isolationist policy it was largely inward-looking and was only slowly moving towards a solution to its economic crisis.

By way of contrast the forcible liquidation of unemployment in the dictatorships was a convincing argument. Since, however, in the case of national socialism this was associated with war preparations, thus lacking the challenging ideological and moral perspectives of social reconstruction and universal equality, the communist experiment continued to rank higher in the sympathy stakes. The 'workers' paradise' was a commonplace which

---

[1] On the above-mentioned (p. 103ff.) underestimation of the 'socialist' component of national socialism especially see also the semi-Marxist theses of Timothy W. Mason (*Arbeiterklasse und Volksgemeinschaft*, Opladen 1975 and 1977) discussed in Ludolf Herbst, 'Die Krise des nationalsozialistischen Regimes am Vorabend des Zweiten Weltkrieges und die forcierte Aufrüstung', *Vierteljahrshefte für Zeitgeschichte* 26 (1978), p. 374ff.; see also, fundamentally, David Schoenbaum, *Hitler's Social Revolution* (New York, 1966), p. 77: the economic consequences of national socialism for the workers were 'a curious mixture of advantages and disadvantages'.

[2] In a particularly extreme form in Tim Mason, 'The Legacy of 1918 for National Socialism', in Anthony Nicholls, Erich Matthias (eds), *German Democracy and the Triumph of Hitler* (London, 1971), p. 215ff.; also preceding footnote.

[3] Friedrich August von Hayek, *The Road to Serfdom* (1944).

never had much bearing on reality but which, at a time of social crisis, could prove an effective counter-Utopia: all shortcomings and sins of civilization were due to capitalism, whose liquidation therefore would give rise to a New Man. Certainly such attitudes and expectations further intensified the extreme polarization between the communist myth of revolution and the national socialist evidence of efficiency with autobahnen, Strength-through-Joy tourism and the Volkswagen as symbols of a practical socialism. Between these two there was little room for positions of moderate thought or for a political Centre, which in any case had become unattractive, all too 'ordinary' and, according to the incessantly repeated slogan of the 'end of the bourgeois era',[1] had long been listed as a moribund political idea.

Mention has already been made of a further aspect of polarization at the expense of moderate political thought: the struggle concerning anti-communism. Here, too, we have a combination of ideological and political elements. Of course there was a well-founded, factually based critique of the reality of communism as well as of the contradictions and untruths of its theory. This 'anti-communism' was a genuine form of scientific and political rationalism, of its philosophical criteria and moral values. But it was devalued and falsified at the time – as indeed it is again today – by its adulteration with an ideological anti-communism of right-wing radical origin, and thus it found itself trapped in the rivalry of hostile totalitarian systems and theories. Here was another similarity between fascism and communism: just as the 'anti-fascism' of liberal, social democratic and indeed conservative origin has lost its anti-dictatorial meaning through the capture of the concept by Marxists and communists, so the anti-communism of democratic stamp has lost some of its libertarian substance through the right-wing radical generalization and monopolization of the term.

Both sides are still deriving considerable political advantage from the manipulation of the slogans of anti-fascism and anti-communism: they render their own anti-ideology respectable and effective in broader circles, and criticism of their own positions can be dismissed as 'ideological', no matter how well founded in fact. The supposedly floating intellectuals, however, are put under pressure and withdraw their criticism of communism for fear of being labelled anti-communist. This accusation in itself was regarded even then – because of the low 'quality' of the right-wing radical ideologies – as defamatory; after the barbarism of national socialism and in view of ever new hopes of a 'communism with a human face' it has remained utterly defamatory to this day.

The accusation of 'folly of anti-communism' or even 'anti-Bolshevism as the fundamental folly of our age', pilloried by an ex-conservative like Thomas Mann in the heyday of the anti-Hitler coalition and of belief in a final reconciliation between east and west, between communism and democracy, was apt to be something like the mark of Cain even in the

[1] See my eponymous article in *Geschichte und Gewalt*, p. 15ff.

thirties.[1] To be anti-communist meant to be akin to fascists and Nazis, and no one wanted to descend to that political, let alone intellectual or moral, level. An equal folly, of course, was the inclination not to criticize communism at all so as not to sully a justified anti-fascism with the stain of anti-communism. For intellectuals like Orwell it was the concept of totalitarianism that broke through this taboo. However, reference to the totalitarian parallels between communism and national socialism crept in only slowly in the thirties, even though the concept had been formulated by liberal and social democratic critics of Mussolini in the early twenties and occasionally used even by Marxists such as Herbert Marcuse as an early description of the anti-liberal trends of his day.[2]

It is true that the Stalinist regimentation of eastern Europe after 1945 caused the scales to fall from many eyes. Totalitarian seduction and threat from both Right and Left were perceived as the real problem of dictatorship in the twentieth century.[3] But it is not fortuitous that a taboo on the totalitarian concept, mainly from the Left, crept in again during the sixties. This went hand in hand with a renewed defusing of the critique of communism, with an over-hopeful ideologization of the policy of *détente*, and with a renewed exacerbation of the charge of anti-communism, designed to intimidate critics or even to impute a new 'fascism' to them. Anti-communism had to be rejected not only because it had figured also in Hitler's ideology but because it was intellectually and morally utterly discreditable, simply because it could not be equated 'qualitatively' with anti-fascism. This argument was, and still is, extremely effective, mainly because it contains a partial truth: the theoretically more substantial tradition of the idea of communism and its greater affinity to moral and human values. But it is, of course, only a partial truth: in practice communism represents a similarly grave but rather more seductive threat to the open, libertarian world of the spirit and of democracy. Anti-communism and anti-fascism, rooted in the libertarian and humanist convictions of the west, cannot simply be polarized but belong together in principle, regardless of their great differences; only thus can their abuse by left-wing and right-wing radicals be realistically resisted. One might even ask whether the manipulation of the two concepts by the two opposing radical ideologies

[1] Kurt Sontheimer, 'Thomas Mann als politischer Schriftsteller', *Vierteljahrshefte für Zeitgeschichte* 6 (1958), p. 39f. (the quotation dates from 1942); see Joachim Fest, in *Aufgehobene Vergangenheit* (Stuttgart, 1981), p. 38ff. On the necessary, though indignantly rejected, connection of anti-communism and anti-totalitarianism see K. D. Bracher, *Zeitgeschichtliche Kontroversen*, op. cit., p. 33, and *Totalitarismus und Faschismus* (Munich-Vienna, 1980).

[2] For example, Herbert Marcuse, *Der Kampf gegen den Liberalismus in der totalitären Staatsauffassung* (1934). Bernard Crick, *George Orwell* (London, 1980), p. 340, Essay on Koestler (1944): the Left wants to be anti-fascist without having to be anti-totalitarian.

[3] See especially Gerhard Leibholz, 'Das Phänomen des totalen Staates', in *Strukturprobleme der modernen Demokratie* (Karlsruhe, 1958), p. 225 (first presented as a BBC broadcast in November 1946); Hannah Arendt, *The Origins of Totalitarianism* (New York, 1951); C. J. Friedrich and Z. K. Brzezinksi, *Totalitarian Dictatorship and Autocracy* (Cambridge/Mass., 1957).

would not make it altogether advisable to replace them both by the concept of 'anti-totalitarian', covering critique both of fascism and of communism.

Certainly this present controversy cannot simply be projected back to the thirties. But its essence nevertheless concerns the issues of that period. Readiness and courage to engage in political thought encountered their limits in forms of 'wishful thinking' and in self-imposed limitation of criticism, which might itself be described as ideological. Just as the writers of the Right, in their thoughts on 'conservative revolution' overlooked the right-wing radical consequences of their ideas, advancing to such abstruse constructs as an anti-western, national-Bolshevik ideology,[1] with Hitler making capital of their concepts and aspirations for his own dictatorial regime, so the writers of the Left, though personally devoted to the utmost freedom, lent the support of their intellectual and moral stature to an ideology of revolutionary dictatorial socialism, of an enforced promotion of social happiness, generously overlooking the consequences of a communist reality – until, too late, they realized their error: the 'God that failed'.[2]

Between the advance of the great ideologies and the retreat of rational political thought existentialism arose during the thirties with the claim to open up new philosophical directions in the clash of progressivism and civilizational pessimism, of war and peace policy, of society and the individual. It was chiefly Jean-Paul Sartre's impact which gathered up the ideas which provided a bridge from the first to the second 'lost generation', from the crisis philosophy of Heidegger, Jaspers and Barth in the twenties to the resistance or 'nothingness' philosophy of the Second World War and its aftermath. Even though philosophical and theological existentialism was not transferred into journalistic day-to-day discussion and produced no further academic or political effect until after 1945, it had nevertheless provided a sharply contrasting background to the foreground ideological struggles and their exhaustion from the thirties. It was a kind of secret tip for those who were not satisfied with the accommodation course of ideologists and intellectuals, moral philosophers and the Churches, and who wished to rediscover the value problem in the 'roots of existence', in the exposed position of the individual amidst rapidly flowing time.

The frequently high-flown language used in particular by the existentialism of Heidegger and his disciples – often degenerating into soliloquies by the initiated – lent these ideas a strangely modish aspect, reminiscent at times of Nietzsche's stylizations. Yet this linguistic element, as proved by the linguistic seductions of the day, was an exceedingly important and integral part of both thought and politics. Herein lies the more general message: behind the pessimism of 'nothingness' the metaphysical hope of 'being'. Sartre himself saw existentialism as an attempt to draw the ultimate conclusions from a consistently atheistic position in the present age. Modern

[1] On Ernst Niekisch, Hans Buchheim, 'Ernst Niekischs Ideologie des Widerstands', *Vierteljahrshefte für Zeitgeschichte* 5 (1957), p. 334ff.

[2] On the eponymous confessional volume see p. 130 footnote 1 above.

man's total loss of orientation in a world 'without God' first produced the despair of his realization of the total loneliness of the individual and the pointlessness of his playing out any social role. This great 'crisis' was necessary, and it was followed by the rediscovery that man nevertheless 'exists', and moreover with the consciousness and capability of endowing the world in its 'absurd' pointlessness, in spite and because of it, with value, just as man alone puts a name to its 'important' pointlessness, reflects on it, and only then judges and establishes values.[1] Existence precedes being – this had been asserted by the Danish theologian Kierkegaard (1813–55), a lonely man in an age believing in progress, and his rediscovery marked the beginning of modern existentialism.

The subjectivism and irrationalism of the age were matched by a form of thought which regarded reason no longer as something pre-established but as an invention of man for the rationalization of the world. This idea was, on the one hand, directed against rationalism and liberalism, but it could be seen also as a declaration of war by the individual, with his own drives of fear and hope, against the collectivist ideologies. As such an alternative philosophy, both to modern belief in progress and to the pressure of political ideologies, existentialism itself, in its many variants, later found itself caught in the wheels of one-sided politicization: as right-wing conservativism (Heidegger), left-wing socialism (Sartre) or even a democratic interpretation of topical value questions (Jaspers). This last interpretation presently also emerged in the Christian theological versions of Barthianism and religious socialism (Tillich, Marcel) and of a Jewish existentialism (Buber). Their contribution to the discussion of values was to prove of fundamental importance. Man's freedom, even as a 'castaway' without God or *vis-à-vis* God, is re-established, at least in a negative sense, having been almost unanimously conjured away by progressivists, cultural critics and ideologists. Kierkegaard had already opposed Hegelian determinism. Now there was the rediscovery of the person in a depersonalized world – even if this was now 'irrational man', rational man having been buried.[2]

[1] See p. 136 above as well as Alexander Schwan, 'Zeitgenössische Philosophie', op. cit., p. 259ff., and *Geschichtstheologische Konstitution und Destruktion der Politik, Friedrich Gogarten und Rudolf Bultmann* (Berlin and New York, 1976). On Albert Camus's 'philosophy of the absurd' see M. Melançon, *A. C., analyse de sa pensée* (Paris, 1976).

[2] William Barrett, *Irrational Man, A Study in Existential Philosophy* (London, 1958). On Martin Buber (*Ich und Du*, 1923) see Hans Kohn, *Martin Buber, Sein Werk und seine Zeit*, 2nd ed. (Cologne, 1961); Michael Weinreich, *Der Wirklichkeit begegnen . . . , Studien zu Buber, Grisebach, Gogarten, Bonhoeffer und Hirsch* (Neukirchen, 1980); Renate Breipohl, *Religiöser Sozialismus und bürgerliches Geschichtsbewusstein zur Zeit der Weimarer Republik* (Zurich, 1971). On Tillich also Thietmar Wernsdoerfer, *Die entfremdete Welt* (Zurich, 1968); Th. W. Adorno *et al.*, *Werk und Wirken Paul Tillichs* (Stuttgart, 1967); Erich Schwerdtfeger, 'Die politische Theorie in der Theologie Paul Tillichs,' doct. thesis (Marburg, 1969); Hans Joachim Gerhards, *Utopie als innergeschichtlicher Aspekt der Eschatologie* (Gütersloh, 1973) (Tillich and Bloch). Finally Gabriel Marcel, *L'Anthropologie philosophique de Martin Buber* (Brussels, 1968); Kenneth T. Gallagher, *The Philosophy of Gabriel Marcel*, 3rd ed. (New York, 1975).

The new personal individualism as a counter to nihilism and catastrophic thought is not therefore conceivable without existentialism, especially religious existentialism. It was basically a challenge to all 'isms', or also (after 1945) a reaction to them. This might lead to very diverse consequences. Yet it provided starting-points which, far from the arbitrarily introverted mannerisms of the disciples of Heidegger or Sartre, might once more confirm man and *his* values in periods of depersonalization. The problem, of course, remained the social dimension: man also is a political creature. A return to the values of natural law, decidedly absent between the wars, might rediscover that dimension. But it was only the new interest in genuinely 'political' thinkers like Aristotle and Kant, and also Montesquieu and de Tocqueville, that once more put the libertarian anti-totalitarian theory of democracy on more solid ground.

In the struggle for viable normative values and reliable political orientations, however, the thirties represented an age of great deceptions and disillusionments. It was a time of striking political misjudgements of fateful consequences: by the conservatives on Hitler's anti-communism (with which they sympathized); by the liberals on the extent of the threat from the Right and the Left, a threat not only to economic but also to political liberalism, leading it into profound crisis; by the Christians about the similarity of the totalitarian threat from the Left *and* the Right, which forbade them to fight the one with the other, even though godless communism was seen as the greater danger; by the socialists about the need to strengthen democratic systems even if these did not match up to their ideas of socio-economic progress. In all these four major instances the problems of orientation had become virtually insoluble. The evident disorientation in the battle of ideas between political decision-makers and their opponents, and indeed in the desperate squabbles of the persecuted and the exiles in the steadily dwindling free parts of Europe, is depressing. When asked about their ideas of salvation for western civilization and its values, against the great ideologies and dictatorships, most of them responded with resignation, scepsis, and critique of democracy. Only in those circles of exile and Resistance which identified the nationalist fragmentation of Europe as the greatest evil of the crisis was a solid basis laid during the war, with the idea of European unity, for a reshaping of politics and its values.[1]

It was only with the challenge of the war and the decisions of the post-war period that the mood of illusions and power-political cynicism gave way to reflection on the basic values of western civilization: reconstruction and order on the basis of freedom, social justice and human dignity. Yet it took the most terrible devastation and barbarism, and finally the inhuman partition of Europe, to refute the ideological errors of the turn of the century

[1] Walter Lipgens, *Europa-Föderationspläne der Widerstandsbewegungen 1940–1945* (Munich, 1968), and *Die Anfänge der europäischen Einigungspolitik 1945–50*, so far Part I (1945–7) (Stuttgart, 1977).

and to surmount their political consequences at the time of the world wars. The remoteness of responsible political thought in the mass age was a problem which continued to confront the old and the new nations alike. This was true even more in view of a global extension of the ideological struggle after 1945.

7. PROBLEMS OF THE DEMOCRATIC IDEA

According to a history of philosophical and political ideas that has become a classic since the thirties, 'A crucial characteristic, and perhaps the most important characteristic of a liberal government, is the negative quality of not being totalitarian.'[1] This is neither an old-fashioned nor an outdated observation. Libertarian democracy is indeed based on the social, and simultaneously moral, idea that politics is the art of the peaceful settlement of diverging interests, and that its method is democratic decision by the majority, ensuring protection for the minority and the right to opposition. However, this clashes totally with those political ideas, and subsequent political and ideological endeavours, which aim at unilinear, comprehensively integrated and uncontroversial solutions to the problems of a plurality of views and interests in the modern state, from Rousseau via Hegel and Marx to the totalitarian theories of communism, fascism and national socialism, along with the state-authoritarian or society-authoritarian technocratic or nationalistic variants of these macro-types.

The struggle for the libertarian form of democracy has been in the centre of political thought ever since the experience of pseudo-democratic dictatorship. Today it is once again derogated by the 'deeper' theoreticians of anti-pluralism (especially of the New Left). After the First World War it was not taken very seriously as a proper subject of political philosophy. It has been mentioned earlier in this book that the exciting arguments between right and left wing, between conservative and revolutionary theories, had been taking place virtually outside the realm of political reality. This reality threw up a multitude of urgent problems. But they were dismissed as undemanding when compared with the traditional or revolutionary themes of political philosophy. Or they were regarded as mere technicalities. Or else, finally, they were regarded as primarily due to the war and used for criticizing the democratic system. This was much to the detriment of political theory formulation generally and of empirical democracy in particular, which only rarely had a mirror held up to its ideas and values. Even then, the

[1] George Sabine, *History*, op. cit., p. 751.

mirror was often a distorting one.[1]

The problems of appropriately modernized democratic thought did not really require the grand speculative schemes which were customary, especially in Germany. Rather they demanded efforts towards a specific understanding and comparative examination. For these, however, both time and patience were lacking amidst the excitements of the period between the wars. This was true especially where libertarian democracy itself had only been granted a short span of life, as in Italy and in Germany. Here indeed it did not last long enough to allow outlines and ideas to mature before the new political form was seemingly refuted by the force of events and by the advance of the dictators. There were, of course, some basic starting-points and problem studies aiming at a comprehension of democracy beyond mere political argument, criticizing or speculation. These were to be found mainly in the emerging empirical social sciences and in a revived science of politics; partially also in the (rather conservative) juridical-constitutional studies completed before the great rupture of the thirties. Mostly, however, these ideas did not become effective in Europe until after 1945, whereas in the USA, where an important part of this 'democracy research' had emigrated or been compelled to emigrate, these studies had been experiencing, and giving rise to, a steady expansion and intensification.[2]

This was not a case of propaganda for democracy or of an uncritical continuation of the idea of progress, as European sceptics contemptuously believed before and after 1945, but a thoroughly critical examination of the problems and value discussions. But unlike the universal, more or less wholesale, 'critique of democracy' practised under the heading of culture critique by intellectuals and philosophers, it did not content itself with a

---

[1] The German scene was dominated not by democratic theory but by critiques of democracy; the paucity of the former was matched by a profusion of the latter. Democratic political science was still underdeveloped, constitutional theory was still struggling with the acceptance of modern democracy generally, and intellectual life was dominated by anti-democratic forays with dazzling and stunning effects, appealing to pre-democratic nostalgia or post-democratic visions of the future. Thus in Germany Carl Schmitt's writings of the early thirties, oscillated between conservative and totalitarian 'alternatives'; and there was interest (albeit critical) in the fascist experiment among liberal democratic observers such as Erwin von Beckerath (*Wesen und Werden des fascistischen Staates* (Berlin, 1927) and Gerhard Leibholz (*Zu den Problemen des faschistischen Verfassungsrechts* (Berlin-Leipzig, 1928).

[2] This can be supported by the names and achievements of (especially) German historians, and social and political scientists. A part was played in this by the beginnings of the Berlin *Hochschule für Politik*, the Frankfurt *Institut für Sozialforschung*, and the Vienna school (alongside the Göttingen and Berlin natural scientists). See the researches of Helge Pross, *Die deutsche akademische Emigration nach den Vereinigten Staaten 1933–1941* (Berlin, 1955); also the admittedly hypercritical balance sheet from the point of view of the 'vanquished' in Hans-Joachim Arndt, *Die Besiegten von 1945* (Berlin, 1978). See also K. D. Bracher, 'Politik und politische Wissenschaft', in *Das deutsche Dilemma* (Munich, 1971), p. 317ff.; also recently Alan D. Beyerchen, *Wissenschaftler unter Hitler, Physiker im Dritten Reich* (Cologne, 1980), p. 19ff. Now the fundamental *International Biographical Dictionary of Central European Emigrés*, 3 vols (München, New York, London, 1980–83).

cheap rejection of 'mass democracy' as such but instead attempted an intellectual assessment of its avoidable problems of development and understanding. For this work de Tocqueville had set a classic example almost a century previously, and Bagehot and Bryce had supplied the British contribution, without, however, finding many followers on the European mainland.

There were three problem areas urgently awaiting intellectual treatment and yet largely neglected by the lofty cerebrations of intellectuals and academics. The first was nationalism as an unbroken force of domestic and foreign politics, its connection with the idea of self-determination on the one hand and of the restructuring of international relations on the other. The second was the present and future form of democracy between separation of powers and concentration of power, the question of parliamentary or presidential structure, its representative or plebiscitarian methods of legitimation. The third was the importance of structural change in democracy, its evolution from a liberal state of notabilities into a state of parties, associations and bureaucracy, together with tendencies towards the social and welfare state.

Although these big issues were frequently raised, they were mostly seen as proof of an insoluble structural crisis, or indeed of the impossibility of democracy generally, and added to the arguments for the decline of western civilization. Analyses of democracy, of parties and associations and of the bureaucracy, beyond purely constitutional treatment, such as those by Robert Michels or Max Weber, Harold Laski or Carl Schmitt, seemed to confirm the pessimistic diagnosis; they point to the clash of democratic and oligarchical trends (Michels), to tensions between democracy, authority and leadership (Weber), to the dissolution of the democratic state into pluralist structures (Laski) or to polycratic zones of conflict (Schmitt).

Behind these there was another string of questions which, connected with the transformation of the modern state generally and not fully understood until after 1945, related to the concept of 'political modernization', even though they had in fact been raised since the turn of the century. These may be seen as three major sets of problems.[1]

Firstly, rationalization of political authority tends to replace a multitude of traditional, religious, family and ethical authorities by one single secular-national authority claiming competence over most other human relationships, both in internal and external politics. The concepts of indivisible sovereignty (externally) and of national integration (domestically) characterize this concentration of the idea of the state. The problem of modern libertarian democracy resides in the fact that it is both a fruit of this rationalization process and its contradiction. On the one hand it demands the internal unity and equality of all citizens, together with national self-

[1] See Samuel P. Huntington, 'Political Modernization: America versus Europe', in Reinhard Bendix (ed.), *State and Society* (Berkeley, 1968), p. 170ff.

determination and independence externally. On the other it is essentially pluralistic, directed towards the free development of the citizen in parties and associations, in a multiplicity of interests and opinions, towards the separation and distribution of powers, being dedicated, alongside self-determination, to the idea of international co-operation. Ultimately therefore it is aimed not only at the solution of internal controversy but also at settlement in the international field, the transfer of democratic principles to foreign politics.

Secondly, the idea of political modernization implies an in-depth change of structures and functions resulting from the progressive specialization and differentiation in state and society. The heightened importance of science and the intelligentsia, of economy and bureacracy, emerges in a quantitative sense. Even more does it become a fundamental problem to democracy in a qualitative sense. It runs counter to the democratic ideal of the all-round competent citizen who, of his free will, (co-)determines policy to see the importance of experts, or expert élites, suddenly and irresistibly growing and exceeding the understanding and influence of the voter and even of his representative in party and parliament. The profound conflict between expertise and politics, a grave conflict also for modern parliamentarianism, is of course an old problem, and one that is not confined to democracy. Yet it emerges more openly and conspicuously in a democracy, while authoritarian and dictatorial systems are able to hide it away or solve it by force. The patent conflict of competences and decision structures in democracy, whether subject-related or political, whether organizationally or personally based, is regarded as one of the 'theoretically' most effective arguments of anti-democratic thought, and was quite especially so in the twenties and thirties; in the intellectual argument of the systems it is used as evidence of democracy's inferiority to authoritarian regimes. The basic discussion about bureaucratization and a professional civil service in a democracy is closely connected with the perpetual tension between its specialized and its political requirements, between generalization of citizenship and specialization of state functions. Scientific-technological and social-economic progress have their price: they compel democratic theory – unless it is to remain bogged down in mere critique and lamentation over the discrepancies between idea and reality – to make a highly unpopular adjustment of the idea of 'government by the people' to theories of the party state, the association state and/or the administrative state – theories which are often used as vehicles of anti-democratic critique.

Thirdly and finally, political modernization intensifies and exacerbates the claim to political participation and co-determination by the citizen. This demand for 'participation', likewise, has not been a militant slogan only since the sixties. In fact it was, for the old and new democracies of the twenties, a central element of the urge for political movement and change, an urge born in the trials of the First World War and the disappointments of its aftermath. It was mainly the radical movements of the Left and the Right which turned that democratic principle against democracy itself by describing it derogatively as a mere Establishment or as the impotent rule by special interests, while orienting their own ideological mobilization towards the ideal of a 'true' government by the people (the proletariat or 'national socialism'). On the other side of the divide the representatives of pluralist democracy, both liberals and social democrats, failed to make adequate use of the new opportunities for political participation by the citizen; on the contrary, the traditional 'defamation of party politics'[1] reached a peak in just that new democratic era. Even the modern facilities for mass communication and broader political education ultimately benefited the critics and opponents of democracy. Their tight organization and the quasi-military 'operations' of their supporters attracted far more attention and engagement, especially among the younger people, than the easily denounced 'horse-trading' and 'dirty business' of parliamentary politics.

If the 'political culture' of a democracy is measured principally by political participation in the hectic domestic movements in the post-war states, their generally heavy polls by comparison with the USA, and indeed the realization of universal suffrage for men and women, and the greater role played by the parties – all these might seem to testify to the liveliness of democratic life in Europe. However, it was soon discovered that participation was not in itself a value. It requires not only accepted rules but also suitable structural prerequisites. Indispensable as citizens' participation is in an age of increased demands and expectations, it can also be readily employed in a non-liberal, non-pluralist sense for an intensified management and control of the population: most consistently in the totalitarian states, where dictatorship governs through pseudo-democratic mobilization and 99 per cent plebiscites, that is, through total citizen participation, eager for such 'empirical' uncontradicted legitimation.[2]

Involvement of the 'masses', their participation from 'below' just as much as their guidance (and manipulation) from 'above', can therefore produce very different results. It was here that political ideologization found a rich field of activity. Contrary to the idea of a continuous and comprehensive political participation of the public, the modern large-area state with its growing complexity of functions only permitted a predominantly representative, indirect, democracy with limited participation by the citizen. To

[1] Erwin Faul, 'Verfemung, Duldung und Anerkennung des Parteiwesens in der Geschichte des politischen Denkens', *Politische Vierteljahresschrift* 5 (1964), p. 60ff, with discussion (p. 81 ff.). On the recent state of comparative party theory see mainly Giovanni Sartori, *Parties and Party Systems* (Cambridge, 1976), p. 3ff.

[2] On the theory and function of 99 per cent elections in communist dictatorships see, on the one hand, Niels Diederich, 'Wahlen, Wahlsysteme', in *Sowjetsystem und Demokratische Gesellschaft*, Vol. 6 (Freiburg/Br., 1972), col. 813ff.; on the other hand, H. Graf and G. Seiler, *Wahl und Wahlrecht im Klassenkampf* (East Berlin, 1971). A classic outline of unity parties is Maurice Duverger's *Die politischen Parteien*, 3rd ed. (Tübingen, 1959; French ed. 1951).

determine the plebiscitarian component of representative democracy[1] and to limit its constantly possible abuse thus remains one of the principal problems of any modern democratic theory. This realization, however, had not yet properly sunk in before the advent of pseudo-dictatorial totalitarian mobilization dictatorships. The further the perfectionist idea of total democracy in Rousseau's sense moved away from the real necessities of moderate, freedom-preserving government, the poorer became the prospects of a realistic democratic theory which would balance the two requirements of participation and authority, freedom and order – and which would, at the same time, check the danger of enforced, compulsory, participation which is but a new form of subjection, now no longer in the shape of pre-democratic absolutism from above but of compulsory participation, as 'voluntary' compulsion of all citizens 'from below' in democratic garb. This more general observation applies equally to political 'democratization' and to its champions, critics and despisers among the educated (to vary a dictum by Schleiermacher): no period in European history experienced such a powerful impact of democratic ideas and developments as the years just before and just after the turn of the century, but at no period, on the other hand, were these the object of greater controversy and fundamental questioning as following their apparent triumph in 1918. This not only burdened liberal democracy in the vanquished countries with the disgrace of its own defeat but also disappointed the extravagant expectations of the victors; it burdened it with the massive mortgages of the war and its aftermath and rendered possible the rise of powerful counter-movements in the plebiscitarian-totalitarian shape of communism, then of fascism and finally of national socialism.

The democratic idea itself, not only its difficult practice especially in the new states, now found itself under attack from two sides. On the one hand there were the old doubts in the democratic camp itself, among liberals as well as among Christians and social democrats. The liberals had already been sceptical about the extension of the suffrage beyond the limits of education and property, simply because they believed democracy possible only as a political system of enlightened and responsible citizens (and taxpayers) and because they had difficulties with the élite problem.[2] Christian state theory for its part regarded the principle of exclusive sovereignty of the

[1] Still fundamental is Ernst Fraenkel's essay *Die repräsentative und die plebiszitäre Komponente im demokratischen Verfassungsstaat* (Tübingen, 1958); also his 'Historische Vorbelastungen des deutschen Parlamentarismus', *Vierteljahrshefte für Zeitgeschichte* 8 (1960), p. 323ff. In German democratic theory the argument, prior to the influx of the neo-radical currents towards the end of the sixties, was mainly between the positions of Gerhard Leibholz (*Das Wesen der Repräsentation*, 1928, 2nd ed. 1960) and Dolf Sternberger (*Lebende Verfassung* Meisenheim, 1956) with a stronger emphasis either on the party-state or on the parliamentary component.

[2] See Kurt Klotzbach, *Das Eliteproblem im politischen Liberalismus* (Cologne-Opladen, 1966) (*Staat und Politik* 9), pp. 10ff., 87ff., 104ff.

people as, if not blasphemy, at least as a threat to the Christian idea of social order; it therefore tried to modify the democratic principle by the idea of a graduated corporate social order, as expressed especially in the Christian-social and corporatist suggestions of the Popes, as an alternative to the Marxist idea of class struggle and to the liberal-laicist as well as the revolutionary-egalitarian concepts of democracy. This was seen in the social encyclicals *Rerum novarum* of Leo XIII (1891) and *Quadragesimo anno* of Pius XI (1931). Not until after 1945 did a marked change occur: in the 1961 encyclical *Mater et Magistra* of John XXIII, the idea of the corporate state was dropped, and John Paul II placed greater emphasis on the human rights idea. Protestantism's attitude was initially marked by equally pronounced mistrust of the ideological pretensions of democracy, although there were great differences between the Lutheran belief in authority and its authoritarian trends especially in Germany (where monarchist and German national influence remained strong) and the views of the Reformed and Calvinist Churches in Britain and Switzerland, and more particularly in the USA, which had substantially contributed to the rise of the democratic idea in the first place and continued to be effective in a secularized form.[1]

In Germany, the social democrats, finally, maintained an ambivalent attitude to bourgeois democracy after 1918, just as they had done before. True, they saw the idea of socialist democracy threatened and discredited by communism which, in the name of socialism, had set up an unprecedented dictatorship; compared with it there was a lot to be said for the civil rights and reformist gains achieved through liberal democracy or as major concessions from it. Even so, the party remained mesmerized for a long time by a Marxist-flavoured programme which obstructed the development of a libertarian democratic theory, even though 'right-wing' social democrats like Gustav Radbruch and (towards the end of the Weimar Republic) Hermann Heller made substantial contributions to it later. However, democratic (self-)doubts of democracy predominated; they supplied further arguments to the intellectual sceptics and adversaries in the bourgeois camp, as well as among the 'socialists'. To the former democracy was already too much, to the latter it was not enough.

On the other side of the pincers in which the democratic idea found itself stood far more determined and resolute enemies, who either regarded the democratic principle as a sign of the decline of the west and called for a conservative restoration or a nationalist revolution, or who, in lieu of the bourgeois-liberal democratic concept, proclaimed a future 'government by the people' in the shape of one-party dictatorship and who intended to put an end, in the name of the people, the class or the nation, to 'multi-party government', that is, to pluralist democracy itself. In this war on two fronts, between its own doubters and ideologists of totalitarian anti-democracy,

[1] See K. D. Bracher, *Deutschland zwischen Demokratie und Diktatur* (Bern-Munich-Vienna, 1964), p. 313ff. ('Demokratie als Sendung: das amerikanische Beispiel').

echoes of pre-war arguments were still heard after 1918, while the flow of new ideas for tackling democratic reality was confined to only defensive attitudes and was soon stifled in pessimism, resignation and forebodings of a new catastrophe.

Although the Great War of 1914–18 had achieved the final breakthrough of democracy in Europe, it also, through its outcome and consequences, lent a new edge to critique of democracy. This went hand in hand with nationalist-militaristic revisionist movements, such as Hitler's, which drew their anti-democratic striking power not only from their struggle against the Versailles and Paris peace treaties and against the 'November Revolution' but also from left-wing critics of the 'unfinished revolution' who put their hopes on social upheaval and international class struggle. In these circumstances the democratic statesmen themselves, in uncertainty and self-doubt, torn between triumphant elation and fear of crisis, constantly threatened and hustled by changes of government, failed to plant any impressive milestones that might have inspired the European public the citizens – or the political intellectuals. There was a lack of eminent personalities with which democratic thought might have identified.

Of course it is something of an improper over-simplification to explain these events mainly in terms of personalities. But the simultaneous decline in authority and lack of democratic leader figures in the democracies certainly was a striking feature of the inter-war years.[1] The European idea, too, containing as it did the seeds of a positive turn in political thought, of supra-national orientations and values, again vanished from the scene with the death of Stresemann (1929) and Briand (1932). Basically, between Wilson's tragic failure (1920), Roosevelt's rise remote from Europe (1933) and Churchill's late hour (1940) there yawned a huge political vacuum which none of the many democratic leader figures in France, Britain or Germany was able to fill. What they lacked was not good will but personal power of persuasion and the ability to steer European democracy from the status and appearance of a transitional solution, from a temporary bourgeois solution between monarchical and socialist-authoritarian forms, into a lasting political system with its own intellectual and moral force of attraction.

That democracy was more than a transitional, or indeed a degenerated, form of history might, at best, be believed in the tradition-buttressed monarchical democracies of Britain and Scandinavia and in the (extremely remote) presidential democracy of America – but not in the crisis-racked parliamentary democracies of the French Third Republic or the rest of

---

[1] A particularly disastrous example was the second presidential election of April 1932, when the eighty-three-year-old Field Marshal Hindenburg was elected – anachronistically and inevitably – with no alternative being left to the democratic parties: K. D. Bracher, *Auflösung*, op. cit., p. 391ff. Alongside the dictators there was only one outstanding figure in the democracies: President Roosevelt. Churchill's day had not yet come. On the personal factors and the problem of authority in democracies see Theodor Eschenburg, *Über Autorität* (Frankfurt/M., 1976), p. 156ff. (with an appendix on 'Antiautoritäre Bewegung'. p. 201ff.).

Europe. As a political form of modernization parliamentary democracy, in particular, with its multi-party system seemed to lack the necessary stability and continuity, and also the inner authority and substance. It evidently did not possess those transrational values of emotion or faith without which no political commonwealth can survive, and democracy least of all, being more dependent than most on the inner participation of its citizens just because it offers so much more scope to self-criticism and opposition than do authoritarian systems of whatever hue.

If the period between the wars is seen as a special period of change and of conflict of values, the failure of politicians and theoreticians to present the fundamental values of democracy convincingly becomes particularly patent. Of course there were formulations and echoes of the great catalogues of human and civil rights in constitutions and legislative texts, and also in political rhetoric, but most of the time these seemed to be just a demand and not the central core or value content of society. States continued to be oriented towards nationalist and ideological objectives on the one hand (macro-politically) and towards the protection of special interests on the other (micro-politically); between these there was a gap which agitators and demagogues utilized for a selfish ideological mobilization of emotions, resulting in an ever-worsening discrediting of a democracy which tolerated such abuse.[1]

Most of the democracies of the twenties were unable to provide signposts for political idealism: the great reservoir of human values, from the individual value of inviolable human dignity to the collective idea of social justice, remained virtually untapped. Its full significance was rediscovered only in the face of totalitarian abuse of political values of belief and was employed for a regeneration and renaissance of democracy – now no longer as a transitional form but as a value-filled realization of human libertarian rights. But that only happened during the struggle against Hitler after 1939 and in the wartime resistance movements, when at times it might seem that political freedom had been expelled from Europe for good. In consequence this was no longer realizable on the same all-European scale that might have been possible after 1918. Now the east of Europe was shunted from one kind of un-freedom into another: the national socialist colour of dictatorship was exchanged for the communist one.[2]

---

[1] Especially in Germany, as previously in Italy, democracy was being discredited as a mere 'bunch of interests', ungovernable polycracy or anarchy. In an efficiency-oriented or autocracy-oriented image of the state such derogation can be made worse by critical socio-political analyses if they lack the sense of values that might bridge the gap between theory and practice, constitution and politics. Typical of the permanent crisis of the German understanding of democracy was, and still is, the assertion and problematization of an alleged conflict between constitution and reality: an extreme theoretical attitude, tending towards ideologization and misjudging the reality of democracy by its perfectionist approach. See, aptly, Wilhelm Hennis, *Verfassung und Verfassungswirklichkeit, Ein deutsches Problem* (Tübingen, 1968), p. 5ff.

[2] See K. D. Bracher, *Europa*, op. cit., p. 269ff.

This charge of 'too late', of a missed opportunity for firmly establishing democratic thought and democratic values throughout Europe, must forever attach to political action and argument of the twenties and thirties. Politicians and intellectuals shared this responsibility to which, under admittedly often difficult and unpredictable circumstances, they showed themselves unequal. The reasons were various: excessive expectations and demands on politics on the part of some; fixation upon old and new dogmas of political and social thought on the part of others; or merely a muddling along, guided by momentary interests and hand-to-mouth politics, in nation-state isolation instead of a timely realization of the interplay of European politics; on all sides, certainly, a misjudgement of the opportunities and limitations of democratization, its chances and its dangers under the conditions of the creation of a free community.

It was a fateful coincidence of overestimation and underestimation of democracy that gripped political thought between the wars and made people look around for false alternatives. A 'third road'[1] between democracy and dictatorship was called for by many conservatives; corporatist authoritarian systems were called for by many Catholics; a monarchical authoritarian state by many Lutherans; a new nationalism and national socialist solutions were demanded by the radical Right; a final social revolution by the radical Left. The approaching end of capitalism was equated with the end of the bourgeois era and of bourgeois democracy. Upon this crisis formula all ideological emotions converged: being largely due to the weakness, colourlessness and intellectual poverty of liberal democracy, it was destined to lead the thirties into the abyss of dictatorship and a new war.

---

[1] The constantly recurring intellectual pattern and ideology of a 'third road' or a 'third force' has in the twentieth century been almost invariably directed against democracy, which it undermines by right-wing or left-wing pseudo-alternatives, and which it derogates by comparison with allegedly more perfect forms of state and society whenever it is not quite ideally unambiguous but pragmatically open to compromise. See on this point George L. Mosse, *Germans and Jews, The Right, the Left, and the Search for a 'Third Force' in Pre-Nazi Germany* (New York, 1970), p. 5ff. Beyond this specific point the old intellectual concept (and propaganda version) has also been of historical and political importance in the pseudo-religious ideas of a third, final, future age, after the past and the present (seen in Joachim of Floris in the twelfth century), these ideas stemming from the concept of the Trinity, as well as in the idea of Russia as the 'Third Rome', of the 'Third Reich', and also in the distinct forms of socialism in the Third World.

8. AUTHORITARIANISM AND DICTATORSHIP: FROM THE FIRST TO THE SECOND POST-WAR PERIOD

The protean concept of the authoritarian state comprises the most varied forms of pre-democratic and semi-democratic 'law-and-order' regimes: historically it figures as the often dreamed-of 'third road' between democracy and dictatorship; at moments of crisis or civil war it is justified as an indispensable emergency form for the salvation of the state; it is, finally, regarded in terms of political evolution as a necessary intermediate form *en route* to the modernization of state and society. Juan Linz, in particular, in his comparative studies of European and Latin American regimes has time and again pointed out that political authoritarianism represents a type of its own between democracy and totalitarianism and not merely an imperfect variant of the one or the other.[1] This applies equally to its historical emergence between the wars and to the surviving and the new dictatorships which predominate especially in the Third World.

It also applies, however, to the ideological dimension of authoritarianism. Its style of thought belongs to the world of dictatorships. It tries to explain and justify dictatorial methods of government. Yet it is often just as far removed from the ideological thought of totalitarian movements as it is from that of democracy, no matter whether it is predominantly traditionally or

---

[1] This premise is not entirely free from problems if one remembers the European instances between the wars: from Hungary (Horthy) and Poland (Pilsudski) through Germany (Hindenburg-Papen, 1932) and Austria (Dollfuss-Schuschnigg) to Greece (Metaxas), Portugal (Salazar) and Spain (Franco). But it seems indispensable in relation to the developing countries of the Third World. A fundamental work is Juan Linz, 'An Authoritarian Regime, Spain', in Erik Allerdt, Stein Rokkan (eds), *Mass Politics* (New York, 1970), p. 29ff.; 'Opposition to and under an Authoritarian Regime, The Case of Spain', in Robert A. Dahl (ed.), *Regimes and Oppositions* (New Haven, 1973), p. 171ff.; 'The Future of an Authoritarian situation or the Institutionalization of an Authoritarian Regime', in Alfred Stepan (ed.), *Authoritarian Brazil* (New Haven, 1973), p. 233ff.; 'Totalitarian and Authoritarian Regimes', in F. J. Greenstein, N. W. Polsby (eds), *Handbook of Political Science*, Vol. 3 (Reading Mass., 1975), pp. 175–411; and most recently with A. Stepan (eds), *The Breakdown of Democratic Regimes*, 4 vols, (Baltimore, 1978), Introduction Part 1, pp. 3–124.

technocratically based.[1] In actual fact, authoritarianism is seen to be oriented mainly towards the dictatorially-based preservation or assertion of social-group, military, economic or tribal power positions through the immobilization of all other forces in the state. Totalitarianism, by contrast, is aimed at the pseudo-religious mobilization of all political forces in the service of a revolutionary monopolist movement and a quasi-religious philosophy with a claim to exclusivity. This rough distinction would have to be further differentiated from case to case: first, according to the preponderance of right-wing or left-wing radical, of national socialist, socialist or imperialist elements and objectives of a dictatorship; next, according to its racial or class-policy concepts of society and community, according to either private enterprise or state economy, or a *dirigiste* or centrally planned economic form; and finally according to its instruments of coercion, oppression and manipulation. An essential criterion would be the question of whether the dictatorship has evolved from a crisis of democracy or from pre-democratic, feudalist-absolutist or autocratic conditions. In every instance the specific historical and political traditions, geographical position and climate, level of development of political and social institutions, as well as the economy, material and spiritual culture, forms of religion and morality would be of considerable importance. Just as the band width of evolution of democratic forms varies from nation to nation, so does the spectrum of ideological variants of justification of dictatorial policy, especially in its authoritarian form.

The constitutional law scholar Carl Schmitt, subsequently to become a champion of the authoritarian Papen-Hindenburg regime and later still of the totalitarian national socialist leadership dictatorship, in his earlier book on dictatorship offered a definition that was significant of the inter-war period.[2] He distinguished between constitutional emergency systems and revolutionary dictatorships. These categories might seem justified on historical grounds but they are, if anything, misleading with regard to modern dictatorship and its political self-image. In terms of constitutional law both constitutional and revolutionary dictatorships retained pseudo-democratic forms; they differed in radicalness of governmental practice and in ideological intensity.

The modern dictatorship concept in fact fluctuates between a crisis or emergency arrangement, requiring rapid decision and action through a concentration of power, though within the framework of the law, on the one hand, and a revolutionary form which 'is a law unto itself'.[3] Yet even the

[1] A still useful ideological distinction between authoritarian-conservative and totalitarian-progressivist regimes (reactionary maintenance or revolutionary change of the value system) was mapped out as early as the fifties by Martin Drath: 'Totalitarismus in der Volksdemokratie', Introduction to Ernst Richert, *Macht ohne Mandat*, 2nd ed. (Cologne-Opladen, 1963), p. xxviiff.

[2] Carl Schmitt, *Die Diktatur, von den Anfängen des modernen Souveränitätsgedankens bis zum proletarischen Klassenkampf* (Munich-Leipzig, 1921; 2nd ed. 1928).

[3] Gustav E. Kafka, 'Diktatur', in *Staatslexikon*, Vol. 2 (Freiburg/Br., 1958), p. 907ff.

historical prototype, the Roman dictatorship of the first century BC, contained just that ambivalence: transition from a constitutionally circumscribed to a comprehensive and permanent dictatorship, the transformation of an authoritarian emergency institution into the governmental principle of an autocratic-order regime. This switch has been repeated time and again in history, especially since the French Revolution. It ranges from seemingly legal, pseudo-democratic forms to caesaristic and totalitarian justifications, from military dictatorship to people's democracy and the dictatorship of the proletariat. Such revolutionary dictatorships can either pursue an authoritarian-conservative policy or act in a progressivist manner. It is just this combination of constitutional-legalistic forms with a pseudo-democratic revolutionary content that enables the dictatorship concept to meet the dual claim of modern authoritarian regimes: their justification through a superior legitimacy in the name of the state and the people, and simultaneously the claim to central organization and concentration of state policy, to social homogeneity and idea-community in the name of distant ultimate goals.[1]

Modern dictatorship therefore differs from the traditional type of monarchistically or theocratically based tyranny or despotism from above. The ambivalence of its functional and developmental potential in modern times is reflected in the broad spectrum of its realizations. Its restricted form, as an emergency institution for the protection of the state and the constitution, is present in the state-of-emergency regulations of democratic constitutions (USA, Britain, Switzerland, France, the Federal Republic of Germany). But there is always the danger that constitutionally founded dictatorial power might be extended by external or internal circumstances and might, justified in a seemingly legal manner, lead to an unconstitutional or anti-constitutional permanent state. This coup-like transformation under the sham legal cover of plebiscites or emergency regulations was accomplished in the course of the French Revolution, in the justification of the 'caesaristic' dictatorships of Napoleon I and Napoleon III, in the fascist seizure of power by Mussolini, in the pseudo-legal totalitarian dictatorship of Hitler, and in the authoritarian transformations of the new republics between the wars into military or leader dictatorships.[2]

A universal drift towards sham-legal dictatorship converted the triumph of democracy in 1918 into a Europe of dictators. After the Second World War this trend continued on a worldwide scale. In the majority of cases, especially in the new countries, the exceptional form has become the normal form. The transfer of democratic systems to the former colonial territories

[1] Just like the concept of revolution (see pp. 89, 107, 117 above), that of dictatorship has likewise become a mixed concept, comprising revolutionary and legalistic, authoritarian and totalitarian forms and contents. See Eleonore Sterling, *Der unvollkommene Staat, Studien über Demokratie und Diktatur* (Frankfurt/M., 1965), p. 189ff.

[2] Karl Loewenstein, 'Die Diktatur Napoleons des Ersten', in *Beiträge zur Staatssoziologie* (Tübingen, 1961), p. 177ff.; E. Sterling, op. cit., pp. 166ff., 210.

of the Third World has almost invariably resulted in (military) dictatorship regimes with socialist and 'people's democratic' or else developmental-dictatorial pretensions to power. Simultaneously there has been an upsurge in the Marxist-Leninist doctrine of the 'dictatorship of the proletariat', likewise with a claim to a superior 'government by the people', with a democratic justification for dictatorship. This form of communist dictatorship, of course – just as the national socialist regime – comes under the heading of totalitarianism, whose ideological unity and total regimentation of state and society, mass party and mass mobilization, far outstrip any historical forms of dictatorship.

An instructive example of the transition from democracy to dictatorship, revealing the ambivalence of the dictatorship concept under the conditions of modern political and social development, is provided by the fate of the Weimar Republic.[1] The first German democracy, with a directly elected Reich President with dictatorial powers, possessed an institution designed to preserve for parliamentary democracy, even beyond the overthrow of the monarchy, the integrating and shielding symbolic force of a supreme and supra-parliamentary power and, at the same time, to control the permanent crises of the young state by the application of a constitutionally-enshrined emergency power.

Here was the point of penetration for the continuing endeavours of a 'national opposition' by the right-wing parties, aiming at the strengthening of these dictatorial powers and at their application in the sense of an authoritarian restructuring or the destruction of the democratic-parliamentary constitutional system in favour of a dictatorial leader state. Originally intended for the protection of the Weimar constitution, and also as a possible counter-weight to a rapidly changing parliamentary government policy, enacted by the Weimar National Assembly in 1919, and indeed used in this spirit by the first Reich President Friedrich Ebert against attempted revolutions by right-wing and left-wing radicalism during the years of crisis from 1919 to 1924, these presidential emergency and dictatorial powers became the basis of government policy and its authoritarian ideologization under Hindenburg's presidency after 1930. Under von Papen's Chancellorship attempts to use this presidential system for a permanent consolidation of an authoritarian-based 'new state' increased in intensity. Hitler's pseudo-legal seizure of power, finally, was achieved by means of presidential emergency decrees (especially the Reichstag fire decree of 28 February 1933) as a permanent state of emergency; national socialist uniform regimentation of the *Länder* and the elimination of the

---

[1] On the intellectual and ideological circumstances of the dictatorship process in Germany see especially Kurt Sontheimer, *Antidemokratisches Denken*, op. cit.; as well as p. 116ff. above. Among the wealth of literature on 'constitutional dictatorship' see now the comprehensive presentation by Heinrich Oberreuter, *Notstand und Demokratie, Vom monarchischen Obrigkeits-zum demokratischen Rechtsstaat* (Munich, 1978), pp. 1ff., 43ff.

constitution was thus very largely performed by the all too easy abuse of dictatorial power provided for the protection of just that constitution.[1]

This escalation of a constitutional dictatorship into an authoritarian one and into the totally arbitrary rule of a leader and his monopolist party, no longer subject to any control, is the extreme instance of the risks inevitably contained in the emergency, martial-law or dictatorship regulations of democratic constitutions. Wherever the constitutional state of affairs is suspended for the purpose of the restoration or the salvation of the state, that danger of a quasi-legal or even illegal switch from limited to unlimited and permanent dictatorship is present. Naturally the formal definition of a dictatorship does not reveal anything about its real face. It may base itself upon a single party (monoparty dictatorship), on the officers' corps (military dictatorship), or even on intellectual-social forces (Church, economy, intelligentsia, bureaucracy). Often it will appear in disguise, seemingly tolerating other political organs alongside itself, though it will extensively control or manipulate these: a monarch (fascism), or a parliament degraded to a purely rubber-stamping organ, or a quasi-suspended ·constitution overtaken by reality, such as the Reichstag and the Weimar Constitution in the 'Third Reich'. It may, after a while, return to constitutional forms by non-violent means like resignation, as in Greece after 1974; or it may remain suspended for a long time in a personality-based intermediate form between traditional authoritarian state and military dictatorship, as in Spain from 1936 to 1976.[2] Or it can, like national socialism, proceed to the extreme political and governmental form of totalitarianism and to total catastrophe.

More recent research into authoritarianism has now also incorporated the theories of development policy: reference is made to 'modernizing authoritarian regimes', which see themselves as transitions to democracy and should therefore be distinguished from conservative-reactionary preservation dictatorships. In all instances, however, political theory is faced with the difficult task of contrasting this (mostly very vague and changeable, and under-researched) authoritarian ideology as a model with a totalitarian philosophy concentrated upon one central key concept. For unlike communism, national socialism and even fascism, authoritarian ideologies do not wish to, or are unable to, assert, either quantitatively or qualitatively, that quasi-religious claim that underlies the central axiom, the identity axiom, of totalitarian ideologies; the fiction or mystification of

[1] To understand the complex processes it is important to bear in mind the interaction of very different factors: constitutional-political and socio-economic ones, intellectual and psychological ones, moral and (pseudo-) religious ones, as well as seduction and coercion. See K. D. Bracher, G. Schulz, W. Sauer, *Die nationalsozialistische Machtergreifung*, 3rd ed. (Berlin, 1974), passim.

[2] On this point, in addition to the mentioned studies by Juan Linz, see especially Stanley G. Payne, *A History of Spain and Portugal*, 2 vols (Madison, 1973) and, *Fascism, Comparison and Definition* (Madison, 1979), p. 139ff., assessing the question of a general concept of fascism (p. 177ff.).

complete political and intellectual identity of leadership, party and people. Thus the lessened role of ideology and unified party – or its absence altogether – as well as the lessened importance of intellectual and political mobilization is a key criterion of this distinction.

Juan Linz's convincing definition, formulated mainly with an eye to Franco's Spain and to Latin America, seems sufficient for the moment:[1] authoritarian regimes are political systems with a limited, non-responsible political pluralism and without an elaborate guiding ideology, but with marked mental attitudes; they do not exhibit any consistent extensive or intensive political mobilization, except possibly at a few special points in their development; and although declared 'leaders' or élitist privileged groups claim for themselves the exercise of power, this is done within certain limits which, while formally ill-defined, are in fact entirely predictable. These are authoritarian mentalities rather than closed ideologies.

From the classic studies of Theodor Geiger[2] the following distinct concepts may be derived: mentality is a mental attitude, a complex of opinions and beliefs, while ideology aims at the substance, at a political theory, no matter how crude or eclectic. Mentality implies psychological disposition, while ideology implies reflexion and self-interpretation; mentality comes first, ideology comes after; mentality is amorphously fluctuating, while ideology is firmly moulded. Above all, ideologies contain a strongly Utopian element, whereas mentalities are closer to the present or the past. Indeed the absence of a Utopian-chiliastic component seems to be a fundamental criterion not only for the theories but also for the forms of dictatorship we are dealing with when we try to distinguish authoritarian ideas and systems from tendentially totalitarian ones. Compared with democracies, however, they all differ on fundamental points: the absence, from idea and practice alike, of human rights, separation of powers, multiparty system and opposition – with all the consequences this may have for the citizens affected.[3]

This 'ideal typology', however, at the same time reveals the difficulty involved in any kind of portrayal of authoritarian ideologies. These are neither dominant nor consistent in themselves; their substance as a rule is as meagre as it is politically meaningless; they only have a secondary, justifying and decorative, character and not the central, representative and determin-

---

[1] Juan Linz, 'Totalitarian and Authoritarian Regimes', op. cit., p. 264.

[2] Theodor Geiger, *Die soziale Schichtung des deutschen Volkes* (Stuttgart, 1932; new ed. 1967), p. 77ff.; and *Ideologie und Wahrheit* (Stuttgart-Vienna, 1953), p. 156ff. Critical of Geiger's earlier position, which was more strongly oriented towards Marxist problems but produced one of the most important contemporary analyses of the Weimar Republic, is Hans-Paul Bahrdt, 'Wünsche, Befürchtungen, Prognosen, Äusserungen Theodor Geigers am Ende der Weimarer Republik', in *Krise des Liberalismus*, op. cit., p. 131ff.

[3] See also the summing-up of the discussion in Mexico in Volker G. Lehr, *Der mexikanische Autoritarismus* (Munich, 1981), p. 28ff.; K. D. Bracher, 'Menschenrechte und politische Verfassung', in *Geschichte und Gewalt*, op. cit., p. 28ff.

ing significance that attaches to the ideologies of national socialism and of communism in particular. If anything, they resemble certain views of fascism. But they are not even comparable with fascism's vague official '*dottrina*', and they differ from actual fascism – in spite of some kinship and sympathy – by the absence of a mass party and of a continuous mobilization.[1]

Thus the principal characteristics of authoritarianism seem to be defined in a negative way: it justifies monocratic or oligarchic exercise of power; in limiting political pluralism and in dispensing with an elaborate ideology it occupies a middle position between totalitarian mobilization regimes and a democratic opening-up of politics; and its main intention is the legitimation of dictatorship by a mixture of traditional and modernization arguments, eclectically garnished with scraps of right-wing and left-wing ideology. Throughout, the state stands at the centre: power props such as the army, the Church, social groups or oligarchic structures serve the strengthening and enhancement of the state's authority.

Like fascism, but quite unlike national socialism or communism, the patterns of authoritarian thought between the wars were directed especially towards the 'true state'. The influential book of the Austrian 'corporate state' theoretician Othmar Spann (1920), which bore that title, provided a basis for the early champions of an organic-homogeneous unification and amalgamation of society and state, whereby conservative anti-liberal and Christian-social ideas were combined with corporatist concepts of the organization of a guided economic and professional hierarchy. It was the idea of the 'third road' between democracy and dictatorship that was realized in the Austrian corporate state from 1934 to 1938.[2] Its intermediate position between fascism and national socialism, on the edge of civil war, was anti-democratic but emphatically non-totalitarian; it also differed from the doctrines of national socialist racialism and the communist class struggle concept, both of which aimed beyond the state, postulating a supranational ideological authority in the key concept of living-space racialism or proletarian world revolution.

In one way or another all authoritarian regimes between the wars

[1] The importance of fascism as a mobilization regime has been examined in particular by Samuel H. Barnes: see his lecture 'Die Rolle des Faschismus in der italienischen politischen Entwicklung' at a conference on Fascism and Democracy, organized by the Universidad Autonoma and the German Cultural Institute in Madrid on 2 June 1976. See K. D. Bracher, *Zeitgeschichtliche Kontroversen*, op. cit., pp. 24–30 (delimited concept of 'fascism'); also Alfred Ableitinger, 'Autoritäres Regime', in *Katholisches Soziallexikon* (Innsbruck-Graz, 1980), p. 210ff.; Konrad Repgen, 'Faschismus', ibid., p. 699; and on the problem of fascism in Spain and Portugal, Stanley G. Payne, *Fascism: Comparison and Definition* (Madison, 1980), p. 139ff.

[2] On this point Adam Wandruszka, *Österreich*, op. cit., p. 852ff.; on the background Gerhard Botz, *Gewalt in der Politik: Attentate, Zusammenstösse, Putschversuche, Unruhen in Österreich 1918–1934* (Munich, 1976).

endeavoured to consolidate the state above all else. From Salazar's Portugal through Franco's Spain, Pilsudski's Poland, the dictatorships in the Balkans and in Greece to the Latin American Caudillo regimes, the aim everywhere was the nationalist consolidation and stabilization of the authority of the state against the crisis of democracy, the totalitarian menace of communism and subsequently national socialism, and also against international-nationalist conflicts or imperial predominance, as feared from the USA in Latin America and between the great powers in Europe.[1]

During the second, the post-1945, phase of authoritarianism much more emphasis was placed on the importance of a state party and on a modernization concept. Moreover, while the inter-war systems saw them-selves as non-democratic or anti-democratic, a claim was now made to democracy, though in the sense of a 'guided democracy', guided from above (as Sukarno's Indonesia). Beyond the previous vague communal ideology and loose organization of political support by the 'masses', the progressive character of the dictatorship and its popular support were now being emphasized. The charismatic character of a leader or a form of populism organized from above would frequently underline the dictatorship's pre-tensions to being a 'government of the people'. Whether traditionalist or modernistic, authoritarianism continued to differ from totalitarian forms by the but secondary role of the state party, by the incorporation of an intensified mobilization into an *étatiste* ideal of stability, and by the subordinate significance of its eclectic ideology, fluctuating between nationalist and state-socialist concepts.[2]

There was also more emphasis on political legitimation through semi-democratic or pseudo-democratic elections, though these served mainly to disguise the actual oligarchy. Between the wars it might have been entirely possible to dispense with reference to democracy, but not so after 1945: thus the anti-democratic ideologies were turned into partially or tendentially democratic justification ideologies, basing the 'third road' between com-munism and democracy much more decisively upon the idea of a 'govern-ment of the people' *sui generis*, bearing a national stamp. Two Latin American instances illustrate the scope within which this evolution of authoritarianism proceeded: Peronism in Argentina (intermittently since 1943) and 'institutionalized revolution' in Mexico (continuously since 1929).[3] Both therefore go back beyond 1945, both include a revolutionary

[1] On the Metaxas case see Anastassios Petrowas, 'Der Weg zur Diktatur des 4. August 1936 in Griechenland', doct. thesis (Bonn, 1980), p. 128ff.; generally Hariton Korisis, *Das politische System Griechenlands* (Hersbruck, 1980), p. 25ff.

[2] See pp. 254ff., 260ff.

[3] See Manfred Mols and Hans W. Tobler, *Mexiko, Die institutionalisierte Revolution* (Cologne-Vienna, 1976); now comprehensively M. Mols, *Mexiko im 20.Jahrhundert* (Pader-born, 1981), pp. 77ff., 416ff.; Volker Lehr, op. cit., p. 51ff. On the categorization of Peronism see Peter Waldmann, *Der Peronismus 1943–1955* (Hamburg, 1974); Hildegard Stausberg, 'Argentinien', in Peter Waldmann, Ulrich Zelinsky (eds), *Politisches Lexikon Lateinamerika* (Munich, 1980), p. 16ff.; and 'Argentinien und die Revolución Libertadora von 1955–1958', doct. thesis (Bonn, 1975), p. 7ff.; Dieter Schneider, 'War der Peronismus totalitär', in Manfred Funke (ed.), *Totalitarismus, Ein Studien-Reader zur Herrschaftsanalyse moderner Diktaturen* (Düsseldorf, 1978), p. 163ff.

claim and a socialist component of modernization, both derive their justification from a state party, trade unions and political election procedures. Yet their own names for themselves reflect the difference that marks these two forms of Latin American authoritarianism: a personalized character on the one hand and an institutionalized one on the other.

Without going into details, it should be said that even a semi-democratic or pseudo-democratic development of authoritarian systems makes no essential change to their dictatorial concept of politics.[1] Typical features are a tremendous preponderance of leadership, government and executive, incompatibility with decentralized or federal state structures, monopoly of political authority held by a person or a group; the movement or party may be more strongly developed but it is understood entirely functionally or instrumentally in the sense of a hierarchy from the top downwards, or at least operated that way. This is true also of most of the 'liberation movements' which embarked on their struggle for power in the era of decolonization following the Second World War, with the postulates of political independence and 'nation building'.[2]

Whatever political conditions and institutional premises the new states had inherited from the colonial era, their main attention, especially in Africa, was necessarily focused on the integration of often very different nations and tribes, and on the concentration of power necessary to achieve state unity. For decentralized structures or those in which power was distributed, such as were bequeathed to them, or recommended to them, by the democratic models of the colonial powers, there was no room at all; in any case the totally unprepared Portuguese colonies of Angola and Mozambique only had their mother country's authoritarian regime to follow. Ideologically, 'socialism' offered itself in all these cases, in national or 'authentic' African form, a motley mixture of mono-party system, personality cult, nationalization and military power, which eliminated its rivals from the liberation struggle and soon, almost universally, was ruled by military dictators.

Here too the peculiarities were revealed which distinguish authoritarian regimes not only from the pluralist democratic concept but also from the communist interpretation of socialism. Just as clearly the authoritarian form

---

[1] V. Lehr, op. cit., p. 38f., lists Left and Right-oriented, technocratic and populist, military-ruled authoritarian systems with or without parties. On the most recent developments see David Collier (ed.), *The New Authoritarianism in Latin America* (Princeton, 1979).

[2] After the voluminous, sometimes rather unhistorical, literature on the issue of 'nation building' in the Third World since the fifties, see now, more realistically, John W. Meyer and Michael T. Hannan, *National Development and the World System: Educational, Economic and Political Change, 1950–1970* (Chicago, 1979). On the significance of military-bureaucratic 'revolutions from above' in various modernization states see Ellen K. Trimberger, *Revolution from Above: Military Bureaucracy and Development in Japan, Turkey, Egypt, and Peru* (New Brunswick/N. J., 1978); Robert Wesson, 'The New Soldier-Ruler in Latin America', in *Hoover Institution Reprint Series No. 39* (*Stanford Magazine* 9/1, 1981), p. 40ff.

of 'national socialism' in the developing countries differs from the racialist and imperialist doctrines of German national socialism and of Italian fascism; at most one might find echoes of Italian fascism in Italy's former colony of Libya, in the power hubris of its military dictator Gaddafi.[1]

The result of authoritarian governmental and system experiments in the course of social and political-military upheavals first in Europe and then in its colonies has been a (theoretically hard to define) mixture of traditionalist and progressivist, national-political and revolutionary-socialist elements, pervaded and held together with ideological fragments from centuries of modern state evolution, with which the new countries are now trying to catch up in a few years. The most difficult boundary line to draw is the one between authoritarianism and, on the one hand, older autocratic tendencies and, on the other, new totalitarian trends whenever that authoritarianism is connected with pretensions to a religious mission and to renewal, particularly in the Islamic dictatorships down to the most recent Iranian upheavals and in the concept of an 'Arab nation', first set into motion, with worldwide political consequences, by Nasser's Egyptian revolution after 1952.[2]

However, there are signs also of liberalizing concepts of authoritarian rule: thus in the further development of Egypt under Sadat and Mubarak. Opportunities along these lines are to be found primarily in economic and social improvements. But, as European experience has shown, they depend also on ideological factors. The degree of uniformity and absoluteness of a political ideology is largely determined by the interpretation, by the scope and by the variability of the political and social order. The fact that, after the end of fascism and national socialism, no ideology with absolute totalitarian pretensions could hope to develop or to succeed, outside the communist power sphere, represents a major hope for the future. The growing attraction of the idea of human rights, penetrating into all the dictatorships, can produce a relaxation, a loosening-up, especially when it goes hand in

---

[1] 'National socialism' emerges most decisively as a version of Arab nationalism: S. A. Hanna and G. H. Gardner, *Arab Socialism* (Leyden, 1969). More specifically, David Ottoway and Marina Ottoway, *Algeria, The Politics of a Socialist Revolution* (Berkeley-Los Angeles, 1970); also Ursula Clausen, *Der algerische Sozialismus* (Opladen, 1969); see Rainer Glagow, 'Islamisch-Arabischer Sozialismus in Libyen', *Afrika heute* (June/July 1973). Historically, Maurice Flory and Robert Mantran, *Les Régimes Politiques des Pays Arabes* (Paris, 1968); E. D. Ologoudou, 'Der Traum eines Dritten Weges, Quellen und Bedeutung des afrikanischen Sozialismus', doct. thesis (Cologne, 1966). See generally, below. On the concept of national socialism as a third road both between the wars and now mainly in the Third World, Hans-Georg Leibbrandt gave an instructive paper in my seminar on political concepts (Winter semester 1976–7): 'Nationaler Sozialismus als Dritter Weg: Konzeptionen und Ausprägungen von der Jahrhundertwende bis zum arabischen Sozialismus' (Seminar records, University of Bonn). An optimistic attempt at a theory was H. C. F. Mansilla (ed.), *Probleme des Dritten Weges, Mexiko, Argentinien, Bolivien, Tansania, Peru* (Darmstadt, 1974).

[2] On the disproportion of clarity and effect in the mobilization concept of an 'Arab nation' see Gerhard Konzelmann, *Die Araber und ihr Traum vom grossarabischen Reich* (1974); as well as the preceding footnote.

hand with a de-ideologization of political thought – and if it survives the setbacks of the sixties. Thcn authoritarianism, as a transitional form of political thought, will again move closer to the democratic idea, as seems to be happening in Mexico and in other Latin American countries.[1] Even totalitarian thought is not safe from such influences; it may well lose credibility in the face of solid reformist progress and its persuasion may suffer when it is seen as a mere façade for coercive rule. In post-Second-World-War Soviet-dominated eastern Europe, especially during the seventies, these consequences emerge in the same measure as the clash between idea and reality, between the communist postulate of human rights and the dictatorial form of government, becomes patent.[2] Contemporary history reveals the truth: it is not communism – as suggested by the words of the Internationale – that establishes human rights but the constitutional idea of moderate libertarian democracy.

[1] In addition to Juan Linz (*Breakdown*, op. cit., p. 7ff.) and Volker Lehr (*Mexikanischer Autoritarismus*, op. cit., p. 294ff.), see the optimistic interpretation in Manfred Mols, 'Parteien und Entwicklungen in der Dritten Welt', in Wolfgang Jäger (ed.), *Partei und System* (Stuttgart, 1973), p. 221ff.

[2] Stimulating, though too optimistic in underestimating the importance of ideology and system preservation in communism, is Peter Bender, *Ende des ideologischen Zeitalters*, op. cit., p. 99ff. See my notes on the totalitarian interpretation of human rights, in *Geschichte und Gewalt*, op. cit., p. 40ff.

PART III
THE PRESENT
De-ideologization and Re-ideologization

The sons eat the fruits
and their fathers slip on the skins.

Albanian proverb

1. POST-WAR EXPERIENCE: RE-EVALUATION AND RECONSTRUCTION

In contrast to the unceasing crisis of ideas after the First World War, there were three major experiences which, after 1945, determined the reconstruction and the political comprehension of a changed world: the experience of totalitarian dictatorship and of the preceding weakness of democracy; the immediate experience of modern war and of ideological genocide; the sobering disillusionment at the Soviet Union's attitude and a renewed totalitarian threat to Europe.

Simultaneously three currents of political orientation emerged during the first few post-war years and, in rapid succession and close interaction, moulded the thought and perception of contemporaries: a conservative yearning for the reconstruction of Europe and its values; at the same time a progressivist turn towards the Left – following the right-wing dictatorships – though this never attained the strength of that following the First World War; and later a sharp reaction to the left-wing totalitarian development in eastern Europe, a development which now no longer presented communism as an interesting intellectual game even to intellectuals but exposed it as a direct threat to freedom – a freedom, moreover, whose existential value had just been appreciated, more immediately than ever before, in the struggle against Hitler. Almost inevitably this led to a hierarchy of values which had been so sadly lacking between the wars.

The concept of the 'free world', no matter how much it was soon to be devalued as a slogan, then described something very real, moreover in a dual sense: liberation from the yoke of Nazi rule and now also defence against new dictatorial subjection.

For the first time in the history of Europe a unanimous opinion began to take shape on the value of libertarian democracy and the community of European interests. Admittedly, this was taking place against the background of utter exhaustion and a crisis mood which coloured the analyses and interpretations of writers, philosophers and theologians more than ever before.[1] But the experience of dictatorship, its destructions and the new threat also provided the prerequisites of a democratic European policy which differed totally from the ideas possible after the First World War. Of course this did not happen overnight. The persistent mental traditions of nationalist and ideological policy continue to survive to this day as massive petrifactions of political life and beliefs. Yet the astonishingly brief span of five years (1945–50) witnessed more than just those great political decisions which have remained decisive to this day as a historic setting of signals. The intellectual and normative decisions of those five years, reflected in constitutions and doctrines, books and discussions, and also in the sudden severances from communism, similarly testify to the emergence of a common-European and common-democratic political comprehension, incomparably more strong and universal than any past political thought permeated by the conviction of the primacy of freedom and human dignity, of the importance of a balance between individual and social rights, and of the unassailable value of pluralistic democracy over all monolithic ideologies and systems.

This is not to say that doubts or differences of opinion on the forms of political life had diminished. But a fundamental concept now was that of the 'open society and its enemies', thrown into the great debate from faraway Australia by the philosopher Karl Popper, a 1938 refugee from Hitler's Vienna. It was a declaration of war on the great ideological dogmas, on past and present closed philosophical systems, and for the unflinching defence of (in the literal sense) open thought and for the (open) society in which alone this was possible – against all cajolement and compulsion. Of course there are controversies over Popper's argument in its philosophical and theoretical details, just as there are controversies about the outlines of a philosophy of freedom now deliberately developed from various quarters from Karl Jaspers to Isaiah Berlin.[2]

---

[1] Walter Z. Laqueur, *Europa aus der Asche* (Munich-Zurich-Vienna, 1970), p. 233ff.; George Lichtheim, *Europa*, op. cit., pp. 307ff., 350ff., Maurice Crouzet, *The European Renaissance since 1945* (New York, 1971). On the significance of the reorientation of the Churches in the light of their past experience of authoritarianism and the post-war demands of democracy see four case studies by Armin Boyens, Martin Greschat (both on German developments), Rudolf von Thadden (significance of Dietrich Bonhoeffer), Paolo Pombeni (Italy), in *Kirchen in der Nachkriegsgeschichte* (Göttingen, 1979); on the specific German argument, Johanna Vogel, *Kirche und Wiederbewaffnung der Bundesrepublik 1949–1956* (Göttingen, 1978). The Christian debate of Marxism under the double ambivalent impact of anti-fascism *and* Stalinism is sketched out by Richard Banks, 'Christianity and Marxism', op. cit., p. 321ff.; see also *Christlicher Glaube in moderner Gesellschaft* (Freiburg/Br., 1981), with comprehensive contributions by Alexander Schwan, Nikolaus Lobkowicz and Henning Ottmann.

[2] Karl R. Popper, op. cit. (first published 1944, American edition 1950, German edition 1957); Karl Jaspers, *Vom Ursprung und Ziel der Geschichte*, 1st ed. (1955); Isaiah Berlin, *Four Essays on Liberty* (1968). See also the detailed survey in Roland N. Stromberg, *After Everything: Western Intellectual History since 1945* (New York, 1975).

Thirty years later this point of departure, the alignment against things totalitarian, is again being challenged by a posthumous generation which no longer thinks or writes from within the same horizon of experience. But this changes nothing about the fundamental importance of the fact that, in the years following 1945, a positive assessment of libertarian democracy and an unambiguous rejection of closed ideologies established itself intellectually for the first time since the turn of the century. Unlike the alienation of the mind from political reality after the First World War, there was now a conviction of the political responsibility of the intellectual; instead of the deep scepsis of the critique of democracy and of cultural pessimism there was now, face to face with actual destruction and the threat to the west, a firmly founded scepsis concerning anything ideological or totalitarian, of the temptations and enticements of Utopian thought, as well as of democracy's self-destructive toleration towards its enemies.

This reorganization of political thought did not, of course, happen out of the blue; at any rate, it also remained controversial in the west, as evidenced by the continued existence of right-wing and left-wing radical ideas, and of strong communist parties especially in Italy and France, and finally by the renewed attraction of dictatorial nationalism and socialism, now on a worldwide scale in the new states of Africa and Asia – not to mention the extension of communism to one-third of the world's population. Nevertheless, the unexpected strength and attraction shown by the reconstruction, as well as the unaccustomed political stability of free Europe, would be inconceivable but for the existential experience of its decision against the totalitarian threat of Hitlerism and Stalinism. This was a case of real decision, of 'crisis' in its original meaning, not just in the way the crisis concept was used in the twenties and thirties, when it frequently and grandiloquently served intellectual self-satisfaction, from Spengler's 'years of decision' through existentialism to the 'socialist decision'. Fundamental confrontations took place between communist sympathizers from Picasso to Sartre, on the one hand, and the champions of freedom of culture, on the other, who included quite a few former 'fellow travellers', from Koestler and Silone to T. S. Eliot.[1] Naturally, under the pressure of great events and in view of the irresistible polarization of the world by the super-powers the once powerful states of Europe, and their intellectuals, now found their importance diminished. But this in turn forced them into a political stock-taking of a kind that had been absent after 1918: a reflection by the nations of Europe on the limits of national-state power politics, and a reflection by the

[1] See W. Laqueur, *Europa*, op. cit., p. 240ff.; Raymond Aron, *Marxism and Existentialism* (London, 1967). On France also the insider's avowal of Louis Aragon, *L'Homme Communiste* (Paris, 1953); see Charles Micaud, *Communism and the French Left* (1963); Annie Kriegel, *Les Communistes français, essay d'ethnographie politique* (Paris, 1969). On old and new problems of alienation between politics, culture and art see Herbert Read, *Art and Alienation: The Role of the Artist in Society* (1969); Edgar Wind, *Art and Anarchy* (1963); Colin Wilson, *The Outsider* (1956).

intellectuals on the fundamental difference between democracy and
dictatorship, rather than the former arguments about 'bad' democracies and
'good' dictatorships, and the flirtation with the latter, merely because of
their ideologically perfectionist visions of the future.

However, 1945 was not simply 'zero hour', regardless of the immensity of
physical and moral destruction. It also represented a great refutation of
political illusions and of left-wing and right-wing revolutionary progressivist
belief. More than ever before was the idea of progress revealed in its
profound ambivalence: faith in an irresistible and automatic improvement
of man in a moral and cultural respect was confronted with the experience of
Auschwitz. Communism, similarly, was no longer sufficient as the quintessence of anti-fascism. After all, the ideological promises of communism
were based on the same old progressivism; and it was there, right in the
Soviet Union, that the inhuman forced labour camps continued to exist.[1]
Cultural critique and pessimism, now that their fears of decline had come
true contrary to expectation, were no longer able to look to strong
individuals or ideological salvation, but instead had to face an immense
exhaustion and disillusionment, and a need for de-ideologization. It was the
period of a seemingly 'sceptical generation',[2] which was seeking its props on
one side or other of by now traditional ideologies in order to ensure not the
great revolution but feasible reform and, most of all, physical and moral
survival.

For the moment, however, there was deep pessimism. The European age
of history seemed to have come to an end, finally, in the destruction wrought
by the war. This was especially true for the Germans: the 'German
catastrophe' (1946) meant to Friedrich Meinecke, the most highly regarded
historian, the end of a German state, and Alfred Weber published in 1945
his *Farewell to Past History*, written in 1944. But even that old progressivist
optimist H. G. Wells was now speculating about the impending end of
human civilization altogether. Incorrigible crisis thinkers such as Heidegger
insisted that it made no difference to European culture whether Europe was
crushed by America or by Russia in the process of technologization and mass
levelling.[3] All hopes of liberation were in fact dashed in eastern Europe by

[1] The discovery and unmasking of totalitarian structures, and hence also the development of
theories of totalitarianism, represented a major upheaval for political progressivist thought.
See Leonard Schapiro (ed.), *The USSR and the Future* (London, 1963); John A. Armstrong,
The Politics of Totalitarianism (New York, 1961). On this point K. D. Bracher, 'Fortschritt –
Krise einer Ideologie', in *Geschichte und Gewalt*, op. cit., p. 211ff.; and especially Raymond
Aron, *Progress and Disillusion, The Dialectics of Modern Society* (London, 1968).

[2] Helmut Schelsky, *Die skeptische Generation, Eine Soziologie der deutschen Jugend*
(Düsseldorf, 1957). On this 'spirit of the fifties' very balanced and informative is Hans-Peter
Schwarz, *Die Ära Adenauer 1949–1957 (Geschichte der Bundesrepublik Deutschland*, Vol. 2)
(Stuttgart, 1981), p. 375ff. See also the numerous different contributions in the symposium
Erwartungen – Kritische Rückblicke der Kriegsgeneration (Munich, 1981).

[3] H. G. Wells, *Mind at the End of Its Tether* (1946); Martin Heidegger, *Einführung in die
Metaphysik* (Tübingen, 1953) (revised lecture from the summer semester 1935 at the University
of Freiburg).

the Soviet Union, and that second start towards an international world order in the shape of the United Nations also ended in disappointment. The atom bomb seemed a symbol of the ultimate possibilities made available by science to a policy of self-destruction: progress no doubt, but usable now for global annihilation.

The apocalyptic perspectives of the last and of a future war, however, might also prove a powerful incentive to avoiding a continuation or repetition of the great mistakes of thought and action that had impressed their stamp on the first half of the century. Their great refutation, Europe's about-turn, a more realistic understanding of political freedom, of human dignity and of the moral values of democracy – these were positive aspects of the catastrophe, aspects ensuring, beyond national differences, a kind of basic consensus throughout the free world, a consensus into which, with unexpected speed, the vanquished Germans and Japanese were included; this, too, very differently from after the First World War.[1]

The establishment of a free Europe in close association with America was the political idea which had been lacking after 1918, when there had been much philosophizing about the decline of the west, while this west had been further confirmed in its political self-dismemberment and ideological self-alienation. It called for firm scales of values which would strengthen and unite Europe against the despotism it had suffered and survived, and was now once more being threatened by, and which would protect the democratic freedoms saved from Hitler in 1945. A stroke of luck helped: an economic resurgence of western Europe, undreamt of even by the operators of the Marshall Plan (1947), raising it within a few years from deepest destitution to new economic prosperity.

This was in sharp contrast not only to the socio-economic crisis experiences of the twenties and thirties, which had contributed so much to the undermining of democracy, but also to the evident inability of the communist systems to accomplish their promised economic and social progress. Never in history has the interaction of economic-social and political thought emerged more strikingly.[2]

[1] It is this positive aspect and not a desperate search for some western, or more particularly American, responsibility for the 'cold war' that should be emphasized in any comparison of the periods following the First and the Second World Wars. Herein also lies the fundamental difference in the subsequent development which, in the first case, led to dictatorship and another war, and, in the second, to a clarification of positions and a renaissance of democracy. See K. D. Bracher, *Europa*, op. cit., p. 284ff.; Klaus Schwabe, 'Die Vereinigten Staaten und der Frieden in Europa 1919 und 1945', in *Historia Integra (Festschrift für Erich Hassinger)* (Berlin, 1977), p. 391ff.; Werner Link, 'Zum Problem der Kontinuität der amerikanischen Deutschlandpolitik im 20. Jahrhundert', in Manfred Knapp (ed.), *Die deutsch-amerikanischen Beziehungen nach 1945* (Frankfurt/M., 1975), p. 86ff.

[2] This context was subsequently called in question and discredited by a revisionist 'in-depth examination' of the Marshall Plan, including its positive importance to the recovery of Europe and of liberal democratic thought, as soon as anyone challenged the clear experience of the Cold War and of anti-totalitarian consequences in arguments with the Left or the Right. Limits

The idea of freedom was favoured by the moment which, by the co-operation of European and American forces, enabled the democracies to rise to a previously unknown prosperity, made more conspicuous by contrast with the repulsive picture of communist coercive rule and coercive economy. The sixties, admittedly, were to reveal that it was chiefly the values of economic, social and military security that were to the fore. It was the other side of the coin of de-ideologization that efforts towards a philosophical and moral foundation of libertarian-democratic policies were lagging behind a pragmatic orientation which could not suffice in the long run. There was the value horizon of a security policy through the trans-Atlantic alliance (NATO), which guaranteed Europe a long period of peace, and of a European policy of the democratic states (the European Community), which replaced international power struggles by co-operation and integration.[1] But the new, the special aspect of these practical values was but slowly and hesistantly perceived in its significance to the history of political ideas: the creation of an awareness was lagging behind the socio-economic and political changes.

The astonishing transformation from which free Europe benefited within a single decade called for new forms of expression. What occurred was a mixture of the old and the new: a link-up with severed thought from the twenties, resumption of the democracy and modernization debate in the social sciences, though now enriched by research into totalitarianism which became an important point of orientation of western self-understanding. It was in fact the continuing argument about the forms and values of democracy and dictatorship, about the 'overcoming' of fascism and national socialism and critique of communism which, rather as a negative delimit-ation of the libertarian-democratic position, formed the horizon of political ideas with its own 'pinpointing of the present'[2] in the fifties.

were therefore set to the leftward shift of 1945; to the extent that intellectual inclinations towards Marxist or semi-Marxist interpretations continued, or were revived, the gap from 1947 to 1950 (the Marshall Plan to the war in Korea) was painfully re-examined in left-wing revisionist and sometimes increasingly anti-American literature and invariably demonized. On the ideological distortions of the great political and spiritual decisions from 1945 to 1950 see now the bibliographical essay for the new edition of Hans-Peter Schwarz, *Vom Reich zur Bundesrepublik, Deutschland im Widerstreit der aussenpolitischen Konzeptionen in der Jahren der Besatzungsherrschaft 1945–1949* (Stuttgart, 1980), p. xxxvff.; K. D. Bracher, *Europa*, op. cit., p. 304ff.; Klaus Schwabe, 'Die amerikanische Besatzungspolitik in Deutschland und die Entstehung des "Kalten Krieges" (1945/46)', in A. Fischer, G. Moltmann, K. Schwabe (eds), *Russland, Deutschland, Amerika. Festschrift für Fritz Epstein* (Wiesbaden, 1978), p. 311ff.; Werner Link, 'Der Marshallplan und Deutschland', *Aus Politik und Zeitgeschichte* 50 (13 December 1980), p. 3ff.

[1] See Alfred Grosser, *Das Bündnis, Die Westeuropäischen Länder und die USA seit dem Krieg* (Munich, 1978), p. 93ff.

[2] Thus the historical-philosophical conclusion of the important liberal sociologist Alexander Rüstow who, after emigrating from Ankara, taught at Heidelberg: *Ortsbestimmung der Gegenwart, Eine universalgeschichtliche Kulturkritik*, 2 vols (Erlenbach-Zurich, 1950–2). On Italy especially the great works of Benedetto Croce and G. De Ruggiero on the history of liberalism, and Guglielmo Ferrero on the demonism of power, see K. D. Bracher, 'Gegen die Politik der Furcht', in *Der Monat* 3/36 (1951) p. 661ff.

The two poles of the discussion are marked by a wealth of political and historical literature: on the one hand, the experience of the seductive and manipulative power of authoritarian and totalitarian dictatorships under the conditions of modernization pressure, and on the other, the arguments about exhaustion and 'the end of ideology'[1], about the feasibility of a value-emphatic while ideology-free political concept in a pluralistic democracy. This orientation debate, admittedly, has basically changed since the mid-sixties, with the advent of a new generation whose horizon of experience was shifted to the later post-war years; it yielded some ground to re-ideologizations which, however, for the most part amounted to a rehash of the old theories of culture and social critique in a 'neo-Marxist' garb.

Political thought in the fifties revolved mainly around illustrations and explanations of the failure of the democracies; it was essentially an attempt to master the past with a view not only to understanding the disaster of the Second World War but also to being prepared for a confrontation with topical problems, no matter whether they concerned actual communism, a possible neo-fascism or the structural problems of democracy. Not only in Germany was the fate of the Weimar Republic seen as a classic example of the political and ideological questions facing the citizen and the state under the conditions of modern industrial society. My *Auflösung der Weimarer Republik*, written between 1950 and 1954, belongs in this ideological and historical context.[2]

The task, however, was not just to prevent a repetition of the self-destruction of democracy by reinforcing it at its most vulnerable points. The task also concerned the new 'frontier situation' in which human civilization found itself since the dawn of the atomic era. Hence the question of progress, too, was posed in a new way. Books like Karl Jaspers' *Die*

---

[1] Thus at the end of the fifties – though soon outdated – one of the leading American sociologists, Daniel Bell, *The End of Ideology, On the Exhaustion of Political Ideas in the Fifties* (Glencoe, Ill., 1960), pp. 265ff., 369ff.; see K. D. Bracher, 'Politik zwischen Theorie und Empirie', *Kölner Zeitschrift für Soziologie und Sozialpsychologie* 13 (1961), p. 525ff.

[2] The author takes the liberty of pointing out that these studies, *Auflösung einer Demokratie*, (1952); *Die Auflösung der Weimarer Republik* (1955), and *Nationalsozialistische Machtergreifung* (1960), even before the widely-featured Fischer controversy on the causes of the First World War and the new debate on fascism in the sixties, had revealed the epoch-historical and structure-historical connection in which the authoritarian state, democracy and dictatorship had to be viewed. Not the sixties but the fifties marked the new start which pointed beyond traditional history. True, the political expansion in the media and universities subsequently resulted in disturbances which ensured incomparably greater publicity to events in the sixties. This is also overlooked by Hans-Ulrich Wehler in his critical account 'Geschichtswissenschaft heute', in *Stichworte*, op. cit., Vol. 2, p. 709ff., which is focused entirely on the Fischer controversy. On the other hand, I would not wish to stop at that once so 'progressive' position. Instead of a modish exaggeration of structure-historical and socio-historical approaches, which have anyway by now become commonplace, it seems to me more important to discuss the totalitarian and not merely the 'fascist' dangers in the relationship of history, politics and ideas. See K. D. Bracher, 'Experience and Concepts', in *A Generation of Political Thought*, *Government and Opposition*, 15/4 (London, 1980), p. 289ff.

Atombombe und die Zukunft des Menschen (1958) as well as the political-moral discussions of the physicists themselves,[1] grasped the problem in its existential significance beyond the scientific-political sphere: the prospect that the enormous progress of science might be linked with the potential for annihilating mankind gave a new dimension to the concept of political responsibility and made supreme demands on the structures and institutions for the safeguarding of peace. Above political strife and issues of ideological creeds there now stood the necessity, as never before, of peaceful resolution of conflicts. The question was merely to what extent this aspect would contribute to a further de-ideologization, or whether the continued existence of the communist challenge with its pretension to an absolute creed would not continue to foil any such tendencies – even after the end of the Stalin era.

In this respect, too, the sixties represent a caesura: intensification of the policy of co-existence, efforts towards bilateral weapons control, and finally the hopes of an active policy of *détente* all seemed to open up new prospects of a peace policy free from ideologies. The point, however, that was too readily missed was that the communist concept of co-existence and peace was anything but free from ideology; indeed the antagonistic character of co-existence has always been stressed. The vaguenesses and contradictions of *détente* were certainly grounded also in ideology.[2]

The hopes of the fifties had, by comparison, been focused much more clearly and fundamentally at a delimitation against communism. As an intellectual and ideological power Stalinism had reached a low point as the brutal regimentations and bloody purges in eastern Europe, Tito's defection, the banishment of millions of troublesome Soviet citizens to a system of prison and forced labour camps (Solzhenitsyn's *Gulag Archipelago*) were destroying the last illusions of the thirties and forties. The revolutionary promise of the future had turned into bureaucratic communism, the intellectual beacon of Marxism had become the power-political military menace of despotism.

The intellectual and moral disenchantment with communism was undoubtedly a factor without which the totally different spiritual climate of the

[1] See, in Germany, the critical 'Göttingen Declaration' of nuclear physicists in 1957: Carl Friedrich von Weizsäcker, *Die Verantwortung der Wissenschaft im Atomzeitalter* (Göttingen, 1957); and worldwide, the discussion of the dilemma of an American 'father' of the atom bomb like J. Robert Oppenheimer (1904–67), which also found dramatic expression: Heinar Kipphardt, *In the matter of J. Robert Oppenheimer* (London, 1967).

[2] On this now the major work by Hans-Peter Schwarz and Boris Meissner (eds), *Entspannungspolitik in Ost und West* (Cologne, 1979), with a critical assessment of *détente* ideas and their limitations in the east, among east bloc dissidents, and in the '*détente* political pluralism' of the west. The possibilities of clinging to the *détente* concept in spite of negative experience are discussed in the volume by Josef Füllenbach and Eberhard Schulz (eds), *Entspannung am Ende?* (Munich-Vienna, 1980). See also my sceptical assessment in *Krise Europas* (1976), p. 357ff., or *Europa in der Krise*, op. cit., p. 417ff., now also separately as *Europa und Entspannung* (Berlin, 1982).

period after the Second World War and the greater stability of western democracies would scarcely be conceivable. The brutal demonstrations of Soviet power politics in Prague (1948), Korea (1950), East Berlin (1953), Budapest (1956) and again Prague (1968), and finally Afghanistan (1979), simultaneously represented defeats for the communist ideology, reminding the world as they did of the deceptive substance of totalitarian thought and beliefs, and preventing a total relapse into the illusions of the inter-war years. The more so as the Soviet Union's entirely imperialist policy of brute force occurred, above all, in countries formerly occupied by Hitler (Czechoslovakia and Poland), for whose liberation in particular the Second World War had been fought. But the domestic system of communism, especially the tyranny and terror of Stalinism, had been so thoroughly revealed in the fifties that the humanist pretensions and future promises of this ideology seemed shattered. Now it was the negative Utopias of a totalitarian future which were applied to the Soviet Union, most impressively in the former communist George Orwell's visions of a totally controlled, despiritualized world and of a global war between two totalitarian world states with no alternative.[1]

To what extent it is also possible to speak of a de-ideologization in the communist sphere continues to be a controversial point.[2] The creed content may have faded, or shrunk to a mere dogma with a cult of Lenin and Marx, but the position and function of the ideology within the framework of continuing mono-party dictatorship have remained unbroken. Their taboo nature and exclusive validity continue to determine the formulations and thought patterns of the communist systems, no matter how bureaucratized or rationalized these may seem. The irrational attraction of communism declined temporarily in the west, but it experienced a revival in the sixties, testifying to the possible revitalization not only of Marxism but also of

[1] See in particular Orwell's books *Animal Farm* (1945) and *Nineteen Eighty-Four* (1949). Orwell's development and assessment in relation to the British Left is discussed by George Watson, *Politics and Literature*, op. cit., p. 38ff. and Bernard Crick, op. cit., p. 306ff.

[2] The range of interpretations extends from the well-founded scepsis of old experts on Soviet communism like Boris Meissner through cautious 'realists' like George Kennan to almost euphoric optimists like Peter Bender. Boris Meissner, in *Entspannungspolitik* (see footnote 2, p. 196) p. 19ff., points to the Soviet thesis of the intensification of the 'ideological struggle' during *détente*, which very much governed the seventies. Kennan fluctuates between a very sober estimate of Soviet policy and an endorsement – not entirely free from contradictions – of *détente*; see his book *On dealing with the Communist World* (New York, 1964). The long line, finally, of those fully backing *détente*, to which they are ready to subordinate almost all other factors, including the experiences of Budapest, Prague and Poland, stretches from Bender to Egon Bahr. How little the revealing books of Solzhenitsyn and many earlier dissenting or emigré writers, or the persecution of intellectual critics such as Sakharov, have affected continuing hopes of *détente* is further evidence of their suggestive power and of the continuing inclination of many intellectuals to give communism, in spite of all criticism, the benefit of doubt, and credit it with good will because of its worthy goals. On the German problem in a state of transformation see Eberhard Schulz, *Die deutsche Nation in Europa, Internationale und historische Dimensionen* (Bonn, 1982).

Leninism. It was only the Soviet monopolist pretension that suffered to some extent as a result of Tito's and Mao's defections – but these were offset by the ideology's worldwide spread. True, the importance of totalitarian communism as a closed creed has been repeatedly questioned, most recently by the emergence of a 'democratic' Eurocommunism in Italy, France and Spain. But a certain degree of polycentrism of 'world communism' does not yet mean the end of its ideological force: on the contrary! And in conjunction with the Soviet Union's military power the belief in the future of communism remains a prime factor in world politics and an indispensable instrument of legitimation for party dictatorships, even if these, as in the countries of eastern Europe, are additionally propped up by military means from outside.[1]

On the other hand, this demystification of communism in the fifties was by no means matched by an ideologization of western democracy, as was subsequently claimed by the neo-Marxist Left. The fact was that de-ideologization referred principally to domestic conditions in the west, leading, at most, to Churchill's well-known observation that other political systems were a lot worse still than parliamentary democracy. A significant aspect, indeed, was the search for modified, stabilizing and crisis-proof forms of 'militant' democracy, such as, above all, the West German Federal Republic (remembering Weimar) in the Chancellor-type democracy as consolidated and moulded by Adenauer, and eventually France in the Fifth Republic, the presidential republic of General de Gaulle, its liberator.[2]

Not enthusiastic approval but a rather sober realization of the necessities and limitations of democratic policy characterized the emergence of consensus in the western countries. After the left-wing experiments of the

[1] The great crises of communism since the East Berlin rising of 1953 reflect the interlinking of military coercive and ideologically totalitarian rule. In this connection greater flexibility in the resolution of totalitarian system crises does not indicate de-ideologization but only a certain measure of modernized adaptation (such as Hungary after 1956) in the forms of cultural life and the breadth of intellectual discussion, which invariably comes up against a barrier the moment issues of governmental or ideological monopoly are touched. For the latest balance-sheet of the extensive discussion and literature see Georg Brunner, 'Die ungarische Revolution – 25 Jahre danach', *Aus Politik und Zeitgeschichte*, B 44/81 (31 October 1981), p. 3ff. On the step-by-step suppression of the 'Prague Spring' of 1968 during the succeeding years see H. G. Skilling, *Czechoslovakia's interrupted Revolution* (Princeton, 1976); Zdenek Hejzlar, *Reform-kommunismus* (Cologne, 1976).

[2] It is, however, significant that these very considerable modifications of 'classic' parliamentary democracy received so little attention in the fifties and sixties. Adenauer's 'Chancellor democracy' and de Gaulle's Fifth Republic were criticized mainly on party-political grounds as presidentially authoritarian, anti-parliamentarian. Only when the 'militancy' of the West German democratic concept was challenged by radical applicants for civil service posts – revolutionaries, as it were, claiming a pension – did fundamental and ideological discussions, getting down to first principles, get under way in the seventies: see K. D. Bracher, *Zeitgeschichtliche Kontroversen*, op. cit., p. 103ff.; also R. Löwenthal and H.-P. Schwarz (eds), *Die Zweite Republik* (Stuttgart, 1974); and now especially Eckhard Jesse, *Streitbare Demokratie* (Berlin, 1980).

first few post-war years a liberal-conservative, non-ideological basic attitude established itself almost everywhere, including Britain and the USA. It was anti-totalitarian but also anti-doctrinaire, focused on the specific, pragmatic aspects and limitations of politics instead of on a replay of the old ideological battles of the nineteenth century which, so it was believed, had finally become anachronistic in the world after the Second War. Nothing revealed this development more clearly than the changed self-image of the social democratic parties. For them the fifties had been a period of reverses; adaptation of their socialist theory (and ideology) to the pragmatic mood of reconstruction and the pluralistically open trend of political thought called for a final break with socialism as an absolute creed. It now became just *one* philosophy among many, and it stood in an entirely positive relationship, instead of atheist opposition, to Christianity as a possible root of socialism: that was the astonishing self-definition performed by the German social democrats in their new 'Godesberg Programme' in 1959.[1]

The British Labour Party and the Socialist International had likewise, at about the same time, formulated their renunciation of the ideological character of socialism and of the old dogma of nationalization. Naturally, this did not take place without considerable internal struggles, and in the sixties it was largely responsible for the re-ideologization phenomena which, temporarily, experienced such a tumultuous upsurge on the Left and among youth. Nevertheless, endorsement of bourgeois democracy together with a socially-coloured capitalism, on the lines of the social market economy in Germany, was something entirely different from the reluctant toleration of democracy between the wars. Admittedly there were attempts at nationalization by the Labour Party in Britain. But the main aspect was no longer ideological but the preservation of freedom and practical reforms through active participation in political power, to prevent abuse of democracy and to avert that danger of power decay and power vacuum which had cleared the road for the dictators to the 'dissolution of the Weimar Republic' (thus my own interpretation in 1952 and 1955).

The real question which greatly engaged political thought in the 'post-ideological' age was the seemingly irresistible extension of the state into vast areas of the economy and of society: the conflict between the (liberal) emancipation of the citizen and his (social) support within the community, a conflict which further accelerated the *étatiste* development while promising to protect the citizen and help him attain his rights. Bureaucracy, already described by Max Weber as an irresistible trend of modern society,

[1] See p. 76 above. On the discussion of the Godesberg Basic Programme of the SPD and its immediate consequences for the sixties and for the subsequent orientation and problems of the SPD between de-ideologization and re-ideologization see Susanne Miller, *Die SPD vor und nach Godesberg* (Bonn, 1974); Helmut Schmidt, *Auf dem Fundament des Godesberger Programms*, 2nd ed. (Bonn, 1974), *Godesberg und die Gegenwart* (Bonn, 1975). Now the comprehensive work by Kurt Klotzbach, *Der Weg zur Staatspartei* (Berlin-Bonn, 1982), p. 449ff.

intervened to an ever-growing degree in the life of the citizen. Thus the argument about the all-caring, all-present welfare state engaged minds far more than the classic ideological confrontation between socialism and capitalism had done. This 'life-ensuring state'[1], this shelter 'from the cradle to the grave', contained within itself both promise and threat: the beginnings of creeping, non-ideological totalitarianism. It was the transformation of the socialist Utopia into an *étatiste* nightmare, the revolt against the super-state which was subsequently invoked also by the anti-system movements of the seventies.

Certainly the exhaustion and demystification of the ideologies also led to a de-politicization, to a withdrawal into the private sphere, to the 'count me out' attitude of the post-war years. Yet this new scepsis towards politics was totally different from the ideological anti-attitudes of the years after the First World War and from the nihilism of the crisis philosophers of that time. Even though the popularity of Sartre's existentialism and his philosophy of *Being and Nothingness* developed into a fashion movement in Paris, it certainly hoped to be accepted far more clearly as a philosophy of individual freedom in a world of collective apparatuses and ideologies, as the salvation of the person in a mass-and-organization world, and as enabling the individual to create his own values amidst a world of shattered beliefs and ideas.

Moreover, contacts between existentialist personalism and Christian renewal movements in the political field were also much more solid than between the wars.[2] Of course, the emergence of Christian democratic parties in most European countries went back to older traditions, especially to Christian social movements. Yet the new strength of Christian democracy and (especially in Germany) its supra-denominational character soon enabled it to adopt a state-supporting role; its self-image as a Christian movement of in-gathering and integration was based also on a changed attitude on the part of the Churches which, after their experiences of dictatorship, had moved from their ambivalent attitude towards secular democracy to an endorsement of philosophical pluralism. The specific political importance of an application of Christian ethics to man's moral and social needs in an industrial society emerged very clearly in the positive key

[1] This almost philosophically sounding term for a soberly bureaucratic state administration of contributions was introduced into the West German discussion in 1953 by the Heidelberg constitutional law expert Ernst Forsthoff. See Forsthoff's writings in *Rechtsstaat im Wandel, Verfassungsrechtliche Abhandlungen 1954–1973*, 2nd ed. (Munich, 1976); *Begriff und Wesen des sozialen Rechtsstaats (Verhandlungen der deutschen Staatsrechtslehrer 1953)* (Berlin, 1954); *Rechtsfragen der leistenden Verwaltung* (1959). But the term was used by Forsthoff as early as in 1938 in *Die Verwaltung als Leistungsträger* (Stuttgart, 1938), *i.e.* under the national socialist state with which he had sympathized, as shown by his early work *Der totale Staat* (1933). This provenance is not without interest in that it spotlights the technocratic-*dirigiste* implications and dangers concealed in an over-emphasis on social-welfare components even in a declared liberal democracy like that of Western Germany.

[2] Thus especially Jacques Maritain (1882–1973): *Christianisme et démocracie* (New York, 1943; Paris, 1945).

role of Christian democratic parties in the restoration of democracy especially in the former dictatorship countries of Italy and Germany, and also in the European policies of France, though initially viewed with suspicion by socialists and social democrats.[1]

Nevertheless, the fifties were deeply involved in bitter arguments about east–west and alliance policy. Both on the Right and on the Left neutralist and anti-American attitudes emerged, reaching their peak in the struggle over the western treaties, over German rearmament and over the further development of nuclear weapons. Yet these never achieved the intellectual or psychological force of the anti-democratic movements of the twenties or thirties. The attraction of communism seemed to have been broken, socialism was engaged in a profound reorientation, concepts like class struggle and nationalism receded against the successes of European reconstruction, and political conservatism, having seen its authoritarian and right-wing radical variants disproved by the disasters of fascism and national socialism, not only accepted the liberal-democratic reconstruction of Europe but quite substantially promoted it.[2]

Undoubtedly pessimistic culture critique continued to represent a powerful undercurrent. Europe's reduction in size and decline in power, its dependence on the relationship of the superpowers, as well as the 'Americanization' of civilization provided fresh nourishment to the idea of decline. Parallels were drawn with classical antiquity, with the fate of ancient Greece vis-à-vis the new Roman superpower, and the decline theories of Spengler and Toynbee attracted renewed attention. But there was also the memory of de Tocqueville who, more than a century earlier, had predicted the rise of democracy and the confrontation between the protagonists of liberty (America) and of serfdom (Russia). His conservative critique of democracy was understood as a constructive alternative to reactionary and authoritarian national conservatism. As for the gloomy comparisons with antiquity and with the decline of Greeks as well as Romans, ancient historians of Christian-democratic orientation soon drew the positive conclusion that the present moment called for the unification of

---

[1] See the portrayals in *Persönlichkeiten der europäischen Integration*, op. cit., p. 257ff. (Adolph Kohler, De Gasperi), p. 291ff. (Werner Weidenfeld: *Konrad Adenauer*), p. 234ff. (Dieter Dettke: *Robert Schuman*); also especially Hans-Peter Schwarz, 'Adenauer und Europa', *Vierteljahrshefte für Zeitgeschichte* 27 (1979), p. 471ff.

[2] It is, however, significant that the most comprehensive conservative volume on *Konservatismus in Europa*, ed. G. K. Kaltenbrunner (Freiburg/Br., 1972), while containing chapters on many countries, has none on post-war Germany. Uncertainty about the concept and essence of a German conservatism has remained considerable in the Federal Republic, even though there have been some demonstrative exponents of conservative political understanding from the start, such as Hans Joachim Schoeps, Otto Heinrich von der Gablentz, Hans-Joachim von Merkatz, whose books, however, tended to refer to historical themes. It is apparent that the anti-democratic, anti-liberal direction, which had marked not only German but continental-European conservatism since the turn of the century, had largely disappeared.

Europe if it was not to suffer the fate of a fragmented Greece.[1]

The idea of close association with America, founded in the wartime and post-war power-political relationships, especially the danger of Soviet imperialism and the division of Europe, was reinforced by the intellectual dispute of the cold war and also by memories of the USA's fateful retreat after the First World War. Even European currents of anti-American colouring, going back to the old arguments of conservative civilizational critique, never attained the strength of the inter-war years. Even Gaullism, combining conservative critique of democracy with France's pretensions to a leadership role in Europe, ultimately – as shown after 1958 – arrived at an endorsement of the new European politics, albeit not in its integrationist form.[2]

Thus the balance-sheet of the fifties was unexpectedly positive not only in material terms. The evolution of political thought likewise revealed a greater measure of readiness for consensus, due probably to the sharpness of east–west confrontation and also to a long-delayed realization of the potential of libertarian politics and constructive reform. The challenges of the sixties, presently, were to be of a different nature. They were to lead to a renaissance of crisis consciousness which once more called the successful policy of reconstruction into doubt – now on a global scale of world civilization, of a north–south conflict and a worldwide revival of ideologies. Belief in revolution, which had receded in the face of the harsh dis- enchantments of the thirties and forties, now returned. Progressivist and decadent concepts once more became criteria of political struggle.

[1] Thus immediately after the war and in the face of the destruction and division of Europe, its total dependence on external powers; with an emphasis on the modern aspect of the tragedy of the Greek city states, see the ancient historian Hans Erich Stier, *Grundlagen und Sinn der griechischen Geschichte* (Stuttgart, 1945). The parallel with ancient history: Europe like ancient Greece, America like ancient Rome, and indeed sometimes communism (Russia) like Christianity and the ancient Germans was a favourite theme during the first post-war years; soon, however, it was overtaken by the incomparable reality of east–west politics.

[2] See Thomas A. Mirow, 'Die europapolitischen Konzeptionen de Gaulles und ihre Bedeutung für die Haltung Frankreichs in der Fünften Republik', doct. thesis (Bonn, 1977), pp. 58ff., 621ff.

2. NEW ORIENTATIONS TOWARDS THE WORLD: IDEOLOGICAL DEPARTURES OF THE SIXTIES

That the decade of de-ideologization would not be the last word was reflected most clearly in the rise of the 'Third World', in the new nationalism and socialism of the developing countries. Europe and America were not able simply to withdraw into a newly won consensus on the libertarian values of western civilization and of its liberal-social democracy. The numerous conflicts which followed the replacement of colonialism, the continuing ideological confrontation of east and west, and the ambivalent consequences of a worldwide extension of American-European civilizational forms together with their concept of progress – all these provided the background of a new challenge to, and a crisis of, the values upon which modern western policies were based.

However, this new questioning of political thought which, in the sixties, led to a wave of re-ideologization, did not come from outside alone. It was a crisis of identity, connected largely with the emergence of a new generation, and it was directed primarily against the conservative and rational character of western reconstruction society, whose achievements were being increasingly criticized as mere restoration and stagnation dominated by grand old men like Adenauer, de Gaulle and Eisenhower. The new, stable and value-conscious democracy increasingly appeared, especially to the young, as an authoritarian system, the successful social market economy as no more than disguised bourgeois-materialist capitalism, and anti-totalitarianism as a mere ideology of anti-communism. A wave of self-criticism swept over the West in connection with the Vietnam war, and with the rapid social transformations brought about by material progress and worldwide communications through new mass media, especially television, whose enormous and growing effect since the mid-sixties it would be difficult to overestimate.

The need of the wartime and post-war generations to 'catch up' prompted an upsurge of sociological and psychological literature. This in turn brought into play a fascinating new process of thought – suspicion of ideology. It concerned an old idea: the ideological content of all thought. But in its application to the de-ideologization phenomenon of the fifties it now gained revolutionary significance. If all ideas of order and value, no matter how successfully tested in practice, could be suspected of ideological bias, then the positive belief in the end of ideologies might itself be declared a mere delusion and fiction.[1]

This external and internal questioning of political thought was accompanied, after the mid-sixties, by an enormous rise in expectations; the problems of the post-war political order and the intellectual pragmatism that went with it seemed the more negative the more the totalitarian experience – the alarmingly clear horizon of experience of the immediate post-war period – was fading. It emerged in this context that the basic problems of political culture were similar in all western democracies, even though the revival of crisis thought and of ideologization revealed distinct traits in different countries. In Germany, because of its national-socialist past and the division between east and west, a special sensitivity to questions of comprehension of democracy, and of totalitarianism and anti-communism, was to be expected; in France and Italy, in view of the unchanged strength of their communist parties, the issue was the importance of communism and the social problem; in Britain and Scandinavia it was mainly the potentialities and problems of the welfare state; in the USA, finally, it was the conflict between worldwide obligations and domestic self-doubt, especially during the war in Vietnam. But the foreign and international context which governed the changes in political thought were directly perceptible also in the Europe of the sixties.

The problems of development policy and interest in the Third World were

[1] The (renewed) upsurge of ideology discussion and of ideologization, especially in Germany, linked up, to an astonishing degree, with the short sharp phase of the twenties, the age of the basic liberal-social analyses of democracy by Max Weber, Karl Mannheim, Theodor Geiger, as well as, controversially, with the cultural-Marxist ideas of the Frankfurt School (Horkheimer, Adorno, Marcuse). It was mainly these latter who, having returned to Europe from exile in 1945, now experienced a revival and, simultaneously, a vulgarization; see Adorno-Horkheimer, *Dialektik der Aufklärung* (1947, but with a much-quoted new edition in 1968), as well as the sympathetic estimate by Martin Jay, *The Dialectical Imagination* (1973). Of the second generation the most influential books were those by Jürgen Habermas with their 'revealing' titles: *Erkenntnis und Interesse*; *Technik und Wissenschaft als Ideologie* (both published in the turbulent year 1968). These were challenged in the 'positivism dispute' mainly by the anti-totalitarian 'positivists' and 'critical rationalists' around Karl Popper and Ernst Topitsch, Hans Albert and Niklas Luhmann, but these only succeeded slowly in forcing back the wave of ancient-and-modern ideologies: see especially Topitsch, *Sozialphilosophie zwischen Ideologie und Wissenschaft* (Neuwied-Berlin, 1961; 3rd ed., 1971); J. Habermas, N. Luhmann, *Theorie der Gesellschaft oder Sozialtechnologie* (Frankfurt/M., 1971); Kurt Sontheimer, *Das Elend der Intellektuellen*, op. cit., p. 67ff.; now also Hans Lenk, Roland Simon-Schaefer, 'Vernunft – Wissenschaft – Praxis, Zur Kritik der "Kritischen Theorie"', *Aus Politik und Zeitgeschichte* B 50/81 (12 December 1981), p. 41ff.; Nikolaus Lobkowicz and Henning Ottmann, 'Materialismus, Idealismus und christliches Weltverständnis', in *Christlicher Glauben in moderner Gesellschaft* (Freiburg/Br., 1981), p. 124ff.

accompanied also by a revival of revolutionary thought.[1] The rise of Maoism as an independent variant of communism, as well as the Castro cult in Latin America, stimulated fresh interest in all left-wing liberation movements which, instead of a transfer of western systems of government to ex-colonial territories, strove for the establishment of an autochthonous 'socialist' form of one-party government. Moreover, the intensification of the policy of *détente* between east and west, no matter how piecemeal and contradictory its results or how deceptive its hopes, likewise contributed to a questioning and, ultimately, liquidation of past systems of orientation now described as outlived and refuted. If communism was now viewed as 'merely' one political state system and one ideology among others, then this meant not just a defusing and 'de-demonization' of totalitarianism but also an increasing relativization of what are, after all, fundamental differences between democracy and dictatorship. Above all, anti-communism, not communism, now came under suspicion of being an ideology.

This upset to the system of political co-ordinates, which has marked political thought since the sixties, was closely linked, in Germany, with the end of the Adenauer era (1963), in Italy with the '*apertura a sinistra*', the opening to the Left (1962), and in France with the diminution of de Gaulle's authority. It reached its climax in 1968. May 1968 saw the great (student) revolt of Paris and a large number of literary revolutionary proclamations, but also the cold shower of the Soviet crushing of the 'Prague Spring' in August 1968.

The political writings of the fifties had been entirely marked by the profound impact of the 'lessons' which, in particular, the weakness of the Weimar Republic and the totalitarian seizure of power by national socialism had on the political stabilization of democracy. One had seen what man was capable of once he submitted to a radicalized political creed. The concept of totalitarianism summed up and generalized Europe's horrifying experience of ideological mono-party dictatorships both of the Right and the Left, no matter how different their provenance or their promises. Decisive rejection

---

[1] Alongside the more general questioning literature it was the militant literature sailing under the flags of anti-colonialism and anti-imperialism that made such headway in the expanding universities and media. Following Castro, Mao for a while became the idol as a Third World hero and as the motor of a cultural revolution which, radiating from China and Latin America into the 'western metropolises', inspired the ideologization process particularly of the young generation. See especially the influential books of the French author Régis Debray, *Revolution in the Revolution? Armed Struggle and Political Struggle in Latin America* (New York and London, 1967) and with Salvador Allende, *Socialism in Chile* (London 1971). An important role was also played, especially in Germany, by the occasionally vehement extra-parliamentarian opposition, notably from Protestant circles; on this an extensive critical-polemical literature came into being: see Chr. Walter (ed.), *Atomwaffen und Ethik, Der deutsche Protestantismus und die atomare Aufrüstung 1954–61* (Munich, 1981); earlier Hans Karl Rupp, *Ausserparlamentarische Opposition in der Ära Adenauer, Der Kampf gegen die Atombewaffnung in den fünfziger Jahren* (Cologne, 1970; 2nd ed., 1980), pp. 9ff., 54ff.

of such ideological movements had therefore been the core of de-
ideologization: an attempt to regain rational standards after the aberrations
of irrationalist policy.

Now, however, radical political belief was once more gaining ground.
Together with the relativization of the critique of communism, strong
criticism was directed at the controversial 'theories of totalitarianism', and
indeed at the concept of totalitarianism generally. In their general political
and political-intellectual significance these criticisms far transcended the
sociological and historical issues of the discussion of a concept. This was a
case of a whole set of semantic shifts which, in the new television age,
produced especially rapid effects, involving the fundamental questioning of
the western idea of order and freedom, and indeed a relapse into the critique
of democracy advanced in the twenties.[1] This was, of course, taking place in
a totally changed world situation, one in which it was no longer – as in the
past – a distant communism and a nearby fascism which appeared as
alternatives, but on the contrary the nearby world-power position of
communism facing a remote 'fascism' which, moreover, was now being
polemically projected into western democracy.

Much as in the twenties, however, the new radical critique of democracy
drew nourishment from reference to the discrepancy between democratic
idea and political reality, and from invoking an alleged crisis of legitimation
in western state systems generally. If their anti-totalitarian character was
denied, or declared to be inessential or a mere ideology of the Cold War, and
if a comparison of the whole idea and reality of communism was dismissed as
anti-communism, then the western democracies lacked a fundamental
element of identification and a criterion to distinguish them from dictatorship. And if the 'quality' of an ideology was made the yardstick and was then
assessed more highly than actual government, then, in spite of all political
differences, the ideological confrontation between 'Marxism' and alleged
'fascism' might well revive the attraction of totalitarian solutions in the
criticized democracies too. For such creeds would now no longer be
accompanied by the cautionary concept of totalitarianism. Libertarian

[1] Sharp criticism of the theory of totalitarianism was practised, among others, by an
American disciple of its principal representative C. J. Friedrich: Herbert Spiro, in *Encyclo-
pedia of the Social Sciences*, Vol. 16 (New York, 1968), p. 106ff.; see on the other hand my
article 'Totalitarianism' in *Dictionary of the History of Ideas*, Vol. 4 (New York, 1973), p. 406ff.
The parallels in the shift of bias and concepts from the debate on totalitarianism to that on
fascism with the revival and intensification of fundamental critiques of democracy since the
second half of the sixties are quite striking. These were chiefly neo-Marxist or Utopian radical-
democratic analyses which (using the old trick of radical right-wing and left-wing critique from
Carl Schmitt to Adorno) confronted the idea with the reality of liberal democracy, and from the
natural discrepancies drew the blunt extremist conclusion that bourgeois democracy had come
to its end. This was invariably accompanied by a 'realistic' refutation or totalitarian-
'democratic' destruction of the principle of separation of powers: once 'the people' were in
power there would no longer be any need for a separation of powers; besides, it was outdated in
terms of government technique anyway. See K. D. Bracher, *Geschichte und Gewalt*, op. cit.,
p. 57ff.

democracy's peculiarity of guaranteeing opportunities for personal freedom and of regarding the balancing of social interests as an essential task, additionally found itself – through unhistorical comparison with developing countries and because of the material growth of its economy – under accusation of being capitalist.

This apparent revival of the left-wing ideological critique of democracy also saw a short-lived companion piece in western Germany in a right-wing radical revival which actually used the democratic concept, though in a nationalist sense. The sudden rise of a 'National Democratic Party' (NPD) proved to be a short-lived protest movement from 1964 to 1971, in the transitional vacuum between the Adenauer era and the social-liberal coalition. The parallel with the Weimar Republic did not go very far.[1] Striking, on the other hand, was the almost avid reception of Marxist social and democratic doctrines with a frantic warming-up of revolutionary theoretical writings and discussions of the twenties and early thirties. These soon found a rich field of application and trial – though also of abuse and destruction – in the rapid expansion and the overhasty reforms and changes in the educational and university systems. The consequences of radical-democratic and neo-Marxist progressivism were soon to be observed throughout the western countries, at mass schools and mass universities, with their mixture of anarchy and bureaucratization.[2]

These waves of re-ideologization may be seen as a consequence of intellectual pressure and an activist need to 'catch up'; this had been brushed aside among the ruins by economic reconstruction and had increasingly piled up during political stabilization. Of course, liberal-conservative contemporaries had similarly spoken of 'neglected reforms' and even 'German educational disaster'.[3] The lagging-behind of social and intellec-

---

[1] The comparisons, which the present author, among others, made towards the end of the sixties (*German Dictatorship*, op. cit., p. 590ff.), gave rise to a wealth of discussion. The most comprehensive collection and overall presentation (up to 1965) is in Kurt P. Tauber, *Beyond Eagle and Swastika, German Nationalism Since 1945*, 2 vols, (Middletown, Conn., 1967); subsequently Hans Maier and Hermann Bott, *Die NPD, Struktur und Ideologie einer 'nationalen Rechtspartei'* (Munich, 1968); H. Bott, *Die Volksfeindideologie, Zur Kritik rechtsradikaler Propaganda* (Stuttgart, 1969); Lutz Niethammer, *Angepasster Faschismus, Politische Praxis der NPD* (Frankfurt/M., 1969); above all Erwin K. Scheuch, 'Politischer Extremismus in der Bundesrepublik', in Richard Löwenthal, Hans-Peter Schwarz (eds), *Die zweite Republik* (Stuttgart, 1974), p. 433ff. However, first in Scheuch and subsequently in other authors the far stronger growth of left-wing radicalism had to be recorded, especially among young people: a re-emergence of the German democracy problem in a different form. See also the concept of the 'romantic relapse' in Richard Löwenthal, *Der romantische Rückfall* (Stuttgart, 1970).

[2] On this subject see the critical observations of an international association of scholars formed in view of these developments in 1970, the International Council on the Future of the University (New York), especially its '*Newsletter*' (1981) and the two reports *On German Universities* (1977) and *On Italian Universities* (1981).

[3] Thus, for instance, one of the co-founders of the CDU in Berlin, the political science professor Otto Heinrich von der Gablentz, in his book *Die Versäumte Reform* (Cologne-Opladen, 1960); very influential was the culture-critically coloured series of articles by the educational philosopher Georg Picht, 'Die deutsche Bildungskatastrophe', in *Christ und Welt* (Stuttgart, 1964).

tual development, the need to reform educational institutions, a hectic urge
for an expansion and total democratization of all social areas all coincided
with the effect of the 'generation gap' and with changes in international
politics, and now acquired an almost revolutionary quality in the self-image
of a student 'intelligentsia' growing at avalanche speed and producing an
increasingly left-wing ideological pressure of expectations. Yet the majority
only talked of progressive reforms, watching the violent radicalization by
activist minorities with an uncertain sympathy and toleration. Indeed some
liberal politicians, partly insecure in their views and partly just hopeful,
made their own not inconsiderable concessions to them.[1] But fundamentally
this was supposed to be a catching-up with the revolution for a 'total
democratization' of state *and* society, of an 'essential' instead of a merely
'formal' basic democracy, to use the jargon of 1968. This, it was alleged,
would have been possible after 1945 but had been prevented by the
'restoration of capitalism' in the confrontation of the Cold War and by
political thought being tethered to the 'anti-communist' concept of totalitarianism. The new order was to be anti-fascist instead of anti-totalitarian –
that was the politically tendentious formula which, needless to say,
retrospectively misunderstood the historical and political reality between
1945 and 1950.

The intellectual circumstances of the ideological upheaval were of a
complex nature. They can be outlined here only briefly. It was a mixture of
excitement and frustration that largely contributed to the feeling of a new
ideological start in the sixties with the mass opening of schools and
universities, and with the rapid professional and social re-stratification of
students, professors and media intellectuals. The nucleus of that mood was a
speedy recharging and heightening of awareness by internal and external
tensions: between quantitative and qualitative objectives, between progressive scientism and mass standardization, between civilizational pressure
to rationality and an activist need for movement, between social stability
and political adventure, between Utopian socialization and moral restraint,
between material abundance in the west and patent shortages in the world.

The origin and spread of radical thought in modern history can never be
explained solely by political causes, as James Billington's fundamental work

[1] A typical contemporary comparative report was that by the English writer Stephen
Spender, *The Year of the Young Rebels* (London, 1969), p. 127ff.; in contrast, the sceptically
assessing critique by George Kennan, *Democracy and the Student Left* (Boston and London,
1968). Spender's optimism at the time was based on an over-emphasis of a 'natural' generation
conflict. On the turbulent May revolt in France, with its many illusions, see Raymond Aron,
The Elusive Revolution (London, 1968); see also Christopher Driver, *The Exploding University*
(1971); David Martin (ed.), *Anarchy and Culture; The Problem of the Contemporary University*
(1969); Sidney Hook, *Academic Freedom and Academic Anarchy* (1971). The first international survey of university protest movements in the stormy year 1967–8, including the
Second and Third Worlds, is in the symposium 'Student and Politics', *Daedalus* 97, No. 1
(Winter, 1968), with a comparative essay by Seymour Martin Lipset and 14 national studies.

has now demonstrated for nineteenth-century western as well as Russian revolutionary thought.[1] Major importance attaches to psychological factors, alongside economic and social ones. In contrast to earlier forms of radicalism, that of the sixties was characterized by a challenge to moral values and by a markedly hedonistic component which was evident also in the anti-authoritarian ideology of progressive educational theory and, even more so, in the 'sexual revolution' of the emancipation movement. New communal forms of Utopian-communist cohabitation came into being; these were instantly formulated in theoretical and political terms and declared to be the future pattern of a far-reaching social revolution beyond family and state, towards an 'ungoverned' society altogether.[2] The tensions between the demand for freedom from violence and violent action of one's own were to be resolved by a theory, soon to become widespread, which simply declared all social and political institutions to be 'structural violence' and which justified any action against them as legitimate resistance.[3] Against the magic formula of 'change', which almost acquired a value of its own and could be used as a universal progressivist justification even for blind destruction as 'a historical necessity', even the emphatic peace theories of the Left soon paled: from the demand for the total liquidation of the causes of 'non-peace' generally to the sanctioning of any revolutionary action as 'liberation' was but a short step.

Of equal importance, however, were the specific background conditions of the Utopian movements – some old, some new – in the turbulent year of

[1] James Billington, *Fire in the Minds of Men*, op. cit., p. 17ff., has special emphasis on the faith and intelligence component, and is instructive also in its comprehensively comparative method and the wealth of processed intellectual history material from the French to the Russian Revolution.

[2] On the 'bio-social' problems of parenthood and upbringing in communes and counter-societies see Alice S. Rossi, 'A Biosocial Perspective on Parenting', *The Family, Daedalus* 106, No.2 (Spring, 1977), p. 13ff.; see J. Rothschild and S. B. Wolf, *The Children of the Counterculture* (New York, 1976). Of great opinion and attitude-forming effect was the 'anti-authoritarian' wave, widely publicized in the Federal Republic by the best-seller of the British experimental educationist Alexander S. Neill, *Summerhill, A radical approach to education* (London 1962). The euphorias of the day were reflected in Thilo Castner, 'Schule und Demokratie, Der Beitrag A. S. Neills "zur Verwirklichung einer freien, antiautoritären Erziehung" ', *Aus Politik und Zeitgeschichte* B 32–33/70 (supplement to *Das Parlament* 8 August 1970), p. 18ff.; see also the (American) discussion in *Summerhill, Pro und Contra* (Reinbek, 1971). Henning Günther, 'Antiautoritäre Erziehung', in *Politisch-Pädagogisches Handwörterbuch* (Munich, 1980), p. 17ff.

[3] The up-to-date formulation of the thesis by the Norwegian mathematician and peace researcher Johan Galtung, 'Violence, Peace and Peace Research', *Journal of Peace Research* 6, (1969), p. 165ff., and *Strukturelle Gewalt*, 2nd ed. (Reinbek, 1977) was anything but new: it has always been the basis of any justification of political-revolutionary violence. But in the garb of an emphatically social-scientific universal principle it gained astonishingly rapid and wide-spread importance at the end of the sixties, even among political scientists: see Peter Graf Kielmansegg, 'Politikwissenschaft und Gewaltproblematik', in Heiner Geissler (ed.), *Der Weg in die Gewalt* (Munich, 1978), p. 69ff.; Peter Waldmann, *Strategien politischer Gewalt* (Stuttgart, 1977).

1968. Major importance attached to the seeming opening-up of the closed system of communism. This facilitated the projection of (at first politically undefined) socially and culturally revolutionary aspirations and expectations into a higher 'socialism' which need no longer, or indeed must no longer, be described as monolithically totalitarian. It seemed like an irony of history that, at the very moment when non-communist socialism, domiciled in the established social democratic parties of the west, began also to dissociate itself ideologically from the Marxist dogma and to draw the necessary conclusions from this de-ideologization, a new wave of ideologization was turning the concept of socialism throughout its breadth and depth into the global battle-cry of youthful rebels in the countries of the west as well as in the Third World.

Communism itself did not remain unaffected. True, official criticism of Stalin's rule of terror, triggered off by Khrushchev's famous 'secret speech' at the Twentieth Party Congress in Moscow, stopped short of ideology and the one-party system: only the 'personality cult', not the basic totalitarian structure of communism, was permitted as a subject for discussion there.[1] Even so, this modest self-criticism revived old and new expectations of 'democratic' prospects not only of Marxism but also of Leninism, as well as new hopes (regardless of all simultaneous and subsequent brutal actions of Soviet communism) of its democratic evolution and readiness for compromise, and indeed of its 'human face'. This applied both to the continually smouldering revisionist and national variants in Moscow's east European satellite regimes and to the separate roads of Titoism, Maoism and Castroism.

The sixties seemed to herald in a progressive decentralization and liberalization of world communism. Its 'de-Stalinization' freed it from a number of outdated dogmatic fetters, while preserving its essential creed content of 'socialism' as the final stage of total democracy. Even the Catholic Church under Pope John XXIII opened up a dialogue with the communist parties in the encyclical *Pacem in terris*. In France and Italy in particular, these dialogues, invoking a special national 'colouring', at times switched to a course of democratic co-operation and in so doing emphasized their own ideological independence. The Italian CP did so especially, with emphatic reference to Antonio Gramsci (1891–1937), the 'Italian Lenin' whose version of democratic communism, developed while in a fascist prison, now made a major impact, although Gramsci and his followers even more so

---

[1] See the discussion in Georg Brunner, 'Abkehr vom Totalitarismus? Wandlungen im Herrschaftssystem osteuropäischer Staaten', in M. Funke (ed.), *Totalitarismus*, op. cit., p. 132ff.; Boris Meissner, *Das Sowjetsystem und seine Wandlungsmöglichkeiten* (Bern, 1976); Annie Kriegel, 'The Nature of the Communist System, Notes on State, Party and Society', *Daedalus* 108, No.4 (Fall, 1979), p. 144ff. ('a "total" system wholly different from our own, not in degree but in kind'). Still of particular value is Leonard Schapiro, *Totalitarianism* (London, 1972), p. 109ff.

clung to the fundamental tenets of Leninism.[1]

To seekers of a faith and to enthusiasts of revolution, who anyway no longer found a domicile within the moderate social democratic parties, these transformations of world communism offered exciting new possibilities of identifying with socialism as a quasi-religion which could, at will, be associated with revolutionary movements or persons of the most various kinds and circumstances, without necessarily having to defend the Soviet Union and its policies. Distance evidently lent enchantment to the view – or so it seemed at times. The attraction of China's violent 'cultural revolution' was its radical rebellion against its own culture as well as the idea of 'permanent revolution' which Maoism, especially student Maoism, attempted to disseminate throughout the world. The attraction of Castro and his Latin American vassals was the application of Maoist guerilla theory with its essentially agro-communist struggle against the capitalist metropolises: on this a whole literature was published, as manuals for European terrorism. The impressive feature of the war in Vietnam, finally, was the successful partisan struggle of a nationalist communism which profoundly shook the assurance of the west's leading power and which, moreover, was masochistically presented on every television screen day after day.[2]

[1] James Joll, *Gramsci* (London, 1977). The ideologically overrated and overrating Gramsci revival of the past one and a half decades, also in Germany, now emerges clearly in the pro-communist large-scale bibliography of Hans Heinz Holz *et al.* (ed.), *Betr. Gramsci, Philosophie und revolutionäre Politik in Italien, Mit einer Bibliographie der Werkausgaben, der deutschsprachigen Gramsci-Literatur und Auswahlbibliographien französischer und englischer Literatur* (Cologne, 1980). See, on the other hand, the apt account by Joseph V. Femia, 'Gramsci, the Via Italiana, and the Classical Marxist-Leninist Approach to Revolution', *Government and Opposition* 14 (1979), p. 66ff: 'A "democratic" interpretation of Gramsci, though not without foundation, is incompatible with his expressed views. And when this interpretation takes the form of equating his thoughts with social democracy, it enters the realm of pure fantasy. Despite his pragmatism and concern for popular support, Gramsci never deviated from a belief in total revolution brought about in part through the intervention of armed force. While some of the currently fashionable doctrines of Eurocommunism do have a genuine basis in his ideas, he himself remained steadfastly committed to the very anti-parliamentarism and insurrectionism the Eurocommunists have repudiated.' (p. 95).

The question remains to what extent Eurocommunist lip-service declarations are altogether compatible with Leninism. Thomas R. Bates, 'Antonio Gramsci and the Bolshevization of the PCI, *Journal of Contemporary History* 11/2–3 (1976), p. 115ff., tends to place emphasis on time-conditioned circumstances (failure of the revolution, fascism and Stalinism). But he too clearly refutes the legend of Gramsci as a democratic Eurocommunist and proves his leading role in the Bolshevization of the Italian communists between 1923 and 1926, when, with support from Stalin and the Comintern, he prevailed over the party leader Amadeo Bordiga in 1924. His subsequent criticism of Stalin, written from his fascist prison, came too late.

[2] The standard works on terrorism are, Walter Laqueur, *Terrorism* (London, 1977); *Guerilla* (Boston, 1976); Fritz René Alleman, *Macht und Ohnmacht der Guerilla* (Munich, 1974), p. 95ff.; Franz Wördemann, *Terrorismus* (Munich, 1977), and Manfred Funke (ed.), *Terrorismus* (Düsseldorf, 1977). On the links between revolutionism and terrorism see especially the studies by Paul Wilkinson, *Terrorism and the Liberal State* (London, 1977); *Political Terrorism* (London, 1974); and his contribution 'Die Drohung des Terrorismus', in W. Hennis, P. Graf Kielmansegg, U. Matz (eds), *Regierbarkeit* (Stuttgart, 1979), p. 310ff. Also H.

Everywhere socialism was on the march. In view of the 'socialist' reality in the Second and Third Worlds it appeared to be the stronger idea, to be *the* alternative of political thought generally – made more confusing but also more susceptible to manipulation by the multiple vagueness of the concept in view of its African, Asian and Latin American special forms (Chile, Peru, neo-Peronism). The fact that all these were dictatorships, with pretensions to liberation and democratization but realized by militant élites through violence, did not seem, in the distortions and confusions of political terminology, to matter any longer. To ideologized thought the distinctions between democracy and dictatorship, pluralism and totalitarianism, become irrelevant, provided its principal need – redeeming safety within a closed system of community and faith – is satisfied. And just this promise had always been held out by socialism and was being held out now (as could be seen after a short interval of de-ideologization) with renewed strength and a worldwide power of attraction. The cult of revolutionary heroes, such as Castro, Che Guevara and Ho Chi Minh, but also of serviceable non-communists such as Nasser and Allende, or of the numerous African liberator-dictators from Nkrumah to Gaddafi, lent further emphasis to the romantic colouring with which socialism was endowed in the Third World.

The charm of the exotic and the mobilization of political sympathies were in fact enormously heightened by the possibility of rapid mass communication, as developed with the globalization of television in the sixties. Ever since, the phenomenon of 'telecracy' has been of supreme importance especially to the propagation of political ideas: a seemingly immediate and irrefutable but in fact thoroughly deceptive and subjective, readily manipulated and scarcely verifiable pictorial information for the masses. To the question of the force of political ideas there was now added the problem of power *over* ideas and their political presentation: a shift in intellectual influencing potential which any topical history of ideas will have to make allowance for in future.[1]

Livingston *et al.* (eds), *International Terrorism in the Contemporary World* (Westport, Conn., 1978); Y. Alexander (ed.), *International Terrorism, National, Regional and Global Perspectives* (New York, 1976); as well as the voluminous bibliography (278 pages!) in U. Tutenberg and Chr. Pollak, *Terrorismus gestern – heute – morgen, Eine Auswahlbibliographie* (Munich, 1978). On Germany also the symposium by H. Geissler, op. cit.; on Italy Alberto Ronchey, 'Guns and Gray Matter: Terrorism in Italy', *Foreign Affairs* 57/4 (Spring, 1979), p. 921ff.; Giorgio Bocca, *Il terrorismo italiano, 1970–1978* (Milan, 1978); as well as the comparative discussion, *Terrorismus in der demokratischen Gesellschaft* (Hamburg, 1978) (*Bergedorfer Gespräch* Nr. 59), p. 22ff. It is significant that there are common factors in terrorism in what were the vanquished countries, Germany, Italy and Japan: military defeat is followed by democracy, and a seemingly rapid change of value systems is then followed by a renewed fascination with anti-capitalist ideologies – amidst an economic boom.

[1] See K. D. Bracher, 'Geschichte und Medium' (in *Geschichte und Gewalt*, op. cit., p. 253ff.); now also the methodological studies in Siegfried Quandt (ed.), *Geschichtswissenschaft und Massenmedien* (Giessen, 1981), p. 5ff., as well as the extensive discussion and literature in the fundamental books by Wolfgang Bergsdorf, *Die Vierte Gewalt, Einführung in die politische Kommunikation* (Mainz, 1980), p. 133ff.; *Sprache und Herrschaft, Studie zur der politischen Terminologie in der Bundesrepublik Deutschland* (Pfullingen, 1983).

The onset of the television age entailed an enlargement but also an indisputable greater crudity of mass communications. Intellectual processing of the unceasing information flow falls (or permanently lags) behind the suggestive power of the pictures. 'The medium is the message' and it is, moreover, focused on new and sensational happenings and opinions. Selection of news and views becomes decisive; all doors are open to manipulation. Thus the ideological disputes especially of the student revolts acquired an impact which frequently burst all bounds and virtually created ideological stars like Rudi Dutschke in Berlin and Daniel Cohn-Bendit in Paris and Frankfurt in 1967–8, and ultimately produced terrorism. Slogans became common currency overnight, values were revalued, ideas were changed and norms upset, without the need for the kind of intellectual penetration and examination required for the laborious writing or refutation of books.

Nearest to the ambivalent effect of television was the mass production and dissemination of leaflets – another record set, especially in the universities, in the late sixties and early seventies. Orientation, of course, proved even more difficult than before in the new crossfire of continuously fluctuating opinion and ideological indoctrination. Swamped by a flood of political information and ever new declarations about the world, many students in the later seventies, when 'the reality of socialism' had so patently disappointed the hopes associated with the idea of socialism, withdrew into metapolitical alternative movements.[1] It had started early and rather exotically as a rebellion by 'angry young men'. John Osborne's disturbing play *Look Back in Anger* was performed in 1956. It culminated in a sociologically and psychologically founded emancipation protest against society *as such*, against its values and taboos, and ultimately as political criticism of the system generally. There were a considerable number of variants, as well as crude over-simplifications and distortions of political thought. One such was that pseudo-legalistic concept of revolution which sophistically differentiated between 'system-immanent' and 'system-overcoming' reforms, or between 'violence against things' and 'violence against persons' – actually supported by philosophers and theologians

[1] On the emergence and assessment of counter-society and alternative movements in the Federal Republic see the attitudes of government and parties, in *Aus Politik und Zeitgeschichte*, supplement to the weekly *Das Parlament* B 39/81 (26 September 1981). On the general international development, especially as a confrontation of technocratic society and youthful opposition see Theodor Roszak, *The Making of a Counter-Culture: Reflections on the Technocratic Society and its Youthful Opposition* (London, 1969). The underlying tendency towards hostility to civilization, virulent since the turn of the century, was summed up by C. P. Snow in 1959 in his much-discussed thesis of the 'two cultures': a scientific one (scientism) and a literary one (literatism), which also marks the ambivalent attitude of the intellectuals. C. P. Snow, *The Two Cultures and the Scientific Revolution* (1959); *The Two Cultures: And a Second Look* (Cambridge, 1965); see F. R. Leavis, *Two Cultures? The Significance of C. P. Snow* (London, 1962).

enthused by youthful ideas (like Helmut Gollwitzer) who now and again made the *sacrificium intellectus* of their pacifism when dealing with the pretensions of alleged emancipational and liberation movements, only to be subsequently disillusioned by the reality of the destruction of moral values by the revolutionaries themselves.[1]

Basically the big noise of the revolt, which reached its first peak in 1968 and the terrorist escalation of the succeeding years, caused a great deal of confusion and disorientation especially among the younger generation. This was all the more the case because of a revival of 'critical theory' and its newer version in books ranging from Herbert Marcuse to Jürgen Habermas, distributed in the form of a rapidly developing and ephemeral pamphlet literature. These 'innovations' in political thought coined, above all, a series of changed concepts and postulates which were adopted also by the political Establishment. De Gaulle's resignation in France in 1969 and the supplanting (albeit by a very narrow electoral margin) of the Christian-Democratic post-Adenauer governments by the social-liberal era in Germany were part of this trend which focused at far-reaching reform and *détente* demands and which, in the upturning and reploughing of the educational system, reflected the massive after-effects of the protest wave and its theories.

Equally important as the immediate political consequences were the psychological and conceptual effects of radical progressivism. The call for 'democratization' in the sense of co-determination was now being heard on all sides, all the way down to the lowest units of organizations, enterprises and schools. There was ceaseless system-critical talk of grass-roots democracy and citizens' initiatives, of latter-day capitalism and latter-day bourgeoisie. The European socialists were once more marching under an ideological banner, reinforced by new adherents from the ebbing student revolt. Minds were dominated and confused by the inflation of the concept of fascism and a corresponding discrediting of the totalitarian concept as 'nothing but' anti-communism.

What remained was an ideological battlefield which today increasingly arouses nostalgic memories. There had been a heavy expenditure of theoretical ammunition and abstract stategic formulas, taken mainly from

---

[1] On the debate on violence with all its questionable distinctions of violence and counter-violence, violence against things and against persons, and the individual-anarchist and collective-communist concepts of violence and terror see Hannah Arendt, *Macht und Gewalt* (Munich, 1970); Ulrich Matz, *Politik und Gewalt* (Freiburg/Br., 1975); *Recht, Gerechtigkeit, Gewalt, Vorlesungen beim 14. Deutschen Evangelischen Kirchentag* (Stuttgart, 1969); as well as the attempt of a Marxist definition of the terror concept, such as in Bruno Frei, 'Die anarchistishe Utopie' and Hans Adamo, 'Über Terrorismus, Ursachen und Funktion des Anarchoterrors in der Bundesrepublik', in *Marxistische Taschenbücher* (Frankfurt/M.1978). Also F. Engel-Janosi, G. Klingenstein, H. Lutz (eds), *Gewalt und Gewaltlosigkeit, Probleme des 20. Jahrhunderts* (Munich, 1977); H. V. Stietencron, *Angst und Gewalt, Ihre Präsenz und ihre Bewältigung in den Religionen* (Düsseldorf, 1979); most recently Jean-Marie Domenach *et al.* (eds), *Violence and its Causes* (Paris, 1981).

the social sciences (which had in part become alienated in a revolutionary direction), where the illusions and disappointments of the time also lived on most conspicuously.[1] However, justified argument involving mere historicism and efforts towards a value-emphatic (though objective) understanding of political and social issues suffered something of a setback through the incursions of an ultimately subjectivist and irrationalist re-ideologization, with its disregard for political experience and impartial objectivity and with its long-term devastation of concepts.

The intellectual profit of this new beginning, mounted with so much enthusiasm and effort, remained controversial, and its further development in the shape of ill-considered and sometimes naïve government measures (in the educational system and the lowering of the age of majority) led to a great many human and political disappointments, as well as violent and terrorist consequences. It was therefore inevitable that, only a few years later, a call for a new 'turn' should have been made.[2] Unlike the abundance of the 'golden twenties', only few new ideas had emerged, and most of these had been mere continuations or appendices of earlier neo-Marxist social and cultural critique, with just a touch of Hegelian hermeneutics,[3] whose

[1] Behind all the ideological hurly-burly and fading visions there emerged from the emphasis on the social and psychological elements of politics some ideas which historians were able to use for a structural-historical understanding of the development. But then these are ideas and problems with which historical political science in the fifties was quite familiar anyway. See the conclusions of Georg Iggers, *Deutsche Geschichtswissenschaft* (Munich, 1971) and *Neue Geschichtswissenschaft, Vom Historismus zur Historischen Sozialwissenschaft* (Munich, 1978); as well as M. C. Brands, *Historisme als Ideologie* (Amsterdam, 1965). These authors also refer to my studies of the Weimar Republik (1952, 1955) and on national socialism (1960, 1964, 1969): thus Brands, p. 239ff., Iggers, pp. 335, 359 (1971); pp. 106, 142 (1978).

[2] Thus, first, a series of lectures in Munich in 1975: *Tendenzwende? Zur geistigen Situation der Bundesrepublik. Mit Vorträgen von H. Lübbe, G. Albers, G. Mann, H. Maier, R. Spaemann, R. Dahrendorf* (Stuttgart, 1975). An important part in the gradual change of the debate was played by the lectures and writings of the philosopher Hermann Lübbe who, though coming from a social-liberal attitude to politics, nevertheless firmly raised his voice against the left-wing decline of political thought; see especially his volume of essays, *Endstation Terror, Rückblick auf lange Märsche* (Stuttgart, 1978). Similarly the decisive arguments conducted against the 'new Left' by until then influential (left-wing) liberals or social democrats like Wilhelm Hennis, *Die deutsche Unruhe, Studien zur Hochschulpolitik* (Hamburg, 1969); *Politik und Praktische Philosophie, Schriften zur politischen Theorie* (Stuttgart, 1977), Heinz-Dietrich Ortlieb, *Vom totalitären Staat zum totalen Egoismus* (Zurich-Osnabrück, 1981); as well as in his role of editor of the *Hamburger Jahrbuch für Wirtschafts- und Gesellschaftspolitik*) and especially, Kurt Sontheimer, *Das Elend unserer Intellektuellen* (Hamburg, 1976).

[3] Jürgen Habermas, for instance, did not originally come from the 'Frankfurt School' but, as a doctoral student of Erich Rothacker, from the 'philosophical' Hegel-Dilthey current. But the mixture of German idealist profundity and the Marxist mania for in-depth questioning resulted in those socio-politically promising explanatory and transformation models which were so typical of the Frankfurt School's instant German and international impact (largely also among Italian intellectuals). Significant, of course, was the subsequent refusal of Adorno and Horkheimer, as well as of Habermas, to accept the political conclusions which followed from their critique of western culture, society and politics. For a critical dispute with Habermas see Wolfgang Jäger, op. cit.; P. Graf Kielmansegg, in *Nachdenken über die Demokratie* (Stuttgart, 1980), p. 38ff.; and especially Kurt Sontheimer, *Das Elend unserer Intellektuellen*, op. cit., p. 199ff., exhibiting, in lucid survey, the principal arenas and 'theories' of German idealist neo-Marxism.

renewed spread, after the break of 1933, especially the massive effect of the Frankfurt school's 'critical theory', proved a highly influential, though in its consequences double-edged, event.

After 1945 its leaders, Max Horkheimer and Theodore W. Adorno, had returned to Germany from their American exile, the former even as Rector of Frankfurt University from 1951 to 1953. But they were regarded as undogmatic, humane-Marxist social philosophers who had made their peace with liberal democracy and its 'capitalist' society. Their critique was academic, warmed by the distant glow of the twenties and the intervening period in America, and even they themselves regarded their exacting critical theory in a purely theoretical light. One of their group, admittedly, did not stick to these rules: Herbert Marcuse who, from his distant California, transferred the old revolutionary message of Marxism in a new formulation not to the former worker proletariat but to the now rapidly growing intellectual vanguard of an 'anti-parliamentarian', anti-system student movement. In doing so in the sixties he hit upon the right historical moment of the student revolt and thereby endowed it with the aura of a philosophical revolutionary ideology; this also revealed some earlier traditional features from Bakunin's and Sorel's anarchist and élite theories.[1]

The different variants of 'critical theory', which also incorporated the sociological, phenomenological and psychoanalytical elements of modern cultural critique in a most fascinating manner, produced a delayed and astonishingly sudden effect. Here was a 'young' Marxism, which did not require identification with the Soviet Union, let alone the GDR, but could derive its legitimation from an American Left which, ever since the student demonstrations at Berkeley in 1964 had been regarded as the forerunner of a western cultural revolution. It engulfed a young generation that was unencumbered by any serious material worries, that was intellectually trained and alive, bored with everyday life, and saw itself excluded from the major decisions of society. The great refusal or progressive violence were the glorified forms of the new politics.

But what had been very specific causes of this revolt in the USA – the genuine problems of racial inequality, the civil rights movements and the Vietnam protest – appeared in Europe, at least initially, as a largely imported revolt. In contrast to the American ad-hoc movements it had a rather theoretical and ideological character and derived its problems very

---

[1] Probably the most influential essay was Herbert Marcuse, 'Repressive Toleranz", in R. P. Wolff, B. Moore, H. Marcuse, Kritik der reinen Toleranz, 6th ed. (Frankfurt/M., 1968). On the Utopian-totalitarian currents and the massive if short-lived effect of the 'new Left' (with bibliography and numerous examples) see Erwin Scheuch, 'Zum Wiedererstehen der Erlösungsbewegungen', in Der Überdruss an der Demokratie (Cologne, 1970), p. 129ff.: here there is also proof of the amazing affinity of left-wing and right-wing radical concepts. The anarchistic component is discussed by David E. Apter, James Joll (eds), The Anarchists (Boston and Toronto, 1964), p. 40ff. ('The Myth of the Revolution'); Erwin Oberländer (ed.), Der Anarchismus (Olten-Fribourg, 1972).

largely from its own educational and career spheres.

The emphatically egalitarian ethos of the protest movement contrasted strangely with its both libertarian and élitarian pretensions; its ideological postulate of the final reconciliation of liberty and equality through an identity of government and governed in the perfect community of a democracy of councils or direct democracy was a return to the chiliastic fictions and fantasies of all totalitarian ideologies.[1] What was first regarded as consistent socialism was later declared to be 'left-wing fascism' when it grew too big for some ideologists and turned violent.

How was this astonishing process of upheaval and reception to be seen? While it had profoundly affected a decade of intellectual rebellion and political self-questionings, there was also the lack of any major independent achievements of that 'cultural revolution', its termination in nihilistic terrorism or in a 'long march through the institutions'. Of course, the discovery and re-evaluation of past intellectual movements is a familiar phenomenon in intellectual history. This was a neo-idealist and (in spite of its eagerness for theory) basically irrational youth movement, a catching-up process, an extended rehearsal of intellectual events before and after the First World War, now greatly magnified by the global perspectives of an anti-capitalist worldwide movement against the 'Establishment' of western civilization and its social and political rules.

In viewing the phenomena of a long-term change of consciousness and values from the angle of the generation change one finds the statistically significant fact that the sixties, on the one hand, reflected the birth boom of the post-war period as a social pressure, while, on the other hand, emancipation and the now practised birth-control must lead to a future reduction in the number of young people. In this respect, too, the period from roughly 1964 to 1973 represents an intermediate period of special character: an eruption of the affluent society and its consequences, a point of rupture between the rising optimism of the fifties and the new austerity of the late seventies.[2]

[1] On the chiliastic feature of egalitarianism, especially since the revolutionary heightening of egalitarian thought in France in the second half of the eighteenth century, see also Otto Dann, 'Gleichheit', in O. Brunner, W. Conze, R. Koselleck (eds.), *Geschichtliche Grundbegriffe*, Vol. 2 (Stuttgart, 1975), p. 1014ff., and *Gleichheit und Gleichberechtigung* (Berlin-Munich, 1981). The medieval religious origins of the model are emphasized especially by Norman Cohn, *Das Ringen um das Tausendjährige Reich* (Bern, 1961), p. 187ff.

[2] Discussion of the generation problem has been on the agenda ever since the Youth Movement (see Gerhard Masur, op. cit.) and the new movements of the First World War; at that time mainly the writings of Karl Mannheim, Sigmund Neumann *et al.* (see Part I above). The revolts and re-ideologizations of the late sixties and the seventies are increasingly viewed as 'generation' problems. An international scholarly survey of certain ancient and modern elements of the debate are presented in the volume *Generations, Daedalus* 107, No. 4 (Fall, 1978); especially the articles by Annie Kriegel, 'Generational Difference, The History of an Idea', p. 23ff.; Noel Annan, ' "Our Age": Reflections on Three Generations in England', p. 81ff.; Carl E. Schorske, 'Generational Tension and Cultural Change: Reflections on the Case of Vienna', p. 111ff.; Morton Keller, 'Reflections on Politics and Generations in America', p. 123ff.; and Harold R. Isaacs, 'Bringing up the Father Question', p. 189ff.

These quasi-revolutionary political phenomena, this demonstration of explosive forces and ideas behind politics and against parliamentary democracy, eventually led to the civilization-critical alternative movements of the late seventies. Deep ruptures and long-term value crises had become obvious. While the certainties of civilized progressive society – that better education will ensure greater prosperity and more freedom and scope for the development of the individual – were being radically questioned by the revolt of the young and by cultural revolt, an allegedly all-penetrating sociologism and psychologism experienced a new upsurge. However, the exuberant ideological progressivism of the 'anti-authoritarian' wave soon got stuck: there emerged a mood of scepsis, fear of the future, a desire for different ways of life, and nostalgia.

This became especially obvious when the oil crisis of 1973 and the resulting energy and environmental debate once more made the limits of growth and the ambivalence of progress the central issue. Now there was a virtual reversal of battle-lines: those who had set out to destroy the 'healthy world' (a term of insult against the fifties) were now emphatically calling for its protection from the consequences of civilization. Left-wingers became 'value conservatives', using the value concept of the 'quality of life' to defend the *status quo* against the dangers of material progress.[1] Past left-wing progressivism now, for its part, came under suspicion of being ideological – the suspicion it had itself directed against the system and security ideas of the post-war world.

The resigned German balance-sheet drawn up at the end of the seventies by progressivist sociological champions of the Left and by some of their more cautious colleagues of the 'spiritual situation of the age' is typical.[2] As once with Karl Jaspers, to whose eponymous book of 1931 the editor Jürgen Habermas refers, there is a preponderance of almost nostalgic critique of the past and scepsis of the future, though now from the Left. In much greater detail and with much more trenchant analysis of the argument, though inbued with a similar culturally pessimistic alienation as that of many intellectuals towards the specific policies of the twenties, we see before us a clear picture of the disillusionment that has followed the high-pitched expectations of ideologists and apostles of change.

---

[1] Thus the claim of a 'left-wing' social democrat like Erhard Eppler, *Ende oder Wende, Von der Machbarkeit des Notwendigen* (Munich, 1976); further examples and positive interpretation in Iring Fetscher, *Überlebensbedingungen der Menschheit, Zur Dialektik des Fortschritts*, (Munich, 1980), pp. 42ff. and 110ff.

[2] Jürgen Habermas (ed.) *Stichworte zur geistigen Situation der Zeit*, 2 vols (Frankfurt/M., 1980).

3. CHANGING OPINIONS AND POLITICAL CULTURE IN THE SEVENTIES

From 1960 to 1975 there was a hectic short-term up and down of de-ideologization and re-ideologization, radical democratization and a cult of violence, cultural revolts and new changes of direction. While the controversial intellectual substance of these 'radical changes' has so far been viewed critically, the limited degree of originality of their idea content should not blind one to the fact that in their effect they represented not just an intermezzo but extreme forms of a long-term development in which deep-rooted feelings and needs were clamouring for expression. Hence also their powerful effect on the younger generation. There has since been talk of a 'silent revolution': changing values and political styles especially in the western sphere, and thus in political views and attitudinal norms of advanced civilization and not just of the developing countries.[1]

The long-term development is emerging more clearly after the dying down of the violent eruptions of the seventies, even though these continue to revive from time to time. What should be noted is that two currents of thought are interacting here: first, a batch of ideas from the twenties, with all those problems of tension between intellectual postulates and political reality which had already been typical of the inter-war years (and their reception of the pre-war ideas of 1880–1914); second, a continual change in the sense of a modernization and institutionalization of social and political ideas, a change which – across the breaks of revolutions and dictatorships – testifies to a unity of the epoch since the turn of the century.

[1] Ronald Inglehart, *The Silent Revolution: Changing Values and Political Styles among Western Publics* (Princeton, 1977). In these rather noisy revolts two currents played the main part: the confrontation of ideological Utopias and myths with scientific and political theory, and the arguments about the 'permissive' society with such catch-phrases as affluent society (Galbraith 1958), anti-authoritarian emancipation and sexual revolution. See Chad Walsh, *From Utopia to Nightmare* (1962); W. H. D. Armytage, *Yesterday's Tomorrows: A Historical Survey of Future Societies* (1968); William Kuhn, *The Post-Industrial Prophets* (1973). Also D. A. Hughes (ed.), *Perspectives on Pornography* (1970); E. M. Brecher, *The Sex Researches* (1969). On the problems of political thought in the sixties see, among others, D. Germino, *Beyond Ideology: The Revival of Political Theory* (1967); also W. G. Runciman, *Social Science and Political Theory*, 2nd ed. (1969).

After each of these breaks – 1914 and 1918, 1933 and 1939, 1945 and 1950, 1964 and 1973 – there arises the question which, it appears, now confronts us finally: are the ideas and values, the political concepts and norms, originating in the eighteenth and nineteenth centuries still valid and serviceable? To what extent have they petrified into mere outward forms, at the mercy of every call for change, and to what degree do they still provide a genuine support to political thought and behaviour?

The shrinkage of ideologies, regarded in the fifties as being at their end, has been followed, after the eruption of the sixties, by a renewed scepsis of ideology. The talk now is of an exhaustion of modernism and its idea of progress altogether. Certainly the negative consequences of scientific specialization, the decline of humanism and the search for religious escapes from the crisis are no new phenomena. But in their worldwide effects they now seem overwhelming. At the moment of greatest extension and highest material achievements, western thought finally seems to be losing confidence in itself, undermined and exploded by its own ideas and their realization.[1]

This pessimistic perspective, of course, takes no account of the adaptability and capacity of regeneration inherent in the pluralism of political thought, with its available alternatives, and which, in the course of our century, has enabled it time and again to overcome or at least to survive the great monolithic excrescences of modernism – fascism, national socialism and communism. The search for an ultimate value, especially in political thought – unless it is superhuman or inhuman – invariably leads back to a multiplicity and variety of human aspirations which have to be met with finite and not with chiliastic solutions. It is here that the long-term evolution of modern democratic thought acquires vital importance, especially in a world overwhelmingly dominated and ruled by unilinear dictatorial political models offering no alternatives.

Our question, therefore, is not crudely: how great is the threat to modern civilization? It is, more specifically and empirically: how exhausted or how appealing still is the idea of democracy which is today invoked by the whole world but whose practical application has remained so controversial and which has been realized in so few countries? The general difficulty of democracy as an idea and reality will be examined in the next chapter. Here we are concerned with the empirical finding which reveals to us the astonishing adaptability and resilience of this most difficult and exacting of all forms of government. In the early sixties its majoritarian support in the free Europe and in the U S A was based mainly on the political and economic

---

[1] On this, impressively, Raymond Aron, *Plädoyer für das dekadente Europa*, op. cit., p. 251ff.; Leszek Kolakowski, 'Selbstgefährdung der offenen Gesellschaft', in *Liberalismus – nach wie vor* (Zurich, 1979), p. 155ff. See also the texts in I. Fetscher, *Überlebensbedingungen*, op. cit., pp. 42ff. and 91ff.: K. D. Bracher, 'Fortschritt', op. cit., p. 229ff.; Leszek Kolakowski, Golo Mann *et al.*, in Hans Rössner (ed.), *Rückblick in die Zukunft* (Berlin, 1981), p. 29ff.

efficiency of democratic institutions. The political process in the party and association state was regulated by a clear representative translation of the 'popular will' into legislative and executive decisions. On this point, as well as on the indispensable position of the opposition, which distinguishes the libertarian democratic concept from all authoritarian and totalitarian variants, there was overwhelming consensus, which, however – in contrast to 'totalitarian' or 'consensus democracy' – never included pretension or coercion to unanimity.

Within a few years this libertarian value-based and efficiency-minded democracy was confronted by a demand for a more comprehensive democratic concept:[1] not the mere functioning of a pluralist system but 'essential' democracy and appropriate 'innovations' were at the focus of the debate. What became obvious in this connection, however, was the importance which attached not only to the various objectives and value concepts but also to the democratic 'rules of the game'. Alongside the 'legitimacy crisis' in the argument about values a second dispute emerged around peaceful or violent forms of realization of political goals; for a while the latter trend, gesturing spectacularly and making greater theoretical demands, attracted greater intellectual acclaim – in the face of which even a lot of politicians retreated!

It was this double dispute that produced all the clamour of the late sixties. It was accompanied by the old, and now freshly posed, question of an improvement, or indeed a revolution, of political participation. 'Citizen participation',[2] the American term, originally conceived in the sense of an activization of political culture, engulfed all institutions. Everywhere the question was raised about replacing representative by plebiscitarian forms, by a 'fundamental democratization', and everywhere the seemingly clear distinction between political democracy (in the state) and efficiently-functioning institutions, susceptible only to limited democratization (in society), proved difficult. Parties and associations, the army and the civil

[1] See the account in Wolfgang Mantl, *Repräsentation und Identität* (Vienna, 1975); see also *Überforderte Demokratie?* (Wirtschaftspolitische Gesellschaft von 1947) (Frankfurt/M., 1975), *e.g.* p. 63ff.

[2] Thus especially the by now classic comparative study of five 'political cultures' (USA, Mexico, Great Britain, Italy, Western Germany) by Gabriel Almond and Sidney Verba, *The Civic Culture, Political Attitudes and Democracy in Five Nations* (Princeton, 1963), pp. 161ff., 230ff. The progressive intensification of the concept is shown by the 1970 symposium, *Partizipation, Aspekte politischer Kultur* (Wirtschaftspolitische Gesellschaft von 1947) (Opladen, 1970); later Ulrich von Alemann (ed.), *Partizipation – Demokratisierung – Mitbestimmung* (Opladen, 1975; 2nd ed. 1978); finally the communal application of a very extensive participation concept, with voluminous empirical material, in Wilfried Nelles, 'Politische Partizipation und kommunaler Planungsprozess . . . am Beispiel einer Stadtsanierung (Andernach)', doct. thesis (Bonn, 1977); also in Wilfried Nelles and Reinhard Oppermann (eds), *Stadtsanierung und Bürgerbeteiligung* (Göttingen, 1979); also Nelles-Oppermann (ed.), *Partizipation und Politik* (Göttingen, 1979), with bibliographies of the rapidly increasing literature on participation.

service, schools, universities and the Churches all depend on an expert internal structure which sets certain limits to the self-determination or the co-determination of all participants. It was these limits that the struggle was about, and the demand for greater participation proved to be a long-term trend.

Certainly its extreme forms, tending as they did towards destruction, were at variance with the smooth functioning expected above all from democratic politics; moreover, it turned out in retrospect that the external image of the revolt, as presented by the sixties, had been overdimensionally magnified by sensationalist reporting in the mass media and by revolutionary self-portrayal of militant groups.[1] However, comparative public opinion surveys in the western countries during the seventies show that if not a 'silent revolution' then at least a profound change in the present political culture was taking place. There was a questioning of existing democracy by an increased demand for participation, leading, in the event of let-down, to a system-critical alternative attitude on the part of many, especially younger, citizens.

This applies not only to the universities, with their rapid increase in numbers and size, and with their new impersonal and mass atmosphere, but also to large sections of the population, especially women. Two major trends emerge in particular: first, a change from a call for predominantly economic growth and security to a demand for an improved quality of life and protection of the environment, and, secondly, an increase in political information and in facilities for participation in the political process, as well as for its disruption.[2] Naturally, considerable differences may be observed in this process, due largely to the arrival of a new generation. In countries like Germany with a repeatedly broken history this generation conflict remains far more serious, even after the dying-down of the violent phase of re-ideologization and system critique, than in the old democracies such as Britain, where political continuity is admittedly at the expense of economic modernization and innovation; in Italy, because of the great regional differences and the but slight degree of social integration, the anti-democratic potential and dissatisfaction with 'the system' have remained especially strong.

However, the most important single factor in the development of the western democracies continues to be the party system. It characterizes and simultaneously determines the degree of political stability in consensus formation and governability, as well as in opposition attitudes within these

---

[1] See the early survey of predominantly left-wing radical trends in Gerd Langguth, *Protestbewegung am Ende, Die neue Linke als Vorhut der* DKP (Mainz, 1971) with the documents, p. 249ff. More comprehensively his *Die Protestbewegung in der Bundesrepublik Deutschland 1968–1976* (Cologne, 1976). On the growing importance of the mass media see Wolfgang Bergsdorf, *Die vierte Gewalt*, op. cit., p. 56ff.

[2] R. Inglehart, *Silent Revolution*, op. cit., p. 363.

democracies, and, as a multiparty system, represents the decisive distinction from the mono-party regimes in the countries of eastern Europe and the Third World: the difference between democracy and dictatorship. All alternative attempts at structuring the process of opinion forming and its translation into politics, whether plebiscitarian or communalistically oriented, have proved to be either threats to libertarian democracy itself or a quasi-anarchist fragmentation resulting in system critique.

That is why democratic theory has been increasingly concerned with the question of how the party-state system can adequately absorb and reflect the changed expectations among the political public. An important part is played in this by the conflict between an older concept of democracy, focused more on economic efficiency and political stability, and the more recent expectation of a qualitative and 'participatory' improvement of politics. A possible compromise between these generation and goal conflicts might be achieved by the reciprocal realization that qualitative goals, no matter how important or noble, first presuppose a considerable measure of economic and political efficiency in order to become realizable at all, and that, on the other hand, the efficiency needed to ensure them must take also account of the increased demands on life and political participation. In order to achieve such a compromise, which will need continuous rebalancing, it is necessary for the political parties to be prepared for it. That is why the non-ideological compromise-and-integration party, the 'people's party' of the post-war period, represents genuine progress.[1] Admittedly, it is time and again put in jeopardy by that need for the non-rational identification of the individual with the mass society, a need less catered for by the rational compromise character of democracy than by the great stylizations and identity shows of authoritarian systems and political substitute religions.[2] Such needs for participation and identification with groups and 'judgements' claiming to fight for higher values frequently come into conflict, because of their absoluteness, with efficiency and with the rules of libertarian

---

[1] On the German debate now especially Peter Haungs, *Parteiendemokratie in der Bundesrepublik* (Berlin, 1980), p. 63ff. (though with an excessively sharp critique, p. 11ff, of the party-state theory of Gerhard Leibholz who was largely responsible for starting the debate in 1952: *Strukturprobleme*, op. cit., p. 93ff.); see Heino Kaack, *Geschichte und Struktur des deutschen Parteiensystems* (Opladen, 1971); Helmut Trautmann, *Innerparteiliche Demokratie im Parteienstaat* (Berlin, 1975), with reference to the small parties; Manfred Rowold, *Im Schatten der Macht; Zur Oppositionsrolle der nichtetablierten Parteien in der Bundesrepublik* (Düsseldorf, 1974), pp. 11ff., 52ff. ('Das Volksparteiensystem').

[2] Time and again the romantic relapse into a particularly pronounced Protestant inward-turned German idealism has disturbed Germany's political development in the modern age: see Richard Löwenthal, *Der romantische Rückfall* (Stuttgart, 1970), tracing this line all the way to the radicalisms of 1969. This is true also of the trends of the new 'peace movements' since 1980, which combine romantically idealistic ideas with some ancient-and-modern Utopias of pacificism and neutralism – with or without communist influence. Note too the apocalyptic title of the latest collection of essays by influential German spokesmen: Walter Jens (ed.), *In letzter Stunde* (Munich, 1982).

democracy which have to be taken into account.

This has in fact happened less and less since the end of the sixties, and the conflict between the demands for participation and for efficiency has not disappeared with the decline of the revolt movements. The attraction of alternative or counter-cultures has by no means diminished; what seems to be lacking is inspiring figures, rather than the attraction of uncompromising social or moral value concepts, to fan once more the smouldering dissatisfaction at the compromise character of 'bourgeois' democracy and its economic instability. At all events Aristotle's ancient question of the pro and contra of open and closed societies, of pluralistic and monolithic political concepts, remains as topical as when Karl Popper newly formulated it in 1945 – since when it has been at the root of all value discussions of political theory.

The strength and attraction of monolithic thought is closely connected with the need for great goals and emotional values in politics also. A longing to transcend the essentially material and compromise-governed character of politics in the pluralist democracies is growing, especially in the industrialized countries whose elementary needs are either saturated or have come up against the limits of growth – and therefore hunger for emotional or spiritual compensation. The outlines of a new romantic idealism are beginning to take shape. Whether it will become mobilizable, or whether the weight of cautionary historical experience in the century of totalitarianism will be sufficient to keep it within bounds, is difficult to predict.

The stock of great political ideas may be regarded as finite: in the history of political thought we do in fact continually encounter similar basic questions.[1] Thus the question about the future of highly developed industrial and communications societies and their political form leads back to a more general problem of democracy, or indeed of politics generally: the problem of the relationship between real and ideal values, between management of the present and visions of the future, between the realization of the goals of the individual and those of society, or community, as a whole.

These are antagonisms calling not for either-or but for as-well-as solutions. Max Weber had described them by the concepts of substantial and functional rationality, the antagonism between values and means: both are equally necessary to the political process. The higher the goals are set, the greater, naturally, are the demands made on the structures and their means. The discrepancy in the ends–means relationship is especially clear in totalitarian systems, where the end invariably justifies the means. Such a tendency to underestimate or violate the reciprocal relation between an absolutely set goal and the manipulation of the rules of human social existence is also found in those newly formulated theories of violence for the sake of achieving 'non-violence' or in the justification of dictatorial rule for

[1] On the following passages see K. D. Bracher, *Schlüsselwörter in der Geschichte*, p. 33ff.

the sake of achieving a 'rule-less' society – perversions of political thought, resulting in lasting destruction and destabilization. The New Left's totalitarian contempt for democracy as a characteristic aspect of revolutionary violation of rules and means was most aptly described by Brzezinski in 1970: 'The sharp edge of the New Left's . . . attacks has been aimed at those American institutions whose normal operation relies most on reason and non-violence . . . leading New Left spokesmen have been contemptuous of free speech, democratic procedures, and majority rule. They have left little room for doubt as to how they would handle their critics if the New Left were ever to gain power.'[1]

Whether the change of values, the implementation of those far-reaching aspirations, remains possible at the same time as the preservation of the structural functioning of democracy, which alone renders such change possible in a peaceful way, or whether the shift and radicalization of the goals bring with it a long-term destruction of its political prerequisites is a question of supreme topicality. After the bitter experiences of the abuse of their liberal values in the radicals' dismantling of liberalism, many of the democratic sociologists and political scientists in America, who are nowadays somewhat misleadingly grouped as 'neo-conservatives',[2] aim at nothing more than the restoration of a much-upset equilibrium. Conservative here signifies, above all, the realization of the necessity to preserve the unassailability of rules which possess the same moral weight as the supreme goals, and indeed are central political values themselves, because humane politics are not possible without humane rules.

What emerges in the disputes of the late seventies is in fact an emphasis, on all sides, on the moral dimension. This applies especially to the problem of progress, raised anew by the crisis of left-wing progressivism in view of the

[1] Zbigniew Brzezinski, *Between Two Ages* (New York, 1970), p. 235.

[2] For instance, such important liberal sociologists as Seymour M. Lipset, Samuel P. Huntington, Daniel Patrick Moynihan, Nathan Glazer, Daniel Bell, Jeane Kirkpatrick and numerous contributors to the periodical *Commentary*. On this change, which had been in the making for some time and which had a clear manifestation in the change of presidency of 1980–1, see the survey 'Du liberalisme au conservatisme', in: Y. H. Nouailhat, *Histoire*, op. cit., p. 93ff.; on this critically, P. Steinfels, *The Neo-Conservatives* (New York, 1979); on the opposite side again with interesting illustrations, Nigel Ashford, 'The Neo-Conservatives', *Government and Opposition* 16 (1981), p. 353ff.; also Friedbert Pflüger, 'Reagan, die Konservativen und die Gefahr der Neuen Rechten', *Sonde* 14, 1 (1981), p. 44ff. This contains a reference to an article by Huntington who as early as in the fifties very shrewdly formulated the (almost necessarily) neo-conservative attitude of a liberal, 'Conservatism as an ideology', *American Political Science Review* 5 (1957), p. 434ff.: 'In preserving the achievements of American Liberalism, American liberals have no recourse but to turn to conservatism. . . . Conservatism is not, as the aristocratic interpretation argues, the monopoly of one particular class in history. Nor is it, as the autonomous school contends, appropriate in every age and place. It is, instead, relevant in a particular type of historical situation. That is the situation in which American liberalism finds itself today. Until the challenge of communism and the Soviet Union is eliminated or neutralized, a major aim of American liberals must be to preserve what they have created.'

oil crisis and the 'limits of growth'. Since that widely discussed eponymous study of 1972[1] the scholarly publications of the international 'Club of Rome' and its critics have invested the debate of a 'global equilibrium' of resources and production, population and environmental problems, with moral-political undertones or overtones. This links up, to a point, with the Third World debate of the sixties but differs from it by the sceptical note which, following the ideological intermezzo with its occasional chiliastic overtones, now once more focuses on the realistic limits both of economic and of social and political expectations.

The anti-technological, anti-modernist current of thought which invokes this changed attitude, however – in a typical about-turn from the highest expectations and demands to the sharpest critique of civilization and resignation – disregards the complexity of real conditions. Forecasts such as those by the Club of Rome in themselves produce, through the publicity and political discussion they give rise to, an intensifying but also a corrective effect. Not only is their scientific determinism modified by specific countermeasures, such as the issues of political dispute in the seventies, but environmental and energy policies become major areas of decision. Even in the world of political ideas and counter-ideas the cost and the consequences of progress, of ever accelerating technological development, are again recognized as a key problem of social and state politics.

In this connection it again emerges that the recurrent ideological prescriptions from the arsenal of classic civilizational and cultural critique are no longer effective. 'Socialism', which profited most from worldwide re-ideologization, is less than ever capable of solving the growing problems, as demonstrated by the economic crises in communism: fixation upon a rigid state-socialist solution, as proposed by communist theoreticians, leads to an inflexible dictated society with declining prosperity and the prospect of political explosions, without any lessening of the environmental problems.[2]

As for our question about the political consequences, the energy and environmental debate, together with its problems of progress, seem to lead to the realization that flexibility and adaptation, pluralism and a balancing of interests are more than ever needed in economy, society and state, as well as

[1] Dennis Meadows *et al.*, *Limits of Growth* (1972). In rapid succession followed: M. Mesarović, E. Pestel, *Menschheit am Wendepunkt, Zweiter Bericht an den Club of Rome zur Weltlage* (Reinbek, 1975); D. Gabor, U. Colombo, A. King, R. Galli, *Das Ende der Verschwendung, Zur materiellen Lage der Menschheit* (Stuttgart, 1976); Jan Tinbergen, *Der RIO-Bericht an den Club of Rome, Wir haben nur eine Zukunft, Reform der internationalen Ordnung* (Opladen, 1977); E. Laszlo *et al.*, *Goals of Mankind, A Report to the Club of Rome on the New Horizons of the Global Community* (New York, 1977); at an earlier date the prolonged discussion in the symposium planned in 1971, *The No-Growth Society, Daedalus* 102, No. 4 (Fall, 1973). See also the comprehensive historical-sociological survey by Raymond Aron, *Plädoyer für das dekadente Europa*, op. cit., p. 253ff. ('Die grosse Furcht von 1973'). Further reports are in the Pergamon Press Publications for the Club of Rome (Oxford and New York).

[2] Thus especially Wolfgang Harich, *Kommunismus ohne Wachstum? Babeuf und der Club of Rome* (Reinbek, 1975).

in the attitude of the citizen. A modern industrial society based on these 'virtues' is also, more than ever before, dependent on their political form, on the efficient working of pluralist democracy, and of course also on the international dimension of supranational co-operation. A non-ideological development of forms of peaceful co-operation and conflict resolution – which is incompatible with any idea of ultimate mission – is clearly, for the first time, becoming a central issue in the debate of political ideas, not only because of the problem of rearmament and war but also in view of the economic and social aspects of a worldwide set of energy and environmental problems.

With a growing sensitivity to questions of a humane shaping rather than an uncontrolled development of the world, the battle-lines of ideas are of course getting infinitely more complicated than in a basic confrontation of capitalism and socialism, reactionary and progressive, conservative and liberal. The linguistically somewhat misleading distinction between 'materialist' and 'post-materialist' values, with which a major empirical study has attempted to sum up important trends of political orientation in the seventies, while pointing to the ideological character of the continual conflict over the right priorities, leaves the political question open.[1] What matters primarily is a balance of ends and means, a compromise between human values and equally human procedures. Ends and means must not conflict fundamentally. Freedom and human dignity, human rights and social justice are equally dependent on economic efficiency and on basic constitutional conditions of social life: these permit only of compromise and not of the assertion of one single will. In the vacuum of ideals or through an attitude of resignation and refusal, these values, no matter whether old and well-tested or newly postulated, can never be accomplished; the only result would be ever new crises and a way clear for dictators. Hence the real difference continues to lie in the issue of democratic or authoritarian policy, or more specifically of, on the one hand, the most libertarian policy possible and, on the other, an (allegedly necessary) directed or enforced policy.

It is here that the old danger of ideological thought arises time and again: a form of thought which, oriented as it was towards political ends, underrated the importance of real political structures, of ways and of means. Reading the ecological disaster literature of the seventies with ideology-critical eyes, one is reminded at times of the sense of hopelessness which made so many intellectuals susceptible to ideologization of thought between the wars. A mesmerization with the 'atom state',[2] intended aggressively or resignedly,

[1] R. Inglehart, *Silent Revolution*, op. cit.

[2] Thus, with considerable influence on the new anti-nuclear and ecological movement, the book by Robert Jungk, *Der Atomstaat, Vom Fortschritt in die Unmenschlichkeit* (Munich, 1977). This is also a point of departure for the new 'peace movement' which, in spite of changed conditions and problems of armaments control in the nuclear age, in many respects represents a return to the western pacifism and unilateralism of the years between the wars. Ideologically, moreover, it shows a misjudgement or disregard of the communist contempt for pacifism. As is

produces, as did the earlier critique of culture, political options which are just as remote from reality and which bypass the emphatically invoked interests of the working people or of the Third World, just as did the earlier socialist Utopia of the proletariat and its supposedly inevitable dictatorship, realized or not (yet) in the Soviet Union.

This escape from reality can take on pseudo-religious traits, it can lead to the ideological undermining of the open society, and in any event it will weaken its resistance to left-wing or right-wing dictatorships. More than ever before one finds conservative nostalgia, withdrawal into nature or into the past, and these may blend with a nostalgic Marxism, with a struggle against large anonymous bureaucracies and multinational concerns, for council-democratic or anarcho-communist community models, and with a sharp critique not only of capitalism but, sometimes, also of 'the actually existing socialism' of the Soviet system.[1]

Left-wing and right-wing anti-capitalism – that intellectual concept of civilizational critique more than a century old – has been revived as a romantic declaration of war on the consequences of progress. Its left-wing alternative, 'socialism with a human face', of course remains an illusion so long as the unilateral communist vision, and hence also the dictatorship, is preserved. Authoritarian nationalism as a right-wing alternative, once reduced *ad absurdum* by national socialism, now once more offers the explosive amalgam of romantic and technocratic features. Both versions hastily and carelessly dismiss the difficult question of a humane ends – means relation. Neo-Marxism and nationalism, social Utopianism and anti-technological neo-mysticism, all again shirk the real question, the question which pluralist democracy alone, with its constitutions and rules, attempts to answer realistically: how can a political system realize humane values without fundamentally violating them in their assertion? Or, the other way round: how can modernization and the concept of efficiency – the prerequisites of scientific and socio-economic progress – co-exist without violent solutions, with that preservation and improvement of the human condition which are the aims of any just social and political order?

The question of power also produces very different patterns in open and

well known, ever since Lenin, pacifism is seen solely as an instrument for party-political goals of a revolutionary minority and is subject to the politically one-sided, power-egotistic classi-fication into unjust (imperialist-capitalist) and just (revolutionary-socialist) wars. This is matched in the general discussion of violence by the arbitrary Marxist-Leninist distinction between reactionary and progressive-revolutionary violence. Thus even a nuclear war now becomes conceivable in GDR theory: see recently this justification doctrine in Wolfgang Scheler, *Gottfried Kissling, Gerechte und ungerechte Kriege in unserer Zeit, (Militärverlag der DDR)* (Berlin, 1981). The fact that Marx and Engels still distinguished between defensive wars and wars of aggression is, of course, being concealed.

[1] Thus the ideal-socialist fantasies of the former GDR theoretician and detainee Rudolf Bahro, *Die Alternative* (Cologne-Frankfurt/M., 1977); *Elemente einer neuen Politik* (Berlin, 1980); *Plädoyer für schöpferische Initiative, Zur Kritik von Arbeitsbedingungen im real existierenden Sozialismus* (Cologne, 1980).

closed systems. While the struggle for power is a basic political concept, its most peaceful possible, monitorable and controllable regulation remains a basic criterion for distinction between political systems. Power, like fear, is one of the basic motivations of all politics: the power-theory interpretation of history and politics has not lost anything in importance since Thucydides and Machiavelli, Hobbes and Montesquieu, Max Weber and Ferrero. That is why a political anthropology which acknowledges power and fear to be 'natural' basic motivations, while freedom and justice are their civilizing regulators, must assign supreme importance to the legal enactment and safeguarding of just these humane regulators.

The struggle for values therefore is and remains primarily a struggle for the methods of politics, a struggle which must not be belittled by any chiliastic or catastrophic visions or counter-prescriptions. Criticism of culture and its degeneration under national socialism and of Marxism and its degeneration into Stalinism both contain lessons on how far humans may go, or be driven, if political ends are placed above the means, or the total idea above consideration of the rights and interests of fellow human beings.

The vital issue remains the discussion of the preservation of our civilization. Its technical realities and potentialities, which go hand in hand with appalling problems of over-population and food shortages, energy and environmental dilemmas, cannot be annulled by a challenge to science and technology, no matter how violent. Any simple 'return to nature' would only make the solution of all problems more difficult; it would further reduce available means and further restrict possibilities of help. Any lowering of performance or efficiency in favour of political participation, no matter how important or desirable, holds the risk of a serious upset of the equilibrium which can only just about be maintained, by further scientific progress and by relieving man of further burdens in the post-industrial society.[1] Any new Luddite tendencies, such as have been gaining ground in political theory since the sixties, are in flagrant contradiction to the social and emancipational demands which are simultaneously being made on our allegedly sick civilization. Third World literature in particular reflects a strange side-by-side existence of primitivism and welfare state ideas. Its political liberation theories, in their Marxist or sometimes theological justification

[1] See Daniel Bell, *The Post-Industrial Society* (New York, 1975), and earlier his article 'The Post-Industrial Society: the Evolution of an Idea', *Survey* No. 2, 79 (Spring, 1971), p. 102ff. – also on the sociologist's ancient temptation to play the prophet or seer. Bell had first introduced the concept in 1959 in an unpublished paper at a seminar of the influential Salzburg Seminar of American Studies. At the same time Ralf Dahrendorf spoke of 'Post-Capitalist Society' (*Class and Class Conflict in an Industrial Society*, 1959), by which he primarily meant the tendency towards a service society, while David Riesman (in *Mass Leisure*, 1958) used the concepts to characterize the problem of increasing leisure for the masses. The concepts, therefore, were in the air at the end of the 'de-ideologizing' fifties but only attained their full impact after the succeeding re-ideologization waves. See also Daniel Bell, 'Liberalism in the Post-Industrial Society', in *Liberalismus – nach wie vor* (Zurich, 1979), p. 205ff.

and orientation, similarly fail to realize the indissoluble connection of the two principal problems: improvement of the standard of living and, simultaneously, safeguarding of human rights. Without modern science and without freedom in the development and assessment of alternatives those problems will become genuinely insoluble.

Here then is an answer to the renewed (self-)accusations of the western democracies, accusations once more aimed at the political system. The spread of western civilization over the entire globe has indeed often enough produced alarming and negative consequences. But what is true of economic development is true also of political development: it was not its effect as such that was bad – the situation of most developing countries was pitiful enough even before the colonial era – but the inadequate implementation of the measures. It was not the transfer of democracy but its power-political and ideological destruction by the allurements – so painfully familiar both in the west and in the east – of dictatorial and monolithic forms of government which made subsequent oppression possible. Ultimately it was either a nationalist or a Marxist friend-foe concept which, as the magic formula of 'total' political integration, swept away the carefully thought-out institutions and constitutions.

There is no doubt that optimistic hopes of the transferability of freedom and democracy have often proved premature. But that does not mean that it is too late – provided the detours and wrong turnings of political thought which in the nineteenth and twentieth centuries accompanied the modernization of western societies and states are not, by our own disaster philosophers, wished upon the Third World.[1] What is needed is a continued comprehensive readiness for assistance. This, of course, must be based on a stable political and economic equilibrium of the west. Only then can developing countries be given the material and spiritual encouragement they need instead of the destructive weapons and ideologies that are, primarily, supplied to them by the dictatorships of the east. Communism, as has again been most recently proved by the economic catastrophe of Poland and the bloody subjection of Afghanistan, offers no alternative, any more than do the old and new despotisms of military or feudalist authoritarianism. We are left with what a man like Winston Churchill, who was not just a conservative but also a last defender of freedom in Europe, reminded us of in an appropriate understatement: that of all the imperfect and indeed bad systems of politics that of libertarian democracy is the least bad.

[1] The self-doubts as well as the responsibility which the highly developed and, simultaneously, democratic west has to bear in this respect are summed up by R. Inglehart, op. cit., p. 392, as follows: 'The changing values and skills of Western publics present alarming aspects. We seem to be witnessing a weakening of institutional restraints, a diminishing reliance on functional rationality and its chief tool, technology – to some extent, even a rejection of them. These trends are alarming because in excess they would be disastrous. But it seems to me that the process represents a redressment of the balance rather than the breakdown of society. The Industrial Era was a time for the development of great means. Post-Industrial Society may provide a time for the application of these means to great ends.'

4. CONTESTED PRINCIPLES OF DEMOCRATIC THEORY

In the course of the twentieth century the confrontation of liberal and totalitarian concepts of the state has passed through a number of phases and forms. But it has invariably also been an argument about democracy and its fundamental principles. Communism had combined its total rejection of the liberal concept of politics with its own pretensions to being both a scientific and a revolutionary political philosophy, while at the same time claiming the principle of democracy, as well as that of dictatorship, for itself. And both Mussolini's and Hitler's dictatorships emphatically declared themselves to be a higher form of government by the people, an allegedly genuine people's community, superior to all pluralist or 'plutocratic' degenerations of 'decadent' democracy.[1]

This 'true' democracy, held up against the liberal 'sham democracy', continues to haunt all theoretical and ideological endeavours for a non-antagonistic model of democracy closed within itself. It is based on the premise that the three great fundamental principles of all democratic theory – majority, liberty and equality – can be reconciled and indeed brought into full congruence. History, however, teaches that, under human conditions, this is possible only within limits, and that any pretension to a perfect solution of the basic conflict between freedom and equality leads to inhuman tyranny with a preponderance of the one over the other.[2]

[1] See Adrian Lyttelton, op. cit., pp. 54ff., 135ff., 149ff.; Renzo De Felice, *Deutungen*, op. cit., p. 226ff.; K. D. Bracher, *NS Machtergreifung*, Vol. 1, p. 472ff. Succinctly J. L. Talmon, *The Myth of the Nation*, p. 542: 'Democratic principles came to be violated in the name of the highest form of democracy.'

[2] See the instances in Gerhard A. Ritter, 'Der Antiparlamentarismus und der Anti-pluralismus der Rechts- und Linksradikalen', in *Der Überdruss an der Demokratie* (Cologne, 1970), p. 51ff. (recently also in Ritter's volume of essays *Arbeiterbewegung, Parteien und Parlamentarismus* (Göttingen, 1976), p. 259ff., as well as p. 292ff. on "Direkte Demokratie" und Rätewesen in Geschichte und Theorie'). The young Marx first postulated 'true democracy' in this totalitarian sense as the total identity of private and public existence; thus his critique of Hegel's state philosophy of 1841–2: Siegfried Landshut, *Karl Marx – die Frühschriften* (Stuttgart, 1953), pp. xxviiff., 47ff. See, on the other hand, the characterization of the not so 'easy' but 'difficult ideology of democracy' in Eva G. Reichmann, *Hostages of Civilization, The Social Sources of National Socialist Anti-semitism* (Boston, 1951); also K. D. Bracher, 'Über die Schwierigkeit der Demokratie', in *Geschichte und Gewalt*, op. cit., p. 289ff. The important work on critique of democracy is Wolfgang Mantl, *Repräsentation und Identität*, op.cit.; Martin Rhonheimer, *Politisierung und Legitimitätsentzug, Totalitäre Kritik der parlamentarischen Demokratie in Deutschland* (Freiburg-Munich, 1979); Eckhard Jesse, *Streitbare Demokratie*, op. cit, p. 23ff.

Even the massive attack launched in the sixties from within the liberally-socially constituted democracies against just these democracies was based on this kind of a perfectionist misunderstanding. It started with revolts and radical resistance against the 'classic' liberal-democratic theory which was criticized as an élitist disguise of real power relations: the discrepancy between its principles, which the critics saw as mere postulates, and an imperfect empirical reality was to be revealed; this demand for appropriate change, for a 'democratization' of democracy itself, was the order of the day for the young rebels, and was rated higher than its stability or smooth functioning.[1]

The glorification of direct democratic action and of total participation, which followed from it, was of course nothing other than the old dispute between idea and reality. The issue, as always, concerns those three basic principles of democracy enshrined in the much-maligned classic theory.

(1) Acknowledgement of the majority principle represents the attempt to make a democracy operational and capable of functioning in the first place.[2] If one were to demand, as postulated by Rousseau and by the totalitarian theory of democracy, complete agreement, total consensus, as the pre-requisite of ideal democracy, then this must inevitably fail as a practicable political system because unanimous decisions are impossible in the long run under free conditions. Otherwise one must forgo the integral principle of freedom of opinion and decision, in which case one arrives in the realm of pseudo-democratic dictatorship, with the fiction of 99 per cent plebiscites and the mono-party system. The way out of this dilemma, out of the antagonisms and the antinomy of the democratic ideas, lies in the readiness of different parties and groups of citizens to make compromises, and their agreement to replace the postulate of complete agreement of the people by an acceptance of the will of the majority, and to stipulate specially qualified majorities for certain kinds of decisions.

Naturally the majority principle contains the danger of the suppression of the minority and might well lead to dictatorship or civil war unless rules for the protection and participation of that minority are simultaneously agreed, and accepted and obeyed also by the controlling majority. The decisive progress, and of course also the problem, of the modern constitutional state lies therefore in the fact that it has channelled the superiority of power into a system of rules: the fruits and the symbol of an advance in human culture and civilization which, in its essence, implies not only the expansion but also the taming of its forces, instead of ruthless exploitation of power. In political terms this means extension of legitimation to the entire people, but at the same time a self-imposed restraint of rule, a tamed democracy instead of an

---

[1] Samuel H. Barnes, Max Kaase *et al.* (eds), *Political Action, Mass Participation in Five Western Democracies* (London, 1979).

[2] On majority, minority, freedom, Carl Joachim Friedrich, *Demokratie als Herrschafts- und Lebensform* (Heidelberg, 1959), p. 57ff., at one time an influential work.

arbitrary dictatorship. One cannot reflect too often on the difficulty and exceptional character of this process in order to understand the constant temptation towards authoritarian or totalitarian action, towards an almost instinctive suppression or even liquidation of opposition, both in the past and at present: although it possesses power, the majority voluntarily abides by the rules which make it forgo the suppression or liquidation of the minority.

In practice this fundamental principle of majority–minority democracy is, of course, far more difficult to implement than any other form of government; it might be called the most difficult of all political ideas.[1] Only its institutionalization and its gradual acceptance by custom can mitigate tensions and pressures, and ensure self-conquest of power. This is done chiefly by the legislative enactment of basic rights and by making them legally enforceable, by a free electoral system and by the separation of powers. But there always remains a vulnerability to the primal urges of unchecked power and unrestrained power politics. In any crisis of democracy there is a risk of a relapse from the self-imposed political restraint into the power enticements of dictatorship. But even in its normal course of operation democracy is under a constant self-threat from arbitrary majority rule, from absolutism or indeed from the 'tyranny of the majority'.[2]

The fact that libertarian democracy, though difficult, is feasible is due not only to moral and civilizational principles but also to the numerous deterrent experiences of dictatorial alternatives. There is such a thing as the correctly understood interest of the citizen and of parties concerned. The more likely they are to be pushed from the majority into the minority, the more concerned will they be with safeguarding an opposition and their own participation, in parliamentary committees or federal institutions for example. Continuous amendments to the electoral law by the majority of

---

[1] See p 231, note 1. On this also the symposium by Ulrich Matz (ed.), *Grundprobleme der Demokratie* (Darmstadt, 1973); also the still valuable books by H. R. G. Greaves, *The Foundations of Political Theory* (London, 1958); Arnold Brecht, *Politische Theorie*, 2nd ed. (Tübingen, 1976); Seymour Martin Lipset, *Political Man* (London, 1960); now especially stimulating is W. J. Stankiewicz, *Aspects of Political Theory, Classical Concepts in an Age of Relativism* (New York, 1976); and his *Approaches to Democracy* (London, 1980), with chapters on (*inter alia*) comparative political violence, value relativism, participation, and pluralism.

[2] Thus first the perspicacious assessment on the instance of an already advanced American development by Alexis de Tocqueville, *Democracy in America* (1835–1840; London, 1967), Vol. 1, ch. 7; on 'omnipotence of the majority' and 'majority tyranny' see J. P. Mayer, *Alexis de Tocqueville – Prophet des Massenzeitalters* (Munich, 1972); Otto Vossler, *Alexis de Tocqueville, Freiheit und Gleichheit* (Frankfurt/M., 1973); recently also Michael Hereth, *Alexis de Tocqueville, Die Gefährdung der Freiheit in der Demokratie* (Stuttgart, 1979). On the limits of the majority principle and the dangers of polarized democracy see the arguments in Jane J. Mansbridge, *Beyond Adversary Democracy* (New York, 1980), with a review by E. J. Dionne Jr. in the *New York Times Book Review* of 22 February 1981, and the conclusion by Robert Nisbet: 'Only powerful local communities with strongly held values of their own can protect us from the collapse of an alienating national democracy into totalitarianism.'

the day are similarly ruled out by the common interest: in tense situations any unrestrained manipulation of electoral law might heighten the danger of political rebellions and explosions, all the way to a civil war situation (as happened in Spain in 1936).[1] On the other hand, modern democracy, accused as it invariably is of instability or inefficiency, has to make an especial effort to remain governable and capable of producing a majority. Defence against opponents of the system and the imperfections of the electoral system are among the main problems of democracy – and the main charges levelled against it.

In the interminable debate about majority versus proportional representation systems the important point is that these electoral systems must, as far as possible, fulfil both functions of all democratic elections: representation of the citizens and the need to form a majority. In more strongly fragmented societies the PR system, though it makes majority formation more difficult, will probably be inevitable: it takes more obvious and 'more just' account of new currents, of major changes, and of important minorities in state and society. The historical and sociological conditions of electoral law call for a considerable range of variation – a circumstance to be noted by all dogmatics of an 'ideal' electoral system.[2]

A restricted application of the majority principle is particularly relevant for the protection of minorities who have no hope of ever becoming a majority, especially religious and ethnic minorities. It is in this area that the permanently safeguarded protection of a minority, as well as of the individual, emerges as a *sine qua non* of democracy. The protection of human rights and a compromise structure are such fundamental elements of democratic policy because the relation between freedom and equality, the basic conflict of the modern state, is reflected in them.

[1] See especially Sten S. Nilson, 'Wahlsoziologische Probleme des Nationalsozialismus', *Zeitschrift für die gesamte Staatswissenschaft* 110 (1954), p. 280ff.; as well as the discussion in K. D. Bracher, *Die Auflösung*, op. cit., p. 326, footnote 10. The vast discussion (see most recently Ulrich von Alemann, *Parteiensysteme im Parlamentarismus* (Gütersloh, 1973); Hans Fenske, *Wahlrecht und Parteiensystem* (1972); also Hans Meyer, *Wahlsystem und Verfassungsordnung* (1978); Dieter Nohlen, *Wahlsysteme der Welt* (1978) has somewhat died down in recent years when it was found that the British two-party democracy as the main model no longer unequivocally supported the arguments in favour of majority elections and that proportional representation was gaining an increasing following even in the mother country of parliamentary democracy (especially among the liberals and the social democrats who had seceded from the Labour Party). Yet the classic arguments are already present in the sixth chapter of John Stuart Mill, *On Liberty* (1859).

[2] That was why the broad spectrum of electoral systems was also adhered to in the first direct elections to the European Parliament in June 1979. British representation, in particular, because of the majority system, does not adequately reflect actual voter intentions (to the detriment of the Labour Party). See Eberhard Grabitz and Thomas Läufer, *Das Europäische Parlament* (Bonn, 1980), p. 233ff.; Institut für Europäische Politik (ed.), *Die erste Direktwahl des Europäischen Parlaments, zusammengestellt und eingeleitet von Emanuel Richter* (Bonn, 1980), pp. 31ff., 232. On research and theory issues Hans-Dieter Heumann, *Europäische Integration und nationale Interessenpolitik* (Königstein, 1980), p. 63ff.

(2) As in the debate on the majority principle and its limitations, so the definition of the principle of freedom and its limits determines the quality of democracy. Post-autocratic or post-dictatorial periods are particularly concerned with this issue: the discussions of the American founding years and the early phase of the French Revolution, the post-Napoleonic era and the revolutionary struggles of 1848, the upheavals of the twenties and the anti-totalitarian upswing after 1945. Nowhere does the difference from a totalitarian concept of democracy emerge more clearly than in the recognition of pluralism of views and aspirations, a pluralism which libertarian democracy endeavours to ensure. However, this unassailable protection of minorities and of individual freedoms against the state and the majority must be matched, on the other hand, by a limitation of freedom which, bearing in mind the lessons of the failure of the Weimar Republic, the authors of the West German constitution, in particular, have emphasized: it is contained in the idea of a reciprocity of political toleration, which denies to the enemies of libertarian democracy its liquidation by the pseudo-legal use of democratic freedoms, as happened in Russia in 1917, in Italy in 1922 and in Germany in 1933. This dual sensitivity of modern democracy, its vulnerability to dictatorial temptations and the possible abuse of its liberties, leads towards a dual determination of the concept of freedom: against its anarchic over-exploitation and against the pressure of the demand for equality.[1]

In contrast to the pre-war period, the freedom component of democracy was formulated after 1945 in more definite constitutional-political terms and thereby also made more susceptible to theoretical formulation. This was done not only by a more substantial emphasis on basic rights but also, and especially, by a further development of the idea of pluralism. Democracy is an agreement to tolerate different views and aspirations, and simultaneously to set limits to them. This characterizes, more clearly than purely formal constitutions and institutions (which may all seem to resemble each other), its difference from all forms of dictatorship. Pluralism means, above all, that the common will is not laid down in an authoritarian or totalitarian manner by the state, but that it is represented and determined by a readiness to set bounds to the plurality of intentions and forces: namely, precisely at the point where the existence or viability of that plurality, its freedom and reciprocal toleration itself are threatened or denied. And conversely, the democratic state can offer full scope for the plurality of aspirations, without being in jeopardy itself, only where that basic agreement is acknowledged.

[1] On the antagonism between freedom and equality see also Leonard Reinisch (ed.), *Freiheit und Gleichheit oder die Quadratur des Kreises* (Munich, 1974); Martin Greiffenhagen, *Freiheit gegen Gleichheit? Zur 'Tendenzwende' in der Bundesrepublik* (Hamburg, 1975); H. J. Eysenck, *Inequality of Man* (London, 1973); D.Guerin (ed.), *Ni Dieu ni Maître, Anthologie de l'anarchisme*, 4 vols (Paris, 1973–6). On this see the older bibliography by René König (on the occasion of Ralf Dahrendorf's *Über den Ursprung der Ungleichheit unter den Menschen*, Tübingen 1961), in *Kölner Zeitschrift für Soziologie und Sozialpsychologie* 13 (1961), p. 497ff.

The controversial issue of the banning of parties arises precisely when political extremism calls the pluralist system itself into question.[1]

The fundamental concept of the state as the plurality of the citizens contains the old wisdom of Aristotle, his rejection of any kind of monomorphic theory of the state. Basic agreement here means recognition of the pluralist principle, and not identical views by all citizens or the fusion of all political trends with regard to the common weal, as demanded by the fictions and constraints of modern dictatorship. On the contrary, it means that all differences of opinion are freely discussed and, provided they find majority support, can also be put into effect against others. The important aspect is respect for the holders of divergent opinions – as so aptly expressed by the English phrase 'to agree to differ'. This is the important principle: the principle of debate and compromise in the political process. While it is impossible to reduce opinions and interests to one formula in advance – as dictatorships demand – libertarian democracy is essentially based on historical experience and on the realization, arrived at through education and not through indoctrination, that only the unfettered discussion of differences of opinion and interests can produce those points of contact which render them suitable and ready for compromise in the common interest.

(3) A prerequisite of libertarian-democratic pluralist theory, of course, was the progressive extension of equal rights to all strata of society: equality and emancipation, initially in the liberal-bourgeois and subsequently in a socialist sense, were the companion piece to the libertarian component of democracy. Herein lies the insoluble relationship and the irremovable antagonism between liberal and egalitarian principles, an antagonism based on the diversity of human beings and of their interests. Democracy attempts to make them susceptible to compromise without forcibly liquidating them. All the critiques of modern democracy, and especially the attacks on its pluralist structure, as they have emerged from theory debates since the sixties, are revolts against the irremovability of those antagonistic relationships between the principles of majority, freedom and equality. There are three main arguments. On the one hand, the democratic argument: Democracy is the majority principle because, within democracy, it ensures the greatest possible measure of equality.[2] On the other hand, the socialist

---

[1] See Eckhard Jesse, *Streitbare Demokratie*, op. cit., p. 15ff. and *Literaturführer Parlamentarische Demokratie* (Opladen, 1981), p. 209ff. ('Streitbare Demokratie in der Krise?'); Manfred Rowold, *Im Schatten der Macht, Zur Oppositionsrolle der nicht-etablierten Parteien in der Bundesrepublic* (Düsseldorf, 1974), p. 52ff.; also the controversies in Manfred Funke (ed.), *Extremismus im demokratischen Rechtsstaat* (Düsseldorf, 1978); Hans Vorländer, *Verfassung und Konsens* (Berlin, 1981), p. 61ff.

[2] Gerhard Leibholz, *Strukturprobleme*, op. cit., p. 151; on the following also his *Die Gleichheit vor dem Gesetz*, 2nd ed. (1959), pp. 16ff., 238ff. The age-old debate on equality, whose radical signposts had been planted by Rousseau and the French Revolution philosopher Babeuf, while warning notices had been provided by Tocqueville, now received new impulses

argument: Freedom of the individual and group rivalry may lead to serious conflicts by further exacerbating those inequalities which are highlighted by the critique of capitalism.[1] But there is also the liberal-conservative argument: Assertion of the principle of equality not only curtails the liberties of the privileged but may, via the bureaucratic-centralist welfare state, lead to unfreedom for all.[2]

All three arguments are sound and yet controversial. The issue of equality as a political problem cannot be understood in terms of conceptual definitions but only in its historical and social context. It has posed itself in very different forms at different periods in history: conditioned by the social, regional and political circumstances prevailing at the time, the concept of equality has been redefined throughout the centuries. Until the establishment of modern democracy the accepted (Aristotelian) view was that every individual must be treated according to his abilities and merits. This 'proportional' or relative equality implied a curtailment of political rights: in the democracy of classical antiquity the citizens represented only a minority; in the Middle Ages they were circumscribed by estates, and in modern times by qualifications of descent, education and property. Suffrage similarly developed in stages. It was only after the middle of the nineteenth century that the idea of equality in principle also prevailed in practice: universal equal suffrage for women, which the great liberal reformer John Stuart Mill had championed, was not realized until after the First World War. And even then a long road ahead remained before women attained genuine equality in

from the re-ideologization of the sixties. Egalitarian democratization demands were opposed by an equality-critical literature: thus, provocatively, Geoffrey Gorer, *The Danger of Equality* (New York, 1966). See recently H. J. Eysenck, *Inequality of Man*, op. cit., earlier J. Sundbom, *Über das Gleichheitsprinzip als politisches und ökonomisches Prinzip* (Berlin, 1962); Ralf Dahrendorf, *Über den Ursprung der Ungleichheit unter den Menschen*, 2nd ed. (Tübingen, 1966); R. A. Newman (ed.), *Equity in the World's Legal Systems, A Comparative Study* (Brussels, 1973); Karl Martin Bolte et al., *Soziale Ungleichheit*, 4th ed. (Opladen, 1975).

[1] See the classic presentation of the problem in Joseph A. Schumpeter, *Capitalism, Socialism and Democracy* (New York, 1942; London, 1977), who subsequently found himself in disgrace with the critics of capitalism, especially of the 'new Left', because of his model of competitive democracy – as indeed the whole libertarian concept of democracy since John Locke. Influential critics of the sixties, in the sense of the egalitarian argument, and also fashionable reading among student protest movements, were C. B. MacPherson, *The Political Theory of Possessive Individualism: from Hobbes to Locke* (Oxford, 1964), *The Real World of Democracy* (Oxford, 1966); Peter Bachrach, *Die Theorie demokratischer Elitenherrschaft* (Frankfurt/M., 1970); Barrington Moore, *Social Origins of Dictatorship and Democracy* (London, 1969). On this, on the other hand, Wilhelm Hennis, *Die missverstandene Demokratie* (Freiburg/Br., 1973); Wolfgang Mantl, *Repräsentation und Identität, Demokratie im Konflikt* (Vienna, 1975).

[2] Gerhard A. Ritter (ed.), *Vom Wohlfahrtsausschuss zum Wohlfahrtsstaat* (Cologne, 1973); Tim Guldimann, *Die Grenzen des Wohlfahrtsstaates* (Munich, 1976); Walter Leisner, *Der Gleichheitsstaat, Macht durch Nivellierung* (Berlin, 1980). On the problems of equality also Douglas Rae, 'The Egalitarian State: Notes on a System of Contradictory Ideals', *The State, Daedalus* 108, No. 4, (Fall, 1979), p. 37ff; see John Logue, 'The Welfare State; Victim of Its Success', ibid., p. 6off.

civic status. Nevertheless, the idea as such of the universal equality of man was founded in ancient Greek teaching of natural law, especially by the Stoics, and subsequently in Christianity. Indeed it was largely a secularization of the belief that all men were equal before God; now they were equal before the idea of humanity and democracy.

This had far-reaching consequences not only for the theory of complete political equality but also for the social structure of modern democracy and for its egalitarian tendencies which, transferred from the idea of political equality to that of social equality, were pushed forward into the revolutionary consequences of totalitarian levelling. The turn towards an egalitarian interpretation of democracy, however, was reflected also in the progressive elaboration and extension of fundamental rights in the liberal-democratic constitutions: the postulate of social and material equality penetrated deep into juridical and political postulates.[1]

Thus the signals are set for that great argument between the liberal and egalitarian concepts of democracy which has been unsettling our century. The social foundations of democracy are changing. The welfare, provision and supply state is on the advance. And with it also the criticism of the excessive or inadequate realization of material and social equality. Warnings against levelling trends and a gloomy cultural pessimism on the one hand, and a call for revolutionary upheaval on the other characterize the dispute around an egalitarian understanding of democracy. It is exacerbated whenever crisis phenomena, generation gaps or social emancipation conflicts demand a modernization or adjustment of the liberty–equality balance: this happened in the second half of the nineteenth century, after the two world wars, after the sixties, and under the emancipation of the Third World.

Yet these recurrent antagonisms and the irresistible advance of social-state elements within a democracy based on freedom and equality are both the result and the price of a modern all-citizen democracy's function of absorbing and transforming new political elements. It has not so much given rise to the problems (as anti-democratic critics maintained, especially before and after the First World War), nor has it failed in their solution (as, on the other hand, radical-egalitarian, socialist maximalists are still complaining). Instead it simply endeavours to absorb and to channel the effects of the industrial-technological revolution and of the population explosion, no matter whether these are directly or indirectly connected with democratic development. And, most of all, it endeavours to reduce rapid social change,

---

[1] See George Brunner, *Die Problematik der sozialen Grundrechte* (Tübingen, 1971) and 'Die östliche Menschenrechtskonzeption', in *Die KSZE und die Menschenrechte* (Berlin, 1977). See J. P. Müller, *Soziale Grundrechte in der Verfassung?* (Cologne, 1973). Klaus Stern, *Das Staatsrecht der Bundesrepublik Deutschland*, Vol. 1 (Munich, 1977), paragraph 21; John Rawls, *Theory of Justice* (Oxford, 1973). Critically also Helmut Schelsky, *Der selbständige und der betreute Mensch* (Stuttgart, 1976); Heinrich Geissler (ed.), *Verwaltete Bürger* (1978).

with its intensification and global generalization of the demand for freedom and equality, to a peaceful political form, one that would check crises, chaos and dictatorship.

Hence the significance of the battle of ideas that is being fought for a continually necessary rebalancing of the relation and combination of the principle of freedom and equality: to take the strain of their antagonism, to transform it in terms of constitutional policy and to cope with it in terms of conflict theory. The formula of the 'social constitutional state', on which the West German constitutional system was based, contains the antagonism and at the same time the compromise which characterize modern democracy. The argument about the relationship between legal and social equality, about its consequences for pluralism and individual freedom, remains a permanent issue of theoretical and political debate on the conflict-managing exercise of power and on divergent concepts of democracy. But this debate takes place within the framework of a compromise system whose denial or denigration by anti-system critics has always been the real threat to democracy.

(4) The profound shift from a liberal to a social form of democracy, needless to say, implies neither the refutation nor the end of its fundamental libertarian concept. It is, of course, true that an increasingly complex social and economic society leads to a network of dependences, state intervention and economic-democratic postulates. Yet neither the council-state nor the corporate-state, nor indeed the orthodox liberal alternatives, accord with the advanced condition of modern society. Its only companion piece is a pseudo-egalitarian authoritarianism or totalitarianism, whose promises of equality have proved either fictitious or destructive. Political surrender of democracy's principles of freedom and majority leads ultimately to the extinction of the citizens' essential equality.

These are therefore reciprocal principles, supporting and conditioning each other in spite of all antagonisms. They represent the three fundamental prerequisites of a properly functioning state – one which manages with a minimum of political enforcement and provides maximum scope for the peaceful resolution of conflicts. First: democracy is majority government, with all votes being equal and free. Second: it makes the greatest possible allowance for the pluralist as well as the egalitarian needs of citizens for freedom of movement and equality of opportunity. Third: it is not, however, radical enforcement of equality or majority absolutism because it remains committed to the protection both of the individual and of the minority, which is not a fixed quantity but may come to power itself.

An exacting and complicated concept, and one that is full of tension! But herein lies the unique humane value of constitutional pluralist and socially-oriented democracy, a value surpassing all theoretical and ideological challenges, and especially the seductive charm of monolithic simplification or of perfectionist Utopias. It alone is guided by the political translation of that moral endeavour which represents the finest fruit of human cultural evolution: to open up yet to restrain itself, to check by effective institutional means the continual temptation of the abuse of power, to resist the age-old imposition of the will of the stronger, and to counterpose to the barbaric 'nature' of political power the political culture of voluntary co-operation and of compromise based on informed interest – yet to be governed by mandatory rules and enshrined in law.

The means to this end, the separation of powers and pluralism, parties and representation, continue to be the main themes in any theory of democracy. Actual implementation of the postulates and principles, admittedly, has to allow for the profound changes to which the idea of separated powers as well as the pattern of parties and associations have been subject in the course of the nineteenth and twentieth centuries. However, confronted with auto-cratic forms and totalitarian models the idea of a regulated share-out of power among several exponents of power, each controlling and checking the other, remains of fundamental importance to the debate on democracy.[1]

Admittedly Montesquieu's rationalistically mechanistic concept of the balance of powers (1749), classically implemented in the American presi-dential constitution of 1787, is now, even in parliamentary democracy, in conflict with a growing concentration of power. Government and parliament interpenetrate each other, and their former confrontation is being replaced by the division of functions between government and opposition. This general observation was much discussed by democratic theory in the fifties.[2] It implies that parties and associations, as well as various levels of political will-formation and decision-making, are now involved in the idea of the separation of powers: in addition to a horizontal separation we now have, especially in federal democracy, a vertical separation of powers. Moreover, with the growing importance of bureaucracy, the administrative state now faces the party state. There is talk also of social, decision-making and temporal separation of powers – all changes testifying to a shift and a complication but not to a disappearance of the separation of powers.

The decisive concept is that of political control. Its effective machinery

[1] K. D. Bracher, 'Demokratie und Gewaltenteilung', in *Geschichte und Gewalt*, op. cit., p. 51ff.

[2] For instance, Martin Drath, 'Gewaltenteilung im heutigen deutschen Staatsrecht', in *Faktoren der Machtbildung* (Berlin, 1952), p. 99ff.; Hans Peters, *Die Gewaltenteilung in moderner Sicht* (Cologne, 1954); Michael Rostock, *Die Lehre von der Gewaltenteilung in der politischen Theorie von John Locke* (Meisenheim, 1974) and *Die antike Theorie der Organis-ation staatlicher Macht* (Meisenheim, 1975). Fundamentally Karl Loewenstein, *Verfassungs-lehre*, op. cit., pp. 12ff., 31ff., 125ff., 422ff.; Dolf Sternberger, *Lebende Verfassung*, op. cit.; Heinz Rausch (ed.), *Zur heutigen Problematik der Gewaltentrennung* (Darmstadt, 1969). On the by now classic impugnment of parties and also democracies as mere oligarchies and élitist governments see, after Mosca, Pareto and Michels (Part I above), now the influential work by T. B. Bottomore, *Elite und Gesellschaft*, 2nd ed. (1969); Peter Bachrach, *Die Theorie demo-kratischer Elitenherrschaft* (Frankfurt/M., 1970); Wilfried Röhrich (ed.), *Demokratische Elitenherrschaft* (Darmstadt, 1975).

continues to be a yardstick of the state of development, the level and the stability of a democracy based on the principle of freedom and equality. Supreme importance attaches to the postulate of the government being responsible to parliament. This was the most effective weapon against the autocratic form of government, and its incorporation in the political process is reflected most clearly in the regulation of constitutional changes of government. That this is accomplished non-violently, as a peacefully regulated event in the political process, and not as the result of unbridled power, *coup-d'état* or revolution, proves the moral and civilizational ranking of a democracy. What it aims at is peaceful and consensus-based control instead of violent autocratic control; compared with this even the chaotic and at times polycratic 'power pluralism' of authoritarian and totalitarian systems, to which critics of anti-totalitarian democratic theory are so fond of referring, is nothing but a relapse into arbitrariness and irresponsibility. Democratic party pluralism is as far removed from such (at best) sham pluralism as is the idea of the separation of powers from the old and new temptations of power concentration.[1]

(5) The importance of the diverse concepts and ideas of pluralism, parties and democracy emerges also from the persisting debate over the principle of political representation, over the representation of the people in parliament, and parliamentary democracy. Here too we find a considerable confusion of concepts, even in present-day anti-parliamentary critiques and movements. Representation of the people through parliaments arose historically from a combination of traditional corporative and natural-law democratic elements. Parliamentary representation, as it developed in England and since the French Revolution, may have become the decisive institutional exponent of modern democracy. But it is feasible and practicable only on two conditions, to which inadequate attention is being devoted in present-day critical argument. On the one hand, parliamentary democracy differs fundamentally from that direct, plebiscitarian, total democracy in which, according to the dreams of ideologists since Rousseau, people themselves would practise government and directly determine and authorize all governmental actions; this explains also the antagonism between the parliamentary principle and the calls for extra-parliamentary co-determination or even self-determination. The French revolutionary

---

[1] See the argument with the old and new polycracy theses which have experienced a significant upswing in recent years, thanks to the polemics against the totalitarian concept, even though basically they hardly contain any new ideas; the authoritarian-anarchist conflicts had been noted also in research on totalitarianism (*e.g.* K. D. Bracher, 'Stufen totalitärer Gleichschaltung', *Vierteljahrshefte für Zeitgeschichte* 4 (1956), p. 42; *NS Machtergreifung*, Vol. 1, p. 306; *German Dictatorships* op. cit., pp. 267ff., 291ff.; *Kontroversen*, op. cit., p. 62ff.), Against spokesmen of polycracy were theoreticians like Hans Mommsen, 'Hitlers Stellung im nationalsozialistischen Herrschaftssystem', in *Der 'Führerstaat', Mythos und Realität*, op. cit., p. 43ff.; now especially Klaus Hildebrand, *'Monokratie oder Polykratie? Hitlers Herrschaft und das Dritte Reich'*, ibid., p. 73ff.

constitution of 1791 summed up this principle in the classic formula: 'The nation, from which stems all power, can exercise it only through delegation.'[1]

Equally important, on the other hand, is the delimitation of the representative-parliamentary principle against the corporate principle, from which parliaments have, historically, developed. In contrast to the corporative constitution, the modern representative constitution is characterized by the fact that parliaments represent not specific legitimated or privileged groups but the people in its entirety. The whole discussion today on 'association democracy', on co-determination through group representation (a negative example is provided by the German universities),[2] but also on a representative's binding mandate as against his freedom of decision, suffers from a failure to bear in mind this distinction, from a mixing-up of plebiscitarian and corporative elements with the principle of representative parliamentary democracy – all this in the name of some supposedly 'true democratization', which in fact falls victim to dictatorial tendencies or even prepares the ground for them.

The possible consequences of this – the plebiscitarian dissolution of the state, or despotic dictatorship, and in either case the destruction of representative parliamentary democracy because it is incompatible with it – can be seen in historical examples such as the radical development of the French Revolution and its abrupt conversion into Napoleonic rule, or the rapid perversion of the council principle into the Bolshevik dictatorship, or on the other hand the manipulation and elimination of parliamentary politics through pseudo-democratic, pseudo-plebiscitarian legitimation procedures of right-wing radical party and leader dictatorships. It is in the wrecking of the representative system behind preserved parliamentary façades that most so-called right-wing and left-wing dictatorships meet and are entirely comparable, however fashionable it may be today to separate these two forms fundamentally by applying differential values to them, or

[1] On the changes in representation theory, Heinz Rausch (ed.), *Zur Theorie und Geschichte der Repräsentation und Repräsentativverfassung* (Darmstadt, 1968) and 'Repräsentation', in Karl Bosl (ed.), *Der moderne Parlamentarismus und seine Grundlagen in der ständischen Repräsentation* (Berlin, 1977), p. 69ff.; Kurt Kluxen (ed.), *Parlamentarismus* (Cologne, 1967); recently also critically Volker Hartmann, *Repräsentation in der politischen Theorie und Staatslehre in Deutschland* (Berlin, 1979), p. 15ff.

[2] An early and perspicacious criticism in the sense of moderate pluralist demoracy, on the eve of the emerging conflicts at the Free University, was by Ernst Fraenkel, *Universität und Demokratie* (Stuttgart, 1967), p. 36ff. On the further development of the arguments, Richard Löwenthal, *Hochschule für die Demokratie* (Cologne, 1971); Ernst Nolte, *Sinn und Widersinn der Demokratisierungen in der Universität* (Freiburg, 1968) and *Universitätsinstitut oder Parteihochschule, Dokumentation zum Habilitationsverfahren Kühnl* (Cologne, 1971); Golo Mann, *Radikalisierung und Mitte* (Stuttgart, 1971); Hermann Lübbe, *Hochschulreform und Gegenaufklärung* (Freiburg/Br., 1972); recently his 'Gruppenuniversität. Revision eines Demokratisierungsprogramms', in *Forum des Hochschulverbandes* (Bonn, 1981), p 13ff.; also Daniel Rhonheimer, 'Demokratisierung aller Lebensbereiche', doct. thesis (Zurich, 1979).

even by disputing the applicability of the totalitarian concept to left-wing dictatorships all the way to the Stalinist one.

There is – and it is important to remember this – a left-wing and a right-wing anti-parliamentarianism, and no amount of historical or ideological differentiation between them can change anything about the fundamental antagonism to parliamentary democracy on which they are agreed: consider the totalitarian right and left-wing front against the Weimar Republic in 1932 or the affinity shown by many present-day left-wing radical theoreticians to the right-wing pro-dictatorial critique of democracy by Carl Schmitt, who opposed democracy because he did not find it ideally realized. The libertarian understanding of democracy stands and falls with the delimitation of representative parliamentarian democracy against all pseudo-parliamentarian 'identitarian' systems.

(6) An important result of the Second, rather more so than of the First, World War was the fact that in the free countries and societies a broad consensus emerged on the minimum requirements of a democratic system: a binding constitution, competing parties, government change through the majority principle and universal free, equal and secret elections, and inalienable freedoms. In this respect all the classic political currents regarded themselves as democratic, after their shocking experience of dictatorship and war. The concept now embraced conservatives and liberals, Christians and socialists, basically all non-totalitarian tendencies and ideas in a pluralist constitutional state.[1] Since then the democracy debate has essentially focused on two areas: delimitation, constantly to be redefined, against authoritarian and totalitarian counter-positions, and controversies about the further development, adaptation, reform and stabilization of democracy in the face of new challenges in the global and post-industrial era.

An important role in the struggle for an adequate concept of democracy (conducted between the wars in the debates on Franklin Roosevelt's 'New Deal' or the theories of John Maynard Keynes for a modification or further development of modern industrial and socially-oriented democracy) was now played by the discussion of reforms to the liberal and social component. Neo-liberalism, with the theory of a 'social market economy', in dispute simultaneously with Keynesianism and with state socialism, marked an advance over classical capitalist liberalism. The social obligation of the market economy system, especially in the new West German democracy, was raised to a basic principle of economic and social reconstruction. The theoreticians of this 'ordo-liberal' concept (thus named after their periodical Ordo (1948 f.)) were Walter Eucken (1891–1950), Wilhelm Röpke (1899–1966) and Alexander Rüstow (1885–1963); its political exponents at a vital time were the West German Minister of Economic Affairs Ludwig Erhard (1897–1977) and his Under-Secretary of State Alfred Müller-Armack

[1] On this especially Alexander Schwan, 'Pluralismus und Wahrheit', in Christlicher Glaube in moderner Gesellschaft (Freiburg/Br., 1981), p. 146ff.

(1901–78). The essential point was the preservation and further development of the competitive principle, but at the same time its adjustment to the demands of planning and of social justice in industrial-egalitarian societies.[1] The philosphically anti-totalitarian current of 'critical rationalism' around Karl Popper similarly stands between that liberal-social and the social democratic trend.

Alongside the modernizing renewal of liberalism which opposed both old and new tendencies towards state collectivism or social-economic collectivism, the further development of an emphatically non-Marxist 'democratic socialism' added its own accents on the democratic debate of the fifties through to the seventies. The development leading to the 'Godesberg Programme' has been mentioned in an earlier chapter. The essential feature here, as in liberalism, was the extension and simultaneous modification of the concept of socialism in a decisively democratic, libertarian and humanist sense, with freedom being placed even above equality as the supreme value. The main efforts of the theoreticians, and even more so of the reform practitioners of democratic socialism, were directed towards correctives to social market economy in the sense of a universally just 'social state'. The debate on the social-welfare component and its limits, on the costs and performance of the welfare state, dominates both politics and theory in all libertarian democracies – and provides fresh fuel to the struggle of the ideologists, a struggle which keeps flaring up because the old social Utopian dreams survive even in the fenced-in world of the civilized constitutional state. Three major hostile movements have, in the main, been operating against this democracy in the sense of 'limited government', undermining it or perverting it: totalitarian nationalism and socialism, authoritarian dictatorship ideas, and anti-western Third World romanticism. No matter whether ideologized as national socialism, fascism or developing-country dictatorship, in their seductive power such anti-liberal 'alternatives' of right-wing or left-wing origin, gaining strength in a power struggle against each other, invariably work together in the destabilization of libertarian constitutional democratic ideas, even if, now more emphatically than ever, they appear under the name of democracy.

[1] See Wilhelm Röpke, *Civitas Humana, Grundfragen der Gesellschafts- und Wirtschaftsreform* (Erlenbach-Zurich, 1944; 3rd ed. 1949); Walter Eucken, *Die Grundlagen der Nationalökonomie* (Jena, 1944); Edith Eucken-Erdsiek (ed.), *Grundsätze der Wirtschaftspolitik* (Reinbek, 1961); Alexander Rüstow, *Das Versagen des Wirtschaftsliberalismus* (Düsseldorf, 1950); Alfred Müller-Armack, *Wirtschaftslenkung und Volkswirtschaft* (Hamburg, 1947). On the history of its effects see Gerold Ambrosius, *Die Durchsetzung der sozialen Marktwirtschaft in Westdeutschland 1945–1949* (Stuttgart, 1977), pp. 29ff., 109ff., 163ff., 184ff.; also Roland N. Stromberg, *After Everything*, op. cit., p. 45ff. (on Hayek, Robbins, Jouvenel, Friedmann et al. as the principal international opponents of Keynesianism and the welfare state). The extent to which the Catholic-liberal dialogue, with its many conflicts, points the way towards the social market economy with its theory of 'subsidiarity' is discussed by Manfred Hättich, *Wirtschaftsordnung und Katholische Soziallehre* (Stuttgart, 1957).

5. BETWEEN COMMUNISM AND DEMOCRACY: TRANSITIONAL VARIANTS OF THOUGHT

The new wave of ideologization in the sixties materialized in five great directions and 'camps', and its further development has also been in five main directions: democracy critique, authoritarianism, nationalism, socialism and communism. This is happening at the very time at which many observers are once more proclaiming the progressive exhaustion of political ideas: following the supposed 'end of ideologies' there is now talk of the 'ageing of Utopias' and of the 'end of the ideological era'.[1] The idea of a new, now worldwide, de-ideologization may of course seem Utopian or at least pointless, considering the lessons of history which suggest the existence of a universal human need (political as well as trans-political) for great ideas and pseudo-religious certainties, especially amidst the conflicts of modern progressivist society.

Two observations would seem to justify the assumption of a new de-ideologization, or at least to justify doubts about the extent of a re-ideologization. The first of these is the fact that the vast majority of mostly new or underdeveloped countries, standing between communist and democratic regimes, have failed to produce any comparable ideology of their own. All that is left now after a period of romantic Third World theories is the harsh reality of rudimentary development dictatorship with, in most cases, socialist embellishments: an ideological vacuum that has become the playground of short-lived nationalist and socialist movements.

The other observation is an impression that ideological communism, which had once more proved so attractive, is experiencing increasing disintegration and a loss of credibility in view of its economic weaknesses, and is eventually becoming a mere façade. The crises over Afghanistan and

---

[1] Thus the titles of the books (previously mentioned) by Daniel Bell (1960) and Peter Bender (1981), as well as the final section of Iring Fetscher (1980), p. 207ff. On the following in particular also Hermann Lübbe, *Fortschritt als Orientierungsproblem* (Freiburg/Br., 1975). See also the demoscopic findings on 'public opinion' formation and malformation as an (ideological) manipulation and intimidation process in Elisabeth Noelle-Neumann, *Die Schweige-spirale, Öffentliche Meinung – unsere soziale Haut* (Munich-Zurich, 1980), p. 59ff. ('Isolations-furcht als Motiv').

Poland are seen as the latest signs of the striking discrepancy between the outward power of the dictatorship and the inner disintegration of the idea of communism. Peter Bender very decisively, though not without some wishful thinking, draws the very confident conclusion, at least with regard to Europe: 'It is no longer ideological struggle or fervour that divides east and west, but perfectly normal conflicts of interests. The problem of European *détente* is no longer the subversion of the west but the internal decay of the east. The east is no longer driven by ideology but by an urge towards modernity.'[1]

Could such euphoric observations have worldwide validity if one were to regard the shift of political emphasis in post-Mao China as a shrinkage of ideology? In an age of worldwide communications, and also in view of the growing threat posed by all states to themselves through further nuclear rearmament and the destruction of the environment, the tendency to reduce politics to factual conflicts of interest would seem to transcend all past ideologies. Admittedly this involves the emergence of new ideological battle-lines in the form of just these ecological, 'value-conservative' philosophies. And there is no doubt that the demands being made on progress in Europe today are very different from those in the age of unlimited expansion and also from those in the developing countries. Yet three questions are fundamental in this context: Does not political thought in terms of ideas represent a constant need, and one that is of particular importance in the television and mass communications age? Is the inner substance of the democratic idea – whose general spread might imply a decline in totalitarian temptations – adequate to the complex demands of such variously developed societies? And is communism as a now classic ideology truly at its end or is it only in a state of transformation?

To start with, even the decline and upsurge of religions never could be predicted purely from external circumstances, and still cannot, as demonstrated by the latest revival of sectarian movements in the west and of Islam in the Middle East. The same is true of political religions with their pretensions to revolution and dictatorship. Experience since the turn of the century has shown that a greater degree of scientific penetration or rationalization of thought does not necessarily provide a barrier. Indeed

---

[1] Bender, op. cit., p. 18: 'Europe is no longer ideologically divided but only politically. Even the conflict between the two super-powers is a perfectly ordinary conflict such as great powers have at all times had with one another.' Is this not an (ideological) underestimate not only of the ideas of socialism and communism but also of the old liberal (human rights) and neo-conservative idealism of the Carter and Reagan administrations. We are faced here with a similar curtailment of the problem of political-ideological change as in the case of the earlier diagnosis of 'post-traditional' Third World societies, when, under the impact of their break with tradition, their continued viability and revival were underestimated: see also the volume on *Post-Traditional Societies, Daedalus* 102, No.1 (Winter 1973), which reveals the considerable differences between Islamic countries and the resulting conflicts of tradition and progress which erupted a few years later.

'modernization' itself was marked by a permanent crisis and by renewed challenges to the libertarian democratic idea, even though, of course, it was marked also by a growing importance of human rights demands. However, the present state of affairs does not suggest an irresistible generalization of a non-dictatorial political concept. One great question remains: is communism really moving towards its own 'Godesberg'? Some believed thus at the time of the emergence of Eurocommunism in the early seventies, suggesting that, in a sense, it was being finally brought to its knees by its economic problems and by the liberalizing effects of the call for modernization.[1]

Here a recapitulation of the essence and effect of Leninism is called for. After all, it is mainly Leninism that, to this day, and indeed more than ever, represents the visiting card of communism. Why has it survived so long, invariably finding new waves of ardent admirers, and why should it now no longer be adequate? This brings us to the long story of disillusionments suffered by credulous and optimistic observers of communism. The strength of Marxism, and even more so of Lenin and Leninism, stemmed principally from the fact that it was able to 'derive specific answers from a dialectical manipulation of abstractions.[2] It was not the logic of the cause but its moral tone that made its quasi-scientific total claim so effective. Social revolution simultaneously as a scientifically inevitable and morally positive idea: was this not the up-to-date, generally humane modernization of the idea of progress, its widening from a policy of personal interest to the social dimension of a sense of egalitarian community? To lend a universal framework to emancipatory aspirations, making them appear as a moral quantity as against mere power politics – therein lay the striking power of Lenin's communism, the power which turned it into a faith with a militant

[1] The wave of declarations and writings on Eurocommunism, which reached its peak about the mid-seventies, died down almost equally rapidly. On the assumptions, hopes and promises – and the wishful thinking which often accompanied them – which were attached between 1975 and 1977 especially to the reformist line of Italian and Spanish communism, see Santiago Carrillo, *Eurocommunism and the State* (London, 1977); also Wolfgang Leonhard, *Eurokommunismus – Eine Herausforderung an Ost und West* (Gütersloh, 1978); Heinz Timmermann, *Eurokommunismus* (Frankfurt/M., 1978); see also, Annie Kriegel, *Un autre communisme* (Paris, 1977); as well as the more realistic analyses and documentations by Martin Steinkühler, *Eurokommunismus im Widerspruch* (Cologne, 1977); Manfred Spieker (ed.), *Der Eurokommunismus – Demokratie oder Diktatur?* (Stuttgart, 1979); on the example of specific European politics Hans-Joachim Veen, *Sozialismus, Kommunismus und die Integration Europas* (Melle, 1978). Lately in particular William E. Griffith (ed.), *The European Left, Italy, France and Spain* (Lexington, Mass., 1979); also (worldwide) Seweryn Bialer and Sophia Sluzar (eds), *Radicalism in the Contemporary Age* (Boulder, Colorado, 1977), 3 vols, with numerous articles on left-wing radical tendencies especially in the contemporary democracies.

[2] George H. Sabine, *History*, op. cit., p. 877. Aptly also Roland N. Stromberg, *After Everything*, op. cit., p. 215, footnote 1: 'Marxist reductionism is obscurantist in so far as it diverts attention from the specific, unique world of politics, which must be understood in its own right and not dismissed as a mere reflection of economic forces.' If one replaces 'economic' by 'populist-racialist' one gets the monocausal reductionism of national socialist ideology: the totalitarian common denominator of the two.

sense of mission and emphatic 'bias', with a readiness to sacrifice for the good cause and with the characteristic sense of a calling among its adherents and sympathizers. One might almost see this as a communist-totalitarian version of the religious and moral sense of mission between Reformation and Calvinism, which was replaced by the individualist-bourgeois attitude of western and American Calvinism and liberalism,[1] and which was now trying to find a new humane content in the shape of the progressivist missionary idea of socialism.

At any event the progressivist slogan of the social revolution has remained on the programme; it extensively dominates the countries of the Third World, in particular, and opens up ever new points of penetration to Leninist tendencies. Admittedly, whereas Calvinist and liberal concepts of progress and mission were directed towards the emancipation of the individual and towards his freedom, communism has so far invariably aimed at a party or leader dictatorship. Fixation upon a single goal, to which all followers and believers have to submit, is typical of every militant progressivism. In the case of Leninism this was based on a 'revolutionary' morality which regarded class struggle and the victory of the proletariat as mankind's only road to final salvation – to that happy ultimate state when, in Marx's vision, everybody would be able to live according to his abilities and his needs, and when the state would be replaced by an association 'in which the free development of each is the condition for the free development of all' as the *Communist Manifesto* put it.

However, no communist revolution ever came anywhere near the fulfilment of this most desirable but equally vague promise of mankind's age-old dream of an earthly paradise. Instead it invariably revealed itself as a power-political goal of its own, and even Marxist 'science', on which it based itself, by no means proved a temporal Bible capable of ultimately satisfying all human needs. What remained was a dogma, assuming the role of morality and religion, while the party claimed the authority of a Church: its leadership possessed the only key to human progress, to political and

---

[1] Especially in early America. See the survey in Y. H. Nouailhat, *Histoire des Doctrines Politiques aux États-Unis* (Paris, 1977), pp. 3ff., 92ff. In this connection my essay 'Providentia Americana. Ursprünge des demokratischen Sendungsbewusstseins in Amerika', in *Politische Ordnung und menschliche Existenz, Festgabe für Eric Voegelin* (Munich, 1962), p. 27ff., also in my *Deutschland zwischen Demokratie und Diktatur* (Munich, 1964); 'Der Frontier-Gedanke, Motiv des amerikanischen Fortschrittsbewusstseins', *Zeitschrift für Politik* 2, (1955), p. 228ff.; 'Fortschritt – Krise einer Ideologie', in *Geschichte und Gewalt*, op. cit., p. 221ff. This older 'civil-theologian' tradition governs not only the liberal idea of a human rights crusade from Wilson via Roosevelt to Kennedy and Carter but certainly also the revival of American liberal-conservatism in the seventies (largely in conformity with classical European liberalism); on this, George H. Nash, *The Conservative Intellectual Movement in America since 1945* (New York, 1974). Strangely enough the earlier American development, in particular, is omitted in the latest German standard work by Fenske *et al.*, *Geschichte der politischen Ideen* (Königstein, 1981). Recently available is the doctoral thesis by Friedbert Pflüger, US-Außenpolitik und Menschenrechte (Bonn, 1982).

economic, spiritual and moral truth.[1]

How was it possible for such a fiction to survive the decades, a fiction on which several generations based their readiness to believe and make sacrifices, no matter how often it was exploded and refuted? The fact that the fanatical faith of the revolutionary generation was transmuted into the continuity of Leninist-communist belief in progress was due to its 'anti-fascist' militant stance between the wars, on which hopes were perennially placed. And after the Second World War it was the new revolutionary situation that was ripening in the countries of the Third World and which invariably masked any disillusionment with Stalinism and Soviet tyranny in eastern Europe. Most of all, however, it was the pluralistic instability and weakness of the west, which to the dogmatic observer of the 'capitalist world' and its open society exhibited the symptoms of early decline. The Marxist schema of progress and decay was once more seen to have been confirmed by victory over fascism and by the end of western colonial rule; the revival of western democracy was only a postlude.

It is still, therefore, the confrontation of pluralistic democracy and revolutionary dictatorship, of political deficiency and perfection, which provides the real basis for the communist ideology and keeps alive the faith of its believers. The Leninist recipe of a progressivist idea of revolution and dictatorship, with its pretensions to socialist-scientific and communist-moral perfection, was not merely raised to the position of a hallowed tradition which outlived all political modifications and ideological 'ageing' of the cults of Stalin or Mao. The revolutionarism and prophetism inherent in that tradition also, in view of the lack of new great progressivist Utopias, serve as a symbolic value for the moral justification of any violent change of social or governmental relations. And such change continues to be on the agenda of most countries of the world – and not only of the communist parties.

There is one other aspect: the tactical and strategic flexibility associated with Lenin's teachings of revolution and dictatorship. In the doctrine of 'peaceful co-existence' this possesses an effective instrument for glossing over the recurrent conflicts between theory and practice, the idea of struggle

[1] The party's exclusive leadership claim is therefore a key thesis which has never yet been abandoned. Even the Italian CP, which goes further than any other in its coalition strategy and 'pluralistic' theory, has always clung to the hegemonist claim of the party; similarly the latest arguments in Poland are coming up against two ideological power-political taboos: the unassailability of the socialist system and the leading role of the party. This is the totalitarian minimum of communism. See also Aryeh L. Unger, *The Totalitarian Party*, op. cit., with apt comparisons and differentiations between NSDAP and CPSU; and Friedrich Ch. Schroeder, *Wandlungen der sowjetischen Staatstheorie* (1979). The same illusionism attaches to the Marxist expectation of the withering away of the state, an expectation repeatedly and massively refuted since the 1917 revolution and the new captures of power after 1945, and yet effective as a deceptive fiction of great ideological attraction to intellectuals and to the New Left: see on this recently Leslie Holmes (ed.), *The Withering Away of the State? Party and State under Communism* (London, 1981). On Stalinism as a revolution from above see Robert C. Tucker (ed.), *Stalinism: Essays in Historical Interpretation* (New York, 1977), p. 77f.

and the idea of peace, antagonism and co-operation, and also for fitting any compromise or reverses into the overall progressivist schema of socialism.[1] Since, significantly, this contains no schedule, and since Marxist predictions all operate without a timetable, no limits are set to the 'dialectics' of achievements and failures: only the (communist) end is, and remains, certain.

Hence any 'socialism' can justify its élitist and violent components by reference to Lenin, or for a while borrow the myth of Leninism and modify it nationalistically or by personalization. At most a competing religion, as in Poland or in the Islamic countries, might deny to Marx and Lenin, those anti-religious founders of a religion, the position of guardians of the grail of a salvationist future. By contrast the 'theology of revolution' which, together with the 'theology of liberation', has been wooing the revolutionary liberation movements of the Third World in Africa and Latin America since the sixties, endeavours to act as a bridge: Christian and communist faith are no longer seen as incompatible, and the ethos of socialist progress is said to be also religiously relevant and legitimizable.[2] A prophetic 'hope principle'

---

[1] The concept was not, as suggested by Soviet communist doctrine, formulated by Lenin but first by Chicherin in 1920. On the development and transformation of the doctrine of co-existence, which was subsequently absorbed into the policy of *détente* but which, contrary to western illusions, always maintained its ideological antagonism, see Boris Meissner, 'Das Entspannungskonzept . . .', op. cit., p. 22ff.; note also Lenin's remarks on the close links between war and peace, which in 1929 the Soviet military theoretician and subsequent Chief of Staff B. M. Shaposhnikov, referring to Clausewitz's dictum, formulated as follows: 'If war is the continuation of politics with other means, then peace is the continuation of war, only with other means.'

[2] Theologies of revolution and liberation as contemporary versions of 'political theology' have been developed in recent years especially with regard to the Church's difficult role in Latin America; this is a classic example of the old problem of the relationship of 'faith' and 'action', religion and public, the religious and the social teaching of the Christian Churches. First opened up about the turn of the century in response to social issues (see Part I above), subsequently reflected in the ambivalent attitude of Christians to the dictatorships of communism as well as fascism and national socialism, the problem has now reached a critical point in revolution theology. Alongside Marxist influence (Ernst Bloch), importance attaches also to reference to theological Resistance fighters like Dietrich Bonhoeffer, though this frequently leads to distortions and false analogies, or even identifications of totalitarian national socialist rule with authoritarian development regimes and to one-sidedly revolutionary interpretations of the Bible. Once again, as in the thirties, there may be the illusion of a Christian justification of violence for social ends. The Christian must admit 'the necessity of violence, and judge the means by its end' (W. H. Auden, 1933).

Among the significant quantity of recent literature see Richard Shaull, 'Die revolutionäre Herausforderung an Kirche und Theologie', in H. Krüger (ed.), *Dokumente der Weltkonferenz für Kirche und Gesellschaft (Ökumenischer Rat der Kirche)* (Stuttgart, 1967); Trutz Rendtorff, *Heinz Eduard Tödt, Theologie der Revolution* (Frankfurt/M., 1968); Jürgen Moltmann, *Theologie der Hoffnung* (Munich, 1964) and 'Gott in der Revolution', in *Evangelische Kommentare* (1968); H. Schöpfer, *Lateinamerikanische Befreiungstheologie* (Stuttgart, 1979); and *Theologie der Gesellschaft* (Bern, 1977); Karl Rahner (ed.), *Befreiende Theologie* (Stuttgart, 1977); P. Hünermann, G. D. Fisher (eds), *Gott im Aufbruch, Die Provokation der lateinamerikanischen Theologie* (Freiburg/Br., 1974); G. Gutiérrez, *Theologie der Befreiung*

(Ernst Bloch, 1954–5) combines the conviction of the inherent corruption of the capitalist world and the expectation of its ultimate disintegration. This view embraces religious and philosophical as well as scientific and ideological arguments, especially in the face of renewed self-doubt and challenges to the liberal-democratic concept of progress from the growth and ecology debate of our day.

Basically, however, the socialist faith, once canonized, needs no short-term empirical proof in order to be seen as a long-term truth which will ultimately prevail. After all, the contradictions of Leninist communism have always been obvious. As a faith in technocratic progress it is also faced with all the problems of industrialization which it ascribes solely to capitalism. Its Utopia is as remote as ever, and the human-bourgeois demands natural to an advancing industrial society are inevitably being raised as the attainment of a higher standard of living and better working conditions appear on the horizon. This system, too, cannot escape the confrontation of idea and reality, a challenge to its totalitarian ideology.

Yet the evolution of Soviet communism since Stalin (from which many western observers, mainly on the Left, derive their repudiation of the charge of totalitarianism) never reached a point where the totalitarian pattern of the power structure or the monopolist pretensions of communist ideology might have undergone some reduction, apart from a slight mitigation of those brutally autocratic methods, reminiscent of the national-socialist mass liquidation system by terror and concentration camps, and in fact the inspiration of the latter. Optimistic hopes of a self-democratization of the system proved deceptive, just as the expectation that a relaxation and liberalization would be the virtually automatic, inevitable result of modernization, the moment the population was able to express its higher aspirations and demands more freely. The fact that not only underdeveloped societies can be ruled autocratically and ideologized in a totalitarian sense was proved by the national socialist regime in a technologically and culturally highly developed Germany.[1]

(Mainz-Munich, 1973); Johann Baptist Metz, *Zur Theologie der Welt* (Mainz, 1977); J. B. Metz, J. Moltmann, H. Deuser, T. R. Peters (eds), *Forum Politische Theologie* (Mainz-Munich, 1981). On the other hand, resolutely, Gustav Kafka and Ulrich Matz, *Zur Kritik der Politischen Theologie* (Paderborn, 1973). Recently also Alexander Schwan, 'Humanismen und Christentum', in *Christlicher Glaube in moderner Gesellschaft* (Freiburg/Br., 1981), p. 57ff. (against 'fashionable currying of favour' and 'absolutization of a partial aspect' of Christianity).

[1] This is not just a problem for all explanations proceeding from the concept of modernization and viewing national socialism purely as a reaction phenomenon. Even a general concept of fascism, which after all specifically regards itself as a socio-economic explanation model, remains controversial so long as it deals simultaneously with underdeveloped and industrialized countries. See K. D. Bracher, *Europa*, op. cit., p. 166ff.; *Zeitgeschichtliche Kontroversen*, op. cit., p. 18ff. Instructive on the ideological manipulations and faulty assessments of Leninist anti-fascism that one totalitarianism can be driven out with another, see David Pike, *Deutsche Schriftsteller im sowjetischen Exil 1933–1945* (Frankfurt/M., 1981). On the (so far inadequately examined) question of national socialist terror and extermination methods having been influenced by Stalinist models of collective persecution see George Watson, 'Rehearsal for the Holocaust', *Commentary* 62 (June 1981) (a more extensive study is expected).

The allure of radical ideologies to this day is thus not simply a function of social conditions. Historical experience and behaviour patterns, well-established institutions and national-imperial traditions are equally important determinants of a country's political culture. In the Soviet Union, however, as in most Third World dictatorships which, unlike the west, have not passed through the experience of liberal pluralist limitation of powers, these factors all support monolithic unified ideologies. And among these, Leninist communism continues to offer the most enclosed, tradition-based and simultaneously revolutionary-mythical version of a political creed. Its 'ageing' could weaken it, but only if accompanied by a restriction of party dictatorship, and of that there can be virtually no question even almost three decades since Stalin's death. A conservative system of government with a revolutionary ideology may seem a contradiction, but there are many instances of institutionalized revolution, especially in the Third World (such as Mexico), and the need for a revolutionary-ideological transfiguration of the mono-party system will find followers in the future – with or without Leninism.

The mixture of rational and irrational, of progressivist and autocratic elements, that makes up the essence of a totalitarian ideology such as Marxism-Leninism, is nevertheless superior to other dictatorship ideologies; it continues to represent the great opposite pole to the concept of pluralistic democracy. The example of the Soviet Union, moreover, however controversial or repulsive the brutal enforcement and maintenance of its regime may be, is effective through its (in the literal sense) forceful rise from developing country to world power. The millions of victims of the dictatorship vanish behind the discipline and single-mindedness with which an industrial state has been created out of the chaos of revolution: a great example of a state-economic system for 'socialist' developing countries for which capitalism and democracy do not seem suitable.

There was, of course, also the experience of classical communism finding itself in conflict in the greatly changed conditions of worldwide development after 1945, in Europe as well as in the Third World. The most striking special case was China. There Mao Tse-tung very successfully argued the thesis of the peasantry as the active exponent of the revolution, and simultaneously that of a novel revolutionary form of guerrilla warfare. The alliance of army and (peasant) people became the instrument of the seizure of power in 1949. The wave of revolutionizations, along the lines of the permanent revolution concept, eventually resulted in ideological conflict with Moscow, the Mother Church of communism. The Chinese road then served as a model for the liberation struggles especially of Cuba and Vietnam: agrarian revolution and guerrilla strategy were the two great forces whose long-range ideological effects included the popular anti-Americanism of Fidel Castro and Ernesto 'Che' Guevara in Latin America, of Ho Chi Minh and General Giap in East Asia, and which also inspired numerous protest and terrorist movements in Europe.[1]

There the modifications of communism manifested themselves in three forms. The first was 'Titoism', the Yugoslav separate development under Josip Broz known as Tito (1892–1980) which, following its rupture with Stalin's claim to sole rule in 1948, aimed towards a more national and self-managing variant, without, however, ever questioning the communist mono-party state. This was done only by Milovan Djilas, for many years Tito's colleague, who criticized the communist bureaucracy as a 'new class' and who was subsequently repeatedly imprisoned, altogether for more than ten years.[2]

A second variant was 'reform communism', which likewise, in Hungary in 1956 and in Czechoslovakia in 1968, turned against Stalinism and, above all, stood for a democratic communism, one 'with a human face' – soon to be revealed as an illusion. Its spokesmen were in Poland the philosopher Leszek Kolakowski; in Hungary, alongside the executed 1956 head of government Imre Nagy, the literary historian Georg Lukács and the sociologist András Hegedüs; in Czechoslovakia Alexander Dubček, the economist Ota Šik, the philosopher Karel Kosík and the writer Ludvík Vaculík. Unsuccessful though these endeavours proved, they certainly continue to be effective, as evidenced by the astonishing rise of the emphatically independent 'Solidarity' trade union movement in Poland from August 1980; this also benefited from a particularly strong continuation of nationalist and ecclesiastical awareness.[3] Admittedly, this too came to an end through renewed dictatorship in December 1981.

[1] On this see Theodore Draper, *Castroism, Theory and Practice* (New York, 1965). Propaganda material for the 'year of revolution, 1968' was provided by numerous pamphlets such as *Materialien zur Revolution*, in *Reden, Aufsätzen, Briefen von Fidel Castro, Che Guevara, Régis Debray* (Darmstadt, 1968); Ernesto Che Guevara, *Guerrilla Warfare* (London, 1969). See F. R. Allemann, *Macht und Ohnmacht der Guerilla* (Munich, 1974), p. 277ff. (Latin America); Tilemann Grimm, *Mao Tse-tung* (Reinbek, 1968); Stuart R. Schram, *The Political Thought of Mao Tse-tung* (New York, 1969); Peter J. Opitz (ed.), *Maoismus* (Stuttgart, 1972); also Wolfgang Leonhard, *Three Faces of Marxism* (New York-Chicago-San Francisco, 1974). Finally Reinhold Neumann-Hoditz, *Ho Tschi Minh* (Reinbek, 1971); and, in time for the turbulent year 1968 the selected writings of the idol 'Ho': *Schriften und Reden 1920–1968* (Reinbek, 1968).

[2] Milovan Djilas, *The New Class* (London, 1966); and, *Conversations with Stalin* (London, 1969). Josip Broz-Tito, *Der jugoslawische Weg, Sozialismus und Blockfreiheit* (Munich, 1976); Vladimir Dedijer, *Tito, Autorisierte Biographie* (Berlin, 1953; there are several enlarged new editions); Andreas Razumovsky, *Ein Kampf um Belgrad, Tito und die jugoslawische Wirklichkeit* (Berlin, 1980).

[3] Works by Kolakowski deserving special mention are *Der Mensch ohne Alternative, Von der Möglichkeit und Unmöglichkeit, Marxist zu sein* (Munich, 1960); see Gesine Schwan, *Leszek Kolakowski, Eine marxistische Philosophie der Freiheit* (Stuttgart, 1971); Alexander Schwan, 'Humanismen und Christentum', op. cit., p. 42ff. Among Lukács's books see also *Marxismus und Stalinismus* (Reinbek, 1970); P. Chr. Ludz (ed.), *Schriften zur Ideologie und Politik* (Darmstadt, 1973). On the Prague Spring, also H. G. Skilling, *Interrupted Revolution* (New York, 1976); also Zdeněk Hejzlar, *Reformkommunismus* (Cologne, 1976).

The third variant, 'Eurocommunism', tended, by comparison, to be overestimated. It was essentially confined to the Romance countries – Italy, Spain and (less so) France – and asserted the compatibility of communism with western democracy and pluralism. Declarations along these lines, however, for instance on the 'dictatorship of the proletariat' and the Eurocommunism book of the Spanish CP leader Carrillo, raised excessive hopes; with their asseverations of an emphatically legal seizure of power they hardly exceed a certain differentiation of communism or its attempts at tactical adaptation to political changes in the world. Ideological faith and the strategic long-term goal are not seriously questioned.[1]

If the political thought in liberal democracies continues to be incompatible with the Soviet system and is there suppressed by totalitarian measures, then this might actually strengthen the growing internal conflicts of a developing Soviet society. Western civilization experience has shown that demands for libertarian democracy characterize the most important developmental stage of an advancing society. Might not, in the face of these contradictions, the western democratic alternative again develop greater strength in the same measure, and fill the idea vacuum caused in Soviet society with its own fundamental political ideas of pluralism, limitation of powers and peaceful resolution of conflicts? It was particularly the great idea of human rights which acquired renewed worldwide significance in the seventies. The after-effects of the Conference on European Security and Co-operation (Helsinki, 1973–5) stimulated libertarian demands and movements in the communist countries of eastern Europe and in the Soviet Union itself, and the increased emphasis on the human rights component in American foreign policy under Presidents Nixon, Ford and Carter revived the old idea for the Third World also.[2]

This also implied a kind of second start, following the failure of the attempt to transfer western democratic system concepts to the new states and developing countries of Asia, Africa and Latin America. The optimistic assumption that these countries, in the wake of independence and modernization, would, as 'development democracies', move towards libertarian constitutional consolidation, had been largely disappointed in the fifties and sixties. What was seen as a purely transitional hitch in the development

[1] See p. 247f., footnote 1 above.

[2] On this point most informative is the work by Friedbert Pflüger, 'US-Aussenpolitik und Menschenrechte', op. cit., doct. thesis, Bonn 1982. See also Claudio Orrego Vicuña, 'Basic Human Rights and Political Development: 15 Years of Experience in Latin America' (paper presented at the Woodrow Wilson International Center for Scholars, Latin American Program, Washington, DC, 15 January 1981); Paula R. Newberg (ed.), *The Politics of Human Rights* (New York, 1980); Lars Schoultz, *Human Rights and United States Policy towards Latin America* (Princeton, 1981). On the form of dissent and the significance of the dissidents in the Soviet Union after Stalin see first Abraham Rothberg, *The Heirs of Stalin, Dissidence and the Soviet Regime 1953–1970* (1972); Robert C. Tucker, *The Soviet Political Mind* (New York, 1972); Roy Medvedev and Piero Ostellino, *On Soviet Dissent* (New York, 1980).

almost everywhere led to authoritarian dictatorship as the 'normal form'. Now a new discussion of this disappointing experience in the transfer of western democracy is getting under way.[1] The process of political integration and nation building, together with the evolution of a viable political culture, is no longer optimistically regarded as an automatic consequence of economic growth and political institutionalization, but is being seen more realistically in the light of research into authoritarianism, which considers the road via development dictatorships as well-nigh inevitable and which is now concentrating on understanding and promoting the transition from authoritarian to democratic political forms at its various potential starting-points.

This required, initially, a comparative study of the various lessons learned from the decline and collapse of western democracies since the First World War. The great work by Juan Linz and his co-workers, concentrating mainly on Europe and Latin America, was a milestone. It was followed by efforts to explore the opposite process: a possible transition from authoritarian to democratic systems.[2] These were concerned with the lessons learned from the introduction (from outside) and the evolution (from within) of democracy in conditions of socio-economic change. These worked from the premises of the political modernization of authoritarian regimes and their gradual democratic transformation from within, instead of artificial institutionalization at a particular point from outside.

The feasibility of this continues to be the subject of controversy. Under the rapidly changing conditions of our age, and contrary to earlier assumptions by political development researchers, there is no such thing as inevitable laws according to which authoritarian development regimes would democratize themselves as a result of a general social modernization process.[3] However, their adaptability has increased, and with it an orientation towards democratic values which, in contrast to the first period of development dictatorships, now exhibit an upward rather than a

[1] See the sceptical balance sheet of a leading politician in this field: David Apter, 'The Passing of Development Studies', in *A Generation of Political Thought, Government and Opposition* 15 (London, 1980), p. 263ff.

[2] Juan Linz (*Breakdown*, op. cit., 1978) has an appropriate sequel volume in preparation; John Herz (New York) is working on a comparative symposium on the restoration of democracies after the First and Second World Wars; the Wilson Center (Washington DC) is organizing numerous studies on the question of 'democratization' of Latin American regimes. It seems altogether that the long neglected scholarly study of Latin America is about to experience an upsurge, partly from the point of view of the debate on authoritarianism (see p. 176ff. above), and in Germany, Peter Waldmann (ed.), *Politisches Lexikon Lateinamerika* (Munich, 1980).

[3] On the example of Mexico see Volker Lehr, op. cit., p. 22; Manfred Mols, *Mexiko im 20. Jahrhundert* (Paderborn, 1981), p. 416ff.; on the example of South Korea, including the issue of legitimation problems in a developing country with rich traditions and strong outside influences, see Hans-Peter Bialas, 'Die Krise der Legitimität im Modernisierungsprozess', doct. thesis (Bonn, 1981).

downward trend. True, the influence of Soviet Marxism and of its specialized Cuban form on the political orientation of the developing countries continues to be considerable. The Soviet–Cuban presence especially in Africa (Angola, Ethiopia) and the revolution-fanning elements of Castroism in Central America (Nicaragua) represent power-political and idea-political competition for democratic versions of the concept of progress. Even so, the general key of most authoritarian regimes since the fall of Allende in 1973 and the Soviet invasion of Afghanistan in 1979 has been less strongly aligned towards Marxist-authoritarian ideologies than in the days when independence and socialism converged and were equated with each other.

Naturally, this is not to say, as mentioned earlier (p. 176 ff.), that anything like automatic transition from authoritarian to democratic regimes is imminent. On the contrary, authoritarianism is increasingly tending towards the development of autochthonous mixed forms and towards justifying these deliberately in terms of ideas and even ideologies. While it is not to be expected that the socio-economic development of Third World countries will approach that of the western industrialized countries in the foreseeable future – population growth and energy crisis seem to militate against this – there remains a patent need for the continual justification of authoritarian solutions to problems of political order. This is just what an earlier western development theory after 1945 had optimistically misjudged – just as it had been wrong with its expectations of democracy in Europe after 1918. Yet even the old and new models of socialism – the Soviet Union, China and Cuba – in most instances had no more than a passing influence; they are paling against the demands for autochthonous forms between 'capitalist' democracy and 'socialist' dictatorship, or indeed between variants of social-reformist and technocratic concepts of the state. In this situation a mediating role might be played by supranational organizations such as the Socialist International, or Christian democratic and liberal associations, by blocs as well as non-committed groupings in the United Nations, or by leaning on the European Community or the Organization of American States.

As early as 1972 Guillermo O'Donnell, in an influential book on modernization and authoritarianism, emphasized the partially successful attempts by Brazil since 1964 and Argentina after 1966 to achieve a relatively high level of modernization by way of 'bureaucratic-authoritarian regimes'.[1] Much the same may even be true of an African developing

[1] Guillermo O'Donnell, *Modernization and Bureaucratic Authoritarianism, Studies in South American Politics* (Berkeley, 1973) and in *Breakdown*, op. cit., Part 3, p. 138ff.; David Collier (ed.), *The New Authoritarianism in Latin America* (Princeton, 1979); John Booth, M. A. Seligson, *Political Participation in Latin America* (New York, 1978); see recently in particular Peter McDonough, *Power and Ideology in Brazil* (Princeton, 1981), pp. 25ff., 109ff.; also M. J. Blachman, R. G. Hellman (eds), *Terms of Conflict: Ideology in Latin American Politics* (Philadelphia, 1977); W. Grabendorff and M. Nitsch, *Brasilien: Entwicklungsmodell und Aussenpolitik* (Munich, 1977); as source books Uwe Holtz (ed.), *Brasilien* (Paderborn, 1981);

country like Nigeria since the civil war in Biafra of 1967–70; admittedly it possesses oil and therefore starts from more favourable premises than most countries of the Third, let alone the 'Fourth World', which are being thrown back further by the energy crisis. Venezuela and Mexico also belong to this favoured group. More than anything else, however, the return to democracy by Greece, Portugal and Spain in the seventies has opened up a prospect of transition that once more offers points of departure for a peaceful and constructive influence by the west.

It is an interesting question to what extent these lessons may be applied also to Venezuela, Peru and Mexico, to Egypt, Turkey and the Philippines – all of them semi-authoritarian developing countries in transition, and each with its own political problems. Certainly they all belong to a different type from the dictatorships which were overthrown by military defeat at the end of the Second World War in Italy, Germany and Japan. But in spite of fundamental differences a historical comparison reveals a number of problems which spring from any transition to democracy – institutional as well as idea problems. One of the principal factors of stabilization, in addition to a system of constitution and political parties, is the ability to enter into political compromise and to achieve a consensus that is based on a minimum of convictions held in common and which will therefore avoid radical ideologization.

The attraction of the democratic idea, moreover, depends very largely on foreign-policy factors. Its effect is enhanced whenever national and civil-rights aspirations towards freedom and economic demands can be brought into a positive relationship through territorially extensive co-operation. The real importance of the European Community and the potential role of North and South American co-operation, and indeed the ideas and forms of European-African co-operation within democratic frameworks should not be underrated. In this context it is again relevant to bear in mind the distinction between authoritarian and (tendentially) totalitarian political concepts – which the praiseworthy authoritarianism research of the sixties failed to do, when it tried to embrace all mono-party systems.[1] To regard authoritarian systems as a type of regime that has to be understood 'in its own terms'[2] at the same time implies that their non-totalitarian elements

Jürgen Puhle (ed.), *Lateinamerika, Historische Realität und Dependencia-Theorien* (Hamburg, 1977); Klaus Esser, *Lateinamerika, Industrialisierungsstrategien und Entwicklung* (Frankfurt/M., 1979), p. 54ff.; A. Rouquié, *Pouvoir militaire et société politique en République Argentine* (Paris, 1978); Hildegard Stausberg, *Argentinien und die Revolución Libertadora*, op. cit., Peter Waldmann, *Der Peronismus*, op. cit. On Nigeria's democracy problems during its (first) transition phase see Patrick E. Ollawa, *Demokratie und nationale Integration in Nigeria (1960–1965)* (Frankfurt/M., 1973), p. 228ff.

[1] On this especially Samuel P. Huntington and Clement H. Moore (eds), *Authoritarian Politics in Modern Society* (New York, 1970).

[2] Thus, after J. Linz, especially James M. Malloy, *Authoritarianism and Corporatism in Latin America* (Pittsburgh, 1977), p. 3.

should be pinpointed and their potential starting-points for democratic developments examined. Equally the potential or real effects of such fundamentally liberalizing political ideas as, during the past few years, the idea of human rights should be borne in mind.

From an overall point of view five main subject areas emerge which seem of particular relevance to ideological development between the fronts of democracy and dictatorship after the ideological storms of the sixties and seventies.

(*1*) Theories of violence and terror as crystallization points of old and new revolutionary concepts; (*2*) Classical and specific nationalism as a basis of political integration theories; (*3*) Old theories of imperialism and the new discussion on dominance and dependence as a debate on economic and political independence; (*4*) The role of spiritual-cultural and religious-ecclesiastical value concepts; (*5*) The position within a continuing or changing east–west conflict.

In all these questions we are ultimately concerned with painful fractures of the idea of progress, with fear of crisis and decline. Between a vacuum of ideas and ideological fragmentation and under the impact of economic and ecological crisis thought in the eighties, we are witnessing the beginnings of worldwide trends towards a revision of classical political concepts. Communications and interdependence have made this world smaller and, apparently, also easier to survey as a whole. Yet it is marked by political tensions extending from the problems of nuclear rearmament by the super-powers to those of food and energy on the part of the non-oil-producing countries. And it is further convulsed by the conflicts of imperial, regionalist and national-state politics which still offer ample scope to ideologization. Even the old question of the connection between war and progress has unfortunately become more topical in the twentieth century as both possibilities are now linked with it in extreme fashion: ever greater technological development renders possible an ever more total annihilation of the earth and of mankind. This nuclear dimension has decisively heightened the problem since the Second World War; even then a colleague of the great American pioneer of war research, Quincy Wright, examined the 'progressivist', role of war in the rise of industrial civilization since the end of the fifteenth century.[1] The connection has been entirely ambivalent from the start. In the nineteenth century also there was an alternation between close connection and pacifist counter-tendencies. Seen ideo-logically, the wars of the French Revolution were both missionary and progressivist, though simultaneously with them enlightenment and incipient industrialization gave rise to something like an anti-war attitude on the part of liberalism, in favour of peaceful engagement in economy, science and technology. Ever since the wars of 1861–5 in America and of 1870–1 in

[1] John U. Nef, *War and Human Progress, An Essay on the Rise of Industrial Civilization* (New York, 1950; reprint 1968); see Quincy Wright, *A Study of War* (1942; new ed. 1965).

France the possibilities of a modern war of annihilation had been taking shape.

The progressive belief that modern industrial civilization would be incompatible with war proved to be a fallacy. Of course all nations were interested in rapid progress – but this was no longer equated with peace. As early as in 1848, in the *Communist Manifesto*, Marx and Engels had introduced this ideological turn in the concept of progress. To them, peace was no longer a moral value but was subordinated to the idea of progress, an idea which acknowledged, and even sanctioned, violence as an instrument: the dictatorship of the proletariat. Progress through peace or through violence – that has been the question ever since, the question posed to political theoreticians, and one which also had a bearing on the economy. Developments since the Second World War have dramatically heightened it in two respects: through a balance of nuclear terror and through a worldwide extension of the centres of conflict. The rise of the Third World was in fact largely due to the ideological and military confrontation of the First and Second Worlds.

6. IDEOLOGIES FROM THE FIRST TO THE THIRD WORLD

The historical and political reasons for the special effect of western ideologies on the Third World and for their modification there are obvious. They were adopted, used and further developed as theories of resistance against western colonial regimes, as patterns of intellectual opposition, of civil disobedience and finally of a liberation struggle. In most cases there was a combination of native tradition and of ideas transferred from the west; the western-educated intellectuals, in particular, attempted to use and remould the ideas of nationalism, socialism and democracy in an independent manner for the legitimation of their own aspirations to independence and a new state form. As ideas for political mobilization and legitimation they achieved a life of their own, seeking specific ideological forms and combinations; however, the most frequent postulate was for a combination of nationalism and socialism. Apart from the diverse conditions under which these national-social emancipatory strivings were realized, the principal factors were the aplomb and the leadership claims of those individuals who got to the top of political movements at the decisive time.

There is in fact an unmistakable difference between the rise of the classical ideologies of nineteenth- and twentieth-century Europe and America, and the part played by ideologies in the developing countries. Having emerged so much later, they are more in the nature of secondary phenomena, not nearly as dominant or comprehensive as the great ideologies, a kind of modernization nationalism which makes existing differences in religious and political conviction or doctrine seem less sharp than at the time of western modernization. The fundamental time-lag between industrialized and developing countries has both an accelerating and a relativizing effect. The emphasis of political thought is very obviously not on its theoretical substance but on the practical function of the very eclectically combined nationalist and socialist ideas. Nationalism, in particular, tends to be rather vacuous. It acquires its qualification solely by its claim to modernization and social integration, a claim it is expected to meet. Essentially, this national 'socialism' is applied as an ideological and political nation-building factor in all instances of artificial, colonially-created 'states without nations'.[1]

There are definite differences in the order of priorities. The top priority, invariably, has been national independence, but the political currents divide on the issue of acceptance of revolutionary or terrorist violence, on the relationship between (western) modernization and emphasis on 'authentic' traditions, on the socialist or bourgeois, industrial or agrarian character of the development. Certainly, it is mainly stereotypes of earlier arguments (about capitalism, for instance) which dominate the ideological field, and the terminology seems to relate less to reality than to current wishful thinking on concepts such as the national state and the social state. There is ample evidence of the inflationary use of the concept of socialism, even with reference to countries exhibiting more of a pre-industrial, feudalist or military dictatorship structure, like African or Arab socialism. This basic inclination to opt for socialist concepts may in effect become significant in the appraisal of 'marginal' crisis situations. In case of doubt the decision will tend to be in favour of economic control rather than freedom, and blame will tend to be placed on foreign capitalist and imperialist powers rather than on their own governments – typical behaviour patterns of left-wing dictatorships. However, most of the developing countries which call themselves socialist, and see themselves as socialist, are in effect less socialist than western welfare states, where the state enjoys far more extensive economic powers.

No less important than socio-economic *étatisme* is the justification of dictatorship-type structures in actual politics. These are not as a rule – as in Leninist communism – based on a totalitarian ideology, but neither are they – as in liberal democratic theory – viewed purely as exceptional situations. Instead, mono-party system and military regime, the two principal forms of development dictatorship, are conceived as occupying a kind of intermediate position, a third road, designed to avoid the disadvantages of both alternatives, the capitalist as well as the communist one. At the same time we may observe a typical alternation of military and civilian regimes, and even the mono-party system is practised flexibly rather than in a totalitarian

---

[1] See recently Heinrich Bechtoldt, *Staaten ohne Nation, Sozialismus als Machtfaktor in Asien und Afrika* (Stuttgart, 1980); instructive comparisons between old European nationalism, regionalism and 'culture-immanent socialism' (D. Rothermund) in the Third World are to be found in the symposium by Otto Dann (ed.), *Nationalismus und sozialer Wandel* (Hamburg, 1978). One of the most influential concepts initially was the optimistic idea of 'nation building' which, in the fifties and sixties, produced a number of theoretical and practical designs for the new countries of the Third World, without, however, being able to exclude the negative consequences of historical nationalism in the Third World's further development. See Rupert Emerson, *From Empire to Nation, The Rise to Self-Assertion of Asian and African Peoples* (1960); first modern beginnings in Karl W. Deutsch, *Nationalism and Social Communication* (1953) (pointing beyond traditional and ethnic factors); recently his *Nationalbildung – Nationalstaat – Integration* (Düsseldorf, 1972). On the 'time lag between industrialized and developing countries' see the eponymous chapter in Rudolf Wendorff, *Zeit und Kultur* (Opladen, 1980), p. 629ff.

manner; the state party allows some scope to various currents and to an internal pluralism. Most importantly, the ideological dreams are retreating before an increasingly sober awakening. The unilateral ideals of unity and equality, progress and modernity are confronted by the harsh facts of instability and compromise, corruption and apathy.

It is certainly an intermediate state between liberation ideology and real power politics, institutional reform and charismatic leadership that determines the picture which the Third World states have of themselves as well as their fluctuation between democracy and dictatorship. This is in line with the old and new dependencies of these materially still underdeveloped countries. But there can be no question of an end to the ideologies which their leaders are making use of. There is far too great a need for an explanation and justification of the major changes which mark both the modernization process and the political struggle for power in areas where no accepted patterns of conflict resolution have as yet been established. That is why the declarations of the first generation of liberation movements in the fifties and sixties are still instructive. They reveal both their basic ideological models and the wide range of variations from continent to continent, country to country, leader to leader. A brief historical and political outline of the most important exponents and ideas will be attempted below.[1]

In Asia the start was made by three very different leaders, whose ideas have governed the development of three great states: the communist Mao Tse-tung in China, the nationalist Achmad Sukarno (1901–70) in Indonesia, and Mohandas K. Gandhi (1869–1948), the philosopher of non-violent resistance, in India. They may be viewed as prototypes of the different currents in which political thought in the developing countries emerged. The communist ideological theses of Maoism initially aimed at alignment with the Soviet Union, but subsequently, with increasingly specific objectives of its own, sought to promote the revolutionization of the Third World. Sukarno and Gandhi's successor Nehru, on the other hand, developed a philosophy of neutrality between east and west, which ultimately led to the movement of non-aligned countries. Tito's communist Yugoslavia, having defected from Moscow, and Nasser's national dictatorship in Egypt gave their support to this orientation in international politics, an orientation which claimed to unite in itself the socialist idea of anti-colonial liberation and the idea of national democratic self-determination.

In his book *On the New Democracy* Mao, as early as in 1940, had tried to

---

[1] See the collection of texts in Paul E. Sigmund, *The Ideologies of the Developing Nations* (New York and London, 1973), p. 70ff.; also Gerhard Grohs and Bassam Tibi (eds), *Zur Soziologie der Dekolonisation in Afrika* (Frankfurt/M., 1973); comprehensively, D. Nohlen, F. Nuscheler (eds), *Handbuch der Dritten Welt*, 4 vols (Hamburg, 1974–8). On colonial prehistory, Rudolf von Albertini, *Europäische Kolonialherrschaft 1880–1940* (Zurich-Freiburg/Br., 1976) and (ed.), *Moderne Kolonialgeschichte* (Cologne, 1970); *Dekolonisation, Zur Diskussion über die Verwaltung und Zukunft der Kolonien 1919–1960* (Cologne-Opladen, 1966).

identify communism with the needs of the anti-colonial revolution and the demand for national independence and economic development. He did this by calling for a dictatorship of all anti-imperialist classes, by extending the Marxist proletariat theory to the entire nation and (like Lenin before him) skipping the stage of capitalism. In the course of the ups and downs of this dictatorship a period of relaxation ('thaw') occurred towards the end of the fifties, when 'a hundred flowers' were expected to 'bloom'; this was followed by the terrorist and extremist phase of the 'cultural revolution', inspired by the theory of permanent revolution. Even before Mao's death in 1976, and more so since, a new turn by the Chinese leadership, with fierce criticism of the personality cult and the cultural revolution, brought an adaptation to co-operative forms of development policy. Its ideological outlines, however, are still entirely vague. Maoism and Mao's theories of guerrilla and people's warfare had a powerful effect on the worldwide revolts and ideologizations of the sixties, right into the western 'metropolises', but this evaporated almost as rapidly.[1]

Whereas Mao's ideology focused on collectivism, class struggle and people's struggle, it was the concept of 'guided democracy' in Sukarno's nationalist liberation theory that acquired special significance for political belief in the new countries. Not communist dictatorship but a national-communal, integral democracy of a new type would characterize the independent development of the Third World. Sukarno's concept, formulated towards the end of the fifties largely for the legitimation of his own permanent presidency, was strongly reminiscent of the classic theory of authoritarianism with a national-revolutionary touch: rejection of the multi-party state, government by a liberation élite, consultative function of a parliament representing different social and economic groups, decision-making by discussion and (guided) consensus instead of multi-party government and majority vote. The mystically transfigured integration concept envisaged a kind of national front (NASAKOM) of all 'progressive' social, religious and political forces, including the communists. The advance of these, admittedly, first led to an unsuccessful communist *coup* in 1965 and then, as a counter-move, to the establishment of a military dictatorship which put an end to the ideas of Sukarno's authoritarian democracy in 1967.[2]

However, Sukarno's idea lived on in a number of Third World semi-democratic semi-dictatorships which tried to legitimate their authoritarian structures by a mixture of 'Jefferson and Marx' (Sukarno's phrase), freedom and guidance, as a leader-and-people government; at the same time they made extravagant claims about their progressivism. This 'progressive' character of the Indonesian revolution was supposed to consist in the fact

[1] See p. 253, footnote 1, above. On ideological changes in the post-Mao period, Helmut Martin, *China ohne Maoismus?, Wandlungen einer Staatsideologie* (Reinbek, 1980).

[2] See Rex Mortimer, *Indonesian Communism under Sukarno, Ideology and Politics 1959–1965* (Ithaca, 1974).

that guided democracy united the progressive elements of all strata and currents of society. Sukarno's concept of a tri-polarity of world politics and of the independence of the Third World, which, full of promise, he termed NEFO (New Emerging Forces), received some special uplift from a first world conference of new states in Bandung, Indonesia, in 1955.[1]

A third type, embodied chiefly in the development of Indian democracy, finally gained stature and prestige from the worldwide role played first by Gandhi's political-religious liberation philosophy and subsequently by the policy of neutrality pursued by Jawaharlal Nehru (1889–1964). Both had studied law in England prior to the First World War and, between the wars, had been active in building up the Indian Congress Party. His idea of passive or non-violent resistance (against colonial rule), to which he stuck even during several periods of imprisonment, earned Gandhi between the wars a charismatic veneration also among the masses; his assassination in 1948 by a religious fanatic shortly after India's independence, moreover, made him into a martyr.

Almost simultaneously with Sun Yat-sen's (1866–1925) attempt to achieve China's independence through reform on the western model,[2] Gandhi was developing what was probably the earliest theory of post-colonial countries. Its core is contained in his *Indian Home Rule* (1909). It has remained topical to this day and has more than once gained new influence through the fact that, in contrast to western as well as communist theories of development, it proclaimed not industrialization as the essence and driving force of modernization, but, alongside the doctrine of peaceful resistance, a moral and human defence of rural indigenous economic and social forms against the sharply criticized evils of western machine civilization.[3]

Admittedly the new India, under Nehru's government of 1947–64, quite substantially deviated from this concept. Its argument with Marxism and with the west was aimed at a specific Indian 'socialism' which differed substantially from Gandhi's traditionalism.[4] India's direction and her problems, too, were determined by political power and technological

[1] On the Bandung Conference and its 'ideology' see, *Die Internationale Politik 1955* (Munich, 1958), p. 786ff.; Herward Sieberg, *Dritte Welt – Vierte Welt* (Hildesheim, 1977), p. 25f.; Rudolf von Albertini, in W. Benz und H. Graml (eds), *Das Zwanzigste Jahrhundert III, Weltprobleme zwischen den Machtblöcken, Fischer Weltgeschichte*, Vol. 36 (Frankfurt/M., 1981), p. 394ff.; there also on the upsurge in the Arab-Islamic world (Erdmute Heller, p. 101ff.); on China (J. Domes and M. L. Näth, p. 276ff.) and Africa (Franz Ansprenger, p. 334ff.).

[2] In his *Three Principles of the People* (Shanghai, 1927); see Gottfried Karl Kindermann (ed.), *Konfuzianismus, Sunyatsenismus und chinesischer Kommunismus, Dokumente zur Begründung und Selbstdarstellung des chinesischen Nationalismus* (Freiburg/Br., 1963).

[3] R. N. Jyer, *The Moral and Political Thought of Mahatma Gandhi* (Oxford, 1973); see Jeoffrey Ashe, *Gandhi, A Study in Revolution* (Bombay and London, 1968).

[4] See R. K. Karanjia, *The Philosophy of Mr. Nehru* (London, 1966); also Dietmar Rothermund, *The Phases of Indian Nationalism* (Bombay, 1970).

development. Nevertheless, the claim to a special position between east and west, between tradition and modernity, has remained. Pacifist alternative groups and ecological 'Green' movements throughout the world, as well as new religious sects, to this day turn their gaze towards India and her own specific world.

The connection between politics and religion is even more pronounced in the development of political thought in the Islamic world. Here, too, a variety of forms is encountered, from the most radical nationalism to the pretension to universal revolution. The strengthening or weakening of the religious component has been of very considerable importance. This has been shown, ever since the twenties, by the new Turkey under Kemal Atatürk, even though it has been but partially successful in assimilating western democracy.[1] Modernist development dictatorship clashes, also in its ideological claims, with Islamic doctrines of government, as witnessed most recently in Iran. Most importantly, however, the real Arabic heartlands are characterized by a permanent political and ideological conflict between the individual states' power politics and the pan-Arab concept of an 'Arab nation'. Though in fact based on very solid ground, such as common language, religion and culture, the concept in fact usually serves the ideological disguise of the power interests of political leaders and systems in the rival states of the Arab League.

The two most important instances are the more secularly ideological claim to leadership by the Egyptian dictator Gamal Abdel Nasser (1918–70) and the fervently nationalistic anti-imperialist stance, inspired by rigorous Islamic missionary ideas, of the Libyan dictator Muammar al-Gaddafi (born 1942), both of them doomed to failure in real political terms but advanced with a considerable ideological charge. Obviously, the Islamic potential has, at the same time, the problem of the adaptation of a deeply-rooted traditional religion to the secular trends of modernization. It reflects the difficulties arising from a combination of western civilizational influences and ideas on the one hand and a native cultural tradition on the other. In consequence, the development of a democratic concept has been less successful in the Islamic world than anywhere else. Even the higher state of development in some of the countries, notably the oil states, has done nothing to lessen the conflicts existing in the Islamic heartlands between a religion conceived in authoritarian and political terms and the trends of modernization, between the idea of Arabism and westernization. Nasser himself tried to mask these problems by his ideology of 'Arab socialism', which added a personal touch to the list of progressivist-nationalist

[1] On the Turkish instance of re-ideologization (made topical again by the terrorism of the seventies) see, at an early date, Serif Mardin, 'Religion as Ideology', in *Abadan'a Armagan* (Ankara University, 1969), p. 193ff. On development problems see Bernard Lewis, *The Emergence of Modern Turkey* (London, 1961); R. E. Ward, Dankwart A. Rustow (eds), *Political Modernization in Japan and Turkey* (Princeton, 1964).

dictatorship theories with supranational pretensions.

We are in fact concerned mainly with proclamations by the dictators themselves – as indeed was the case with the dictators between the wars. The history of political thought in the Third World in most cases shrinks to a string of propaganda statements by liberation leaders. Nasser's 'philosophy of revolution' of 1952 admittedly is an early instance of a non-Marxist concept of socialism, but in spite of its further evolution on the basis of a mono-party system and the goal of an 'Arab socialist union' (1962), and in spite of its radical policy of expropriation of foreign companies, most memorably over the Suez Canal, and of its clamorous anti-Israeli course, it never really acquired a clear political profile. Under his successor, Anwar El Sadat (1918–81), the policy then developed into a moderate authoritarian system with leanings towards the west. Nasser's role as one of the Great Three of neutralism (the others being Nehru and Tito) and his idiosyncratic policy of oscillation between west and east display Nasserism as a very personal creation of limited ideological import, even though for a time its international prestige was high. His attempt to reconcile Islam with modernization, an attempt made in tune with a rising stratum and enforced through the suppression of conservative groups, such as the Moslem Brotherhood, eventually remained confined in Egypt.[1]

It is also typical that the Arab dictators are nearly all military figures: as strong men they promise a synthesis of the old and the new. It remains true in the case of the short-lived attempt made by General Ayub Khan in Pakistan to introduce a land reform and establish a system of 'grass-roots democracy' by means of a state-of-emergency dictatorship, again in the name of modernization of Islamic social and state theory. Ayub Khan's ideological declarations of 1959–60 were much more strongly oriented towards actual co-operation with the west, but this did not rule out a subsequent intensification of relations with China. The practical demands of a position between the Arab states and India characterized the increasingly pragmatic aspect of Pakistan's further endeavours to formulate an Islamic version of development dictatorship on the fringe of the Arab world.

Positioned between military dictatorship, anti-colonialism and anti-

[1] On this F. Tachau (ed.), *Political Elites and Political Development in the Middle East* (New York, 1975); Fritz René Allemann (ed.), *Die Arabische Revolution, Nasser über seine Politik* (Frankfurt/M., 1958); Rainer Büren, *Nassers Ägypten als arabisches Verfassungsmodell* (Opladen, 1972); N. Rejwan, *Nasserist Ideology, Its Exponents and Crisis* (New York, 1974). Since then radicalizing impulses have come mainly from Palestinian, Libyan and Iranian liberation movements: see Alexander Flores, *Nationalismus und Sozialismus im arabischen Osten, Kommunistische Partei und arabische Nationalbewegung in Palästina 1918–1948* (Münster, 1980); Bassam Tibi, *Die Krise des modernen Islam, Eine vorindustrielle Kultur im wissenschaftlich-technischen Zeitalter* (Munich, 1981); Said Amir Arjomand, 'Shi'ite Islam and The Revolution in Iran', *Government and Opposition* 16 (1981), p. 293ff.; M. M. J. Fischer, *Iran from Religious Dispute to Revolution* (Cambridge/Mass., 1980); Hans A. Fischer Barnicel, *Die islamische Revolution, Krise einer religiösen Kultur als politisches Problem* (Stuttgart, 1980); Bernard Lewis, 'The Return of Islam', *Middle East Review* 12 (1979), p. 17ff.

communism is an important movement, which developed as a socialist party for Arab renewal (Ba'th) in Egypt and Syria as early as the forties and subsequently also in Iraq and in Jordan. Its ideological postulates are Arab unity, neutralism, democracy and socialism; the role of Islam figures rather less prominently (indeed one of the party's founders was a Christian). Its marked emphasis on democratic and pre-Marxist socialist objectives naturally clashes with dictatorial practice in the Arab countries, in which Ba'th has at times functioned as the only ruling party. The party's programme, therefore, was aimed mainly at the idea of a united Arab nationalism culturally as well as politically, with the state's dominant role amounting to an authoritarian system in all practical demands for reform. Three fundamental principles override all else: the unity and freedom, the special character and the mission of the Arab nation. The principles of educational policy are equally radical and nationalist, aiming as they do at the abolition of private and foreign educational institutions and at restricting the teaching profession (except at universities) to Arabs.[1]

However, the numerous versions of 'Arab nationalism' differed so much in the various member countries of the Arab League (founded 1945), from Iraq to Morocco, that the idea more often resulted in political and ideological conflict than in unity; frequently hostility to Israel was the only effective common bond. The front lines kept shifting. In addition to a confrontation of conservative and progressivist, of monarchist and 'socialist' state doctrines, the spiritual influence of the former colonial power, France, played a part especially in the north African countries. The moderate 'gradualism' of Tunisia's permanent president Bourguiba contrasted with the more radical revolutionism of the Algerian military dictatorships; this, moreover, was soon to exert a worldwide influence through Frantz Fanon's *Wretched of the Earth* (1970), endowing revolutionary and terrorist movements with an ideological halo. Here the transfer of Marxist theory from an industrial-socialist to a peasant-nationalist liberation ideology for developing countries had been accomplished in the example of Algeria's struggle for independence; liberation movements and their radical theoreticians in Latin America, in particular, derived their inspiration from it.

The two most recent versions of Islamic governmental and revolutionary ideology are still too confused and chaotic for reliable characterization in this book. But both the 'Islamic socialism' since 1969 of the Libyan military dictator Gaddafi, favoured as he is by his country's oil wealth, and the Iranian revolution of the Shi'ite religious leader Khomeini since 1979 clearly demonstrate the totally unexpected political and ideological patterns which may arise from the clash of traditionalism and modernization, of Islamic and

---

[1] See Kamel S. Abu Jaber, *The Arab Ba'th Socialist Party, History, Ideology and Organization* (Syracuse, 1966); also Horst Mahr, *Die Bath-Partei, Porträt einer panarabischen Bewegung* (Munich and Vienna, 1971); *Lexikon der arabischen Welt* (Zurich-Munich, 1972), p. 229ff.

socialist ideas.

Unlike Asia and the Arab countries, the new states of Africa had neither a common religion nor a pre-set political ideology to guide them. It is there that we witness the fiercest clash between transferred forms of government from the colonial era and emphatically progressivist socialist-nationalist ideas with traditional cultural and social ties, which cleared the way for strong individuals. Three main types of liberation and governmental ideologies may be distinguished. First, a moderate authoritarian pro-western social-national doctrine with an emphasis on a specific African character (on 'authenticity' and 'négritude'), as represented especially in ex-French Senegal by the francophile author and head of state Léopold Sédar Senghor (born 1906). The second type is a radical theory of 'democratic dictatorship' with occasional pro-communist leanings and influences, seen initially in Sékou Touré, the dictator of Guinea, and his colleague in Mali, Modibo Keita, with his defence of the united party and the unified-party system; nowadays the former Portuguese colonies of Angola and Mozambique also belong to this category. In between these types stand those leader figures whose ideological pretensions to being their nations' saviours and redeemers serve them as justifications of their own power positions – pretensions, as in the case of Ghana's first ruler, Kwame Nkrumah, trumpeted forth with considerable emphasis far and wide.

In Senghor's political theory the concepts of 'African socialism' and 'négritude' occupy a central position. Senghor distances himself both from the totalitarian anti-religious features of Marxism and from its 'scientific' mispredictions; at the same time he seeks to define a possible applicability of European socialist theories to a disparate African reality.[1] His 'democratic socialism' for Africans largely emphasizes the early socialist, extra-Marxist, co-operative and spiritually humanist elements of the idea of socialism, especially their French tradition 'from Saint-Simon to Léon Blum'. To him, moreover, the nation stands above 'class': his critique of Marxism emphasizes the significance of the ideals of the French Revolution, which (he says) Marx had scoffed at and underestimated. Senghor finally speaks of a 'third revolution' beyond the capitalist and communist ones, by which the coloured people would have to make their own special contribution to the 'new planet-wide civilization'.

A key role in this is assigned to the concept of 'négritude'. The negative experience, or rather the failure, of assimilation gave rise to the positive rediscovery of pre-colonial indigenous traditions and to the experience of a

---

[1] In his book *Nation et voie Africaine du Socialisme* (1961); see L. S. Senghor, *Négritude und Humanismus* (Düsseldorf, 1964) and *Rede zur Verleihung des Friedenspreises* (Frankfurt/M., 1969); also J. J. Hymans, *L. S. Senghor, An Intellectual Biography* (Edinburgh, 1972). On the latest state of intra-African development discussion see the recent symposium: *Black Africa, A Generation After Independence*, *Daedalus* III/2 (Spring, 1982). The quotations according to P. Sigmund, op. cit., p. 240ff.

coloured 'collective soul'. *Négritude* to Senghor means here the 'entire complex of civilizational values – cultural, economic, social and political – which characterize the black people, or, more accurately, the negro-African world'. The concept is defined in a highly emotional and intuitive manner, in the sense of an irrational community myth, but differentiated at the same time from national socialist racialism: Senghor admittedly, with significant vagueness, speaks of 'anti-racial racialism'. The problem of inverted racialism emerges here; it is to be resolved by a full realization of the values of *négritude* and by effectively integrating them into mankind's civilizational evolution. It is acknowledged in this connection that the colonial era with its European influence had fructified the notion of *négritude*. This expresses itself no longer as opposing, but rather as supplementing, European values: European values are used for arousing the dormant values of *négritude*, which can then be channelled into a universal civilization (though their character remains controversial so long as the non-European cultures are regarded as merely 'exotic'). Basically Senghor, in line with certain currents of French cultural philosophy, views *négritude* in a series of great 'myths', of the archetypal 'images' around which the lives of people are organized and legitimated in civilizations: on one plane with dynamic 'myths' such as communism, democracy, or the free market economy – a peaceful co-existence reminiscent of Georges Sorel. This is also the final reason why, in Senghor's opinion, European civilization should not be imposed unmodified on other people and continents. What is needed is an organic fusion or amalgamation with its own substance, which is thereby enriched.

This cultural theory actually contains the whole problem of the transferability of ideas and institutions. It is, in fact, the problem of modern nationalism: that old observation that different countries have different customs and ideas, as classically described by Montesquieu in his *Ésprit des Lois* (1748). Time and again it will clash with the aspirations of all great ideas and systems towards universal validity – the permanent conflict between national independence and internationalism, between authoritarian state order and supranational human rights.

The idea of 'African socialism', however, has been claimed most emphatically by the Tanzanian head of state Julius Nyerere (born 1921). A Roman Catholic, a one-time student in England, with less affinity to Europe than Senghor but equally critical of Marxism, Nyerere founded his concept of socialism mainly on the traditional extended family as a responsible alternative form to profit-oriented capitalist or collectivist communist social policy: his (not exactly original) concept, which is reminiscent of the social-authoritarian ideas of the inter-war period, envisages limited property and organized community. Original or not, it is interpreted – and herein lies its decidedly ideological significance – as a thought and behaviour pattern of 'our traditional African socialism', that is, as the indigenous basic orientation of Africa's historical type, the type of the extended family. How this can be squared with modernization and social transformation remains to be seen.

Just as effective was Nyerere's justification of the one-party system by his theory of the 'National Movement' which within its ranks permitted full freedom of opinion but not the formation of factions. The main argument was based on the view that a plurality of parties was the result of class conflicts – which did not exist in Africa. Questionable though this double assumption may be – not all parties are class parties, and African society is by no means homogeneous – as a 'theoretical' confirmation of the widespread tendency towards the mono-party system it exercised a good deal of influence. Nyerere, finally, also described the role of the trade unions as part of the 'National Movement' in the sense of political integration, and emphatically drew attention to the antagonistic connection between nationalism and pan-Africanism – an area in which, in spite of the Organization of African Unity, progress has been slight, though declarations grand. Europeans will find painfully familiar the basic idea that the new nationalism must avoid the mistakes of the old (European) nationalism and must regard itself as an instrument of African unification and not partition: this means that African nationalism, too, becomes meaningless, dangerous and anachronistic unless it is, simultaneously, pan-Africanism.[1]

On the issue of the development of models and of their transfer to developing countries the communist model, too, time and again exhibits a good deal of attraction. Historically and politically this is entirely understandable and should not be dismissed as a mere whim. What really matters is the extent to which it will prove possible to separate development-technical aspects from totalitarian implications and consequences. Certainly the attempts of many developing countries and, especially, ideologists of liberation movements to draw on the communist example as an alternative to democratic and authoritarian modernization strategies should be taken seriously.[2]

[1] See Franz Ansprenger, 'Quellen und Programme des afrikanischen Sozialismus', in *Civitas* 4 (1965), p. 88ff.; and *Auflösung der Kolonialreiche* (Munich, 1966); W. H. Friedland, C. G. Rosberg (eds), *African Socialism* (Stanford, 1964); Marion Mushkat, 'Der afrikanische Sozialismus', in *Politische Vierteljahrsschrift* 12 (1971), p. 220ff. Of particular interest A. James Gregor, 'African Socialism, Socialism and Fascism, An Appraisal', *The Review of Politics* 29 (1967), p. 324ff.

[2] On this point several articles in the interesting volume *Protagonists of Change, Subcultures in Development and Revolution*, ed. A. A. Said (Englewood Cliffs, 1971), on the USA, Soviet Union, China and others as 'models of development', with an essay by Hans Morgenthau, 'A Rational Policy of Development and Revolution' (p. 165ff.). See also the standard works, K. G. Riegel, *Politische Soziologie unterentwickelter Gesellschaften: Entwicklungsländer* (Wiesbaden, 1976); M. Bohnet (ed.), *Das Nord–Süd-Problem, Konflikte zwischen Industrie- und Entwicklungsländern*, 4th ed. (Munich, 1977). (The North-South concept itself is meanwhile becoming an ideology.) From the Left recently a sympathetic compilation by R. Falk, P. Wahl (eds), *Befreiungsbewegungen in Afrika, Politische Programme, Grundsätze und Ziele von 1945 bis zur Gegenwart* (Cologne, 1980).

In the other region of the Third World, in Latin America, the conditions for the formation of political ideas are again very different, even though the problems of development and modernization are entirely comparable. The strong European (mainly Spanish and Portuguese) character of the cultural and political élites, which followed the classic disputes between left-wing and right-wing ideologies, contrast sharply with underdeveloped structures of society and state, which have persevered in their late-colonial forms. Christian-democratic, socialist and communist doctrines are facing realities marked by wealthy large-scale landownership and a poor rural population, by uneven industrialization and strong foreign influence on the economy. The pattern of contrasts differs from country to country, and the phases of economic development have not unrolled as consistently as expected.[1] Nor have they led to a stabilization of democracy but, predominantly, to authoritarian forms.

However, the intellectual argument about reform or revolution has remained fierce; following Castro's rise under the banner of emphatic 'anti-imperialism' the argument gave a new impetus to ideologization. Terrorism and guerrilla warfare also found particularly articulate intellectual support in Latin America during the sixties; from there its influence went out to the European Left's debate on violence and terrorism, and in Latin America itself, in turn, soon resulted in an authoritarian justification of a policy of anti-terrorist violence imposed from above. Ideological conflicts reached a particular peak in connection with the rise and the overthrow of the radical regime of the socialist Allende in Chile. Since then Latin America's intermediate position between the west and the developing countries of Asia and Africa has emerged mainly in an intensified human rights debate and in the role of the (Catholic) Church which, traditionally conservative, is greatly agitated by the discussion of social problems and by the upsurge of liberation theology.

The connection between human rights postulates and political modernization, or stabilization, and their importance has to be indicated again and again. The past fifteen years have shown the extent to which an intensification of the human rights debate can simultaneously raise the question of the legitimation of authoritarian regimes, and to which, on the other hand, revolutionary movements can benefit from it – movements which for their part hope to use the liberation slogans for establishing their own left-wing dictatorships. The Cuban example continues to act as an inspiration, as witnessed by the latest insurrectionist movements especially in Nicaragua and El Salvador. It is here that the entire dilemma of a specific human rights policy is revealed, such as confronted US Latin America policy during the transition from Carter to Reagan, operating as it did between authoritarian

[1] In a once-famous book by Walt W. Rostow, *The Stages of Economic Growth* (1960), with the declaratory subtitle *A Non-Communist Manifesto*; see also his *Politics and the Stages of Economic Growth* (London, 1971).

regimes and terrorist movements. Strictures on the former, in the name of human rights under Carter benefit the latter, while priority for anti-terrorism under Reagan may on the other hand strengthen the authoritarian structures.[1]

It is this dilemma within any Latin America policy that also determines political ideas on stability and progress. But it also contains a few positive prospects. One of these is a deliberate differentiation between totalitarian (Marxist) and authoritarian (conservative military) regimes. This breaks with the fatal inclination of many American intellectuals to accord – by tabooing the concept of totalitarianism – a bonus (of a 'good' revolution) to left-wing dictatorships. Any justification or legitimation of political systems must make allowance for the values of the society concerned. And on this point the Christian and liberal traditions of Latin America carry a far greater weight than in other regions of the Third World. Their political culture, fragmented and partially anarchist, and indeed at times anachronistic though it may seem, nevertheless exhibits a strong awareness of infringement of rights. Ideological sanctioning of violent terrorism from below in the sixties continued to be just as controversial as state terrorism from above in the seventies. The Left's hope of a spread of revolutionary Castroism did not materialize; on the other hand, the right-wing theories of violence by state authority have been exposed to fierce attacks in the human rights debate. From a traditionally rhetorical subject this debate has turned into a topical political issue, gaining increasing attention and hence also legitimation weight. Its most recent highlight was the award of the 1980 Nobel Peace Prize to an Argentinian human rights champion, Adolfo Pérez Esquivel.

In consequence both the right-wing and the left-wing dictatorial ideologies have moved into the spotlight. In Latin America the latter never had a consistency that was anything like the European forms of totalitarianism. On the other hand, admittedly, Latin America, after the Second World War, lacked a similar profound political experience as that left upon Europeans by fascism, national socialism and Stalinism. Not until the sixties did the turbulence arrive: left-wing and right-wing radical terrorism, the experience and the consequences of the Vietnam war, dissident movements in eastern Europe and Russia, all sharpened political perception across

---

[1] On the USA's human rights policy in Latin America under Carter see Friedbert Pflüger, op. cit., Ch. VII and VIII; for the transition to Reagan *Sonde* I, 81, op. cit., p. 40ff. Also the special issue *Aus Politik und Zeitgeschichte*, supplement to the weekly *Das Parlament* B 32/81, 8 August 1981, with articles by Manfred Görtemaker (western Europe), Wilfried von Bredow (theoretical critique) and Hans Rühle (comprehensive processing of attested trends). Of particular importance are the articles by leading 'neo-Conservatives' in the periodical *Commentary*, including those by its editor-in-chief Norman Podhoretz, such as 'The New American Majority' (January 1981, p. 19ff.); or by Jeane Kirkpatrick (now US representative in the UN) also on the appraisal of Left-Right forms of dictatorship on Soviet influence ('Security and Latin America', ibid., p. 29ff.). See most recently the symposium *Human Rights and American Foreign Policy*, *Commentary* 72/5 (November 1981), p. 25ff.

traditional ideological battle-lines. With regard to this development in Latin America the sixties may be said to be characterized by belief in an imminent revolution, and the seventies by nostalgia for the clear-cut fronts of the Cold War.[1] At the same time, however, a politically moderate, non-ideological concept of human rights gained increasing strength, a concept championed with growing success mainly by Christian democrats and reformist socialists against left-wing and right-wing authoritarianism, étatisme and revolutionarism.

This trend, admittedly, suffered a lot of reverses, from the failure of the leading Christian democrat Eduardo Frei in Chile to the precarious intermediate position of Christian democrats like José Napoléon Duarte in El Salvador in the Central American confrontations between right-wing military dictatorships and left-wing guerrilla movements. Nevertheless, that moderate current may confirm the experience, especially for Latin America, that authoritarian regimes in developing countries are by no means more efficient in the long term than liberal democratic ones. Indeed it was liberal democratic regimes (originally mainly in Argentina, Chile, Uruguay and Costa Rica) which enabled their populations to enjoy a higher standard of living, while traditionally more dictatorial states (like Haiti, Bolivia and Paraguay) exhibited the lowest socio-economic standards. Even the special case of Cuba, which prior to Castro's revolution was one of the more highly developed countries, contrary to its communist propaganda, has not been nearly as successful as a development regime as it has been as a system of oppression – as proved by the most recent flight of its own population in 1980, a flight which has socio-economic as much as political motives. Indeed some of the newer democracies, such as Venezuela and Colombia, prove that the preservation of political rights and civil liberties – whatever authoritarian regime propaganda may say – stands a better chance of effective opposition to theories and actions of violence than pure dictatorial counter-violence.

The problem here, as elsewhere, is that the idea of human rights should not be surrendered to the Left but should be kept, and claimed anew, for libertarian democracy, which alone is capable of enshrining it in its political system, instead of just using it for ideological propaganda, as progressivist dictatorships are doing by invoking higher goals. The problem of Latin America is still the relationship of authoritarian and liberal, dictatorial and democratic elements. And this relationship continues to be on the horns of the dilemma of human rights policies and suppression of terrorism invariably clashing with each other.

Historical experience, of course, reminds us of the importance of fighting extremism by political means. Just as the Weimar Republic had suffered shipwreck through a disastrous narrowing down of political options, due to

[1] Thus the analysis (somewhat oversimplifying on this last point but generally very impressive) by Claudio Orrego Vicuña, op. cit., p. 23ff. (manuscript, Wilson Center).

an increase in right-wing and left-wing radicalism, so the new Latin American efforts to resolve system crises are hampered by the 'veto capacity of the extremes'.[1] A typical controversial example, to this day, was the extreme political radicalization and the army putsch in Chile in 1973, when the restricted scope for movement on both sides had rendered a negotiated solution impossible. It was a classical power vacuum: Allende was handicapped by pressure from the extreme Left, which regarded any compromise as treason to the socialist revolution; Eduardo Frei and the Christian Democrats were under pressure from the extreme Right, which opposed any compromise by pointing to the communist danger. Extreme polarization and shrinkage of the scope for manoeuvre and negotiation intensify the tendency to violent alternative solutions and eventually sanction dictatorship. The Chilean example is of major, on the whole rather negative, importance to political thought in Latin America. On the one hand it seems to prove that deep-going social reforms can be accomplished only by revolutionary political violence; on the other hand it appears to support those who doubt that a liberal democracy, in the final count, is capable of surviving a social and political crisis in the face of the communist menace, and who therefore regard the authoritarian solution as inevitable or even as desirable. In reality a non-dictatorial system stands and falls by its maintenance and development of the non-extremist virtues of moderation, self-control, toleration and pragmatic readiness for compromise. The real threat is from extremist ideologizations with the result of militant intolerance, irreconcilable goal conflicts and class struggles, and total friend-foe attitudes.

The democratic hope that may spring from these reflections is, of course, bound to remain a delicate plant so long as the Latin American dilemma is viewed principally as a question of development dictatorship. It is for this reason that the human rights issue acquires growing importance, an importance which – regardless of all historical, political and cultural differences – may well be likened to its role in communist eastern Europe. In this respect Latin America's special position among Third World countries emerges clearly. Equally clear, admittedly, is the hitherto unbroken survival of a military-dictatorial concept which at times, as in Peru in 1968, even regards itself as revolutionary-progressivist or in many cases, especially in Brazil and Argentina, as a technocratic development dictatorship; these dictatorships as a rule justify themselves with anti-communist arguments and sanction their own violence as anti-terrorist pacification. Whether it will

[1] Ibid., with reference to Chile 1973 (Allende's overthrow): 'Extremes from the left and the right were pretty successful in impeding any political agreement viable, and this plunged the country to the military solution, of which both sides thought they could get the best.' On the classic situation of the power vacuum as the forefield of dictatorship see K. D. Bracher, *Demokratie und Machtvakuum*, op. cit., p. 109ff. (also in *Geschichte und Gewalt*, op. cit., p. 93ff. on Austria); Artura Valenzuela, *Chile* (Linz-Stepan, *Breakdown of Democratic Regimes*, Vol. iv), especially p. 45ff.

be possible to translate the demand for profound changes into peaceful and libertarian-social forms will largely depend on the future attraction of the human rights debate. One of the most important aspects, however, will be the extent to which political thought among Latin American intellectuals can free itself from traditional polarization and radicalization and the extent to which it succeeds in widening the area between Right and Left, between radical demands for change and rigid defence of old structures. Both extremes have repeatedly paralysed the states' ability to function and have led to domestic oppression and external conflict.[1]

Western Europe represents a most important example to Latin America by its successful liquidation of an international civil-war situation. Ideas of supranational co-operation, at times well advanced but invariably relapsing into national-authoritarian *étatisme*, are as important for Latin America as they are in Europe. This may also take the strain off relations with the USA, much as the Atlantic community has operated against European anti-Americanism. It seems rather an anachronism that a continent which, unlike Europe, is linguistically almost homogeneous, has not so far produced a comparable Latin American community idea, or that it has scarcely moved beyond the nationalist stage of very much younger developing countries in other continents.[2]

The European legacy, with its class structure and nationalism, has been in the nature of a liability to political thought in this 'Latin' continent. But European support by political parties, as in Portugal's and Spain's transition to democracy, might turn the example into an asset. Alignment on Europe and the disappearance of authoritarian systems in the Iberian mother countries of Latin America may well convey a more favourable picture of democracy than in the past. The same is true of the constructive political ideas behind European integration and Atlantic co-operation. No continent stands a better chance than Latin America of similarly outgrowing the developmental stage of dictatorship.

Even at its termination, our century still remains an age of ideologies and their totalitarian temptations. The conclusion drawn from the refutation of

[1] In addition to my studies on radicalism in the Weimar Republic and in Europe between the wars, see especially the further case studies on Latin America in Linz-Stepan, *Breakdown*, op. cit., Part III. This also demonstrates the significance of the totalitarianism concept for the tabooing of any comparison of right-wing and left-wing radicalism. Significant and effective titles are Helga Grebing, *Linksradikalismus gleich Rechtsradikalismus, Eine falsche Gleichung* (Stuttgart, 1971); see, on the other hand, the discussion in the symposia by Manfred Funke (ed.), *Extremismus* (1977), *Terrorismus* (1977), as well as the volume *Extremismus, Terrorismus, Kriminalität* (1978) in the series of the Federal Centre for Political Education. On the totalitarianism debate see, most recently, *Totalitarismus und Faschismus* (Munich, 1980); E. A. Menze (ed.), *Totalitarianism Reconsidered* (London, 1981).

[2] On this, especially, the symposium by Manfred Mols (ed.), *Integration und Kooperation in Lateinamerika* (Paderborn, 1981), with instructive chapters on the historical, bureaucratic, economic, ecclesiastical and regional aspects of the integration problem.

'fascism generally', from the crises of the liberal idea of progress, and from the degeneration of Marxist and communist theses has proved premature: the conclusion that the nineteenth-century ideologies, which had so substantially propelled our social and political reality up to the middle of our own century, had spent their radical motive force. That forecast of the sixties, which is being repeated today, is not even true of the west, where disillusionment and de-ideologization had advanced furthest, let alone of east–west or north–south problems.[1]

Now more than ever does the present author believe that his scepsis of over twenty years ago is still justified, the scepsis with which, even before the headlong rise of the Third World and fierce worldwide re-ideologization, he regarded the slogan of the 'end of ideologies'.[2] That sceptical appraisal of 1961 has remained topical, not only in retrospect to the ideological waves of the past fifteen years, but also in the face of a tendency towards 'alternative' crisis theories and towards neo-Left and neo-Right strictures on civilization – strictures which from a century of growth and progress conclude a future of decline and global catastrophe.[3] Fractures in progress, theories of crisis, Utopias of a totally different life – everywhere the issue of ideology has

[1] At the same time, on the eve of an apparent *détente* and de-ideologizing policy of co-existence, the CPSU in its 1961 programme confirmed that 'peaceful competition between socialism and capitalism on an international scale' represented 'a specific form of the class struggle between them' – *i.e.* of the topical ideological struggle in the west and in the Third World. The real issue, therefore, was not, and is not, co-existence instead of world revolution, but 'world revolution through co-existence', as so aptly put by Klaus Horning, *Der politisch-revolutionäre Krieg der Gegenwart* (Munich, 1980), p. 79ff.; see J. E. Fjodorow, 'Internationale Beziehungen und ideologischer Kampf', *Deutsche Aussenpolitik* (East Berlin), No.9 (1981): 'In the ideological struggle, however, there is no peaceful co-existence, nor can there be any. It is uncompromising . . .'

[2] See my essay of 1961, 'Politik zwischen Theorie und Empirie', *Kölner Zeitschrift für Soziologie und Sozialpsychologie* 13 (1961), p. 525ff. In the Third World these waves may at times give way to ideologies of industrialization and modernization, of pan-movements and of post-colonial nationalisms which differed in their instrumental, anti-intellectual character from the universal intellectually-grounded ideas of the western tradition. Economic development and national power became the central ideals, replacing classic civil rights. It is in this respect that Russia and China, quite independently of their early ideological premisses of Marxism-Leninism, may well become mesmerizing models, rebounding on the west.

Any evidence of an exhaustion of the old ideologies soon finds itself confronted with the experience of the survival of ideological driving forces in the emancipation of new states. Though these may be classified as 'spurious' instrumentalist ideologies in the hands of ambitious people's tribunes, they are nevertheless imbued and inspired with feverish expectations and passions – and they seem scarcely less determined to change the world than were the totalitarian ideologies in Europe when faced with the crisis of liberal and democratic thought. Naturally the Utopian concepts as well as the ideological concepts are subject to time and change, and have largely degenerated into material aspects. Even so, their effect was at no time totally exhausted. Thus my critical comments (on Daniel Bell, op. cit.) in 1961.

[3] On this point see Iring Fetscher, *Überlebensbedingungen der Menschheit – Zur Dialektik des Fortschritts* (Munich, 1980), p. 42ff.; also my articles 'Fortschritt – Krise einer Ideologie', in *Geschichte und Gewalt*, op. cit., p. 211ff., and 'Angst vor der Zukunft?', *Scala* 4 (1982), p. 42ff.

remained acute. As a counterpart to universal technological development and as a gap-filler in a world of secularization, of crises of purpose and orientation, ideologies continue to exert an attraction of prime political significance in an age of ever greater enlightenment and emancipation. They remain a permanent challenge to all efforts to order the citizens' political and social existence in accordance with the idea of human rights and of civilizing force, to make possible that 'good life' and that moderate form of government which political thought on freedom, right from the time of Aristotle, has held high against the ideologists of the perfect state and of totalitarian rule.

From the civic ideal of Greek city-state democracy to the 'pursuit of happiness' of American democracy and to the 'limited government' of the modern constitutional state with its separation of powers and its open society – this is the great design of the humane alternative to despotism. As yet the great struggle between the world principles of liberty and serfdom remains undecided – no more and no less. Its outcome invariably depends on the readiness to resist the enticements of the totalitarian idea, and on the ability to compensate for the fallibility of man and his world by continually renewed efforts towards an order of peaceful compromise. And, moreover, to regard this not as a necessary evil but as a value superior to all those promises of an earthly paradise which have been used, from time immemorial, to justify inhuman force and destroy free human communities.

INDEX OF NAMES

GENERAL INDEX